THE GIG ECONOMY

This edited collection examines the gig economy in the age of convergence from a critical political economic perspective. Contributions explore how media, technology, and labor are converging to create new modes of production, as well as new modes of resistance.

From rideshare drivers in Los Angeles to domestic workers in Delhi, from sex work to podcasting, this book draws together research that examines the gig economy's exploitation of workers and their resistance. Employing critical theoretical perspectives and methodologies in a variety of national contexts, contributors consider the roles that media, policy, culture, and history, as well as gender, race, and ethnicity, play in forging working conditions in the "gig economy." Contributors examine the complex and historical relationships between media and gig work integral to capitalism with the aim of exposing and, ultimately, ending exploitation.

This book will appeal to students and scholars examining questions of technology, media, and labor across media and communication studies, information studies, and labor studies as well as activists, journalists, and policymakers.

Brian Dolber is Assistant Professor of Communication at California State University San Marcos. He is the author of *Media and Culture in the U.S. Jewish Labor Movement: Sweating for Democracy in the Interwar Era* (2017). He is also the author of several journal articles published in venues such as *Communication, Culture and Critique*, *Communication Theory*, and *Democratic Communiqué* and book chapters. His ongoing research focuses on the gig economy, particularly the organizing methods and media strategies of Rideshare Drivers United in Los Angeles.

Michelle Rodino-Colocino is Associate Professor of Media Studies in the Donald P. Bellisario College of Communications at Penn State University. Her research, teaching, activism, and creative work span feminist media and critical cultural studies, with special interest in labor, new media, and social movements. Her scholarly articles have been published in journals such as *Communication and Critical/Cultural Studies*; *Communication, Culture, and Critique*; *Critical Studies in Media Communications*; *Feminist Media Studies*; *New Media & Society*; and *Women's Studies in Communication*, among others.

Chenjerai Kumanyika is a researcher, journalist, and artist who works as an assistant professor in Rutgers University's Department of Journalism and Media Studies. His research and teaching focus on the intersections of social justice and emerging media in the cultural and creative industries. He has written about these issues in journals such as *Popular Music & Society*; *Popular Communication*; and *Technology, Pedagogy and Education* and in *The Routledge Companion to Advertising and Promotional Culture*.

Todd Wolfson is Associate Professor in the Department of Journalism and Media Studies at Rutgers University. His research focuses on the convergence of technology, inequality, and social change. Todd is author of *Digital Rebellion: The Birth of the Cyber Left* (2014) and co-editor of *The Great Refusal: Herbert Marcuse and Contemporary Social Movements* (2017) as well as over a dozen peer-reviewed articles. He is currently working on a book focused on new forms of worker organizing in the gig economy. Todd is co-director of the Media, Inequality & Chance Center (MIC), a partnership between University of Pennsylvania and Rutgers University.

THE GIG ECONOMY

Workers and Media in the Age of Convergence

*Edited by Brian Dolber,
Michelle Rodino-Colocino,
Chenjerai Kumanyika,
and Todd Wolfson*

NEW YORK AND LONDON

First published 2021
by Routledge
605 Third Avenue, New York, NY 10158

and by Routledge
2 Park Square, Milton Park, Abingdon, Oxon, OX14 4RN

Routledge is an imprint of the Taylor & Francis Group, an informa business

© 2021 selection and editorial matter, Brian Dolber, Michelle Rodino-Colocino, Chenjerai Kumanyika, and Todd Wolfson; individual chapters, the contributors

The right of Brian Dolber, Michelle Rodino-Colocino, Chenjerai Kumanyika, and Todd Wolfson to be identified as the authors of the editorial material, and of the authors for their individual chapters, has been asserted in accordance with sections 77 and 78 of the Copyright, Designs and Patents Act 1988.

All rights reserved. No part of this book may be reprinted or reproduced or utilised in any form or by any electronic, mechanical, or other means, now known or hereafter invented, including photocopying and recording, or in any information storage or retrieval system, without permission in writing from the publishers.

Trademark notice: Product or corporate names may be trademarks or registered trademarks, and are used only for identification and explanation without intent to infringe.

Library of Congress Cataloging-in-Publication Data
A catalog record for this book has been requested

ISBN: 978-0-367-69021-2 (hbk)
ISBN: 978-0-367-68622-2 (pbk)
ISBN: 978-1-003-14005-4 (ebk)

Typeset in Bembo
by Apex CoVantage, LLC

CONTENTS

About the Editors viii
About the Authors x
Acknowledgments xv

I
Introduction: The Gig Economy: Workers and Media in the Age of Convergence   **1**

    The Gig Economy: Workers and Media in the Age of Convergence   3
    Michelle Rodino-Colocino, Todd Wolfson, Brian Dolber, and Chenjerai Kumanyika

II
History: We Were Always Gig Workers   **17**

  1 Behind the Wheel and in the Streets: Technological Transformation, Exit, and Voice in the New York City Taxi Industry   19
      Hannah Johnston

  2 More than a Gig? Ride-hailing in Los Angeles County   34
      Tia Koonse, Lucero Herrera, Saba Waheed, Janna Shadduck-Hernández, Ana Luz Gonzalez-Vasquez, and Kean Flowers

3 Care in the Platform Economy: Interrogating the Digital
   Organisation of Domestic Work in India   47
   Ambika Tandon and Aayush Rathi

4 Sex Work/Gig Work: A Feminist Analysis of Precarious
   Domina Labor in the Gig Economy   58
   Lauren Levitt

III
Ideology: Thinking Like a Gig Economist   73

5 "The Future Demands We All Become Prolific
   Artists": Cultural Ideals of Gig Work in Popular
   Management Literature   75
   Juhana Venäläinen

6 "Uber for Radio?": Professionalism and Production
   Cultures in Podcasting   92
   John L. Sullivan

7 Good People "Belong Anywhere": Airbnb's Emerging
   Neofascism   107
   Brian Dolber and Christina Ceisel

8 'Uber' University and Labor Recomposition: Struggling
   Notes on (Dis)organized Academia   124
   Marco Briziarelli and Susana Martínez Guillem

IV
Media: Negotiating the Gig Economy   139

9 "¿Qué hay detrás de todo?": Opacity, Precarity, and the
   Unwaged Labor of Latina Audiobook Narrators   141
   Ruth L. Nuñez

10 Liquid Assets: Camming and Cashing In on Desire in the
   Digital Age   159
   Kavita Ilona Nayar

11 This is Gig Leisure: Games, Gamification, and Gig Labor   177
    Randy Nichols

12 Uprooting Uber: From "Data Fracking" to Data Commons   190
    Stephen E. Rahko and Byron B Craig

V
Struggles: Organizing in the Gig Economy   **205**

13 Platform Organizing: Tech Worker Struggles and Digital
    Tools for Labour Movements   207
    Enda Brophy and Seamus Bright Grayer

14 Competition, Collaboration and Combination:
    Differences in Attitudes to Collective Organization
    Among Offline and Online Platform Workers   223
    Kaire Holts, Ursula Huws, Neil Spencer, and Matthew Coates

15 Precarity Beyond the Gig: From University Halls
    to Tech Campuses   239
    Tamara Kneese

16 The Cycle of Struggle: Food Platform Strikes in the
    UK 2016–18   256
    Callum Cant and Jamie Woodcock

VI
Conclusion: We Are All Gig Workers   **269**

   Conclusion: We Are All Gig Workers   271
   Michelle Rodino-Colocino and Chenjerai Kumanyika

Bibliography   *279*
Index   *312*

ABOUT THE EDITORS

Brian Dolber is Assistant Professor of Communication at California State University San Marcos. He is the author of *Media and Culture in the U.S. Jewish Labor Movement: Sweating for Democracy in the Interwar Era* (2017). He is also the author of several journal articles published in venues such as *Communication, Culture and Critique*, *Communication Theory*, and *Democratic Communiqué* and book chapters. His ongoing research focuses on the gig economy, particularly the organizing methods and media strategies of Rideshare Drivers United in Los Angeles.

Chenjerai Kumanyika is a researcher, journalist, and artist who works as an assistant professor in Rutgers University's Department of Journalism and Media Studies. His research and teaching focus on the intersections of social justice and emerging media in the cultural and creative industries. He has written about these issues in journals such as *Popular Music & Society*; *Popular Communication*; and *Technology, Pedagogy and Education* and in *The Routledge Companion to Advertising and Promotional Culture*.

Michelle Rodino-Colocino is Associate Professor of Media Studies in the Donald P. Bellisario College of Communications at Penn State University. Her research, teaching, activism, and creative work span feminist media and critical cultural studies, with special interest in labor, new media, and social movements. Her scholarly articles have been published in journals such as *Communication and Critical/Cultural Studies*; *Communication, Culture, and Critique*; *Critical Studies in Media Communications*; *Feminist Media Studies*; *New Media & Society*; and *Women's Studies in Communication*, among others.

Todd Wolfson is Associate Professor in the Department of Journalism and Media Studies at Rutgers University. His research focuses on the convergence of technology, inequality, and social change. Todd is author of *Digital Rebellion: The Birth of the Cyber Left* (2014) and co-editor of *The Great Refusal: Herbert Marcuse and Contemporary Social Movements* (2017) as well as over a dozen peer-reviewed articles. He is currently working on a book focused on new forms of worker organizing in the gig economy. Todd is co-director of the Media, Inequality & Chance Center (MIC), a partnership between University of Pennsylvania and Rutgers University.

ABOUT THE AUTHORS

Marco Briziarelli is an associate professor in the Department of Communication & Journalism at the University of New Mexico, USA. He explores intersections of political economy of media and cultural studies.

Enda Brophy is an associate professor in the School of Communication and an associate in Labour Studies at Simon Fraser University. He is the author of *Language Put to Work: The Making of the Global Call Centre Workforce*, which won book of the year awards from the Canadian Communication Association and the Canadian Association of Work and Labour Studies in 2018.

Callum Cant is author of *Riding for Deliveroo* and a PhD student at the University of West London, where his project focuses on Marxist theories of class composition and workers self-organisation in the service sector.

Christina Ceisel is Assistant Professor of Communications at California State University, Fullerton. She is the author of *Globalized Nostalgia: Tourism, Heritage, and the Politics of Place* (Routledge, 2018).

Matthew Coates is Statistical Consulting Associate at Hertfordshire Business School at the University of Hertfordshire in the UK.

Byron B Craig holds a PhD in Communication and Culture from Indiana University-Bloomington. He is currently an assistant professor at Illinois State University in the School of Communication and serves as an affiliate faculty for the African American Studies program.

Brian Dolber is Assistant Professor of Communication at California State University San Marcos. He is the author of *Media and Culture in the U.S. Jewish Labor Movement: Sweating for Democracy in the Interwar Era* (Palgrave, 2017).

Kean Flowers is a social worker in Los Angeles, California, where he provides mental health services and resource support for children and families. He holds a master's degree in social welfare from the UCLA Luskin School of Public Affairs. In both his research and practice, he explores and intervenes upon sociopolitical systems that impact individuals carrying intersectional identities.

Ana Luz Gonzalez-Vasquez is a project manager at the UCLA Center for Labor Research and Education in the Institute for Research on Labor and Employment. She holds a PhD and master's in urban planning from UCLA.

Seamus Bright Grayer completed his MA in communication from Simon Fraser University in January 2020. He is currently working as one of the chief stewards for the Teaching Support Staff Union.

Susana Martínez Guillem is Associate Professor in the Department of Communication & Journalism at the University of New Mexico, USA. She draws on discourse studies and cultural studies to study the ideological dimensions of everyday practices in relation to immigration, place, space, social movements (anti)racism, and multilingualism.

Lucero Herrera is a senior research analyst at the UCLA Labor Center, where she conducts sectoral and applied research on low-wage service industries. She holds a master's in urban and regional planning from UCLA.

Kaire Holts is a postdoctoral researcher at Ragnar Nurkse Department of Innovation and Governance at the Tallinn University of Technology in Estonia. She was a senior research fellow at Hertfordshire Business School at the University of Hertfordshire in the UK when this chapter was written.

Ursula Huws is Professor of Labour and Globalisation at Hertfordshire Business School at the University of Hertfordshire in the UK.

Hannah Johnston is a postdoctoral fellow at Northeastern University. She received her PhD in Geography from Queen's University, Canada, where she studied the collective organizing strategies of New York City taxicab drivers.

Tamara Kneese is an assistant professor in the Department of Media Studies and Program Director of Gender and Sexualities Studies at the University of

San Francisco. Her book about the platform infrastructures of digital afterlives is under contract with Yale University Press.

Tia Koonse is the Legal and Policy Research Manager at the UCLA Labor Center. She holds a law and a master's degree ('11) in urban planning from UCLA's Epstein Program in Public Interest Law and Policy, with concentrations in critical race studies and community development and housing.

Chenjerai Kumanyika is a researcher, journalist, and artist who works as an assistant professor in Rutgers University's Department of Journalism and Media Studies. His research and teaching focus on the intersections of social justice and emerging media in the cultural and creative industries. He has written about these issues in journals such as *Popular Music & Society*; *Popular Communication*; and *Technology, Pedagogy and Education* and in *The Routledge Companion to Advertising and Promotional Culture*.

Lauren Levitt is a PhD candidate in communication at the University of Southern California. Her dissertation project examines the alternative economic practices and kinship structures of sex workers and sex workers' rights activists in New York and Los Angeles.

Ruth L. Nuñez is an information studies doctoral candidate at UCLA. Her research is at the intersection of digital technologies, Latinx communities, media, and social justice.

Kavita Ilona Nayar is a doctoral candidate in the Department of Communication at the University of Massachusetts–Amherst. Her research focuses on gendered labor at the intersection of intimacy, commerce, and technology.

Randy Nichols is Associate Professor in the Division of Culture, Arts & Communication in the School of Interdisciplinary Arts & Sciences at the University of Washington Tacoma. He is the author or editor of three books, including *The Political Economy of Media Industries: Global Transformations and Challenges* (2019), co-edited with Gabriela Martinez.

Stephen E. Rahko holds a PhD in communication and culture from Indiana University-Bloomington. He is currently a lecturer at Indiana University-Bloomington in the Kelley School of Business.

Aayush Rathi researches the socio-legal-political aspects of contemporary technological systems. More particularly, his research engages with questions of labour, gender, and surveillance. He is currently affiliated to the Centre for Internet and Society, and BBC Media Action.

Michelle Rodino-Colocino is Associate Professor of Media Studies in the Donald P. Bellisario College of Communications at Penn State University. Her research, teaching, activism, and creative work span feminist media and critical cultural studies, with special interest in labor, new media, and social movements. Her scholarly articles have been published in journals such as *Communication and Critical/Cultural Studies*; *Communication, Culture, and Critique*; *Critical Studies in Media Communications*; *Feminist Media Studies*; *New Media & Society*; and *Women's Studies in Communication*, among others.

Janna Shadduck-Hernández, EdD, is a project director at the UCLA Center for Labor Research and Education. She teaches in UCLA's labor studies major and the Graduate School of Education and Information Studies.

Neil Spencer is Professor of Applied Statistics at Hertfordshire Business School at the University of Hertfordshire in the UK.

John L. Sullivan (MA, PhD, University of Pennsylvania) is Professor of Media and Communication at Muhlenberg College in Allentown, PA. His research explores the links between media industries and systems of social and economic power.

Ambika Tandon is a senior researcher at the Centre for Internet and Society, India. She has co-led several projects exploring the intersections of gender and technology, including implications on women's work, data rights, and digital access. She has also consulted with institutions such as BBC Media Action and City University, UK.

Juhana Venäläinen is Assistant Professor of Cultural Studies at the University of Eastern Finland, Joensuu. His current research interests revolve around the societal transformations and cultural interpretations of work and the economy, including concepts such as the sharing economy, the platform economy, and the gig economy.

Saba Waheed is Research Director at the UCLA Labor Center. She has two decades of research experience developing projects with strong community participation. She received an MA in anthropology from Columbia University.

Todd Wolfson is Associate Professor in the Department of Journalism and Media Studies at Rutgers University. His research focuses on the convergence of technology, inequality, and social change. Todd is author of *Digital Rebellion: The Birth of the Cyber Left* (2014) and co-editor of *The Great Refusal: Herbert Marcuse and Contemporary Social Movements* (2017) as well as over a dozen peer-reviewed articles. He is currently working on a book focused on new forms of worker organizing in the gig economy. Todd is co-director of the Media, Inequality & Chance Center (MIC), a partnership between University of Pennsylvania and Rutgers University.

Jamie Woodcock is Senior Lecturer at Open University, UK. He is the author of *Working the Phones*, a study of a call center in the UK inspired by the workers' inquiry.

ACKNOWLEDGMENTS

We wish to thank the authors who worked tirelessly to tell the stories and struggles of gig workers and media. We also thank Sheni Kruger and Emma Sherriff at Routledge as well as anonymous reviewers for their useful insights and for approaching this project with thoughtfulness and urgency. This book could not have been possible without the many gig workers who told us their stories and inspired the editors to work as scholar-activists to engage our research, teaching in service in the pursuit of equity, fairness, and justice. We stand in solidarity with gig workers everywhere.

Brian would like to thank his co-editors for being supportive colleagues and comrades in taking on this project as a collaborative effort. He thanks Todd Wolfson again, and Victor Pickard, for their support of his work with Rideshare Drivers United through the Media, Inequality and Change Center. He also thanks the Canadian Social Sciences and Humanities Research Council for their ongoing support of research on platform organizing through an Insight Grant, and his collaborators on that project—Enda Brophy, Lily Irani, Tamara Kneese, Alesandro Delfanti, Jamie Woodcock, Seamus Bright Grayer, and Mark Dunn. Brian is grateful for support from his colleagues in the Department of Communication, Julia Johnson, and Dr. Elizabeth Matthews, Interim Dean of the College of Humanities, Arts, Behavioral and Social Sciences at CSUSM. He also thanks his colleagues on the Union for Democratic Communications steering committee for continuing to create space for meaningful scholar-activism. Brian is honored to struggle alongside Ivan Pardo, Tina Givens, Eric Dryburgh, Nicole Moore, and the organizing committee of Rideshare Drivers United, who have consistently reminded him that we can, and will, win. He is forever thankful to his partner, and now co-author, Christina Ceisel for love, support, and inspiration. Brian dedicates this book in memory of his mother, Elaine, who spent many years doing essential gig work as an early intervention special education teacher, and to his infant daughter, Eliza, who has already made the world a better place.

Chenjerai would like to thank his co-editors—Brian, Michelle, and Todd—for inviting him to this project and for their relentless, insightful work on it. He would also like to thank his partner, Saadiqa Kumanyika, whose labor is always a key part of what he's able to accomplish. Next, he'd like to thank his comrades in 215 People's Alliance for allowing him the time to pull back from some areas of their organization to focus on this book. He'd like to thank Daphne Lawless for her fast and precise formatting work and finally to all of the workers whose unseen underpaid, labor, creativity, and personal sacrifice is required to power the techno-extractive labor arrangements that we use. Let this acknowledgment and the truth-telling and interventions in this book be contributions to more substantive solidarity.

Michelle would like to thank Brian, Chenjerai, and Todd for their positive energy, keen intellects, dedication to seeing this project to fruition, and inspirational work as organizers in movements for social justice. She is grateful for their friendship and shares joy in speaking truth to power. She also thanks her colleagues, friends, and students at Penn State University and University of Cincinnati, as well as friends in Union for a Democratic Communication (UDC), International Communication Association (ICA), and National Communication Association (NCA). Michelle thanks Marie Hardin, Dean of the Donald P. Bellisario College of Communications; Shivaani Selvaraj, Director, Penn State Center, Philadelphia; and John Christman, Director of the Humanities Institute, for funding portions of the research and the writing of this project. Michelle thanks Pooja Nerkar for her research assistance as well as App-Based Driver Association's Takele Gobena; Philadelphia Drivers Union's Angela Vogel and Ali Razak; and Rideshare Drivers United's Brian Dolber (again!) and Nicole Moore for sharing their insights organizing in the gig economy. Special thanks to Jewel Davis, Gregory Lioi, Osborne Hart, and Chris, Gloria, and Michael for sharing their experiences as gig workers and allies. Thank you to Marcus Courtney, for welcoming her first to study and then to organize at WashTech, an early union for contingent tech workers. Special shout out to her students who see a better world, and to all of the activists, artists, and friends who have taught her how to "yes, and." Michelle is extremely grateful for the love, joy, and support that Todd, Stella, Mom, Dad, and Grandma have generously shared, and for Jellybean and Bob for their supportive naps. Michelle dedicates this book to Todd, for all of the love, labor, and delicious dinners he has lovingly prepared, and to Stella, who has already found her voice: may this book help you use it.

Todd would like to thank his fantastic co-editors that have made this project a joy to work on. Todd would like to give special thanks to all the intrepid cab drivers in the Taxi Workers Alliance of Pennsylvania that have been fighting over the gigification and platformization of point-to-point transportation for decades, including Ronald Blount, Mohammad Shukur, Tekle Gebrehdhim, Patrick Anamah, and many other amazing leaders. Todd would also like to thank the leaders of the Philadelphia Drivers Union, mentioned earlier, as they carry this fight forward. Todd is indebted to his mischievous crew—Woody, Sebastian, Rosa, and Levi—and his extremely generous partner Alison. Their love, joy, and magnanimity make him believe another world is possible.

I
Introduction
The Gig Economy: Workers and Media in the Age of Convergence

THE GIG ECONOMY

Workers and Media in the Age
of Convergence

*Michelle Rodino-Colocino, Todd Wolfson,
Brian Dolber, and Chenjerai Kumanyika*

"If we don't band together, it's only going to get crappier," Gloria told Michelle and Pooja as she stood in front of the metal parking lot divider at the Philadelphia Airport on an overcast Tuesday in May 2019, the day before a global strike against Uber and Lyft.[1] That day was like many for the 54-year-old African American woman, who had been waiting 90 minutes, app on, for Uber to connect her with a passenger. Gloria—like the hundreds of gig workers that the editors of this book have interviewed and collaborated with in Philadelphia, Los Angeles, New York, Seattle, and London—worked long hours, many of them unpaid. Her story epitomizes the exploitation of people working by the "gig," a labor arrangement that the US Department of Labor defines as "a single project or task for which a worker is hired, often through a digital marketplace, to work on demand."[2] Characteristic of gig work, Uber and Lyft pay drivers only for miles driven with a passenger in the vehicle, not for time they wait for fares or driving to and from jobs, nor for vehicle maintenance and insurance expenses, nor for the ill health effects of working hours on end.[3] Having completed over 3,000 miles in her first year as a full-time driver for Uber's basic service, Gloria cited shrinking pay and longer wait times as reasons for striking. Other drivers amplified Gloria's message. In preparation for the rally, drivers produced a massive collection of handwritten posters and other signs, which they stacked in the Philadelphia airport lot in the hours before the rally. These signs captured specific demands. "WE DEMAND A LIVING WAGE," "DRIVER SAFETY MATTERS," and "WE DESERVE SAFETY TRANSPARENCY."

Drivers struck on May 8, 2019, in dozens of cities around the world, with coordinated actions timed to disrupt Uber's IPO two days later. They demanded living wages, secure, dignified work, and transparent management. On the eve of the strike, six driver-led grassroots organizations across the US released a joint statement titled, "Why We Are on Strike," outlining the rationale for the May 8 actions:

> We are calling for a National Day of Action Against Uber, Lyft, and all other App-based For-Hire-Vehicle companies on Wednesday, May 8th to shine light on how Uber and Lyft's flawed business model pushes hard-working drivers across the US and the globe into poverty and desperation. . . . Driver-led grassroots organizations across the entire nation are unified in our call for a strike against Uber corporate greed. . . . Drivers will never back off or fade into the night. Our movement will only grow stronger.[4]

One of the organizations that authored the statement, Rideshare Drivers United (RDU), a fledgling drivers' union in California, called the strike after Uber slashed mileage rates by 25 percent in Los Angeles. Co-editor Brian Dolber helped organize and coordinate the strikes around the US. With support from the Media, Inequality and Change Center, co-directed by another editor, Todd Wolfson, RDU built its membership base throughout the prior year, using a hybrid online and face-to-face organizing strategy that integrated communications across an organizing app they developed in-house with advertising on social media, text messaging, phone calls, and one-on-one conversations. Throughout 2019, RDU organized events like the May 8 strike and demonstrations supporting passage of AB5, California legislation that recognizes drivers' and other gig workers' status as employees of Uber and Lyft.[5]

Although the strikes did not significantly disrupt service, they did damage Uber's IPO, as media questioned the company's $90 billion valuation, and shares fell over 30 percent in the following weeks.[6] While Silicon Valley elites used "algorithmic management" to hide how they exploit workers, rideshare drivers talked back collectively, also with the help of new media technologies.[7] Using apps, smartphones, social media, and text messaging as organizing tools, the strikes showcased the convergence of media in workers' struggle for control over their work, fair hours, and fair pay.

More than an example of workers targeting an exploitative company, the strikes also demonstrated the convergence of workers' solidarity in and beyond the gig economy.[8] Recognizing their common interests, taxi drivers joined Lyft drivers who joined striking Uber drivers, recognizing common interests among point-to-point transportation workers and the correspondent need to build a larger shared struggle. Food couriers and nannies—also contracted by "gig" companies—showed up to support striking drivers across the globe, offering a window into an even broader coalition of gig and direct hire workers.

During the rally in Philadelphia, Michelle and Pooja spoke with Walmart workers who joined striking drivers in solidarity as exploited, low-waged, insecure workers. "We face the same conditions," explained Chris, a Walmart stocker.

Chris compared the low wages at Uber and Walmart, arguing that the low wages "make it impossible for you to bring up a family." Recognizing the shared conditions and economic exploitation across industries, Chris and a co-worker noted that some of his Walmart co-workers are Uber drivers. May 8 demonstrated the potential for "solidarity unionism," workers' supporting each other's rights and demands via direct actions, organized outside of formal union contract negotiations and by workers without bargaining status.[9]

The urgency of workers' demands and the social forces driving them came into even clearer focus as business and travel screeched to a standstill during the coronavirus pandemic of 2019–2020. Without employees' rights and with scant social provision, gig workers joined hourly, part-time, tip, and undocumented workers who had little recourse as the pandemic unfolded.[10] Gig employers offered employees unemployment compensation to provide for work disruptions during the pandemic, but drivers and their unions found that they fell short and were irregularly accessible. In the US, Uber's pandemic hardship response has been inadequate and riddled with loopholes, including requiring drivers to provide proof they have tested positive for the virus or have been "personally asked" to be quarantined or placed in isolation.[11] Uber and Lyft have also continued to challenge California's AB5 law that recognizes drivers as employees, even during the pandemic. In response, RDU has demanded immediate recognition of drivers' rights as employees, including immediate access to unemployment and extended sick pay, temporary basic income, and an eviction moratorium, among others.[12] The actions on May 8, 2019, amplified gig workers' demands and evidenced the worker solidarity that underlies them. The COVID pandemic has made both more urgent.

What's New About the Gig Economy?

The global day of action against Uber highlights the converging contradictions and possibilities explored in this book. On the one hand, the technology and venture capital firms that facilitated the rapid expansion of the gig economy leverage new technologies to "disrupt" existing markets and regulatory frameworks that ensure basic rights for workers. These same firms harness big data and algorithms to wipe out a managerial class of workers while putting service workers (as "independent contractors") under the thumb of a black box platform. On the other, workers in these industries—Uber and Lyft drivers, food couriers, package delivery drivers, and nannies—utilize new communications technologies to resist, adapt, and forge collective power. Walmart workers, long the exemplars of the exploited service class, have joined in solidarity with app-based gig workers.

The May 8 strike attracted other low-wage workers and sympathetic consumers because they recognize that Uber and Lyft drivers, and workers across platforms, are the latest canary in the coalmine. The captains of data-mediated capitalism are experimenting with new ways of lowering labor costs, new strategies of surveilling and controlling workers, and novel ways of discouraging worker organization. The very workers disempowered by these practices are forced to participate in their development. Many of these strategies continue to be tested on workers in industries beyond the gig economy's traditional boundaries. For this reason, although platform workers are a small segment of the overall labor force, the condition of these workers attracts the attention of workers across the economy.

Our conversations with Gloria and drivers in Seattle, Los Angeles, and Philadelphia reveal that their turn to gig work represents less their preference for flexible over secure employment and more as a means to survive in an exploitative economy. As Gloria explained, only by comparison to her prior employment as an underpaid, overworked health care aide—working 100-hour weeks with naps in the facility where she assisted patients—is driving for Uber "easy-breezy." Gloria was not alone in characterizing gig work as better than alternative jobs with long hours and low pay. Contemporary gig work, then, should be understood as a survival strategy within an economy in which acceptable, livable working conditions are scarce.

As critical scholars, we illuminate the gig economy's contours so that we may develop new strategies to change them. We explore intersections and divergences in how the "master's tools"[13] are being used in organizing strategies across sectors. With techno-utopian promises of the freedom to work "anytime, anywhere," venture capitalists and tech companies justify exploitative practices that are as old as capitalism itself.[14] Faced with the material reality of being squeezed to work long, unpaid, and underpaid hours, however, gig workers across the globe are coming together to organize and change conditions. Emerging gig worker unions are using the media and communication tools that were developed or appropriated by Silicon Valley elites to organize a conscious, powerful working class in the digital age.[15] These struggles converge with anti-racist, pro-immigrant, and feminist movements, making the gig economy a site for exploring intersectional movement building in our current conjuncture. In the meantime, the media and cultural industries are increasingly guided by gig economy logics and processes, creating potential solidarities between workers in the service and creative sectors. Indeed, as scholar-activists we are drawn to these paradoxes and possibilities as we recognize our own academic institutions in these dynamics.

What is new about the "gig economy" is not its contingency, its gendered, racialized character, or its supposed flexibility. It is the ways in which technologies of management, automation, control, and collection are deployed in the workplace and by workers. These are the stories we share in this book.

Convergence in the Gig Economy

At the heart of these struggles and this volume are questions of convergence: What does convergence mean? How do managers and workers in the gig economy harness it? Why is it important? Traditionally, media studies scholars have understood convergence as the "flow of content across multiple media platforms, the cooperation between multiple media industries, and the migratory behavior of media audiences who will go almost anywhere in search of the kinds of entertainment experiences they want."[16] In this view, technological processes drive, if not dictate, social arrangements within the media system, and it downplays how media are developed socially and politically in accordance with accumulation and surveillance strategies. Privileging technology in accounts of convergence and the gig economy obfuscates more than it illuminates. As Ben Tarnoff puts it, discourse around the "gig economy" implies a convergence between "platform" and "gig" that elides labor relations and forms of exploitation.[17] Discourse around platforms cultivates a "comforting sense of technical neutrality and progressive openness."[18] In so doing, "platform" is positioned to appeal to customers, regulators, advertisers, and investors.

This book considers convergence more broadly and more critically than do analyses that cast the nebulous "platform" as an agent of change. We define convergence as the coming together of social, economic, political, cultural, historical, and technological forces. This volume, more specifically, takes a critical political economic approach to explore broader questions around convergence that foreground their history, relationships to wider systems of power, including capitalism, as well as struggles for social justice.[19] Thus, contributors explore how media and telecommunications systems long integral to the extraction and circulation of value under capitalism continue this work in new contexts and with new possibilities for creating a fair economy.

Furthermore, we define convergence in the gig economy as the intersection of technological and political economic forces with forms of management, labor, and labor struggle that have advanced the logics of capitalism. The concept "platform capitalism"[20] enables scholars to craft typologies of data-driven, digital applications that gig and non-gig employers have used to manage production following economic crises of the 1970s. We push the date of the key economic forces back even further, to capitalism's very inception on the backs of unpaid and forced slave labor, as well as to industrial capitalism's employment of cheap, temporary workers that managers overworked and underpaid. As an arm of the gig economy, we understand "surveillance capitalism"[21] is simply the latest means to extract value from media consumers who constitute what Dallas Smythe called the "audience commodity."[22] Today, companies like Google and Facebook have made billions from data extraction while expanding the social factory, "blurring the lines between labor and leisure, between democratic engagement and individualized consumption."[23] These are the kinds of promises Uber and Lyft make when they claim drivers can move seamlessly between "earning" and "chilling."[24]

We disentangle what is novel about the gig economy from long-standing power relations and struggles over conditions of production. Contributors take up Sarah Banet-Weiser's call for analyses of convergence culture that go beyond media content's flow across platforms and instead examine "contradictions" and "possibilities" of an array of converging forces and spaces.²⁵ In the context of the gig economy, what happens, for example, as transportation services converge with Silicon Valley wealth and entrepreneurial ideologies? As the "creative class" converges with service workers? As new forms of gender and racial discrimination converge, creating what Safiya Noble calls "algorithmic oppression" and "technological redlining"?²⁶ As old modes of labor discipline and exploitation converge with new technological regimes? As visible forms of labor converge with less visible forms that are "behind the screen" and behind algorithms?²⁷ As neoliberal techno-fetishism converges with new labor organizing models? This volume explores the concept of convergence through this critical lens to understand the gig economy. Before turning to the plan of this book, we provide context by discussing the gig economy's converging histories and editors' intentions and scholar-activism.

Converging Histories of the Gig

Although labor organizing secured hourly wages for white working-class men in the late 19th and early 20th century, insecure, contingent arrangements reminiscent of today's gig economy logic are a hallmark of capitalism's extraction of surplus value from workers. As Marx put it, "Capital has one sole driving force, the drive to valorize itself, to create surplus-value, to make its constant part, the means of production, absorb the greatest possible amount of surplus labor."²⁸ Contingency lowers costs and maximizes profits that workers generate by directly limiting earnings and frustrating efforts to organize against low wages, long hours, and intense, unsafe working conditions. High turnover marked industrial capitalist work, even into the early 20th century; in 1913 Henry Ford hired over 52,000 workers to keep a steady 14,000-member workforce at his Highland Park plant.²⁹

Contingent arrangements have also long been the refuge for workers locked out of high-paying, secure work due to discriminatory hiring practices and union job protectionism. Whether they were pickers paid by the pound, musicians paid by the gig, or sex workers paid by the "john," gig workers have disproportionately been working-class women, men, and women of color, new immigrants, and migrant workers. Their exploitation has long been justified through patriarchal and white supremacist ideologies and institutions of oppression.³⁰ Journalists and commentators in the mid-19th century, for example, touted working-class (immigrant and native-born) women's "outwork," such as hat making at home, for preventing "'idleness'" and as a sort of side hustle "'in scant times, when there is not much to do.'"³¹ One 1971 ad appearing in business magazines for Kelly Girl, a temporary office agency, touted its white working-class "Never Never Girl" who "never takes a vacation or holiday," "never asks for a raise," and "never fails to please."³² New immigrant women who have come to the US for decades, to work as nannies and housekeepers, have created a globalized domestic labor force that institutions treat as "disposable."³³ Despite their precarity, domestic workers and industrial home workers have fought for legal recognition of their labor, fair pay, and safe working conditions.

The presentism of social commentary emphasizing the novelty of the "precariat" stems from a white androcentrist neglect of this gendered, raced, classed history. African American women in the telecommunications industry experienced exploitation similar to contemporary gig workers. Between the 1960s and 1980s, AT&T replaced white women with African American women as telephone operators not because the company cared about hard-fought equal employment rights, but because the company viewed black women employees as cheap and expendable labor at a time when it was digitizing and downsizing operator work.[34] Thus, it is important to recognize that histories of technology are ones in which "innovation" has been mobilized to reconfigure labor processes, justify them, and distract us from gendered, raced, and classed divisions of labor that constitute these same histories.[35]

It is this gendered, raced, and classed historical amnesia that enables commentators to glamorize the gig economy as cutting edge, technologically driven, and therefore neutral and perhaps even progressive from a political economic standpoint. Consequently, today's multibillion dollar global "gig economy" corporations like Uber, Lyft, and Amazon emphasize their ingenuity in leveraging online technologies and new media to create gigs not jobs, platforms not workplaces, entrepreneurs not workers. Recycling the entrepreneurial ideology promoting "venture labor" that dotcom-era tech workers undertook and Neff explored, these companies marshal techno-utopian promotional discourses to attract workers.[36] They suggest being a gig worker means being "your own boss" and, echoing Duffy, assert the "extra money" you earn as a gig worker can help you "do what you love."[37] Uber promises drivers will move from "earning" to "chilling" with just one click, making it easy to "get your side hustle on." Rival Lyft assures, "you're free to drive, earn and get paid when you choose."[38] The discourse of technological innovation enables these companies to hide behind technology, masking their true relationship to customers and the workforce. This sleight of hand allows them to avoid basic regulations, remaining financially unencumbered, minimizing workers' ability to express their collective interests, and thwarting efforts to unionize.

Gig Worker Activism

This is an unapologetically engaged volume. Taking up communication scholars' calls to engage in activism for social justice,[39] we hope to inform policy, organizing, and movement building around the struggles of gig workers and a growing segment of precarious workers more broadly. The editors are scholar-activists, as are many of the contributors.

Additionally, each of the editors has researched the gig economy and supported gig work organizing. Brian Dolber began researching the gig economy while in between academic posts, completing his first book on media and labor history[40] and driving for Uber. Brian drew on his expertise in labor studies and previous years as a labor organizer to research Uber and Lyft, and as a member of the organizing committee of Rideshare Drivers United-LA, to pioneer new strategies for using online platforms to organize workers. Brian has been part of two strike actions for Uber and Lyft drivers in Los Angeles.[41]

Chenjerai Kumanyika works on the executive and steering committees of 215 People's Alliance, a multiracial collaborative fighting for equity and justice in Philadelphia at the ballot box and in the streets. His interest in precarious working conditions in the "gigification" of journalism and emerging media grew out of his experiences and observations as a writer for NPR, a primary contributor to Scene on Radio's "Seeing White" series, and his work as executive producer and host of Gimlet Media's Peabody-winning podcast, Uncivil. After Chenjerai's departure from Uncivil, workers there formed the podcast industry's first union. During the 2020 pandemic, Chenjerai used podcasting to raise awareness about gig and gig-like conditions in solidarity with the Instacart worker's strike.[42]

Michelle Rodino-Colocino has been a scholar-activist since she was a student and labor organizer in the late 1990s and early 2000s in Seattle with WashTech, the Washington Alliance of Technology Workers/CWA Local 37083. That experience informs her present research on new media and labor management and activism, for which she has interviewed over 60 drivers and organizers in Seattle, detailing 80-hour workweeks and unpaid time spent waiting for calls.[43] Her research has supported organizing at the App-Based Drivers Association, the first chartered local for drivers (affiliated with Teamsters 117), and inspired her participation with the Philadelphia Drivers Union in the May 8, 2019, Uber strike.

Todd Wolfson has been involved in community and labor organizing for two decades. Todd co-founded Media Mobilizing Project (MMP) in 2005 and was part of the executive and steering committee of 215 People's Alliance. As part of his work with MMP, Todd began supporting cab drivers when they struck over the imposition of GPS machines in 2006. Since then Todd has worked closely with the Taxi Workers Alliance of Pennsylvania and more recently with Philadelphia Drivers Union. Alongside his organizing work, Todd is conducting research with gig workers in Philadelphia and London, studying the organizing models of rideshare drivers and food couriers.

As engaged scholars we intend for this volume to deepen our understanding of the promise and perils of "participant activism," a methodology for scholar-activists that Michelle has explored to describe research in which scholars "participate as activists" in the very movements and struggles for social justice that they study.[44] Far from a position of detached "spectatorship" where "contemplation" is the object,[45] participant activists seek to advance social justice through their research.

Embracing research that advances social justice enables us to stake out space for academics, political and community organizers, social movement activists, legislative regulators, consumers, and workers across industries to build solidarity in and through scholar-activist work. Creating such spaces is important in the present political-economic climate marked by a decades-long redistribution of resources upwards to a small elite with massive power, erosion of workers' rights and living conditions, and creeping fascism in the US, Brazil, India, the Philippines, and elsewhere. The particular assault on academic freedom in Turkey and Hungary forces us to consider the dangers of combining staunch neoliberal economic policies with reactionary, authoritarian politics. In this context, we aim to produce knowledge that supports broader struggles for justice.

Working Through the Gig Economy: The Plan of This Volume

This volume expands on calls that editors have previously made for academic solidarity by providing such a space here, where we engage *with* and *as* gig workers.[46] In the context of the neoliberal university, we see ourselves "as part of the same mode of production as those with whom [we] collaborate." We work to bring radical perspectives to our scholarship "while developing social relationships that challenge dominant modes of production."[47]

We draw together research that examines the experience of and resistance to exploitative aspects of the gig economy with a range of expertise in the communication discipline (critical/cultural studies, policy studies, technology studies), employing multiple theoretical perspectives (political economy, critical race, feminist) and methodologies (ethnography, history, discourse analysis, community-based participatory research) in a variety of national contexts. We consider the roles that media, policy, culture, and history play as well as gender, immigrant status, ethnic background, and racial identity in forging working conditions in the "gig economy."

The following chapters range from empirical to theoretical to practical with an understanding that neither past nor present is static, nor are workers and consumers passive (nor necessarily discrete), and that even the most hyperbolic claims for the newness of gig work have antecedents in the past.[48] The first section, "History: We Were Always Gig Workers," troubles the notion that the gig economy is something novel, rooted strictly in technological change. These chapters provide historical context by looking at labor that has long been precarious—as well as gendered and racialized—such as taxi driving, domestic work, sex work, and academic work but where modes and experiences of exploitation and resistance are shifting in the contemporary context alongside digital technology.

The second section, "Ideology: Thinking Like a Gig Economist," critically explores how gig work has been justified through discourses of creativity, independence, and flexibility. By examining popular management literature, work cultures within the podcasting industry, corporate lobbying efforts, and academic labor, the authors demonstrate how gig work has been sold to workers and the public as a progressive transformation in the political economy.

The third section, "Media: Negotiating the Gig Economy," attends to workers' experiences, exploitation, and reconceptualization of relationships to gig work particularly within the media sector. The media sector serves as an important site of gig work for multiple reasons: it has a long history of relying on contingent labor; it has been particularly impacted through digitization; and it has long been infused with the ideology of the entrepreneurial self that characterizes gig work. Through studies of the videogame industry and gamification, cam models, and audiobook readers, we see how gig workers confront the notion that their work is "just a gig" and develop strategies for coping with amateurization, raced and gendered marginalization, and unpaid labor. One chapter suggests workers should democratize data, transforming it into a commons.

In the fourth section, "Struggles: Organizing in the Gig Economy," authors chronicle and critically analyze efforts and barriers to collectively organizing as gig workers. These struggles occur in paradigmatic gig occupations, such as rideshare and delivery, and in academia. Authors discuss how workers draw upon the political economic and technological contradictions embedded in the existing system to transform industries and challenge late neoliberal capitalism. We conclude by considering how the COVID-19 pandemic converged with gig labor to create new class formations around "essential work" that put workers' lives and livelihoods at additional risk, highlight enduring exploitation, and point to new paths for creating solidarity and systemic change.

We hope that this collection offers a window onto the burgeoning literature poised at the intersections of technology, labor, and resistance. Contributors to this book critically engage with the gig economy and the transformation of work and technology that it signifies. In this vein, we also see this volume as a humble step in the development of praxis that contributes to Paolo Freire's call for "reflection and action directed at the structures to be transformed."[49] Amid the growing immiseration of working people at the hands of Wall Street and Silicon Valley, we look to authors, organizers, and workers to provide a spark of renewal that lights a path forward.

Notes

1. Michelle Rodino-Colocino and research assistant, Pooja Nerkar, spoke with over two dozen Uber and Lyft drivers and the lead organizers of the Philadelphia Drivers Union (PDU) during the week of the May 8, 2019, global strikes against Uber. Names of interviewees are pseudonyms to protect anonymity.
2. Elka Torpey and Andrew Hogan, "Work in a Gig Economy," *BLS.gov*, May 2016, www.bls.gov/careeroutlook/2016/article/pdf/what-is-the-gig-economy.pdf.
3. Michelle Rodino-Colocino, "Uber's $9 Billion IPO Rests on 80-Plus Hour Workweeks and a Lot of Waiting," *Salon*, April 30, 2019, www.salon.com/2019/04/30/ubers-9-billion-ipo-rests-on-drivers-80-plus-hour-workweeks-and-a-lot-of-waiting_partner/.
4. "Why We Are on Strike," *NYTWA.org*, last updated May 13, 2019, www.nytwa.org/statements/2019/5/13/joint-national-statement-on-why-we-strike-from-may-8th-2019-striking-cities-released-5819.

5. Brian Dolber, "From Independent Contractors to an Independent Union: Building Solidarity through Rideshare Driver United's Digital Organizing Strategy," Report for The Media, Inequality & Change (MIC) Center, October 3, 2019, www.miccenter.org/wp-content/uploads/2019/10/Dolber_final-2.pdf.
6. Kate Conger and Michael de la Merced, "Uber Aims for Valuation of Up to $91 Billion in I.P.O.," *The New York Times*, April 26, 2019, www.nytimes.com/2019/04/26/technology/uber-ipo-valuation-price-range.html; Conger and de la Merced; Kate Conger, Vicky Xiuzhong, and Zach Wichter, "Uber Drivers' Day of Strikes Circles the Globe before the Company's I.P.O.," *The New York Times*, May 8, 2019, www.nytimes.com/2019/05/08/technology/uber-strike.html; DeMAnuelle-Hall, Joe, "Strike by Drivers Disrupts Uber Launch," *Labor Notes*, May 31, 2019, www.labornotes.org/2019/05/strike-drivers-disrupts-uber-launch.
7. Dolber, "From Independent Contractors."; Rodino-Colocino, "Uber's $9 Billion IPO."; Alex Rosenblat, *Uberland: How Algorithms Are Rewriting the Rules of Work* (Berkeley: University of California Press, 2018).
8. Todd Wolfson, "Introduction: Class Struggle Before Class," *South Atlantic Quarterly* 119, no. 2 (2020): 394–400.
9. Conger et al., "Uber Drivers' Day of Strikes."; Dolber, "From Independent Contractors."; Veena Dubal, "Gig Worker Organizing for Solidarity Unions," *Law and Political Economy*, June 19, 2019, https://lpeblog.org/2019/06/19/gig-worker-organizing-for-solidarity-unions/; Staughton Lynd, *Solidarity Unionism: Rebuilding the Labor Movement From Below* (Oakland, CA: PM Press, 2015).
10. Eliza Berkon, "How D.C.'s Hourly and Gig Workers Are Grappling With New Economic Realities Under Coronavirus," *WAMU.org*, March 17, 2020, https://wamu.org/story/20/03/17/how-d-c-s-hourly-and-gig-workers-are-grappling-with-new-economic-realities-under-coronavirus/; Loh Dylan, "Gig Economy Workers Fall on Hard Times in Singapore and Australia," *Nikkei Asian Review*, April 8, 2020, https://asia.nikkei.com/Economy/Gig-economy-workers-fall-on-hard-times-in-Singapore-and-Australia2.
11. "Supporting You during the Coronavirus," *Uber.com*, last modified March 17, 2020, www.uber.com/blog/supporting-you-during-coronavirus/.
12. "Demand Coronavirus Relief for Platform Workers," *Drivers-United.org*, https://drivers-united.org/a/demand-coronavirus-relief-for-platform-workers?r=2uHzpZoN&fbclid=IwAR3bm6gxqqhU27sQYf1dLEpCGZhOf3JQBHeAonJou2BpjHfDTe7ZFm9BWiI.
13. Audre Lorde, "The Master's Tools Will Never Dismantle the Master's House," in *Sister Outsider: Essays and Speeches* (Berkeley: Crossing Press. 2007), 112.
14. Michelle Rodino-Colocino, "Technomadic Work: From Promotional Vision to WashTech's Opposition," *Work Organization, Labour and Globalization* 2, no. 1 (2008):104–16.
15. Wolfson, "Introduction: Class Struggle."
16. Henry Jenkins, *Fans, Bloggers, and Gamers: Exploring Participatory Culture* (New York: New York University Press, 2006), 2.
17. Ben Tarnoff, "Platforms Don't Exist," *Metal Machine Music* (newsletter), November 22, 2019, https://bentarnoff.substack.com/p/platforms-dont-exist.
18. Tarleton Gillespie, "The Politics of 'Platforms'," *New Media & Society* 12, no. 3 (2010): 360.
19. Janet Wasko, Graham Murdock, and Helena Sousa, "Introduction: The Political Economy of Communications: Core Concerns and Issues," in *The Handbook of Political Economy of Communications* (London: Blackwell, 2011).
20. Nick Srnicek, *Platform Capitalism* (Hoboken, NJ: John Wiley & Sons, Ltd, 2016).
21. Shoshana Zuboff, *The Age of Surveillance Capitalism: The Fight for a Human Future at the New Frontier of Power* (London: Profile Books, 2019).
22. Dallas W. Smythe, "On the Audience Commodity and Its Work," in *Dependency Road: Communications, Capitalism, Consciousness, and Canada* (Norwood, NJ: Ablex, 1981).

23. Brian Dolber, "Blindspots and Blurred Lines: Dallas Smythe, the Audience Commodity, and the Transformation of Labor in the Digital Age," *Sociology Compass* 10, no. 9 (2016): 748.
24. Rodino-Colocino, "Uber's $9 Billion IPO."
25. Sarah Banet-Weiser, "Convergence on the Street: Rethinking the Authentic/Commercial Binary," *Cultural Studies* 25, no. 4–5 (2011): 643.
26. Safiya Noble, *Algorithms of Oppression: How Search Engines Reinforce Racism* (New York: New York University Press, 2018), 1, 4.
27. Sarah T. Roberts, *Behind the Screen: Content Moderation in the Shadows of Social Media* (New Haven: Yale University Press, 2019).
28. Karl Marx, *Capital Volume I*, Marxists.org, www.marxists.org/archive/marx/works/1867-c1/ch10.htm.
29. David Roediger and Philip Sheldon Foner, *Our Own Time: A History of American Labor and the Working Day* (New York: Verso, 1989), 191.
30. Eileen Boris, *Home to Work: Motherhood and the Politics of Industrial Homework in the United States* (Cambridge: Cambridge University Press, 1994); Chang Grace, *Disposable Domestics: Immigrant Women Workers in the Global Economy* (Cambridge, MA: South End Press, 2000); Evelyn Nakano Glenn, "From Servitude to Service Work: Historical Continuities in the Racial Division of Paid Reproductive Labor," *Signs: Journal of Women in Culture and Society* 18, no. 1 (1992): 1–43; Erin Hatton, *The Temp Economy: From Kelly Girls to Permatemps in Postwar America* (Philadelphia: Temple University Press, 2011); Louis Hyman, *Temp: How American Work, American Business, and the American Dream Became Temporary* (New York: Viking, 2018); Daniel H. Pink, *Free Agent Nation: How America's New Independent Workers are Transforming the Way We Live* (New York: Warner Books, 2001); David R. Roediger and Elizabeth D. Esch, *The Production of Difference: Race and the Management of Labor in US History* (Oxford: Oxford University Press, 2012).
31. Christopher Clark, *The Roots of Rural Capitalism: Western Massachusetts, 1780–1860* (Ithaca: Cornell University Press, 1990), 186.
32. Hatton, *The Temp Economy*, 51.
33. Chang, *Disposable Domestics*.
34. Venus Green, *Race on the Line: Gender, Labor, and Technology in the Bell System, 1880–1980* (Durham, NC: Duke University Press, 2001).
35. David Noble, *Forces of Production: A Social History of Industrial Automation* (New York: Alfred A. Knopf, 1984); Todd Wolfson, "The Gig Economy and Class (De) Composition," in *The Routledge Companion to Media and Class*, ed. Erika Polson, Lynn Schofield Clark, and Radhika Gajjala (New York: Routledge, 2019), 192–202.
36. Gina Neff, *Venture Labor: Work and the Burden of Risk in Innovative Industries* (Cambridge, MA: MIT Press, 2012).
37. "Drive Toward What Matters," *Lyft.com*, accessed February 20, 2020, www.lyft.com/drive-with-lyft; Brooke Erin Duffy, *(Not) Getting Paid to Do What You Love: Gender, Social Media, and Aspirational Work* (New Haven: Yale University Press, 2017).
38. Rodino-Colocino, "Uber's $9 Billion IPO."
39. Dana Cloud, "The Only Conceivable Thing to Do: Reflections of Academics and Activism," in *Activism and Rhetoric: Theories and Contexts for Political Engagement*, ed. JongHwa Lee and Seth Kahn (New York: Routledge, 2010), 11–24; Cathy J. Cohen and Sarah J. Jackson, "Ask a Feminist: A Conversation with Cathy J. Cohen on Black Lives Matter, Feminism, and Contemporary Activism," *Signs: Journal of Women in Culture and Society* 41, no. 4 (2016): 775–92; Patricia Hill Collins, *On Intellectual Activism* (Philadelphia: Temple University Press, 2012); Brittney C. Cooper, Susanna M. Morris, and Robin M. Boylorn, *The Crunk Feminist Collection* (New York: The Feminist Press, 2017); Lawrence R. Frey and Kevin M. Carragee, eds., *Communication Activism*, 2 vols. (Cresskill: Hampton Press, 2007); Peter Nien-chu Kiang, "Crouching Activists, Hidden Scholars: Reflections on Research and Development with Students

and Communities in Asian American Studies," in *Engaging Contradictions: Theory, Politics, and Methods of Activist scholarship*, ed. Charles R. Hale (Berkeley: University of California Press, 2008), 299–318; JongHwa Lee and Seth Kahn, *Activism and Rhetoric: Theories and Contexts for Political Engagement, Second Edition* (New York: Routledge; 2019); Steve Macek, "From the Weapon of Criticism to Criticism by Weapons: Critical Communication Scholarship, Marxism, and Political Activism," in *Marxism and Communication Studies: The Point Is to Change It*, ed. Lee Artz, Steve Macek and Dana Cloud (New York: Peter Lang, 2006), 217–42.

40. Brian Dolber, *Media and Culture in the US Jewish Labor Movement: Sweating for Democracy in the Interwar Era* (New York: Springer, 2017).
41. Dolber, "From Independent Contractors."
42. Chenjerai Kumanyika, "The Instacart Strike and Gig Work during the COVID-19 Pandemic," *Soundcloud.com*, accessed November 27, 2020, https://soundcloud.com/chenjeraikumanyika/instacart-strike.
43. Rodino-Colocino, "Uber's $9 Billion IPO."
44. Michelle Rodino-Colocino, "Participant Activism: Exploring a Methodology for Scholar-Activists Through Lessons Learned as a Precarious Labor Organizer," *Communication, Culture & Critique* 5, no. 4 (November 9, 2012): 544.
45. Kevin M. Carragee and Lawrence R. Frey, "Introduction: Communication Activism for Social Justice Scholarship," in *Communication Activism: Vol. 3: Struggling for Social Justice Amidst Difference*, ed. Lawrence R. Frey and Kevin Carragee (New York: Hampton Press, 2011), 1–67.
46. Michelle Rodino-Colocino, "Communication Activism| Critical-Cultural Communication Activism Research Calls for Academic Solidarity," *International Journal of Communication* 10 (2016), https://ijoc.org/index.php/ijoc/article/viewFile/6007/1753.
47. Brian Dolber, "Precarity and Solidarity at Neoliberalism's Twilight: The Potentials of Transnational Production Autoethnography," *Cultural Studies Critical Methodologies*, February 22, 2019, 4, https://doi.org/10.1177/1532708619829781.
48. Tim Strangleman, "The Nostalgia for Permanence at Work? The End of Work and Its Commentators," *The Sociological Review* 55, no. 1 (2007): 81–103.
49. Paulo Freire, *Pedagogy of the Oppressed*, trans. M. B. Ramos (New York: Herder and Herder, 1970).

II
History
We Were Always Gig Workers

1

BEHIND THE WHEEL AND IN THE STREETS

Technological Transformation, Exit, and Voice in the New York City Taxi Industry

Hannah Johnston

"There is not enough work for everybody . . . This is SLAVERY NOW," veteran black car driver Doug Schifter posted on his Facebook page mere hours before dying by suicide in front of New York's City Hall. His note implicated the city for failing to regulate the for-hire vehicle (FHV) industry in which he worked for 44 years. Schifter explained how years of unregulated FHV growth caused a vast oversupply of drivers resulting in his, and other drivers', financial ruin. Unable to pay his bills and having maxed out his credit cards, he anticipated losing his house. Schifter concluded by sharing his intention to bring his and other drivers' pain to light, "I see no point to continue trying. I hope with the public sacrifice I make now. . . [to bring] some attention to the plight of the drivers and the people."

The degradation of the FHV industry that Schifter bemoaned was exacerbated by Uber's 2011 entry into New York City. Since 2011 the total number of FHVs has tripled, flooding the market and increasing competition and road congestion. For years, worsening working conditions were compounded by unregulated driver pay rates and app-based company pricing policies that routinely undermined drivers' wage share. However, six months after Doug Schifter died, the New York City Council reversed course, passing unprecedented legislation that limited the number of app-based FHVs and established a citywide minimum fare for app-based drivers. Workers heralded the new regulations as an important step towards improving job security and working conditions throughout the sector. The City Council's decision was a result of a multiyear campaign by the New York Taxi Workers Alliance (NYTWA), a grassroots union[1] representing FHV transportation workers throughout the city.

This chapter charts the entry of Uber into New York and drivers' financial demise. I offer two arguments. First, longstanding industry exploitation, and in particular neoliberal reforms in the New York taxi market that began in the 1970s, paved the way for the adoption of app-based services. Second, when app-based services ultimately compounded driver precarity through debt, NYTWA was uniquely positioned to achieve sectoral reform because of its commitment to inclusive organizing.

In this chapter, I introduce the New York Taxi Workers Alliance. Then I present an overview of New York's FHV sector. While I focus on the years surrounding the introduction of app-based services (2010–2018), I also reference the neoliberal reforms of the 1970s that laid the groundwork for the success of app-based services. I then examine drivers' responses to the impact of app-based transportation companies. Drawing on Hirschman's concepts of exit, voice, loyalty, and neglect (EVLN),[2] I analyze a series of 31 interviews and a survey of over 300 app-based drivers conducted in New York City between 2016 and 2018.[3] A key finding points to an unfortunate irony: the app-based services that attracted drivers with the promise of better working conditions perpetuate many of the objectionable behaviors that workers hoped to escape. Additionally, drivers' acquisition of work-related debt foreclosed their exit option by frustrating their ability to leave the industry. Work-related debt, however, did catalyze collective participation in voice-based strategies aimed at regulatory reform. I then examine NYTWA's role in cultivating collective voice and campaigning to ensure professional drivers' ability to earn a living from the for-hire transport sector. In conclusion, I argue that given the industry-wide effect of app-based services, sectoral reform is the best way to ensure decent working conditions for all.

The New York Taxi Workers Alliance

Founded in 1998 as a member-led organization to support the needs of drivers working in New York City's FHV sector, NYTWA has developed an approach to driver advocacy that addresses economic inequality. The organization's early work, under the banner of "The Lease Drivers Coalition," began in 1992 as a project spearheaded by a nonprofit called the Committee Against Anti-Asian Violence.[4] This work reflects NYTWA's longstanding ties in South Asian immigrant communities—notably Pakistani, Bangladeshi, and Indian immigrants—who comprise a large portion of taxi sector workers.[5] Since establishing itself as an independent organization, however, NYTWA has sought to create broad-based solidarity across the FHV sector yielding a diverse membership with regard to race, ethnicity, gender, and driver status.

NYTWA is growing at a time when labor markets are in transition, when nonstandard forms of work are on the rise, and when trade union membership and collective bargaining coverage in the United States are at an all-time low. While many labor unions are grappling with how to respond to these labor market transformations, NYTWA has been leading the way for over two decades, improving conditions for workers legally classified as self-employed who, as such, do not have collective bargaining rights. For this reason, NYTWA is commonly associated with the worker center movement.[6]

Over the past two decades, worker centers like NYTWA have emerged as a new type of institution advocating for worker rights.[7] Operating independently and often within a limited geographical scope, they provide social services and labor resources to workers in a variety of different, and frequently nonstandard, forms of employment to help facilitate improved social and economic integration.[8] For example, NYTWA fights against predatory loans targeting driver-owners, launches campaigns to improve working conditions broadly (i.e., demanding taxi stands), and offers ticket assistance and driver training programs.

Within New York City's FHV sector, high levels of municipal regulation over the terms and conditions of driving work afford drivers little control over their quotidian work experience. Consequently, NYTWA has identified a need for worker unity and collective power, although it has had to develop methods and strategies to achieve this absent collective bargaining. Like other worker organizations that promote leadership development from the worker base,[9] most members of NYTWA's board, organizing committee, and staff are current or former drivers. Competition resulting from the entrance of app-based transportation companies to the NYC market in 2011 has hurt the viability of driving as a profession and has thus become a central theme addressed by NYTWA.

Before Uber: Employment Status, the Great Recession, and Drivers' Structural and Associational Power

There is a historical correlation between the FHV labor market and overall economic conditions. During the early 2000s, the yellow cab industry was the most reliable, competitive, and lucrative sub-sector to work in. However, an expanding economy also meant that low-skilled workers had myriad job opportunities, making the yellow cab industry—marked by long hours and dangerous working conditions—relatively unattractive. Following the 2008 financial crisis, however, the number of licensed drivers reached an all-time high as slack labor market conditions and the relative ease of entry into the driving profession absorbed workers displaced from jobs in struggling sectors like construction and transport.[10]

Similar trends occurred decades earlier during the Great Depression, leading to early industry regulation. The Haas Act, introduced in 1937, limited the number of registered vehicles to 13,595 and designated control of licensing and industry oversight to the city. It "came about during [a] threat of fare wars that would push drivers and garages into ruinous competition" and helped ensure that drivers could make a viable income by limiting the number of available vehicles on the road.[11] The act also included an owner-operator component, which kept medallion prices down.

Efforts to balance power in the industry eroded over the subsequent decades, particularly during the 1970s and 1980s. While the capped medallion market ensured that taxi supply did not outstrip demand, private transfer of medallions was permitted, drastically increasing the price of both fleet and owner-operator permits.¹² Medallions became an attractive investment leading to inflated values and financialization—exemplified most clearly by Medallion Financial, a company that underwrites loans for taxi medallions and trades publicly on the NASDAQ (TAXI). When Uber entered New York City in 2011, medallions sold for as much as 1.2 million USD; however, since this time, medallion prices have fallen dramatically to less than 200,000 USD. For taxi barons and speculative investors, this has resulted in millions lost.¹³ For individual owner-operators, this depreciation has left them with toxic assets—a sizeable debt to either repay or discharge. It has also left many with the fear and stress that typically accompanies financial insecurity.

The platform economy's most notable disruption has been in the taxi industry. The early success of platforms in this sector was well primed by neoliberal industry reform that began systematically shifting employment related risk onto the shoulders of drivers decades earlier. Prior to the 1970s, the taxi industry was characterized by full-time employment and strong trade unions. As employees, drivers were paid a fixed wage, and fares that accumulated on the meter were typically shared between drivers and cab owners. Drivers also had access to standard employment benefits like unemployment insurance, wage and hour protections, and the right to collectively bargain. Neoliberal reform changed all this.

At the end of the 1970s, leasing was introduced in New York and in cities across the United States.¹⁴ Under leasing, drivers were reclassified as independent contractors—the same employment status that characterizes platform economy work. Leasing required drivers to pay a fixed sum up front to rent a medallion (and typically also the car that it is affixed to); in turn, drivers would keep all fares earned during their shift. Thus, adverse conditions with monetary implications—such as bad weather, low passenger volume, and traffic—became risks borne exclusively by the driver. Lessors, on the other hand, maintained a stable and guaranteed income.

Leasing has repercussions on both the structural and the associational power of NYC FHV drivers. Structural power is largely determined by the location of the industrial relations actors within the economic system. Myriad factors, including product and labor markets, labor substitutability, payment and management control systems, and the structure and sophistication of collective organizing, influence the extent of workers' structural power.¹⁵ Under leasing, labor markets became fragmented, work relationships more informal, and collective bargaining obsolete, transforming employees into free-agent workers with few rights.

Factors that contribute to tighter labor markets give workers greater structural power by making them less substitutable. Conversely, workers can be encouraged to accept adverse terms and conditions "by the knowledge that any worker who demands too much can be replaced by someone else from the 'reserve army' of the unemployed who can do the same work more cheaply or more compliantly."¹⁶ In the years preceding app-based FHV services, burgeoning unemployment led to a growing reserve of licensed drivers, undermining their ability to be selective about who they leased from. Additionally, while drivers previously needed to demonstrate a basic level of knowledge regarding the city's road infrastructure, app-based technologies' algorithmically determined routes contributed to the profession's deskilling.

Leasing also directly impacted associational power, limiting drivers' collective rights and redefining the scope of possibilities for collective action. Self-employed drivers found themselves beyond the purview of the National Labor Relations Act (NLRA) and exempt from key labor rights such as the right to unionize and bargain collectively. Union membership rates, or participation rates in collective institutions such as worker centers and works councils, are often used as a proxy for associational power because membership generally confers strong levels of unity. However, the need and desire for collective association persisted, and NYTWA has sought to cultivate associational power by uniting drivers under a single sectoral organization.

In the absence of collective bargaining, NYTWA has developed a multipronged approach involving legislative action, administrative rule making, direct action protests, and media engagement. While this approach has influenced NYC's Taxi and Limousine Commission's rules, enforcement remains a perpetual challenge. The establishment of lease caps, for example, assures drivers can earn a viable living and are protected from overcharges. Yet despite such rules, overcharging and extraneous and unsanctioned fees, such as early vehicle pick-up charges and cleaning fees, continued.[17] For years, precarious drivers, eager to ensure that there would be a car available to lease, felt that they had little choice but to pay in excess of the legal limit.

Uber: An Alternative?

Unfavorable working conditions in the traditional taxi sector paved the way for the introduction of app-based dispatching. While some drivers were attracted to companies like Uber under the pretense of high earnings and flexible schedules,[18] many left after experiencing longstanding dissatisfaction with their working conditions in more traditional sectors, and in particular, lease overcharges. In a series of interviews I conducted in 2016, few respondents were new to the industry, having worked previously in other low-wage jobs, for example as store clerks, janitors, or security agents. Most had a long history of driving and all had experience leasing vehicles. Of those with industry experience, all mentioned past dissatisfaction with the conditions under which they procured a vehicle.

These findings are based on 31 interviews with app-based FHV drivers. Interviews were guided by a set of questions designed to capture demographic characteristics and work experience, including industry tenure, reliance on income from driving, why drivers chose to work for app-based dispatching services, and their job satisfaction and outlook. Interviewees were invited to participate at the NYTWA office, were contacted via snowballing, or were identified via their online media presence. Their anonymity was ensured (all have been given aliases), and they were free to withdraw or refuse to answer any question. Interviews were conducted in person when possible and over the phone when not.

Drivers who chose to move from traditional FHV sectors to app-based dispatching services can be examined through a framework first presented by Albert Hirschman in 1970. Hirschman highlighted EVLN as a range of possible responses of employees or consumers who experience dissatisfaction.[19] Exit is observed as quitting, resigning, or seeking employment elsewhere. Voice may include making formal complaints or participating in social dialogue, such as collective bargaining or workplace cooperation, and is aimed at improving unsatisfactory conditions. Loyalty is expressed passively by patient workers who optimistically await improved conditions. Neglect can be observed in behaviors such as absenteeism or reduced work effort and productivity.

For experienced lease drivers, Uber's arrival created an illusion of choice, especially when compared to garages who were largely indistinguishable in their exploitative practice of overcharging. Their switch from the regulated yellow cab industry to app-based dispatching services was an exercise of the exit option, fueled, in large part, by exploitation in traditional FHV sectors. That traditional cab drivers and app-based drivers were both considered independent contractors made this transition all the more seamless.

Industry overcharges and inflated lease prices were particularly infuriating for experienced drivers and are best understood through the experiences of individuals. Miguel, born in 1968 in the Dominican Republic, started driving a yellow cab in May 2002. In May 2014, he purchased a car and began working full time for Uber.

> At the garage we used to pay too much money to rent a medallion. I was working with someone who would rent the medallion but had worked with the garage to finance [the purchase of] his car. He showed me his receipts and said "look how much money I am paying for this car." This guy was paying $54,000 for a car that would have cost about $38,000 from a dealer—all inflated from the garage. This was incredible. On top of financing his car he was renting the medallion for almost $1,400 per week.

Even though his friend had borne the brunt of high charges, Miguel expressed that these types of experiences were emotionally draining and defeating. They both made the switch to Uber.

Garvin was born in Colombo, Sri Lanka, and spent 10 years as a yellow cab driver before switching to Uber in 2012. As a yellow cab driver, he purchased his own car, painted it yellow, and installed a partition, though he rented a medallion. He felt this arrangement created an opportunity for bigger financial gains.

> You buy your car and this is your investment so you take care of your investment. Once the car is paid off, maybe after two or three years, you

will gain a little bit more money [because then you only have the medallion payment] and you could have the car for as long as five years.

Nonetheless, his investment also placed him at greater risk of exploitation. As the economy worsened and the demand for medallions increased, "there was no security because at any time, they could come and take the medallion and say, you are not driving with us anymore." He would have been obliged to pay off his vehicle debt, but without a street-hail permit, he would have no income. For Garvin, Uber meant that he didn't have to worry about permits or the threat of having them rescinded, thus providing more reliable market access.

Alvin never bothered to buy a vehicle. Instead he leased a yellow cab for five years from a garage before briefly switching to Uber and then to Lyft and Gett. He described aspects of the garage that he really liked, but he had no patience for inflated and predatory lease pricing.

> I liked driving a yellow cab. What I didn't like was the management of the garages and how they dealt with me. I liked driving yellow though, I liked going to the garages, hanging out with the other drivers, that kind of thing was fun, you know. [But] the whole mentality with the dispatchers at the garage was something that I got tired of. The final straw was one garage that really ripped me off. They gave me a weekly lease (car and medallion) at one price and then half way through the lease they upped the price. They told me if I didn't like it I could f-off, so that's what I did.

Nick, like Alvin, was born in New York and grew tired of unpredictable and indignant garage managers. He got his taxi license in 2005 during a summer break from college. In the 10 years he drove a yellow cab, he worked at six different garages. The first garage was his favorite because

> they had the best [most reliable] cars in New York City. . . . Their problem was that the owner is kind of known to be the real version of Danny DeVito in the old taxi driving TV show. Some days you would catch him on a good day and he would be smiling and making jokes, and the next he is telling you to fuck off and never work here again. You should have the right to not show up when you don't want to work. It's like a rental car company, you know? You're a customer, not an employee. So I would call them a day in advance to tell them I wasn't coming in. Then I would show up the next day and they would be cursing me and anyone else who took time off. Meanwhile these guys are making millions of dollars.

Despite his self-employed status, Nick found that his working conditions were dictated by the garages and that he had very little flexibility. Uber's promise of flexibility was a hopeful improvement compared to what he experienced at the garage.

Like most markets, Uber entered NYC with large-scale incentives to attract drivers. While media coverage and court rulings suggest that promises of 90,000 USD annual earnings attracted drivers to work for the company, interviews with experienced drivers reveal they had grown tired of exploitative leasing arrangements in other FHV sectors. Unfortunately, the hope that Uber would provide better working conditions was short lived. Uber's corporate approach to deregulation flooded the market with cabs, and the company regularly changed drivers' contract terms by taking larger commissions or introducing discounted services like UberPool and requiring drivers to accept these hails, despite paying them less per mile driven. These conditions affected the entirety of the labor market and exacerbated the already precarious situation of many drivers.

Taxi 2.0: Uber Exploitation, Driver Debt, and Voice

The hope that Uber would provide a viable alternative to the exploitation that characterized the taxi industry didn't last. As more drivers affiliated with Uber, Lyft, and other app-based services, they began to find they were working a greater number of hours for the same or less money. When comparing their experiences with others, it became clear that the factors contributing to poor working conditions were as much a market problem as they were a firm problem. Redress required a market-wide solution.

My interviews, paired with a 2017 survey of drivers, show that drivers' acquisition of job-related debt coupled with Uber's market dominance stripped them of viable exit options. While there were a growing number of apps through which drivers could sell their labor, the quotidian work experience was strikingly similar irrespective of which firm they chose. Some apps too popular and costly to avoid; drivers often had to multihome, working simultaneously through multiple apps, to ensure that they could make a living. The lack of meaningful exit options helped steer drivers to voice-based behaviors and participation in the major campaign that resulted in the first vehicle cap placed on app-based services in North America.

Since the introduction of ride-hail technology in New York, NYTWA has received visits and calls from app-based drivers who testified to crowded roads, an oversupply of drivers, and declining wages. NYTWA created venues for yellow cab drivers and medallion owners, like Mr. Singh, to explain the deterioration of his financial stability directly to presiding TLC Commissioner Meera Joshi. Expressing frustration with the city's lack of sufficient regulation during a public meeting that was held at NYTWA's office, Mr. Singh said,

> I have been unable to find someone to drive with me and my [monthly] mortgage [payment] is about 5,000 dollars. I also have three kids. In the month of April, the bank seized my medallion because I was unable to pay the mortgage. I borrowed money from my friends and my family and I paid

the bank and I got it back. These are the letters I am getting from the bank. They say I will lose my house—so even though I am working, it looks like I will be homeless very soon.

Some of Mr. Singh's challenges were attributed to competition. Apps introduced e-hails into lower Manhattan, where yellow cabs formerly held the exclusive right to work. At the same time, as former yellow cab lease drivers exited the sub-sector, drivers who owned medallions found it increasingly difficult to find a driving partner, thus adding to their individual financial burdens.

To better capture a sense of driver characteristics, opinion, and experience, NYTWA administered a qualitative survey in November and December of 2017. These survey findings, paired with my qualitative interviews, shed light on how gig work is experienced by drivers throughout the sector and highlight the need for sectoral reform to address shortcomings in the unregulated market. The survey results presented here are from 307 drivers who identified themselves as primarily driving in the "app-based dispatch FHV" sector and were surveyed at NYC airports.

App-based drivers in New York have a longer driving record than have app-based drivers elsewhere, averaging approximately 26 months.[20] Existing research suggests that one in six workers in the gig economy each month is new and that more than half of on-demand workers leave their job within 12 months.[21] Research on Uber drivers specifically reveals a national average of driving tenure of a mere 6.7 months.[22] Labor market growth in the gig economy, including the taxi industry, is largely attributed to the low barriers to market entry. While it has been argued that lifting restrictions that limit market access benefits workers and allows market growth, these statements falsely infer that market exit is equally fluid. Indeed, while transportation applications in New York City have permitted a larger number of individuals to enter the market,[23] vehicle ownership was heavily promoted by companies like Uber. Given the city's low rates of vehicle ownership generally, it is notable that 75 percent of respondents obtained financing in order to acquire their work vehicle. Like taxi drivers trapped by toxic medallions, vehicle debt accrued by app-based drivers makes it difficult for them to leave the market at will.

Given that, for those who have financed cars, debt limits their ability to exercise the exit option, one might argue that, with the growing number of app-based services, moving from one app to another is an expression of exit. However, abandoning popular apps can be too costly, and many must multihome to acquire sufficient work (74 percent).[24] The tendency toward multihoming reveals that loyalty, as conceived of by Hirschman as an optimistic allegiance to a particular brand or employer, is not a motivating factor for drivers to stay with one particular app provider. In fact, multiple interviewees indicated that they saw little distinction between main app competitors and that they decided which app they would work with based on wherever they got the first hail.

What imbues workers and consumers with power under Hirschman's framework is the ability to exercise the exit option with immediacy. This immediacy, however, does not exist for app-based drivers who think of exit as a medium- or long-term plan. For example, when asked if they would continue driving over the next five years, 25 percent of drivers indicated that they would not, 36 percent indicated they were unsure, and the remaining 39 percent indicated that they would.[25] Among those who said that they would continue to work in the industry, almost all (90 percent) indicated that they would continue to drive what they were driving currently—an indicator of some level of optimism about their future job prospects. Roughly half of drivers who indicated that over the next five years they would not continue driving noted insufficient earnings as their reason. This sentiment was also reflected in interviews. Hasan, a young Uber driver from Pakistan, explained that he had three more years to pay off his car. In 2016, after Uber dropped their fares, he stated that he was not earning the living he had hoped to. "It is like Taxi 2.0. . . . As soon as my car is paid off, I am getting out."

Take-home pay is low despite long hours. While Uber and similar ride-hail apps tout their scheduling flexibility, drivers across all platforms spend significant time behind the wheel, averaging 56.74 hours per week with a median of 61 hours.[26] The high volume of hours worked is consistent with industry standards. Standard yellow medallion leases are 12 hours per day, and the other research on transportation apps suggests that, among full-time drivers, practices including nudging[27] and driving incentives contribute to similarly high hours.[28] These hours demonstrate that most drivers work in the industry in a full-time capacity (95 percent of respondents); less than 5 percent have a second job.[29]

Having established that many drivers lacked both immediate exit opportunities and loyalty toward a particular app provider, two other possible responses remain under the Hirschman framework: neglect and voice. Responding by way of neglect, drivers can endure current conditions and attempt to distance themselves from a particular app. However, neglect is a passive response that can result in worsening conditions, a situation that is likely to fuel a race to the bottom when it comes to working conditions and pay. Voice, on the other hand, offers a more proactive method to address deteriorating conditions.

As NYTWA witnessed deteriorating conditions in the industry writ large, the union began work towards a campaign to develop app-based FHV regulations. Raj, for example, struggling to make his payments expressed frustration to the TLC commissioner in a 2016 meeting, "We (drivers) went to the TLC meetings, we have given rallies, but why are we not being listened to? What can we expect from you? Nobody wants to listen to us. Why are we being punished?" Indeed, the city seemed either blind or unwilling to hear drivers' calls until February 2018 when Doug Schifter charged the city with bringing financial destitution upon drivers that led him to utter desperation:

> I have no more health insurance and am not enjoying good health.
> No more vehicle as my GM engine failed twice this year as well as the transmission.

No more income to pay bills and maxed out credit cards I cannot pay.
I will lose my house and everything else.
I see no point to continue trying.

And so Schifter tried to make the only difference he knew how, by his "public display of a most private affair," posting this statement on social media, driving to the steps of city hall and ending his life with a shotgun.

Suicide Is No Exit: Collective Voice and Industry Reform

NYTWA had long sought to amplify collective expressions of worker voice. When it came to app-based dispatch services specifically, NYTWA organized protests in opposition to legislation that would regularize Uber's practices—even driving as a caravan to attend hearings at the state capital to voice opposition to Governor Cuomo's introduction of a bill that would permit ride-hailing statewide. NYTWA staff and members also regularly attended TLC meetings, offering feedback and proposals for rulemaking procedures with the aim of improving the terms and conditions of drivers' work, a strategy that they had developed over the previous decades with much success.[30] Uber's strong lobbying efforts, however, had effectively quashed prior proposals to regulate app-based ride-hail services, even in New York.[31]

As a union, voice has always featured centrally in NYTWA's approach and strategy, but it was only in the wake of driver suicides that NYTWA was able to compel its industry counterparts to act. Media coverage of the suicides played a large role in stimulating meaningful conversation around industry reform. Media interviews accompanied expressions of collective action and voice. For example, NYTWA organized a vigil for Doug Schifter and issued several public statements that clearly linked his financial distress, feelings of entrapment, and loss of hope to the struggles of thousands of other drivers that visited the office daily. In their announcement of the vigil, NYTWA wrote,

> every day we get hundreds of calls and visits to our office from drivers who are in financial desperation—black car, yellow cab and green car drivers, including Uber and Lyft drivers themselves. Incomes have plummeted and foreclosures and bankruptcies are on the rise. Drivers call in the middle of the night in crisis, needing referrals to homeless services and suicide prevention resources.

From my own time as a participant observer in the NYTWA office, I knew this to be true. It weighed heavily on the shoulders of the staff and organizers. In the wake of Doug's suicide, NYTWA vowed, "Today we mourn, tomorrow we organize."

With organizing came more tragedy. By the summer, a total of six New York drivers—Doug Schifter, Nicanor Ochisro, Danilo Corporan Castillo, Alfredo

Perez, Kenny Chow, and Abdul Saleh—died by suicide. Tragedy did not distinguish between industry sub-sector. Yellow, black, green, and app-based driver suffering was indiscriminate.

The suicides proved a catalyst for action. If exit was impossible and neglect was likely to result in deteriorating conditions, voice was the only remaining option. The families of fallen drivers spoke out about financial distress, falling incomes, and heightened competition that now characterized the industry. At the same time, NYTWA ramped up its campaign and directed their attention at New York City officials. It was the inaction of these representatives, NYTWA charged, that had contributed to dire working conditions. In an interview with labor columnist Chris Brooks, NYTWA executive director Bhairavi Desai stated that Doug Schifter's suicide humanized the struggle of FHV drivers. She continued, "One of the most important progresses we made is putting the drivers back in front—as the visible face of their industry and in the organizing campaigns to regulate these companies."[32] The quest to put drivers at the front of campaigns made the antagonistic debate between tech enthusiasts and taxi moguls obsolete. Instead, the public debate shifted to the issues of longstanding import to NYTWA: working conditions, remuneration, and drivers' right to work with dignity.

Vigils and demonstrations helped to keep the campaign in the spotlight and in the media and NYTWA's campaign demands, including a vehicle cap and a minimum industry-wide fare that would be based on the yellow cab meter. NYTWA's campaign demands were directly informed by the race to the bottom that affected drivers across all sectors—drivers who, if not already trapped by the predatory loans of the traditional taxi market, had become trapped by a tech-enhanced illusion of a better opportunity. Instituting minimum standards that would be enacted sector-wide was the only hopeful path forward.

Conclusion

On August 8, 2018, New York City became the first city in the United States to institute a FHV vehicle cap limiting the number of ride-hail vehicles in the city. This restriction, temporary for one year, was accompanied by the introduction of a minimum fare for FHV operators aimed at ensuring earnings on par with the city's commitment to a living wage. According to Joshi, these regulations would "raise driver earnings by an average of $10,000 per year, and require companies to be more transparent about how they calculate pay and car leasing costs."[33] Both achievements were direct results from NYTWA's organizing work and their campaign for economic justice, drivers' livelihoods, and ultimately lives. Moreover, these successes were made even as Uber and Lyft spent over one million dollars in the first half of 2018 lobbying against NYTWA's demands.[34]

Drivers' propensity to join the collective call for industry reform resulted directly from deteriorating conditions because none of the available exit options were tenable. Apps had done nothing to raise industry standards; instead, they were fueling a race to the bottom. In comparing individual firms, their business models were nearly indistinguishable; thus, changing between FHV sub-sectors or app companies provided drivers no relief. What is more, drivers from all sectors were increasingly saddled with debt and faced fierce competition. For this reason, NYTWA's proposal sought to unite drivers across all sub-sectors and to improve industry standards for all.

The outcome of August 8 was a remarkable victory, but this is also a story of victory marked by tragedy. Even as the city moves towards greater regulation, the echoes of years of deteriorating working conditions reverberate loudly. In October, just days after a *New York Times* feature article about drivers' continued concerns about mental health amidst insurmountable debt payments, a seventh driver—Fausto Luna—ended his life.[35] Nonetheless, the terms of the sector-wide wage have been introduced, and the vehicle cap, though temporary, has been extended as the city engages in a comprehensive study on the impact of app-based FHV services. Drivers, under the banner of NYTWA, are maintaining collective momentum, pushing to ensure that the outcome will bring meaningful change, and directing their efforts towards debt forgiveness for those mired by toxic assets.

Notes

1. Though legally classified as a nonprofit, NTYWA was the first affiliate of the AFL-CIO to represent nonstandard self-employed workers. As such, NYTWA does not participate in collective bargaining and drivers fall outside the purview of key pro-worker labor legislation. Nonetheless, the group identifies as a union and boasts a strong union culture.
2. Albert Hirschman, *Exit, Voice, and Loyalty: Responses to Decline in Firms, Organizations, and States* (Cambridge: Harvard University Press, 1970).
3. These data are a subset of two larger datasets collected during the same period that examined driver sentiment industry-wide including yellow cabs, green cabs, and black car services.
4. Monisha Das Gupta, *Unruly Immigrants: Rights, Activism, and Transnational South Asian Politics in the United States* (Durham, NC: Duke University Press, 2006).
5. Bill DeBlasio and Meera Joshi, "2016 NYC Taxicab Factbook," in *NYC Taxicab Factbook* (New York: Taxi and Limousine Commission, 2016).
6. Ruth Milkman, and Ed Ott, *New Labor in New York: Precarious Workers and the Future of the Labor Movement* (Ithaca: Cornell University Press, 2014).
7. Janice Fine, *Worker Centers: Organizing Communities at the Edge of the Dream* (Ithaca: ILR Press/Cornell University Press, 2006)
8. Janice Fine and Jennifer Gordon, "Strengthening Labor Standards Enforcement Through Partnerships With Workers' Organizations," *Politics & Society* 38, no. 4 (2010): 552–85.
9. Nik Theodore, "Rebuilding the House of Labor: Unions and Worker Centers in the Residential Construction Industry," *WorkingUSA* 18, no. 1 (2015): 59–76.
10. Eric A. Morris, "Cash and Cabbies," in *Freakonomics* (New York: NPR, 2009), http://freakonomics.com/2009/10/29/cash-and-cabbies/.
11. Graham Russell Hodges, *Taxi!: A Social History of the New York City Cabdriver* (Baltimore: The Johns Hopkins University Press, 2007), 66.
12. Biju Matthew, *Taxi!: Cabs and Capitalism in New York City* (Ithaca: ILR Press, 2008).

13. Andrew Prokop, "Michael Cohen's Taxi Business Partner Just Agreed to Cooperate with Investigators," *Vox*, May 22, 2018, www.vox.com/2018/5/22/17382138/michael-cohen-evgeny-freidman-taxi-king.
14. Veena Dubal, "The Drive to Precarity: A Political History of Work, Regulation, & Labor Advocacy in San Francisco's Taxi & Uber Economies," *Berkeley Journal of Employment and Labor Law* 38, no. 1 (2017): 73–136; Matthew, *Taxi!: Cabs and Capitalism*; Hannah Johnston, "Workplace Gains beyond the Wagner Act: The New York Taxi Workers Alliance and Participation in Administrative Rulemaking," *Labor Studies Journal* 43, no. 2 (2018): 141–65.
15. John Kelly, *Rethinking Industrial Relations: Mobilisation, Collectivism and Long Waves* (New York: Routledge, 2012).
16. Ursula Huws, *Labor in the Global Digital Economy: The Cybertariat Comes of Age* (New York: New York University Press, 2014), 31.
17. People of the State of New York Office of the Attorney General Labor Bureau. In the Matter of the Investigation of Eric T. Schniederman Attorney General of the State of New York of 28th Street Management Inc., Downtown Taxi Management LLC, Tunnel Taxi Management LLC, Woodside Management Inc. AOD No 13–501. New York, 2013.
18. Alex Rosenblat, *Uberland: How Algorithms Are Rewriting the Rules of Work* (Berkley: University of California Press, 2018).
19. Jaesub Lee and Amy L. Varon, "Employee Exit, Voice, Loyalty, and Neglect in Response to Dissatisfying Organizational Situations: It Depends on Supervisory Relationship Quality," *International Journal of Business Communication* 57, no. 1 (2020): 30–51; Eleni Aravopoulou, Fotios V Mitsakis, and Charles Malone, "A Critical Review of the Exit-Voice-Loyalty-Neglect Literature: Limitations, Key Challenges and Directions for Future Research," *International Journal of Management* 6, no. 3 (2017): 1–10.
20. $N = 288$.
21. Diana Farrell and Fiona Greig, "Paychecks, Paydays, and the Online Platform Economy: Big Data on Income Volatility," *Proceedings. Annual Conference on Taxation and Minutes of the Annual Meeting of the National Tax Association* 109 (2016): 1–40, https://www.jstor.org/stable/26816593.
22. Jonathan V. Hall, and Alan B. Krueger, *An Analysis of the Labor Market for Uber's Driver-Partners in the United States* (Cambridge, MA: National Bureau of Economic Research. 2016).
23. Todd Schneider, "Taxi, Uber, and Lyft Usage in New York City: Open TLC Data Reveals the Taxi Industry's Contraction, Uber's Growth, and the Scramble for Market Share," *Todd E. Schneider*, April 5, 2016, http://toddwschneider.com/posts/taxi-uber-lyft-usage-new-york-city/.
24. $N = 307$.
25. $N = 301$.
26. $N = 279$.
27. Nudging is the practice of dispatching the subsequent ride before completion of the current ride. This encourages drivers to stay logged into the app and to continue working.
28. Juliet B. Schor, and William Attwood-Charles, "The 'Sharing' Economy: Labor, Inequality, and Social Connection on For-Profit Platforms," *Sociology Compass* 11, no. 8 (2017): e12493.
29. $N = 294$; $N = 302$.
30. Johnston, "Workplace Gains Beyond the Wagner Act," 141–65.
31. Joy Borkholder, Mariah Montgomery, Miya Saika Chen, and Rebecca Smith, *Uber State Interference: How Transportation Network Companies Buy, Bully, and Bamboozle Their Way to Deregulation* (New York, NY: National Employment Law Project, 2018).

32. Chris Brooks, "Meet the Militant Taxi Drivers Union That Just Defeated Uber and Lyft," *Working in These Times*, August 15, 2018, http://inthesetimes.com/working/entry/21386/militant_taxi_drivers_union_uber_lyft_alliance_new_york_city.
33. Peter Holly, "New Rules Guarantee Minimum Wage for NYC Uber, Lyft Drivers," *The Washington Post*, December 4, 2018, www.washingtonpost.com/technology/2018/12/04/new-rules-guarantee-minimum-wage-nyc-uber-lyft-drivers/?noredirect=on&utm_term=.e243e179e3cb.
34. Brooks, "Meet the Militant Taxi Drivers Union That Just Defeated Uber and Lyft."
35. Emma Fitzsimmons, "Suicides Get Taxi Drivers Talking: 'I'm Going to Be One of Them'," *The New York Times*, October 2, 2018, www.nytimes.com/2018/10/02/nyregion/suicides-taxi-drivers-nyc.html; Tyler Pager and Emily Palmer, "Uber Driver's Death Marks Seventh For-Hire Driver Suicide Within a Year," *The New York Times*, October 7, 2018, www.nytimes.com/2018/10/07/nyregion/uber-driver-suicide-for-hire-taxis-new-york.html.

2

MORE THAN A GIG?

Ride-hailing in Los Angeles County

Tia Koonse, Lucero Herrera, Saba Waheed, Janna Shadduck-Hernández, Ana Luz Gonzalez-Vasquez, and Kean Flowers

In 2019, the California legislature passed Assembly Bill 5 (AB5), extending labor protections and other workplace benefits such as healthcare and the right to collective bargaining to gig workers formerly classified as independent contractors.[1] The law codified *Dynamex Operations West, Inc. v. Superior Court* case, and adopted the so-called ABC test that makes independent contractor classification illegal unless companies demonstrate that the worker is free of the company's control, is doing work outside of the company's usual course of business, and has a trade, occupation, or business in the field.[2]

Unsurprisingly, arguing that classifying drivers as employees would dramatically change their business model and negatively impact their bottom line, transportation network companies (TNCs), such as Uber and Lyft, pushed back against AB5, spending hundreds of millions of dollars on a ballot proposition. With the recent passage of Proposition 22, drivers are now exempted from AB5 permanently classifying them as independent contractors under state law.

From the onset, the TNC business model has largely relied on misclassifying drivers as independent contractors. Misclassification has deprived drivers of legal protection from discrimination and sexual harassment; has excluded them from recent labor gains, such as a higher minimum wage, paid sick time, and fair scheduling practices; and, significantly, has prevented them from engaging in collective bargaining to address these issues, as independent contractors are not protected from retaliation for these activities and can be "deactivated" from their Uber and Lyft accounts.[3]

This chapter illustrates the working conditions and experiences of TNC drivers, preceding the passage of AB5. It portrays the reality of TNC drivers in the so-called gig economy, foregrounds the experience of drivers, and describes what this labor actually entails. It is based on 260 surveys and eight in-depth interviews with ride-hailing drivers in Los Angeles County conducted in 2017, as well as an extensive policy and literature review. Many of the drivers we interviewed and surveyed relied on their TNC "gig" work as their primary or as a significant source of income, invested considerable resources in securing such work, and enjoyed flexible hours but wanted the control and benefits afforded to regular employees. We conclude by calling on policymakers to establish fair working conditions, ensure greater transparency and oversight of the sector, and allow for worker organizing.

Ride-Hailing in Los Angeles

Los Angeles is an ideal site for on-demand ride-hailing companies, also known as TNCs. In a city with over 8,000 people per square mile and decades-late investment in public transit, TNCs have flourished to accommodate the deficiencies of Los Angeles's neglected public transit options.[4] Given the simplicity, reliability, and convenience that Uber advertised to Los Angeles residents,[5] it is no surprise that TNCs were widely welcomed into the city's confines.

According to the National Center for Sustainable Transportation, about 32% of Angelenos have adopted ride-hailing, making Los Angeles one of the largest ride-hail markets in the US.[6] Los Angeles has been particularly receptive to an expanded ride-hailing driver base and an increased consumer demand for multiple reasons, among them the city's expansive geography, urban sprawl, and limited public transit coverage for many neighborhoods.[7] Though public transportation infrastructure is expanding, recent estimates indicate that only 9% of commuters take public transportation to work, and 70% drive to work alone.[8] Local government support of ride-hailing platforms to meet regional mobility needs has also contributed to the rise of TNCs in Los Angeles,[9] and many concede that the rise of these platforms has generally made mobility smoother for consumers.

Precarity in Gig Work

Gig work is the latest iteration of casual, contingent, and precarious work—work that is nonstandard, is often temporary, and has lower wages, income instability, job insecurity, and higher rates of workplace injuries and health issues.[10] The work's "invisibilization of money exchanges between driver and rider, non-branded fleet, and volunteeristic labor" obscures its labor *as labor*.[11] These conditions render drivers vulnerable to exploitative work conditions, particularly for those who rely on it as a primary job and source of income. TNCs often engage in aggressive marketing strategies to lure prospective drivers "with the promise of bonuses of several hundred dollars and high five-figure annual income, but without revealing the costs and risks associated with ride-hailing."[12] A 2015 Uber study asserted that drivers averaged more than $19 an hour before expenses.[13] Other studies that incorporate the cost of driving find that gross earnings are between $8.55 and $11.77—the bottom fifth of wage earners and less than the lowest-paid service sector worker.[14] As platform services and rates frequently shift, uncertainty becomes standardized, as do drivers' income insecurity and absence of benefits.[15] This uncertainty does not decline over time, as drivers are generally not better compensated due to seniority or tenure.[16]

Such working conditions produce an alienated precarity characterized by irregular, insecure, and isolated work, which fails to provide drivers with lasting financial and social mobility.[17] This precarious labor model has been a wider trend in neoliberal, late capitalist societies for decades.[18] The growth of TNC platforms such as Uber and Lyft is predicated on indirect employment and precarious work arrangements that have relied on technological capabilities to optimize and manage labor through data collection.[19] The simplicity of activating an app as a consumer or driver and being linked to a service makes such a platform appealing. However, lack of regulation and oversaturation of drivers has led to further problems that exacerbate the precarity of such work. Often, drivers must remain on call due to the accessibility of a smartphone and a saturated market that drives down working conditions, causing drivers to work more hours for less income.[20]

Drivers also face conditions that are stressful and can compromise their health and safety. Drivers report that they feel pressure to accept rides and extend their working day to avoid deactivation, or job loss.[21] (Because drivers were working excessive hours, Uber recently implemented limits to ensure rest.[22]) In fact, some studies have shown increased risks related to kidney failure, back pain, and respiratory illnesses.[23] These illnesses have resulted in disabilities due to poor working conditions that push workers toward more hours, fewer breaks, and physical deterioration that makes driving unsustainable.[24]

Methodology

The study uses a multimethod research approach that includes surveys, interviews, and academic and policy research. In August and September 2017, UCLA students conducted face-to-face surveys with 260 TNC drivers throughout Los Angeles County. The survey collected information on drivers' work experience, attitudes toward driving and navigating platform work, earnings and expenses, working environment, and preferences and expectations for the future. To complement the survey data, students also conducted in-person interviews with eight TNC drivers in Los Angeles. Interviews covered topics such as working conditions, employment classification, organizing, and job satisfaction.

Findings

More Than a Gig

Many of today's gig apps materialized during the Great Recession, which created the conditions necessary for those who were unemployed or underemployed to turn to the gig economy[25] and monetize their cars, driving skills, or homes. For

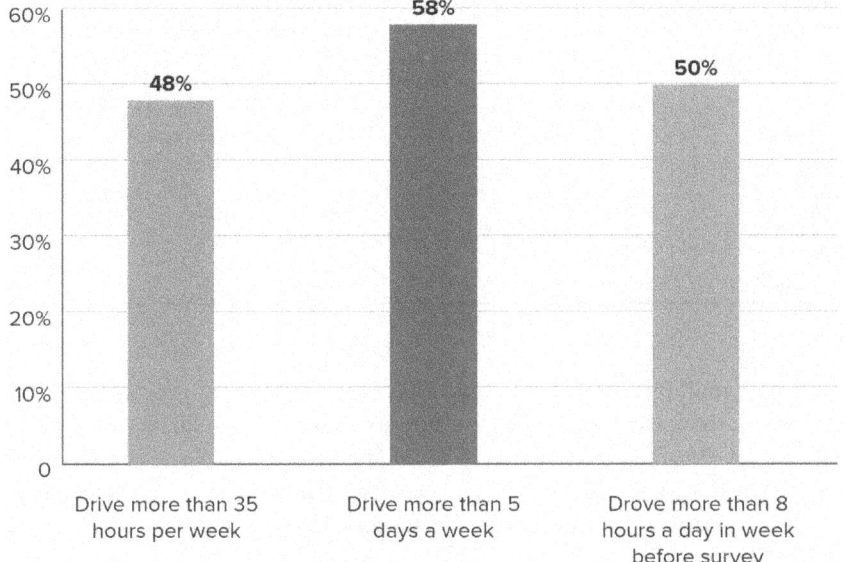

FIGURE 2.1 Days and hours of driving

some, driving is a necessary bridge between other jobs or ways to supplement their income. Since the recession, many workers who once held high-wage jobs, within a diminished field of opportunity, have taken low-wage work.[26] This may explain why gig work is continually expanding as unemployment is reaching record lows.[27] A number of studies have reiterated the part-time nature of this work: one found that workers spend about 12 hours of platform work per week,[28] and another found that half of drivers work 15 hours or fewer a week.[29] Yet our study establishes that many drivers stay in this work longer and work more hours per day. Thus, we question whether this work is actually short term, as many in our sample describe TNC work as their full-time, primary employment.

Our survey found that 47% of respondents drive for a TNC as their only job. Even for those with other jobs, driving for a TNC is a significant source of income. Among all drivers in our sample, 66% depend on driving as their main source of income. Almost half of those surveyed reported driving 35 hours or more a week, and three in five drive more than five days a week. On average, respondents reported driving seven hours a day, with half stating that they drove more than eight hours a day during the week before the survey (Figure 2.1).

Drivers use their earnings to sustain both themselves and family members. Over half support at least one other person in their family, and over one-third of drivers support their family with at least one child present. Our survey also found that nearly one in five drivers receive some form of public assistance, such as food assistance, housing subsidies, and other assistance programs for low-income families.

TABLE 2.1 Selected driver characteristics

	Full-time driver (more than 34 hours per week)	Part-time driver (34 hours or less per week)
Average age	39 years	32 years
Female drivers	11%	26%
Tenure	1.8 years	11.1 months
US-born	50%	79%
Support at least one child in family	46%	25%

Though multiple studies have noted high rates of turnover,[30] our survey found a lower rate of driver exit within the first six months: only about one-third of those surveyed had driven for their current TNC for less than six months, while almost two out of 10 had driven between six months and one year, and more than half had driven for over a year. On average, TNC drivers have been on the job for 13 months.

There are commonalities among those for whom driving is their main source of income, who drive full-time hours, and who have driven for more than a year: they tend to be older and are more likely to be immigrants, to hold driving as their primary job, and to stay in the profession for a longer time span. There are, however, distinct differences between part-time and full-time drivers and in driving tenure. Part-time drivers are usually younger than their full-time counterparts, are more likely to be US-born and have shorter driving tenures, and are less likely to support a child. Those that have driven for less than a year are more likely to be younger than their counterparts, work part-time hours, and not rely on driving as their primary job (Table 2.1).

The Cost of Driving

While taxis have a set meter rate based on an array of factors, such as the cost of living, TNC fares vary widely. Generally, TNCs create fixed, non-negotiated formulas that include a base fare plus per-minute and per-distance rates for the time and distance from pickup to drop-off, surge pricing, the company's fee, and whether other fees are applicable.[31] Recent studies have noted discrepancies between what the companies advertise as average hourly pay and what drivers actually earn.[32] Drivers, meanwhile, endure costs such as wear and tear on their vehicles, gas, car insurance, repairs, car maintenance, taxes, and additional expenses such as AUX cables, candy, and water. Estimates on work-related expenses incurred by drivers are difficult to measure. While studies on earnings are widespread, less is known about the hidden costs of driving.

The gig economy emerged during a period of national economic recession, and monetizing one's resources became a way to navigate that uncertainty. The majority of drivers in our sample use their own car, with about a quarter leasing their cars. Over a third of drivers, however, purchased or leased their car in order to drive for the company: 22% of the drivers purchased and 14% leased in order to drive for the TNC. This heavy financial investment necessarily locks drivers into their work, and those who purchased or leased their car to drive for the company are more likely to work longer hours. More than half of those who purchased, and almost two-thirds who leased to drive for the company, work 35 hours or more a week.

In addition to paying for general maintenance costs for their vehicles, drivers incur other major expenses, such as gas and insurance, and almost half of drivers report experiencing difficulties paying for these various work-related expenses. Many drivers incur additional expenses by purchasing accessories for their riders. Over three-quarters provide amenities such as water, candy, and AUX cables, and eight in 10 purchased cell-phone mounts and mats. These are provided at no extra charge to riders, and some have come to expect them and file unfavorable ratings to drivers who don't provide them.[33] An Uber driver expressed his concerns over these expectations: "When passengers ask for water, I feel like I have to provide [it] as if it were conditions of a contract, even though it's not. I don't like how passengers think drivers should provide these for them."[34]

In order to pay for these additional expenses, drivers report having to work more hours, using their credit cards, asking parents/friends for a loan, or taking out loans with another third party, and employing other means including using savings, working more hours at a second job, or picking up additional gigs through other on-demand platforms such as Postmates.

Out-of-pocket expenses significantly diminish drivers' earnings. A recent Economic Policy Institute study found that Uber drivers earn less than the minimum wage in many major urban areas, including Los Angeles.[35] When we asked drivers if they would prefer to earn a set hourly wage after expenses, more than half said that they would. Among those who would like to receive a set hourly wage, the majority want a guaranteed hourly rate of $15 or more. About one in three drivers would like to earn $21 an hour or more, and only 13% would like to earn less than $15 an hour. The median hourly wage that drivers would prefer to earn is $19.

The pressure of the job is a significant, if less quantifiable, cost of the work. Much of the work of app-based drivers is monitored and evaluated on the app through which they work. Poor rider reviews, low acceptance rates, and customer complaints can deactivate drivers from their work entirely. This essential fact underlines the precarity of this form of work and necessarily endangers the well-being of the driver. Both Uber and Lyft ask riders to rate their driver following the use of their service. Individual scores are then used to calculate an average score for each driver, and if a score falls below a certain point, then the company may issue a warning or deactivate—fire—the driver from the platform. Our survey found that over half of drivers feel pressured to elicit good reviews, though the majority have received negative reviews. Drivers can be also suspended or deactivated if a passenger files a complaint. Over one-third of drivers have had a customer complain to the company, and only half were able to address it. Among those who have had a passenger complaint sent to the TNC, 20% were deactivated. Almost one-third of respondents fear deactivation.

Driving the Conditions of Work

While drivers generally find flexible work schedules appealing, studies have found that many contingent workers would actually prefer to enter or rejoin the permanent workforce but are prevented from doing so for multiple reasons: the rules of temporary employment agencies, a lack of choices due to economic need, or gaps in knowledge about the conditions of independent contract work.[36]

Our research finds that drivers want control over their work but also the benefits of employee status. For example, close to two-thirds of drivers surveyed said the company was not their boss, yet over half said they would like to become TNC employees. Even among those who would like to retain their status as independent contractors, most want the workplace benefits associated with traditional employment. Four in five drivers, for instance, want workers' compensation, which provides workers with wage replacement and medical benefits if injured on the job, and health insurance. About 79% would like to receive overtime pay, while 74% would like paid sick leave and access to a retirement plan.

Drivers in our survey also want greater control over their contracts. Despite a business model that depends on drivers, Uber and Lyft often unilaterally change terms and conditions of their contracts at will.[37] More than half of the drivers we surveyed had experienced a modification in their contract at least once, and for nearly 40% of workers, it changed three or more times. Drivers cannot pick up passengers until they agree to the terms of contracts the TNC dictates.[38] In addition, each new contract includes language around arbitration from which drivers must opt out. If they have not opted out before, the previous arbitration agreement is retained.[39] While contracts are now exclusively developed by the TNCs, 81% of drivers in our study want to be able to negotiate the conditions of their contracts (Figure 2.2).

Drivers also report additional ways in which the companies exert control over their daily activities. Many experience stress from a TNC's ceaseless communication, which is a form of "soft control" that encourages them to drive. Almost half receive a notification when the app is off and one-quarter feel stressed from the contact. In addition, 39% feel pressure to drive when they receive notifications of surge pricing. A 2016 study found that the Uber app's use of algorithmic labor logistics shapes drivers' approach to their work, performs electronic surveillance, and is instrumental in developing policies for performance targets.[40] Half of the

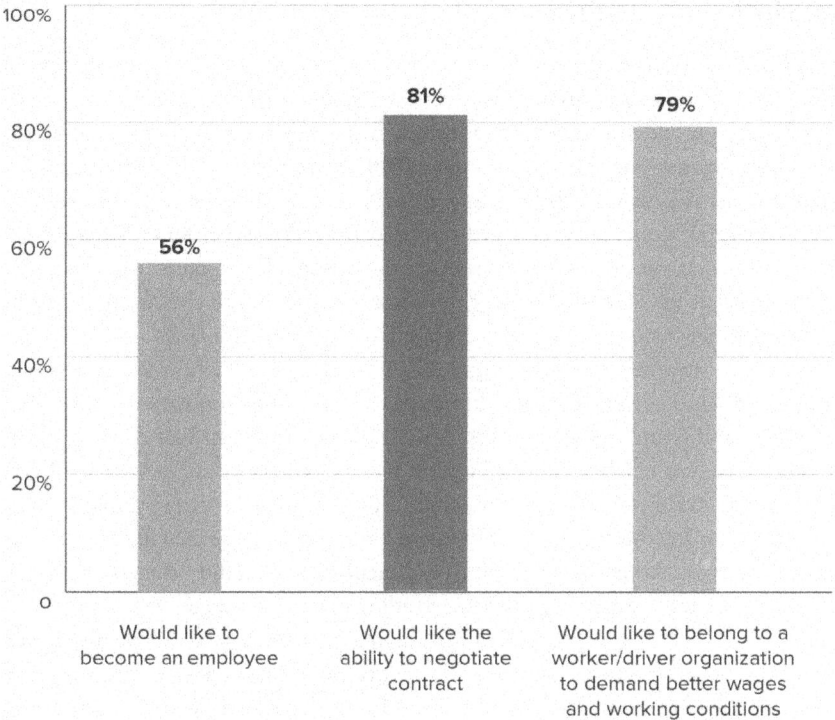

FIGURE 2.2 Drivers' attitudes about working status

surveyed drivers are concerned about how the company apps track and surveil them.

Without the employment protections granted in AB5, drivers may be fired for organizing to improve their working conditions, as long as the TNC companies continue to treat them as independent contractors. Drivers we surveyed adamantly want the ability to come together with other drivers to advocate for themselves; eight in 10 drivers want to join a worker or driver organization. One driver reported,

> [I] really would like to see the ridesharing crowd come up with their own independent union . . . I think that specific representation would be essential and crucial to representing our interests like a specific labor sector. I would like to see that happen, and if that did I think it would be very positive in getting things done because I think it would be more representative of our beliefs.

Consistent with these survey responses, the past five years have brought about significant traction in the growth of various informal driver organizing groups such as Rideshare Drivers United and Gig Workers Rising.[41]

Conclusions and Recommendations

Working conditions in the gig economy have grown increasingly dire during the COVID-19 pandemic. Misclassified gig workers who lack paid sick leave, access to unemployment insurance, healthcare, workers' compensation, company-provided personal protective equipment (PPE), and income predictability faced a heightened risk of COVID-19 infection, food insecurity, and homelessness.[42] Meanwhile, gig companies invested hundreds of millions of dollars into Proposition 22—even though many of these same companies remain unprofitable—to continue to avoid reclassifying their workforce as employees or paying into unemployment insurance, workers compensation, or payroll taxes.

With the November 2020 passage of Proposition 22 in California, these companies are able to exempt their workforce from AB5. The proposition is unsettling for worker rights and organizing. It sets a dangerous precedent that companies can buy their way out of labor laws and upend the checks and balances between labor, government, and business. The proposition further maintains substandard working conditions for the gig sector; the limited benefits in Prop 22 fall well beneath what drivers would receive as employees. Finally, some studies suggest that many drivers won't even receive the health subsidies and higher wages promised.[43]

Our study showed this work is more than a gig. We found that many drivers stay in the work for longer durations and work more hours per day than do their traditional gig counterparts. We also found that drivers make significant financial investments into vehicles, accessories, and other amenities while covering expenses for car maintenance, gas, and insurance. Our findings show that while gig workers in Los Angeles value flexibility, they also desire a measure of predictability, safety, and income security, protections long available to other workers. With Prop 22 in effect, these drivers will be operating under gig-like employment terms while they provide part-time and full-time work.

Arguably, the proliferation of gig work has produced a system of unstable and unregulated labor founded upon the exploitation of drivers and capitalist business models that prioritize profit over worker rights.[44] Policymakers may consider the following recommendations to create an environment where technology benefits both consumers and workers.

First, policymakers must ensure safe and dignified working conditions in the sector. With the passage of Prop 22, the independent contractor classification shields TNC companies from responsibility for many of the basic standards afforded to employees. Policymakers must (1) continue to challenge the exploitation of workers in the sector, such as refusal to pay workers for time spent waiting and driving to pick up passengers; (2) curb the expansion of misclassification into other gig work; (3) consider ways to create joint liability and expand the definition of "employer" to hold accountable corporate entities with deep pockets for wages, safety, and other working conditions; and (4) provide oversight and documentation of the conditions of work. Regular evaluation and monitoring of current and future TNC practices will facilitate enforcement of regulations as well as a greater understanding of how this labor model impacts workers, consumers, other businesses, public transportation, and the environment.

Second, policymakers should encourage democratized gig work, featuring greater transparency, less concentrated ownership, and proactive approaches to preventing displacement by technology. Platforms that allow workers to network with one another can be developed. These technologies could facilitate transparency around issues such as appeals processes for deactivation and could create systems for worker input. Cooperatively-owned apps controlled and/or co-owned by workers might channel fees into programs and direct services for workers. Given the imminent possibility of driverless cars, policymakers may also consider proactive policies that will support transitions to other forms of work.

Finally, workers need to be able to organize independently and advocate for their working conditions. Policymakers and worker advocates must develop strategies that remove barriers to organizing, such as retaliatory deactivation, and support institutions that center and lift up worker voices. Without a strong worker presence, power will continually fall on the company side, removing the checks and balances needed to ensure that worker rights, not profits, are driving decisions and policy agendas.

Notes

1. Kate Conger and Noam Scheibe, "California Bill Makes App-Based Companies Treat Workers as Employees," *New York Times*, September 11, 2019, www.nytimes.com/2019/09/11/technology/california-gig-economy-bill.html.
2. Dynamex Operations West, Inc. v. Superior Court of Los Angeles, S222732 Cal. Sup. Ct. (2018).
3. Denise Cheng, *Is Sharing Really Caring? A Nuanced Introduction to the Peer Economy* (Washington, DC: Open Society Foundation, 2014), 12–13, https://static.opensocietyfoundations.org/misc/future-of-work/the-sharing-economy.pdf.; Natasha Singer, "In the Sharing Economy, Workers Find Both Freedom and Uncertainty," *New York Times*, August 16, 2014, www.nytimes.com/2014/08/17/technology/in-the-sharing-economy-workers-find-both-freedom-and-uncertainty.html.
4. Michael Storper, "The Neo-Liberal City as Idea and Reality," *Territory, Politics, Governance* 4, no. 2 (2016): 241–63, https://doi.org/10.1080/21622671.2016.1158662.; Laura J. Nelson, "L.A. Is Hemorrhaging Bus Riders—Worsening Traffic and Hurting Climate Goals," *Los Angeles Times*, June 27, 2019, www.latimes.com/local/lanow/la-me-ln-bus-ridership-falling-los-angeles-la-metro-20190627-story.html.
5. Travis Kalanick, "Uber LA Officially Launched," Uber Blog, March 8, 2012, www.uber.com/blog/los-angeles/uber-la-officially-launched/.
6. Giovanni Circella, Farzad Alemi, Kate Tiedeman, Susan Handy, and Patricia Mokhtarian, *The Adoption of Shared Mobility in California and Its Relationship With Other Components of Travel Behavior* (Davis: UC Davis National Center for Sustainable Transportation, 2018), https://escholarship.org/uc/item/1kq5d07p.
7. Laura Bliss, "Cities Have to Get Creative When Uber and Lyft Won't Release Trip Data," *The Atlantic*, January 13, 2018, www.theatlantic.com/business/archive/2018/01/uber-lyft-cities-data/550433/.
8. US Census Bureau, "Census Reporter Profile: Los Angeles, CA," accessed January 23, 2019, https://censusreporter.org/profiles/16000US0644000-los-angeles-ca/.

9. Emily Alpert Reyes, "At L.A. City Hall, It's the Visionary vs. the Lawmakers," *Los Angeles Times*, August 18, 2015, www.latimes.com/local/california/la-me-adv-sharing-economy-20150818-story.html.
10. Veena Dubal, "The Drive to Precarity: A Political History of Work, Regulation, & Labor Advocacy in San Francisco's Taxi & Uber Economics," *Berkeley Journal of Employment and Labor* (2017): 73, 75, https://repository.uchastings.edu/cgi/viewcontent.cgi?article=2588&context=faculty_scholarship; Arne Kalleberg and Steven Vallas, "Studying Precarious Work," *Work in Progress*, December 20, 2017, https://workinprogress.oowsection.org/2017/12/20/studying-precarious-work/.
11. Julietta Hua and Kasturi Ray, "Beyond the Precariat: Race, Gender, and Labor in the Taxi and Uber Economy," *Social Identities* 24, no. 2 (2018): 276, https://doi.org/10.1080/13504630.2017.1321721.
12. Lawrence Meyers, "Towards a Cost Estimate of a NYC UberX Driver: A White Paper," June 10, 2015, https://nyctaxinews.com/uber_white_paper.pdf.
13. Jonathan V. Hall and Alan B. Krueger, "An Analysis of the Labor Market for Uber's Driver-Partners in the United States," *IRL Review* 71, no. 3 (May 2018): 725, https://doi.org/10.1177/0019793917717222.
14. Alison Griswold, "Uber Drivers Make About as Much Money as Minimum Wage Workers," *Quartz*, May 16, 2018, https://qz.com/1278707/the-uber-economy-is-actually-just-the-low-wage-economy/; Lawrence Mishel, *Uber and the Labor Market: Uber Drivers' Compensation, Wages, and the Scale of Uber and the Gig Economy* (Washington, DC: Economic Policy Institute, 2018), 2, www.epi.org/files/pdf/145552.pdf.
15. Cheng, "Is Sharing Really Caring? A Nuanced Introduction to the Peer Economy"; Singer, "In the Sharing Economy, Workers Find Both Freedom and Uncertainty."
16. Orly Lobel, "The Gig Economy & the Future of Employment and Labor Law," *University of San Francisco Law Review* (2016): 66–67, https://papers.ssrn.com/sol3/papers.cfm?abstract_id=2848456.
17. Robert MacDonald and Andreas Giazitzoglu, "Youth, Enterprise and Precarity: Or, What Is, and What Is Wrong with, the 'Gig Economy'?" *Journal of Sociology* 55, no. 4 (2019): 724–40, https://doi.org/10.1177/1440783319837604.
18. Ibid.
19. K. Sabeel Rahman and Kathleen Thelen, "The Rise of the Platform Business Model and the Transformation of Twenty-First-Century Capitalism," *Politics & Society* 47, no. 2 (2019): 177–204, https://doi.org/10.1177/0032329219838932.
20. MacDonald and Giazitzoglu, "Youth, Enterprise and Precarity: Or, What Is, and What Is Wrong with, the 'Gig Economy'?"
21. Samantha Allen, "The Mysterious Way Uber Bans Its Drivers," *The Daily Beast*, January 15, 2015, www.thedailybeast.com/the-mysterious-way-uber-bans-drivers; Avery Hartsman, "10 Ways Uber Drivers Can Get Kicked Off the App," *Business Insider*, July 23, 2017, www.businessinsider.com/uber-is-recommitting-itself-to-putting-its-drivers-first-2016-11; Biz Carson, "Uber Is Making Changes to Eliminate the Fear Factor for Drivers," *Business Insider*, November 27, 2016, www.businessinsider.com/uber-is-recommitting-itself-to-putting-its-drivers-first-2016-11.
22. Faiz Siddiqui, "Uber Mandates a Six-Hour Rest Period for Frequent Drivers," *The Washington Post*, February 12, 2018, www.washingtonpost.com/news/dr-gridlock/wp/2018/02/12/uber-mandates-a-six-hour-rest-period-for-frequent-drivers/?utm_term=.a11e95f2d9b7.
23. Hua and Ray, "Beyond the Precariat: Race, Gender, and Labor in the Taxi and Uber Economy."
24. Ibid.
25. Nicholas Kacher and Stephan Weiler, *Inside the Rise of the Gig Economy* (Fort Collins: Colorado State University Regional Economic Development Institute, 2017), 2, https://redi.colostate.edu/wp-content/uploads/sites/50/2017/06/REDI-report-April-gig-economy.pdf.

26. Beth Gutelius and Nik Theodore, "The Future of Work: Urban Economies in Transition," in *Jobs and the Labor Force of Tomorrow: Migration, Training, Education*, ed. Michael A. Pagano (Urbana: University of Illinois Press, 2017), 3–22, www.jstor.org/stable/10.5406/j.ctt1v2xtk2.4.
27. Abha Bhattarai, "Now Hiring, for a One-Day Job: The Gig Economy Hits Retail," *The Washington Post*, May 4, 2018, www.washingtonpost.com/business/economy/now-hiring-for-a-one-day-job-the-gig-economy-hits-retail/2018/05/04/2bebdd3c-4257-11e8-ad8f-27a8c409298b_story.html.
28. Intuit Tax and Financial Center, "Dispatches from the New Economy: The On-Demand Workforce" (2016), 4, https://intuittaxandfinancialcenter.com/wp-content/uploads/2017/06/Dispatches-from-the-New-Economy-Long-Form-Report.pdf.
29. Jonathan V. Hall and Alan B. Krueger, "An Analysis of the Labor Market for Uber's Driver-Partners in the United States," *National Bureau of Economic Research*, www.nber.org/papers/w22843.
30. Rosaria M. Berliner and Gil Tal, "What Drives Your Drivers: An In-Depth Look at Lyft and Uber Drivers" (poster presentation, STEPS Symposium, Davis, CA, December 2017), https://steps.ucdavis.edu/wp-content/uploads/2017/12/12.-BERLINERWhat-Drives-Your-Drivers-An-In-Depth-Look-at-Lyft-and-Uber-Drivers.-Rosaria-Berliner-Gil-Tal.pdf; Annette Bernhardt and Sarah Thomason, *What Do We Know About Gig Work in California? An Analysis of Independent Contracting* (Berkeley: UC Berkeley Labor Center, 2017), 16, https://laborcenter.berkeley.edu/what-do-we-know-about-gig-work-in-california/.
31. "Uber Help," Uber, accessed May 15, 2018, https://help.uber.com/; "Lyft Help Center," *Lyft*, accessed May 15, 2018, https://help.lyft.com/hc/en-us/articles/115013080008-How-and-when-driver-pay-is-calculated#calculations.
32. Griswold, "Uber Drivers Make About as Much Money as Minimum Wage Workers"; Mishel, *Uber and the Labor Market: Uber Drivers' Compensation, Wages, and the Scale of Uber and the Gig Economy*, 12–13.
33. Kat Kane, "The Big Hidden Problem With Uber? Insincere 5-Star Ratings," *Wired*, March 19, 2015, www.wired.com/2015/03/bogus-uber-reviews/.
34. Saba Waheed, Lucero Herrera, Ana Luz Gonzalez-Vasquez, Janna Shadduck Hernández, Tia Koonse, and David Leynov, *More Than a Gig: A Survey of Ride-Hailing Drivers in Los Angeles* (Los Angeles: UCLA Labor Center, 2018), https://irle.ucla.edu/wp-content/uploads/2018/05/Final-Report.-UCLA-More-than-a-Gig.pdf.
35. Mishel, *Uber and the Labor Market: Uber Drivers' Compensation, Wages, and the Scale of Uber and the Gig Economy*, 2, 15.
36. Alice De Wolff, *Breaking the Myth of Flexible Work: Contingent Work in Toronto* (Toronto: Toronto Organizing for Fair Employment, 2000), https://files.eric.ed.gov/fulltext/ED458428.pdf; Arne L. Kalleberg, "Flexible Firms and Labor Market Segmentation: Effects of Workplace Restructuring on Jobs and Workers," *Work and Occupations* 30, no. 2 (2003): 170, https://doi.org/10.1177/0730888403251683.
37. Brishen Rogers, "The Social Costs of Uber," *University of Chicago Law Review Online* 82, no. 1 (2015): 98, https://chicagounbound.uchicago.edu/cgi/viewcontent.cgi?article=1037&context=uclrev_online.
38. Ben Z. Steinberger, "Redefining Employee' in the Gig Economy: Shielding Workers from the Uber Model," *Fordham Journal of Corporate & Financial Law* 23, no. 2 (2018): 585, https://ir.lawnet.fordham.edu/jcfl/vol23/iss2/5/.
39. Ibid.; "Lyft Terms of Service," *Lyft*, accessed May 18, 2018, www.lyft.com/terms.
40. Alex Rosenblat and Luke Stark, "Algorithmic Labor and Information Asymmetries: A Case Study of Uber's Drivers," *International Journal of Communication* 10 (2016): 3777, https://ijoc.org/index.php/ijoc/article/view/4892/1739.
41. Sarah Holder, "Why L.A.'s Ride-Hail Drivers Went on Strike," *Bloomberg*, March 26, 2019, www.bloomberg.com/news/articles/2019-03-26/inside-l-a-uber-and-lyft-drivers-25-hour-strike#:~:text=Why%20L.A.'s%20Ride%2DHail,higher%

20wages%20and%20fairer%20treatment; Johana Bhuiyan, "Uber Wants to Redefine Employment. More Than 50 Labor Groups Are Fighting Back," *Los Angeles Times,* April 8, 2020, www.latimes.com/business/technology/story/2020-04-08/labor-groups-ask-congress-to-reject-uber-ceo-plea.

42. Lucero Herrera, Brian Justie, Tia Koonse, and Saba Waheed, *Worker Ownership, COVID-19, and the Future of the Gig Economy* (Los Angeles: UCLA Labor Center, 2020), www.labor.ucla.edu/wp-content/uploads/2020/10/UCLA_coop_report_Final-1.pdf.

43. Ken Jacobs and Michael Reich, *The Uber/Lyft Ballot Initiative Guarantees Only $5.64 an Hour* (Berkeley: UC Berkeley Labor Center, 2020), https://laborcenter.berkeley.edu/the-uber-lyft-ballot-initiative-guarantees-only-5-64-an-hour-2/.

44. MacDonald and Giazitzoglu, "Youth, Enterprise and Precarity: Or, What Is, and What Is Wrong with, the 'Gig Economy'?"

3

CARE IN THE PLATFORM ECONOMY

Interrogating the Digital Organisation of Domestic Work in India

Ambika Tandon and Aayush Rathi

Paid domestic work is witnessing the entry of digital intermediaries, affecting millions of workers in a sector that is informal and outside the domain of legal protections across the world. In India digital platforms providing domestic work services have grown at a rate of 60 percent month on month.[1] We understand paid domestic work as including tasks performed inside the home—cooking, cleaning, washing, and child and elderly care—and typically by low-income women. This occupational or task-based segregation can also result from the sexual division of labour that relegates women to performing domestic tasks inside the household or the 'private sphere'. With socio-economic norms around reproductive work treating it as economically unproductive and thus not *work*, the relegation to the private sphere contributes to the invisibility and lack of recognition of domestic work as paid labour.

In India, as in other parts of the global south, domestic labour has historically been invisibilised, undervalued, and feminised. Undervaluation stems partly from the type of workers engaged in domestic work—workers in this sector are predominantly Dalit, Bahujan, and Adivasi women, who have migrated from rural areas in search of work.[2] In addition, much like other manual tasks in the informal sector, it has been delegated to 'unskilled' work in the hierarchy of labour in the neoliberal economy—which is critically contingent on the "head versus hand hierarchy . . . encoded in caste with mental labour assigned to dominant castes and physical labour to oppressed ones."[3]

The similarity in precarity and the informal nature of this relationship across gig work and domestic work has led to the labelling of domestic workers as the "original gig workers".[4] A debate, however, has taken shape among those who see potential and those who see enduring exploitation in platformised domestic work. Proponents of the platformisation of domestic work in India argue that digitisation will act as a step towards bringing formalisation to the sector, while critics argue that platforms could leave workers open to exploitation in the absence of protections. Similar debates around lack of protections and precarity have also taken place in other occupational sectors of gig work such as transportation and food delivery.[5]

Very little literature assesses platforms' impact on domestic workers, especially regarding their identities, labour conditions, employment relations, and potential to collectively organise. Assessing digital platforms as an alternative to placement agencies and word-of-mouth placement becomes important as the domestic work sector is set to grow further[6] and provide a significant source of livelihood for women from low-income groups with low levels of education, in a context where they may be unable to find work in other sectors in the informal economy.[7]

There is a similar dearth of research on other labour placement agencies in India, and the lack of regulation or even registration implies that there is almost no data about the number of such agencies that operate nationally. N. Neetha's work, which remains one of the most exhaustive sources on placement agencies in northern India, finds that they commonly charge exploitative commissions from workers, withhold wages, and are complicit in bonded labour and human trafficking.[8] Gajjala describes these dynamics as creating a context in which workers' exploitation escapes critique; "displaced bodies are absorbed into a consumer base and also made available for various deskilled (and underpaid) forms of labour, while their forced mobility is characterized as progress".[9]

In this chapter we examine the shifts platformisation has brought to the employment relationship in domestic work. In doing so we seek to further an understanding of domestic work, specifically, and gig work, broadly, such that it may inform workers' collective struggles. We explore domestic workers' alternating identities between 'self-employed' and 'employed' that may frustrate and yet offer new opportunities for collective organising. We argue that design and operational logics of digital platforms play a key role in worker identity, as does workers' imagination of digital platforms through their interaction with corporate digital and analogue infrastructures. We also argue that collectivisation will be contingent on the workers' potential to overcome the isolation inherent to the platform economy and align with collective identities. As our interviews with workers suggest, workers are meaning-making subjects who view their employment relationship in contradictory ways that both impede and generate new possibilities for domestic worker organising. The sections of this chapter explore models of employment relationships in the platform economy, platforms as negotiators, and the logics of platforms, as these dynamics inform domestic platform workers' contradictory identities. Before turning to this analysis, we discuss our methodology.

Methodology

This chapter draws from a larger project that explores the contours of the platform domestic work economy, including models of employment relationships, the ways that platforms negotiate working conditions, and what we identify as the logics of platformisation. We supplement this structural analysis with an investigation of the perspectives of platform managers, state government officials, and workers on platforms, through 60 semi-structured in-depth interviews we completed between June and November 2019. In this chapter, we focus on how the platform economy and the perspectives of workers interact.

We selected New Delhi and Bengaluru as the field sites for the study because both cities have historically functioned as prominent destination nodes in the placement network of domestic workers in the country, and consequently, the largest concentration of digital platforms in this sector are operational in these cities. The interviews in Delhi were carried out by the authors, while interviews with workers in Bengaluru were undertaken by union members from the Domestic Workers Rights Union with no prior experience of research. Thus, we integrate feminist principles of participation in the research process by co-designing the research project with on-ground organisers and workers.

Structures of Domestic Work in the Platform Economy

Global literature on the gig economy in the domestic work sector points to two kinds of digital platforms—*marketplace* and *on-demand*.[10] *Marketplace platforms* are virtual job boards, where the function of the intermediary is limited to information exchange between the customer and worker. The intermediary controls the kind of information available about—and therefore visibility of—each entity in the transaction. It also matches workers and employers, which is most often an algorithmic decision, and could collect feedback about workers. We did not find any instances of marketplace platforms that collect feedback about employers from workers.

On-demand platforms provide short-term services, closest to the 'Uber model' of the gig economy. It is worth noting that of the tasks we consider as comprising paid domestic work, that is, cooking, cleaning, washing, and child and elderly care, on-demand platforms only hire workers for providing cleaning services. UrbanCompany, the only platform company that ventured into provision of other domestic work, such as cooking and care services on an on-demand model, spoke of the unprofitability of these services because of the lack of demand, since customers largely require full-time workers.

In the on-demand model, workers are algorithmically matched to customers, with the terms of service, including wages, set by the intermediary. Workers do not negotiate any part of their contract but are treated as independent contractors by most platforms. Apart from wages, companies determine the tasks to be performed, provide uniforms, collect extensive feedback, and surveil workers through various means while they perform their tasks.

The final category we identify, *digital placement agencies*, is not present in previous literature and is perhaps unique to the Indian context. They replicate the business models of traditional placement agencies. They create a database of workers, who are manually or algorithmically matched with employers based on their requirements. Unlike marketplace platforms which work on subscription-based models, digital placement agencies demand a high one-time fee for providing employers access to as many workers as is necessary until the employer is satisfied.

As the following sections describe, platforms' structural choices are key determinants of the access to, performance of, and experience of digitally mediated work. We organise key findings of this project such that platforms' roles in shaping gainful labour market outcomes for workers is highlighted. As such, we disaggregate these outcomes to understand how, and how much, each of three models of platforms similarly and distinctly impact the securing of the outcomes.

Platforms as Negotiators

Platform companies can negotiate conditions of work on behalf of workers, or can even set the terms and conditions of work for both workers and employers. There is wide variation within platforms' roles as negotiators for domestic workers, with both weak and strong models of intervention in the employer-employee relationship. On one end of the spectrum are marketplace platforms, with minimal intervention in the recruitment process compared to on-demand platforms that exact control over each aspect of work on the other. Digital platforms have reconfigured the conception of intermediaries in the domestic work sector, functioning as next-generation placement agencies. As such, they may provide workers with agency or reinforce their powerlessness in setting the terms and conditions of their work.

Most marketplace platform companies prefer to act as distant intermediaries, positioning themselves as job boards or listing sites rather than demonstrating active interest in the nature of work that workers are being placed in. A smaller minority of marketplace platform companies negotiate conditions of work that are easier to regulate, such as enforcing minimum wage standards. These marketplace platforms are able to function as strong intermediaries that offer grievance redressal systems to workers—especially for cases of harassment and non-payment of wages—and negotiate wages, hours, and tasks on behalf of workers or offer tips on location-based expectations for wages.

We found that marketplace platforms are designed to match workers and employers 'efficiently'. Further, we found that the agency to exercise choice through platforms was differentially distributed to workers based on three characteristics of workers: (i) digital access and literacy and therefore a relatively better understanding of the functionality of the platform, (ii) physical mobility and the resources to bear indirect costs that were outsourced to them, and (iii) preference for flexibility without being dependent on the platform for primary income. Women workers tend to be disadvantaged on all three counts, possibly limiting their agency and capacities to reap the benefits of the platform economy.

On-demand platform companies determine conditions of work, including wages and tasks to be performed with the goal of standardising the customer experience. They claim to offer flexibility by allowing workers to accept or decline tasks, which also allows the positioning of platform companies as intermediaries rather than employers. Rather than empowering workers to negotiate decent conditions of work, on-demand platform companies do not address workers' concerns, including harassment, and extraction of additional unpaid labour.

> Pavan (showing the mobile application): See for yourself, how much I have earned this week. It's as good as nothing! I have been coming here (to the office), travelling for hours, for the last 3 days for mandatory training even though I have been doing this for 3 years now. They threatened that my account will be deactivated if I don't come. They don't even compensate us for our time, or even provide us food when we have to be here all day.
> —*Pavan, worker with an on-demand platform providing cleaning services, New Delhi*

In addition, constant feedback collection and worker surveillance weakens negotiation power as workers are forced to please customers at any cost to retain their work with the platform company. The only instance we found of a platform company that also collects feedback on employers from workers is Quikr, which incorporates a call-in feedback mechanism that allows workers to raise their concerns with the same team that deals with customer complaints. However, this feature does not affect the ability of the customer to use the platform in the same way that workers' publicly visible monthly ratings affect their ability to receive work—the consequences of negative feedback are much harsher for workers.

The design of the third type of platform—digital placement agencies—is such that it is well placed to form and enforce decent conditions of work in contracts for workers. Digital placement agencies negotiate workers' contracts, which allows them to set conditions for exploitative or decent work. They do not regulate or surveil workers in their day-to-day tasks but offer a platform to address grievances if they arise. We find instances where platform companies are willing to negotiate better wages on behalf of workers, ensure timely payment of wages, and intervene in case unpaid labour is being extracted. Such willingness, however, does not imply that workers are able to access job security or basic benefits, thereby reinforcing precarious work conditions.

Across different platform models, we find that the existence of an approachable intermediary increases agency among workers, as they are able to negotiate with employers on issues such as non-payment of wages, extraction of unpaid labour, and harassment and violence with the recognition that there is an intermediary that can be approached if employers are exploitative. That being said, we recognise that agency does not operate in a binary of presence and absence and is not a marker of the absence of coercion. On the contrary, we find that aspects of platformisation that enhance agency and contribute to workers' exploitation exist simultaneously. Accordingly, workers narrated experiences where certain aspects of platform design led to gainful work outcomes; at the same time, expansive surveillance and management practices led to disempowerment.

Logics of Platformisation

The construction of domestic work platforms as a technological artefact becomes severely limiting as it enables the imagination of 'solving' social problems. Indeed, most domestic work platforms posture as 'social ventures'. The platform economy reconfigures and continues some historical forms of exploitation, while others are challenged. What remains clear is that platforms in the domestic work sector adopt the logics of this sector, more than the converse.

In making sense of platformisation, we reject its conceptualisation as a project with universally agreed upon objective goals. Understanding it begs the question: platformisation *of what*? What we are witnessing in the global south is the corporatised platformisation of informal economies—driving, logistics, or care work—in urban spaces.

> Akash: They call us partners, but that is just a misnomer. Eventually, they do what they want to do and we have no option but to obey. Is that what a partner is?
>
> —*Akash, worker with an on-demand platform providing cleaning services, New Delhi*

Platformisation is conflated with formalisation, and it is within this vector, that of shifting to formality from informality, that platforms operate. Within the logic of formalisation that platform companies promote, the paternalism of privileged class and caste is parsed technologically in the form of the platform. Formalisation is understood in a limited sense, where technological channels of hiring are created to enable an intensive commodification of domestic and care work. The benefits that are stated to accrue to job seekers are dependent on participation in this commodification process. These benefits do not take the form of protections that are supposed to be the central function of formalisation processes. Instead, the so-called benefits are intended to transform domestic workers to participate within the logics of the market without adequate protections. Workers participating in labour markets through platforms, for example, are often required to have bank accounts, the ownership of which appears as the enabling role that platforms play in formalisation. Such logic is wrongheaded, however, because this notion of financial inclusion stops at financialisation of vulnerable populations without calling for systemic changes that would enable the accruing of any gains to these vulnerable populations, such as access to credit.

At the same time, platformisation of informal economies is different from that of the formal sector. Van Doorn highlights several useful questions to be used in the research of platformed labour.[11] Some of the questions posed are: (a) What is the nature of work performed? (b) What is the social situation and legal status of the worker? (c) What is the worker's relationship to/investment in the work? These questions become pertinent, as these are the axes on which the contours of the platformisation in occupations takes place. The platformisation of domestic and care work, then, takes a very different form than it has for, say, driving or delivery work. The scholarly analyses of platformed labour emerging from the 'Uberisation' framing is of limited use in understanding the platformisation of domestic and care work.

Moving away from the conception of gig work—of the male experience of driving and engaging with a socio-technical intermediary—is necessary. Platforms are deeply embedded in the history of sectors that they seek to 'disrupt'. The multiplicity of models and the many failures of platforms to 'crack' the sector are possibly indicative of how the strategies of control and care by platforms are designed. This dynamic is best indicated by the typology of domestic work platforms. The on-demand model, which is premised on the fungibility of work being platformised, is a far cry from the way in which paid domestic and care work is historically and currently organised in India. A central characteristic of work arrangements in India is the familiarity that is required to be built between paid domestic and care workers with their employers. Consequently, such work arrangements exist for months, if not years.

The piece rating of tasks through on-demand platforms could have important ramifications for domestic and care workers in India, as it stands to reshape the cultural boundaries within which they have historically operated. Platforms also, in their attempts to account for these cultural contours, have begun to offer longer term arrangement bearing resemblance to the archetype of paid domestic work in India as the presence of digital placement agencies indicate. In doing so, platform models in India replicate the existing social order that mediates domestic and care work arrangements. However, they too intervene only at limited points in the provisioning of domestic and care work, thereby raising pressing questions regarding the sustainability of improved working conditions through digital mediation.

Meaning-Making Subjects

Informal sector workers have historically been sidelined in the trade union movement, which has focused on the exploitation of wage labour. Moreover, within the formal/informal demarcation carved out in the workforce, greater focus has been placed on the small formal sector.

There is widespread purchase of the view that globalisation, with freely mobile capital as its central tenet, has led to the weakening of labour movements globally. This view has not gone unopposed, with the fragmentation of the global system of production touted as making capital more vulnerable than before. Concomitantly, the expansion of the informal sector is characterised by a break away from capitalist production relations that are rooted in the alienation of labour from capital. This has led to self-employment, as opposed to wage employment, emerging as the prevalent form of labour relations.

> Prabhu: They are not giving us anything [to start with], we have to invest our own money. I invested Rs. 3000 to start. When I started out, the pay was good, but after they onboarded more workers the orders got distributed. Per day, I only got 2 to 3 orders. I want to earn Rs. 30 to 40 thousand a month. In my old job I used to earn Rs. 28,000 per month. When I started here, they said you can earn Rs. 50,000 monthly. But now it's reduced a lot. I even had to invest my own money to buy products, which they cut from my pay. I thought it would be better to work independently than with the company because of all this, since I'm investing this amount anyway.
>
> —*Prabhu, worker with an on-demand company providing cleaning services in Bengaluru*

Acknowledging these changes, a growing body of scholarship, globally and in India, underlines the requirement for a new imagination of trade union activism. New approaches would need to grapple with structural changes that the trade union movement is going through and arrive at how labour activism efforts need to be reimagined to factor in the salience of informal sector workers. It can be argued that self-employment, characteristic of the platform economy as well, similarly provides new locations and forms of labour activism to emerge—not from those who are traditionally exploited (that is, at sites of extraction of surplus such as factories), but from those who are economically dispossessed without becoming proletarianised.

> Interviewer: Have you heard about trade unions?
>
> Rajeshwari: I had gone for a union meeting once in my area. They told us a lot of rules, and we had to follow whatever they said. They told us to ask for higher salaries and bonuses. But we can lose employers' trust through all this. Some workers ask for these things, they want the benefits. But I am happy with the work I do with CrewOnJobs, it is flexible and part-time, I can earn money beyond my monthly salary. I have decided not to go for union meetings.
>
> —*Rajeshwari, worker with an on-demand company providing cleaning services in Bengaluru*

Such an exercise could commence by approaching domestic workers subjectively through their actions as meaning-making human subjects whose identities (and behaviour) are shaped by objective sets of relations within which they act. Domestic workers are also a part of the valorisation process themselves, as providers of labour-power that structurally aids the continued generation of capital by aiding the reproduction of middle- and upper-class employers who work in capitalist firms. On the other hand, many domestic workers also see themselves quite differently, as self-employed workers negotiating their own terms of work selling their 'service' to potential buyers (their 'patrons' in the households where they work).

The way in which domestic workers confront their employers then uncovers the slippages in their subjectivities between self-employed workers and wage workers. This duality is an integral framework for the construction of a new language of labour activism in the context of not just domestic workers, but also other informal or 'gig economy' spaces. The duality for other workers in the platform economy may be in a different form. The duality, then, need not even be necessarily as fundamentally divergent as in the case of domestic workers, but it is essential to understanding precarity—across the informal sector and in the platform economy.

Acknowledging worker subjectivities then makes interrogating the sufficiency of the employee-independent contractor dualism of legal worker categories. As Dubal highlights, many immigrant and racial-minority taxi drivers eschewed meaning making as employees despite the promised land that the employee categorisation supposedly is.[12] It raises pertinent questions around the taken for granted naturalness of this classification, when "the legal binary reflects neoliberal cultural and political trends and ideologies—particularly, the veneration of the working-class entrepreneur."[13] As legal consciousness theorists point out, it is the individuals' perception of the law and legality that affects how they mobilise it.[14] The tension between how workers are understood in law and how workers identify themselves is surfaced in discussions around the treatment of domestic workers and is now amplified in the case of the platform economy.

Conclusion

In this chapter, we find that platforms' operational logics will play a key role in shaping workers' determination of their material employment conditions. Our typology of platforms mediating domestic work includes three types—(i) marketplace, or platforms that list workers' data on their profile, provide certain filters for automated selection of a pool of workers, and charge a fee from customers for access to workers' contact details, (ii) digital placement agency, or platforms that provide an end-to-end placement service to customers and identify appropriate workers on the basis of selection criteria and negotiate conditions of work on behalf of workers, and (iii) on-demand platforms, or companies that provide services or 'gigs' such as cleaning on an hourly basis, performed by a roster of workers who are characterised as 'independent contractors'. We find that this typology is critical to understand whether a platform acts as a weak or strong intermediary, based on the level of control they exercise over negotiating conditions of work and its performance.

Two central implications of the platform typology in shaping domestic work relationships emerge. First, despite the rhetoric of neutral efficiency that platform companies propagate, there exists vast potential for platforms to intervene, positively or negatively, in the work relationship. In other words, platforms exist in, and shape, the political economy of labour relationships that they claim only to mediate. Different aspects of each platform model determine their impacts, including negotiation of contracts, outsourcing of costs, grievance redressal, and so on. Further, platforms exist with occupational histories proper. Even with an overt acknowledgement of the impact of the informality and exploitation typical to the domestic work sector, platforms often end up reifying these histories.

Our analysis points to the challenges in collectivisation of domestic workers in the gig economy. Historical debates around the meaning making of domestic workers' collective identities are similar to those becoming popular in the discourse around gig work. These debates relate to the categorisation of the gig work within existing classifications of formal labour—either as employment or as independent contractors. However, our chapter shows domestic workers' marginal social positions and occupational histories often lead to experiencing domestic work as fluid employee-contractors. Future research must capture the manner in which workers themselves mobilise these concepts to arrive at appropriate policy interventions and collectivisation strategies. Finally, it is critical for collective labour action to further a worker-centred understanding of platform work, such that sites of resistance may be imagined, and with them, effective challenges to understandings of platform work may be mounted in the domestic work sector, and elsewhere.

Acknowledgements

This chapter is largely an excerpt from a forthcoming report by the authors, to be published by the Centre for Internet and Society, India. The report collects the findings of a year-long study on digital mediation of domestic and care work in India, led by the authors. The study is a part of and supported by the Feminist Internet Research Network, hosted by the Association for Progressive Communications (APC), and funded by the International Development Research Centre (IDRC). Authorship for this chapter is listed in reverse alphabetical order.

Notes

1. P. Kadakia, "Bai on Call: How Home Service Apps Are Changing Domestic Help Market," *Hindustan Times,* February 21, 2016, www.hindustantimes.com/more-life

style/bai-on-call-how-home-service-apps-changing-the-maids-market/story-s6zz6kmWw1aEamZ1yLxjaL.html.
2. S. Bhattacharya and S. Sinha, *Domestic Workers in India: Background and Issues* (New Delhi: ILO, 2009).
3. A. Basolne, "The Skilled and The Schooled," *The Caravan*, 2018, www.magzter.com/article/News/The-Caravan/The-Skilled-And-The-Schooled.
4. G. Geymonat, S. Marchetti, and Kyritsis Penelope, "Out from the Shadows: Domestic Workers Speak in the United States," *Open Democracy*, 2017, www.opendemocracy.net/en/beyond-trafficking-and-slavery/out-from-shadows-domestic-workers-speak-in-united-states/.
5. J. Ticona, A. Mateescu, and A. Rosenblat, "Beyond Disruption: How Tech Shapes Labor Across Domestic Work & Ridehailing," *Data & Society*, 2018, https://datasociety.net/wp-content/uploads/2018/06/Data_Society_Beyond_Disruption_FINAL.pdf.
6. KPMG for Ministry of Skill Development and Entrepreneurship, *Human Resources and Skill Requirements in the Domestic Help Sector* (2013–17, 2017–22), www.ugc.ac.in/skill/SectorReport/Domestic%20Help.pdf.
7. Labour Bureau, Ministry of Labour & Employment, *Report on Fifth Annual Employment—Unemployment Survey, Volume I* (2015–16), http://labourbureaunew.gov.in/UserContent/EUS_5th_1.pdf.
8. N. Neetha, "Contours of Domestic Service: Characteristics, Work Relations and Regulations," *The Indian Journal of Labour Economics*, 52 (2009): 489–506.
9. R. Gajjala, "The Problem of Value for 'Women's Work'," *GenderIT*, 2017, www.genderit.org/node/4907/.
10. Ticona et al., "Beyond Disruption."
11. N. van Doorn, "On the Conditions of Possibility for Worker Organizing in Platform-based Gig Economies," *LogOut!* 2019, https://notesfrombelow.org/article/conditions-possibility-worker-organizing-platform
12. V. Dubal, "The Drive to Precarity: A Political History of Work, Regulation, & Labor Advocacy in San Francisco's Taxi & Uber Economies," *Berkeley Journal of Employment & Labor Law* 38, no. 1 (2017), https://repository.uchastings.edu/faculty_scholarship/1589.
13. Ibid.
14. See Patricia Ewick and Susan S Silbey, "Conformity, Contestation, and Resistance: An Account of Legal Consciousness," *New England Law Review* 26 (1991): 731; Austin Sarat, "' . . . The Law Is All Over': Power, Resistance and the Legal Consciousness of the Welfare Poor," *Yale Journal of Law & Humanities* 2 (1990): 343.

4

SEX WORK/GIG WORK

A Feminist Analysis of Precarious Domina Labor in the Gig Economy

Lauren Levitt

Fifty professional dominas work at Dungeon X, a commercial dungeon in a large city in the northeastern United States, on any given day.[1] These women are not protected under labor law. Consequently, they have little job security, receive no hourly wage, and generally take home less than 50 percent of the value of their services. As independent contractors, these women are responsible for paying self-employment tax in addition to federal income taxes. Like other workers in the gig economy, they are ineligible for workplace benefits such as healthcare, retirement plans, overtime, or paid leave. Moreover, despite wages being unreliable and benefits nonexistent, the dungeon's management forbids these women from working at other dungeons or conducting independent sessions with clients. Because their work occupies a legal grey area (laws regarding bondage and discipline/dominance and submission/sadism and masochism [BDSM] sex work are open to legal interpretation), dominas are vulnerable to arrest, contributing to their stigmatization as sex workers and BDSM practitioners.[2] Furthermore, unlike independent dominas, they have little control over vetting their clients, making them especially susceptible to violence and arrest by undercover police officers. If a client assaults them, it is unlikely management will report the incident to law enforcement or take punitive action such as barring the perpetrator from the dungeon.

Like other gig workers, the lives of these women are marked by economic precarity and deeply impacted by neoliberal policies that withdraw public support for welfare, low-income housing, Medicaid, food stamps, and other programs. Because they do not earn an hourly wage, employees at the dungeon lack a reliable income stream, and when business is slow they can go for months without having a single session with a client. Since Dungeon X's owner does not report income, it is difficult for workers to pay taxes or keep money in the bank, making it difficult for them to build credit or even provide proof of income, frustrating efforts to secure housing. If they work at the dungeon full time or without a day job, their resumes might also reflect significant gaps of time without conventional employment, a problem that makes finding work in the future onerous. However, these examples of economic precarity in sex work are not unique to the sex industry but are instead characteristic of the gig economy as a whole. In this sense, their labor entails certain kinds of risks not unlike those taken on by Silicon Alley entrepreneurs.[3]

Although sex work stands apart from official definitions of the gig economy, they are in fact inextricably linked.[4] Sex work operates according to the logics of the gig economy, demanding multiple sources of income, independent contractor status, low wages, flexibility, and a premium on creativity. Many sex workers also participate in the gig economy to make ends meet. To function, the mainstream economy depends on the underground economy, which includes but is not limited to sex work. Despite this dynamic, little has been written about the relationship between sex work and the gig economy. What, then, is the relationship between the sex industry and the gig economy? Specifically, what are the similarities between sex work and gig work, and what can these commonalities tell us about the relationship between the underground economy and the mainstream economy more generally? Drawing on interviews with 16 female-identifying sex workers, the following chapter answers these questions, contributing to feminist research on the gig economy by sharing omitted stories. As the following interviews put into sharp relief, sex workers embody the connection between the underground economy and the mainstream economy.

Relevant Literature

Considering the relationship between sex work and the mainstream economy, a number of sex work scholars have found that the growth of the sex industry is connected to broader shifts in the labor market. According to Elizabeth Bernstein, the entry of white, middle-class women into the sex industry coincided with the rise of the service economy; relatively privileged and highly educated women turned to sex work because they could make more money offering sexual services than they could otherwise.[5] Black women are likewise drawn into the porn industry by the lack of more desirable work opportunities in the face of neoliberal cutbacks and the feminization of labor, according to Mireille Miller-Young.[6] Furthermore, Heather R. Berg maintains that the precarity faced by porn performers is symptomatic of late capitalism more broadly, which "increasingly relies on a flexible and itinerant workforce" and fails to provide "basic benefits and protections."[7]

Scholars of the gig economy also view gig work as part of broader trends in the labor market. For example, Austin Zwick uses Uber as an example to show how gig economy companies "enact the neoliberal playbook, including (a) (mis) classifying workers, (b) engaging in regime shopping, and (c) employing the most economically vulnerable."[8] Valerio De Stefano proposes that the gig economy is part of broader economic trends including "casualization of the workforce, informalization of the formal economy, and the so called 'demutualization of risk.'"[9] Joshua Healy, Daniel Nicholson, and Andreas Pekarek situate the gig economy in the context of increased job and income insecurity and the loss of employment benefits since the 1980s, particularly in the United States, and Jeremias Prassl sees gig work as following "a broader trend of fissurization" in the mainstream economy.[10] Finally, Jim Stanford characterizes the gig economy as part of "a broader shift in capitalist employment relations" to "precarious work practices."[11] The present analysis builds on past studies of the gig economy and sex work by making their connection explicit, contributing to and inviting further feminist analyses of gig work.

Methodology

Ethnographic methods, including in-depth interviews, have proven especially productive for feminist scholars studying sex work. Miller-Young, for example, used ethnographic interviews and participant observation in conversation with textual analysis in her study of black women in pornography because, as a feminist, she wanted to understand the experiences of black women in mainstream pornography, an industry geared toward straight, white, male desire. Speaking to black women in the porn industry allowed Miller-Young to let them "speak for themselves," an aim which is not alien to this chapter.[12] Wendy Chapkis also conducted interviews with women working in the sex industry, in addition to participant observation and secondary research on commercial sex, in her comparative study of the sex industry in the United States and the Netherlands. Chapkis conceded that one of the weaknesses of qualitative research is its susceptibility to biases of the researcher. Chapkis attempted to counteract this tendency by intentionally including material with which she did not agree. However, she recognized that her research participants exercised agency by revealing or withholding information, necessitating the critical interpretation of their narratives.[13]

Following the work of Chapkis and Miller-Young, I crafted the methodology of this study to reflect my desire to understand the experience and context of workers at Dungeon X. This chapter, more specifically, draws on in-depth, semi-structured interviews conducted with 16 current or former female-identified sex workers in July 2018. Fourteen of these women were working at Dungeon X between May 2013 and July 2015, and the remaining two have worked as an erotic dancer and an erotic masseuse in the same city. Interviews lasted approximately one hour and covered relationships with coworkers, types of support given and received, hierarchy at work, relationships with friends and family, and work history. Interviews were then coded according to ad hoc and emergent coding schemas using qualitative data analysis software, NVivo, with codes relating to difference, labor, and precarity. Like Chapkis, I too tried to remain open to viewpoints that challenge my own, while allowing myself to interpret the words of my research participants through my own perspective.

Sex Work and the Gig Economy

Since its emergence with the 2009 financial crisis, the gig economy has been linked with economic precarity. According to *The Financial Times*, the term "gig economy" was first used to refer to the practice of working multiple part-time jobs in order to get by.[14] Although the gig economy is now synonymous with working for online "sharing economy" applications like ride-sharing apps Uber or Lyft, these jobs are also precarious because of their short-term status, low wages, and lack of workplace protections or benefits. The gig economy is also closely connected to creative labor that, as Angela McRobbie argues, is critical to the neoliberal economy.[15] Previously referring to the musical engagements of jazz musicians in the 1920s, the term "gig" today is more commonly used for any type of short-term engagement, particularly those of a creative type.[16]

Sex work shares many characteristics of the gig economy and, in doing so, highlights the exploitative nature of all labor under capitalism. Scholarship on the gig economy identifies misclassifying employees as independent contractors as one of the defining features of the gig economy.[17] Like gig workers, sex workers are frequently considered independent contractors, but as Berg's writing on porn work shows, the label "independent contractor" is often nominal.[18] The weekly schedules that many sex workers hold, for example, should legally render them employees of the business.

Several of my interview participants nonetheless identified themselves as independent contractors. Erin,[19] a holistic bodywork practitioner, noted that as an independent contractor in an illegal business she is automatically isolated from other workers. Lily, an independent escort who worked at Dungeon X for one year, compared doing sex work to working in bars and restaurants because in both cases you are an "independent contractor" who makes your own schedule. Finally, Miriam, a direct support professional who worked at Dungeon X for two years, wondered why skilled workers or independent contractors do not have more say over their wages, though many independent contractors do not either.

Like independent contractors, many sex workers lack workplace benefits such as health insurance or paid leave. As Leona, who worked at Dungeon X for two years, related, "My new job, which is a straight job, is significantly more economically viable and has things like benefits, which are nice, which we did not have [at Dungeon X]." The absence of health insurance is particularly difficult for workers with disabilities like Natalie and Miriam. Natalie, an independent domina and performance artist, seriously injured her back and suffered a series of psychotic breaks during her five-year tenure at Dungeon X. Natalie did not seek the care she needed after she injured her back because she did not have health insurance, instead expending much of her income on sliding-scale doctors and eventually becoming hospitalized, where she was finally put on Medicaid. Similarly, Miriam, who struggles with bipolar disorder, depression, and anxiety, was paying entirely out of pocket for her psychiatric treatment, including multiple psychiatric medications, until three women at Dungeon X, including Natalie, convinced her to sign up for public healthcare through the Affordable Care Act. Others had not been so lucky.[20]

The lack of paid leave also poses problems, especially for those with chronic health conditions. Shortly after being released from the hospital for the second time, Natalie was brutally attacked and sexually assaulted. She had to return the following week, however, because she could not afford to take more time off work. Even without paid leave, it could be difficult for some to take extended periods off work for necessary medical treatment. Natalie faced resistance from management when she requested time off work for her back surgery. The dungeon's owner even attempted to convince her not to undergo the surgery by admonishing her that she did not need it. Her manager too had questioned her need for surgery, advising her to take up yoga.

De Stefano argues that gig economy workers may lack basic worker protections beyond leave and health insurance.[21] Companies misclassify gig economy workers as independent contractors to deny them protection under labor law.[22] Like gig work, sex work frequently denies workplace rights such as a minimum wage, maximum weekly hours, or protection against discrimination. The majority of women I interviewed began doing sex work because they needed money; only three out of 14 did not mention financial concerns as a reason for engaging in sex work. Seven of the 12 women I interviewed who worked at Dungeon X had responded to an ad on Craigslist. Janice, an actor and entertainer who worked at Dungeon X for eight years, recalled the ad's promise of high wages that, for most interviewees, never came.

For many the promise of earning extra money rang hollow. Six of the 12 women who worked at Dungeon X mentioned some form of wage exploitation in their interview. Leona and Jane, a pharmacy counterperson who worked at Dungeon X for five years including one year as a manager, stated that the money was not particularly good there. For Leona, some of the "straight" jobs she had were more "lucrative and economically sustainable" than working at the dungeon, and she mentioned that workers with little interest in BDSM would often leave quickly when they realized "it's not actually the most profitable job you could take." Natalie observed that at Dungeon X, like the other male-run dungeon she had worked at, workers received the smallest cut of the money—$80 as compared to $140 for the house—explaining that the owner's systematic overhiring practices further exacerbated the dungeon's already low wages and high turnover.

Several of the women I interviewed also mentioned that clients failed to tip them adequately. Gretchen, an independent dominatrix who worked at Dungeon

X for six years, mentioned that clients would often try to take advantage of new workers by tipping them less for particular services. Jane similarly remarked, "You know, your two to four was just struggling to make money and having to fend off a bunch of creeps who obviously weren't gonna pay for what they were asking for." Miriam also mentioned an incident in which a client badly beat her and only tipped her $50. Liz, who worked at Dungeon X for a year and a half, noted that even at the new dungeon where she works clients sometimes do not tip and then are reprimanded by management.

Miriam, however, saw low wages as endemic to the sex industry as a whole. She initially began sex work as a "sugar baby"—typically a young woman, who dates and often becomes intimately involved with someone else, frequently an older man, in exchange for either money or goods and services—with an allowance of $400 per night. Though finding this amount "shamefully low," Miriam could not find anyone else who would pay more. Before Dungeon X, she had worked at a different dungeon which hosted foot parties where "no one really pa[id] enough for anything," adding, "That's kinda the standard." Dissatisfied with inadequate compensation, Miriam ultimately left Dungeon X to work independently, attributing wage exploitation in the sex industry, especially for women of color, to the presence of sex trafficking.

Sex workers are also exploited through long working hours. Erin related how, at the first bodywork studio she worked in, the owner would overschedule and overwork the staff. "All of us worked five to six days a week . . . four to seven days a week," she explained. Natalie recollected a similar experience at the first dungeon where she worked: "It was an afterhours place, so we were working midnight to six, and we were required to do five days a week, which is a lot in sex work, Jesus Christ." Those demanding hours led many to use heroin.

Finally, sex workers were not protected against workplace discrimination, particularly racial discrimination. A racial hierarchy of desirability meant that white women and lighter-skinned Latina women were more in demand than were black women. Yanna, a stay-at-home parent who worked at Dungeon X intermittently for six years, remembered a black Columbian coworker who was rarely picked for sessions because of her skin color. Miriam was especially vocal about racism in the sex industry, a problem she specifically linked to anti-blackness. Miriam also noted that sex workers of color were often responsible for contributing financially to their families. "And that makes them more vulnerable, then, to be coerced into services or sex acts that maybe they didn't want to do as much," she expanded. To illustrate this point, Miriam, who is Asian and white, spoke of a coworker who attended the same college she did: "I feel like we were similar people, and she's black, though. And, so, she was treated differently, disrespected and needed to give money to her mom and just had this context of reality that I did not."

Miriam also objected to racial discrimination from management. She accused one manager of frequently stealing money from black workers but almost never from white workers, noting that this particular manager would mistreat black workers by making them redo tasks like cleaning up a room. Such racial intimidation was "mostly used to intimidate lighter skinned or white folk," Miriam claimed. These gratuitous demonstrations of power prevented more privileged workers from speaking out against discrimination for fear of being next. Furthermore, Miriam maintained that black and darker-skinned Latina workers would be fined two or three times as frequently as she was for infractions such as being late, adding, "And managers are often the one who show their discretion with that."

Moreover, as "independent contractors" many sex workers are responsible for any injuries sustained on the job. Miriam, Liz, and Yanna recollected an incident when a coworker had a seizure at work and management ordered that she be carried out to the sidewalk before calling an ambulance. Miriam, who was on shift at the time, expressed guilt over her complicity in the situation, while Liz, who actually called the ambulance, articulated more condemnation for management.

Jobs in the gig economy tend to be temporary or piecework, and many sex work jobs are also short term.[23] Although the women I spoke with worked at Dungeon X for at least one year, it is worth considering the significance of over-hiring and its impact on turnover. Yanna told me, "The owner of the place just hires anybody at any time 'cause he just wants as many girls so that he can make money." According to Natalie, over-hiring also led to high turnover: "There were so many people and not enough clients and not enough rooms. And there would just be new people added daily because most of them would quit, but a lot of them would quit because there [were] more new people coming in constantly." Megan, an independent dominatrix who worked at Dungeon X for a year, speculated that the reason it took so long for the more senior workers to accept new people was because of the high turnover rate, and other women who worked at Dungeon X confirmed Megan's theory. Emily, a marketing and customer experience manager who worked at Dungeon X for a year and a half, Janice, Miriam, and Natalie gradually stopped engaging with new workers over time. Emily articulated, "Having worked there, there's such turnover that you begin to realize there's no point in getting to know most people because they'll be gone in a week or two anyway, so you just don't want to engage with them." Although she acknowledged that some of the senior women at Dungeon X could be really "bitchy," the longer Emily worked there, the more she "understood that people stumbled through there so often, not everyone's gonna be your best friend." Janice likewise remarked, "You see a lot of people come through there, so it's hard to try and care for everybody 'cause people come and go so fast."

This dynamic increased the competition between workers and led to a hostile work environment, particularly for new hires. "When new people would come in, it wouldn't be welcoming. It would be like, 'What the fuck is this shit?'" Natalie explained. Yanna even recalled treating new workers as rudely as possible to encourage them to quit. Likewise, Venus, a nonprofit worker who worked at Dungeon X for about a year, described how some of the more senior workers would not speak to the new workers and behaved as if the latter did not exist. Similarly, De Stefano found that competition undermines solidarity between gig workers.[24]

Janice grew so frustrated with the lack of appreciation for her voluntary labor that she stopped training new hires. "So I stopped doing a lot of the free information. It became, you know, not that you had to be in the club, but you had to show that you were serious [about the job]," she recalled. Yanna echoed this sentiment when she said that she would only warm up to the new workers after they had demonstrated that they were there to work and because they were passionate about the job, not for the cachet of being a dominatrix. Like Janice, however, Natalie eventually ceased training new workers after many of them quit anyway, and even Miriam, who always trained and helped new hires until she left Dungeon X, eventually limited her efforts to interact with them.

In addition to hiring practices and worker attitudes, the rapid replacement of workers at Dungeon X resulted from workers who were unprepared for the requirements of the job. For instance, Yanna recounted hearing about women running out of their first sessions crying. For this reason, Janice always advised new workers to figure out their boundaries straight away and to articulate them as specifically as possible. She reasoned,

> I feel like I had to make a lot of decisions that I wasn't prepared for, and that's what I always wanted to let the new girls know because if you're prepared for it, then it's harder to second guess yourself and then feel bad about it later, which is I think why a lot of people leave is because they make decisions that they don't feel proud of.

Beyond Dungeon X, the sex industry has a high turnover rate because workers do not know what to expect. As Laurie, a stay-at-home mother who was as an erotic dancer off and on for six years, revealed, "There's always girls that come and go, kinda stay for a week and then they realize they're not really cut out for it." Because sex work is "not for everyone," just as in the gig economy, there is always a fresh stream of workers cycling through the industry, keeping competition high and wages low.

Sex Workers as Active Agents

Despite exploitative working conditions, Dungeon X workers are not simply victims of their environment. All of them have chosen to work at the dungeon because they prefer it to other types of work available to them. For example, work at the dungeon affords flexible work hours; if a worker needs a day off to go on a job interview or care for a sick child, she simply finds someone else to cover her shift. Other workers appreciate how the job allows them to multitask, permitting them to take on freelance projects in areas such as marketing, graphic design, or journalism in their downtime between sessions. And for still others, especially for low-skilled workers, the job offers better compensation than strenuous, low-paying work in the service industry, with the lack of steady wages offset by the potential to make a lot of money in a short period of time.

Additionally, many of my interview participants, especially those engaged in independent sex work, saw freelance work as preferable to full-time work, in no small part because of the flexibility it offers. Megan remarked that working independently gives her more control over her schedule, clients she accepts, her image, and how much she charges. By the same token, Lily prefers being an "independent contractor" to a full-time employee because of the "flexibility of schedule" it provides. Lily began working at Dungeon X because she was waiting tables at a restaurant and needed a second job with a flexible schedule. Now that she works independently, she no longer works evenings or weekends unless she wants to, and she has a "flexible daytime schedule."

Natalie much prefers working independently to working at a Dungeon X because she can do her own bookings. "And I'm able to structure my schedule around my life rather than structuring my life around my schedule, so it just makes a lot more sense," she explained. In fact, flexibility is so important to Natalie that she quit a previous job as a regional makeup artist because the company would not give her weekends off to practice roller derby. Gretchen prefers working independently to working at Dungeon X because of the "peace of mind" it gives her by allowing her to work less and on her own time. She hopes to become a freelance art curator and thinks that this will allow her to travel more and have more freedom. Lana, an independent dominatrix who worked at Dungeon X several times over the course of six years, enjoys her day job, which is commission-based and where she can make her own hours, like working independently, and she is proud that her friends at Dungeon X were "self-employed doing what they love." Jane, who still occasionally works as an independent BDSM player, informed me that working independently is better money than working at a house "and you can set your own hours." Even Miriam, who was unable to work independently for more than six months after she left Dungeon X for mental health reasons, granted that working independently allowed her to work less and earn more money, although she had to "hustle" for it.

Nonetheless, even interviewees who did not work independently appreciated the flexibility of sex work. Janice started working at Dungeon X "because it was so easy to work around the schedule, because I can focus on my main goals and do this." Leona and her coworkers at Dungeon X "were pursuing it either as an outlet or as a monetary source that [lent] flexibility." Yanna also appreciated that she was able to set her own schedule and hours at Dungeon X. Erin concurred, saying that sex work "allows you the flexibility to live your life in the meantime." Abi Adams, Judith Freedman, and Jeremias Prassl report that women are more likely than men are to prefer self-employment because of its flexibility.[25] Perhaps this preference stems from women's taking on the lioness's share of unpaid familial labor and the lack of other high-paying, flexible-hour job options, but given this reality for many women, sex work provides a way to negotiate this structural inequity.

Finally, like gig work, sex work is associated with creativity. Both Megan and Lana felt that sex work constituted creative labor. "I'm creating a lot with my domming, and I enjoy that, doing the creative part, like taking photos and making things for that. I just mean exploring sexuality and doing that in a creative way," Megan expressed. Likewise, Lana sees working as a dominatrix as "performance art," and she takes pride in the fact that many of her friends from Dungeon X were also creative. She called Dungeon X "a host for creative female misfits scrambling to make a life in the last creative cornerstones of [the city where I live]."

Other sex workers had engaged in different types of creative labor. Erin has worked for a number of artists, including a sculptor and a painter, in creative assisting and fabrication roles, and she is also a seamstress, making clothing and costumes for circus and theater. Furthermore, Erin is a fine artist in her own right, with a studio a few blocks from her house that pays for itself through the creative work she does. She argues that doing sex work has boosted her artistic career because she can now afford to turn down less highly paid work.

Like Erin, Miriam is also an artist and a seamstress. She has two associate's degrees, one in fine art and one in costume design, and she has designed costumes for theater. Miriam was formerly a member of a do-it-yourself artists' collective, where she hosted her own life-drawing event. Janice also studied fine art at college and, while working at Dungeon X, taught art to children at a Jewish Community Center (JCC). Moreover, Janice works in entertainment, and she has done some media consulting work related to her job as a dominatrix. At the time of her interview, she was considering marrying sex work with entertainment by embarking on a career as an intimacy director, choreographing sex scenes for television and film. Venus runs her own event production company. Gretchen recently went back to school to become a contemporary art curator and decided to work in the nonprofit sector, someday hoping to "merge art and curatorial . . . studies with advocacy, non-profit, and community outreach work."

Still other sex workers engage in creative pursuits in their free time. Liz and Natalie are performance artists and produce a collective, female-led performance art show. In addition to creating through her dominatrix work, Lana makes visual art inspired by BDSM. She elaborated, "Before this I didn't have a subject to paint. I didn't know what I wanted to paint. I had no idea. I was painting abstract things, and then I walk into the dungeon. I see leather and latex and this world that of fetish that transfixed me."

More Than a Dominatrix

Gig economy workers must often rely on multiple income streams to make ends meet.[26] In addition to sex work structurally resembling gig work in terms of workers' "independent contractor" status, temporary labor, desire for flexibility, and creativity, sex workers also utilize multiple income streams to survive. The need for sex workers to hold multiple jobs at once reflects a wider economy in which this is increasingly the case, for legal as well as criminalized workers. Having access to multiple sources of income may involve performing various types of sex work simultaneously, working a "straight" job in addition to a sex work job, or doing sex work at the same time as other gig jobs. As Berg shows, porn workers often perform other types of sex work such as erotic dancing, webcam modeling, and escorting, to supplement their unreliable income, or they use porn as a calling card for work in these adjacent industries, allowing them to demand higher wages for their labor.[27] An example of a porn performer working in a number of related sex industries, Vanessa Blue has worked as "a porn actress, exotic dancer, phone sex worker, fetish model, dominatrix, and private escort."[28]

The interviews discussed here also illustrate the fact that workers move in and out of different sectors of the sex industry, sometimes performing different kinds of sex work simultaneously. More than half of my research participants reported doing more than one type of sex work.[29] In addition to practicing bodywork, Erin has been as an erotic photography model and sometimes works as an escort. Gretchen worked briefly as an erotic masseuse as well as a dominatrix. Jane and Miriam were both sugar babies in addition to being dominatrices, and Miriam was also an escort. Although Laurie was mainly an erotic dancer, she worked briefly in a fetish club, and Yanna performed at a lap-dancing club in between two of her stints at Dungeon X. Sarah had been a fetish model before working at Dungeon X, and Natalie sometimes does erotic dancing as well as working as an independent dominatrix. However, Lily has done more sex work jobs than any other participant has. In addition to working as a dominatrix and an escort, she has done erotic dancing, erotic massage, porn, and nude modeling, and she is a hostess in a sex club.

Additionally, sex workers perform other "gig" jobs. As well as being a seamstress and an artist, Erin has worked at events as a coat check attendant, door person, and bartender, and she framed her freelance work as a "hustle," a black working-class strategy for survival, according to Robin D. G. Kelley.[30] Janice has also hosted trivia, karaoke, and speed dating in addition to working in entertainment. Furthermore, a number of participants were self-employed. Natalie and Liz run their performance art show, and Gretchen works "freelance." Emily summarized this point, saying, "We all have side gigs or main gigs and this was our side gig."

Finally, sex workers perform jobs in the mainstream economy, regularly and on an occasional basis. Many workers have "day jobs," or ongoing employment outside the sex industry. As mentioned earlier, Emily had a full-time job the entire time she was a sex worker, as did Lana and Venus. Liz works as a receptionist in a funeral home part time at the same time as being a dominatrix, and Erin works for a nightclub while practicing bodywork. When Lily began working at Dungeon X, she was a server in a restaurant, and Janice taught art to kids at the

JCC while working at Dungeon X. Miriam worked as a cashier, had a job on her college campus, and sold hats while doing sex work. According to Yanna, many of the dancers at the club where she worked were "professionals" of some kind.

Sex Work Supports the Mainstream Economy

These interviews demonstrate the parallels and convergences between sex work and the gig economy. Women dungeon workers are overlooked in analyses of the gig economy. Thus, undertaking such an analysis makes a modest but significant contribution to feminist scholarship. Like other forms of caring labor, sex work is feminized (predominantly performed by women), and exploitation in the sex industry is highly gendered, raced, and classed, as is exploitation in the wider gig economy. Just as the majority of sex workers are women, many sex workers are people of color and working class. There are numerous middle-class and high-end sex workers and plentiful poorly paid gig jobs, and according to Zwick, the largest demographic of gig workers in the United States are 18- to 29-year-old people of color.[31] However, in general, there are more prestigious and/or middle- to high-income jobs in the gig economy than the sex industry, and gig work spreads more easily across racial and ethnic lines than does sex work. This economic reality suggests that exploitation depends on one's position at the intersection of systems of oppression.[32] Members of marginalized groups such as women, people of color, and low-income workers are more likely to experience labor exploitation than are their more privileged counterparts, in gig work as in sex work.

Sex work is *one form* of gig work that predated the "gig economy," but sex work has its own unique characteristics. The primary difference between sex work and other forms of gig work is the matter of criminalization and stigmatization; most gig workers do not experience stigma or face incarceration because of their job. As Juno Mac and Molly Smith suggest, criminalization only intensifies economic exploitation.[33]

The resemblance between gig work and sex work and the fact that sex workers, like gig workers, must work multiple jobs to make enough money to live suggest that sex work is more closely connected to the gig economy than has previously been theorized. Not only can sex work be gig work, but sex work often subsidizes the low wages, lack of benefits, and job insecurity of the gig economy. In this way, underground economies, including sex work, undocumented labor, and the black market, are crucial to the functioning of the mainstream economy. The exploitation present in these underground economies reflects and supports labor exploitation under global capitalism more generally.

This last point is significant because in order to address labor exploitation in the sex industry and the gig economy, we must first address it in the mainstream economy. Because the gig economy is inseparable from the mainstream economy, better conditions for all workers will improve conditions for gig economy workers, and the same holds true for sex workers.[34] When sex workers have access to mainstream jobs that are flexible, well paid, and include benefits, they will have less incentive to endure labor exploitation in the sex industry. Furthermore, gig work must be recognized as labor in order to combat the commodification and dehumanization of gig workers, and this is also true of sex work.[35] Only when gig work and sex work are recognized *as work* can legislation protect these forms of labor.

Notes

1. Dungeon X is a pseudonym.
2. Gayle Rubin, "Thinking Sex: Notes for a Radical Theory of the Politics of Sexuality," in *Pleasure and Danger: Exploring Female Sexuality*, ed. Carole S. Vance (Boston, MA: Routledge, 1984).
3. Gina Neff, *Venture Labor: Work and the Burden of Risk in Innovative Industries* (Cambridge, MA: MIT Press, 2012).
4. Elka Torpey and Andrew Hogan, "Work in a Gig Economy," BLS.gov, May 2016, www.bls.gov/careeroutlook/2016/article/pdf/what-is-the-gig-economy.pdf.
5. Elizabeth Bernstein, *Temporarily Yours: Intimacy, Authenticity, and the Commerce of Sex* (Chicago: University of Chicago Press, 2007), 9.
6. Mireille Miller-Young, *A Taste for Brown Sugar: Black Women in Pornography* (Durham, NC: Duke University Press, 2014).
7. Heather R. Berg, "Porn Work: Adult Film at the Point of Production" (Doctoral diss., University of California, Santa Barbara, 2016).
8. Austin Zwick, "Welcome to the Gig Economy: Neoliberal Industrial Relations and the Case of Uber," *GeoJournal*, 83 (2018): 679.
9. Valerio De Stefano, "The Rise of the 'Just in Time Workforce': On-Demand Work, Crowdwork, and Labor Protection in the "Gig-Economy," Proceedings from *Crowd-Sourcing, the Gig Economy, and the Law* (Philadelphia, 2015): 3, accessed July 3, 2019, http://ssrn.com/abstract=2682602.
10. Joshua Healy, Daniel Nicholson, and Andreas Pekarek, "Should We Take the Gig Economy Seriously?" *Labor and Industry* 27, no. 3 (2017); Jeremias Prassl, *Humans as Service: The Promise and Perils of Work in the Gig Economy* (Oxford: Oxford University Press, 2018), 9.
11. Jim Stanford, "The Resurgence of Gig Work: Historical and Theoretical Perspectives," *The Economic and Labor Relations Review* 28, no. 3 (2017): 392.
12. Miller-Young, *A Taste for Brown Sugar*, 22.
13. Wendy Chapkis, *Live Sex Acts: Women Performing Erotic Labor* (New York: Routledge, 1997).
14. Leslie Hook, "2015: A Year in a Word: Gig Economy," *The Financial Times*, December 30, 2015.
15. Angela McRobbie, *Be Creative: Making a Living in the New Creative Industries* (Cambridge: Polity Press, 2016).
16. Hook, "2015."
17. De Stefano, "The Rise of the 'Just in Time Workforce'"; Healy et al., "Should We Take the Gig Economy Seriously?"; Prassl, *Humans as Service*; Zwick, "Welcome to the Gig Economy."
18. Berg, "Porn Work."
19. Erin is a pseudonym; this study replaces interviewees names with pseudonyms to protect anonymity.
20. Two other former Dungeon X workers recalled a schizophrenic colleague who had stopped taking her medication and had to be taken to the hospital.

21. De Stefano, "The Rise of the 'Just in Time Workforce.'"
22. Prassl, *Humans as Service*; Zwick, "Welcome to the Gig Economy."
23. Stanford, "The Resurgence of Gig Work."
24. De Stefano, "The Rise of the 'Just in Time Workforce.'"
25. Abi Adams, Judith Freedman, and Jeremias Prassl, "Rethinking Legal Taxonomies for the Gig Economy," *Oxford Review of Economic Policy* 34, no. 3 (2018).
26. Adams et al., "Rethinking Legal Taxonomies"; Healy et al., "Should We Take the Gig Economy Seriously?"
27. Berg, "Porn Work."
28. Miller-Young, *A Taste for Brown Sugar*, 276.
29. Nine out of the 16 women I interviewed told me that they had done more than one *kind* of sex work. Four more had held more than one sex work job.
30. Robin D. G. Kelley, *Race Rebels: Culture, Politics, and the Black Working Class* (New York: Free Press, 1996).
31. Zwick, "Welcome to the Gig Economy."
32. Kimberlé Crenshaw, "Demarginalizing the Intersection of Race and Sex: A Black Feminist Critique of Antidiscrimination Doctrine, Feminist Theory and Antiracist Politics," *University of Chicago Legal Forum* (1989).
33. Juno Mac and Molly Smith, *Revolting Prostitutes: The Fight for Sex Workers' Rights* (London: Verso, 2018).
34. Healy, Nicholson, and Pekarek, "Should We Take the Gig Economy Seriously?"; De Stefano, "The Rise of the 'Just in Time Workforce.'"
35. De Stefano, "The Rise of the 'Just in Time Workforce.'"

III
Ideology
Thinking Like a Gig Economist

5

"THE FUTURE DEMANDS WE ALL BECOME PROLIFIC ARTISTS"

Cultural Ideals of Gig Work in Popular Management Literature

Juhana Venäläinen

This chapter analyzes the cultural ideals of gig work through the lens of popular management literature. As the notion of the gig economy has become fashionable in the media and the consulting parlance,[1] there is also a growing number of authors who have taken the opportunity to write guidebooks for people interested in going for the brass ring and escaping the dullness of wage labor.

> There's a huge new game in town that's having a profound effect on worldwide workforces. Monumental changes will occur in how companies recruit, hire and manage employees. Perhaps even more drastic changes will take place for the workers themselves. The new game of course is called the Gig Economy.[2]

Although these guidebooks may genuinely help current and prospective "giggers" to learn the demands of the new work order, they also set out expectations that are often ambivalent and unattainable.

At the political level, the debate continues about how to react to the so-called alternative and contingent employment arrangements, of which the gig economy is an example.[3] For some, these arrangements represent the deterioration of "regular work," whereas for others, they appear as prospects of growth and employment. This dichotomy observes the dynamics of work mostly from a top-down perspective, easily overshadowing how a similar tension between optimistic and dystopian interpretations evolves in the ambivalent expectations laid on the gig workers themselves.

The aim of this inquiry is to deepen understanding about how novel "structures of feeling"[4] of work now emerge. The approach builds upon and contributes to the sociological and cultural analyses of new work,[5] paying attention not only to the macro-scale restructuration of contemporary capitalism but also to its subjective repercussions and the intricate ways of constructing the working subject. As a case in point, the analysis focuses on a particular cultural form—*popular management literature*—to unravel how workers are primed to the era of the gig economy. As will be argued, gigging guidebooks operate as tools of personal transformation: they educate workers to accept the fundamental uncertainty of employment and the thorough melting together of life and work. The books prepare the workers to push their limits, submit to unrealistic expectations, and conceive success and failure as individual rather than structural.

What kind of skills and qualities does a worker require to cope and thrive in the gig economy? Before looking further into that, the chapter introduces the literary genre of pop-management and elaborates how the evolution of the gig economy is explained in it. After that, five traits of an idealized gig worker (*entrepreneurialism, self-development, malleability, prudence,* and *communicativeness*) will be examined. The chapter concludes by discussing the ambivalences between the different traits and illuminating how pop-management literature contributes to molding a hyper-individualized, entrepreneurial subjectivity.

Data and Methods

The research material consists of 13 electronic gig economy guidebooks, published in 2016–2018,[6] that were collected from Amazon.com Kindle Store through a keyword search with the search phrase "gig economy" in the order given by Amazon's "Featured" algorithm. Non-guidebook items, such as academic, journalistic, and fictional titles, were excluded. For tracing the evolution of a relatively recent concept such as the gig economy, the e-book market is a fertile field, as it reacts to debates faster and with a wider discursive variety than does the conventional print book market.

The books were analyzed through a qualitative categorization and coding process theoretically informed by critical discourse analysis.[7] This approach highlights the ideological functions and effects of language in constituting the social world. Simultaneously, it seeks to unveil the intimate connections between language and power.

Three questions were considered in the coding and analysis process: (1) How is the gig economy defined? (2) What kind of recurring terms and concepts are utilized in portraying the transforming landscape of work? and (3) What kind of expectations for gig workers do the texts manifest? Data excerpts related to each question were tagged using keyword-based and manual methods. The excerpts were coded inductively, and the codes were grouped together to formulate analytical categories. Figure 5.1 illustrates the analytical structure for the third research question, which is in this chapter's focus. The five resulting categories were formed by grouping lower-level codes that ultimately link back to individual data excerpts.

Cultural Ideals of Gig Work **77**

FIGURE 5.1 The traits expected from an ideal gig worker. The radius of the circle and the numbers in parentheses indicate the frequency of codes in the analysis.

Pop-Management as a Genre

In the book *Dead Man Working*, business scholars Carl Cederström and Peter Fleming describe pop-management as literature that one would expect to find at the paperback shelves of just about any airport departure lounge bookshop in the world.[8] This well-marketable genre of nonfiction expresses business ideas in a lighthearted manner, often making provocative statements, introducing new concepts, and challenging old ones. In opposition to traditional management doctrines, the books express an openly anti-corporate and anti-bureaucratic attitude,[9] proclaiming the era of a "frictionless capitalism."[10]

The ideological roots of pop-management literature can be traced back to the concept of *liberation management*.[11] In this discourse, the credo is that management should not be about telling employees what to do, but rather about unleashing their creative potential and helping them to find their "true selves."[12] This resonates strongly with the guidebooks analyzed in this chapter: they speak not only about managing a business but also about managing *life* and guiding personal transformation.

What the gigging guidebooks proclaim is not merely a theory of management or a documentary account of what happens behind the scenes, but a shamelessly instrumental take on how to profit from the current transformation of work. The books combine elements from the genres of *self-help*[13] and *getting things done*.[14] They encourage the reader to pursue "the life you want"[15] and to concentrate on things that "you care about doing."[16] At the same time, the titles emphasize the imperative to succeed ("*Thrive in the Gig Economy . . .*"; "*Make Great Money. . .*") and promise to advise the reader on how to do so ("*Complete Guide to Getting Better Work. . .*"; "*How to Thrive and Succeed. . .*"; "*450 Moneymaking Ideas. . .*"). To be sure, the picture painted is somewhat optimistic. In the analyzed texts, the gig economy is depicted as

> a truly amazing, fulfilling, dynamic, limitless way to live out one's dreams and be fully engaged, happy and productive person, contributing one's best to the world[.][17]

The overarching sentiment of the analyzed guidebooks contrasts starkly with the research that emphasizes the exploitative aspects of the gig economy: growing precarity and the eradication of collective bargaining power,[18] legal barriers to recognizing gig workers as workers,[19] shifting of economic responsibility from employers to employees,[20] the asymmetry of risks and benefits,[21] and the gender- and race-based discrimination within the platforms.[22]

Defining the Gig Economy

> The ground will shift beneath your feet and you must be nimble enough to jump to the next patch of solid earth and not fall through the cracks.[23]

In the analyzed books, the gig economy is typically portrayed as a drastic and abrupt transformation in work, the economy, and lifestyles: a "seismic shift in the way we work,"[24] an "amazing force that normalizes all types of project and temporary work,"[25] and a "disruptive and rapidly changing landscape."[26] Other times, the phenomenon is positioned in a longer trajectory of transforming work regimes. While these texts assume that the gig economy is "here to stay,"[27] it is still considered to be in its infancy and evolving as part of a "shifting cultural and business environment."[28]

Thus, there is some ambivalence between and within the books about the precise nature of the change that the gig economy brings about. Some authors see it as an irreversible and unforeseen event, others as a logical continuum of developments that have been around for a longer time.[29] Evidently, the two interpretations are not mutually exclusive: some aspects can be considered genuinely novel (such as the extensive use of digital platforms), while others (such as the blurring boundary between the categories of employee and entrepreneur) might be "old wine in new bottles."

In addition to defining the gig economy as a transformation, the texts underline the rapid growth of the phenomenon and the different aspects of how gigging contributes to a wider reconfiguration of the working life. The texts often discuss the close resemblance of the gig economy to other new "economies" (on-demand, sharing, access. . .) and highlight the "skills-based" nature of the new formation.[30] However, these new skills do not appear as a finite set of expertise, but rather as abstract expectations about the suitable "mindset" for personal growth. In the following sections, these *traits of the ideal gigger* that constitute the complete "gig mindset" will be identified and scrutinized.

Entrepreneurialism: Adapting the "Gig Mindset"

[A] simple change of mindset can make all the difference for your career.[31]

Becoming a successful gigger is not only about acquiring a specific set of skills, the texts insist, but also about cultivating a particular attitude and adopting a certain way of looking at things. This is what the books refer to as the "gig mindset,"[32] "project mindset,"[33] " 'plug and play' mindset,"[34] "opportunity mindset,"[35] or the "freelancer mindset."[36] A successful gigger does not simply subscribe to a pre-existing social, cultural, or legal form (because none would readily fit) but rather practices continuous experimentation, "reinvention," and "disruption,"[37] always looking for ways of going beyond the status quo.

What markedly sets gig work apart from ordinary entrepreneurship is the extent and intensity of personal branding. The gig mindset is materialized in entrepreneurial self-promotion: identifying one's "core skills"[38] and embedding them into a personal brand. The focus is not so much on entrepreneur*ship* as contrasted to wage labor, but in entrepreneurial*ism* as a whole way of life. While entrepreneur*ship* still implies a categorical difference between the entrepreneur and the enterprise, in the notion of entrepreneurial*ism* that the gig economy represents, this gap is bridged. To illustrate the point: we can imagine a grocery store entrepreneur who is a hundred percent committed to the business and even harnesses their unique personality for marketing the business. However, there is still—at least theoretically—a possibility to separate the product to be sold (the foodstuff) and the person selling it, whereas in gigging, the worker and the work, the life and the business, the person and the product, seem to melt together. Essentially, what the giggers are selling is *themselves*: the unique combination of skills and personality.

Embracing a gig mindset involves learning to "monetize a passion."[39] Placing passion at the heart of the business, the books argue, makes work meaningful. It creates a "long-term thriving practice" and a "sustainable competitive advantage"[40] over the ones who are only working for money. This advantage emerges almost spontaneously, as one of the books explains under the rubric of "Rule #1: Love what you do,"[41] because one who works for passion "will work harder, be more purposeful and achieve better results."[42]

For passion to become rebranded as a competitive instrument, it has to be transformed into a distinguishable selling point, a "unique value proposition".[43] The notion of finding one's uniqueness—the thing that makes one *different*—demonstrates the ultra-individualist social ontology within the representations of gig work: the game is you against *everyone else*—and in the digital realm, that means globally.

Self-Development: Learning as an Imperative

According to gigging guidebooks, the ideal gigger should focus on learning and updating certain core skills but not get too *fixed* to them. Texts advise readers to attune themselves to the changing demands of the market, which, ultimately, are marked by constant change: "the parameters continue to be defined and the opportunities are being uncovered daily."[44] Thus, the only way to thrive, or to survive, is to commit to continuous self-development.

The texts bluntly point out the shift in which the opportunity of lifelong learning (as a sort of humanistic ideal of self-cultivation) is transformed into an individualized economic imperative for coping. The books are also not secretive about the fact that it is at least as much laborious as it might be rewarding to stay up to date and to "remain relevant"[45] in the gig market. Rather, the texts address the reader with outspoken directions, even providing checklists for assessing whether one "has what it takes":

> You may need to learn completely new skills to stay valuable in the marketplace. Get used to it[.][46]

[] I am curious. [] I never stop learning. [] I take time to learn new, useful, and relevant tools or skills.[47]

One of the analyzed books, citing another business guidebook *Reinventing You* by Dorie Clark,[48] reminds that not everyone is fond of the idea of engaging in a "continuous career campaign"—of updating skills as well as marketing them and integrating them into one's personal brand. However, the people who fail to do that, writes Clark, are the ones "who will lose," because "[w]hether or not you want to play the game, it's happening around you."[49]

The continuous project of self-development includes a process of self-reflection where the individual thinks through the different elements of their life and ponders which elements of it would be "gig-able."[50] This self-development calls for perfection, as the global gig market requires one to focus on activities where they are not only better but *the best*.

Malleability: Be Yourself—and Then Transform

While the guidebooks strongly recommend exploring one's unique strengths, a cautious undertone keeps reminding the reader that one day, the skills may become obsolete and worthless in the market. In this event, gig workers arrive at square one to rethink the fundamentals of their "lifestyle business."[51] Thus, the individual worker is required to adapt to a version of *flexible specialization*[52]: a mode of production where the self-enterprise invests in highly specialized product development but, simultaneously, prepares to make unexpected changes that call for an immediate reconfiguration of the personal production line. The ideal gigger vacillates between attachment and unattachment, learning to "let something go without resisting."[53]

At the surface, there is nothing particularly novel in this story: it reminds of what sociologist Richard Sennett already two decades ago wrote about "the corrosion of the character"[54] or Catherine Casey of the "post-occupational" condition.[55] However, the negative connotations of "corrosion" are now even more heavily being replaced by positive-sounding terms, from "flexibility, autonomy, and meaning"[56] to "customized" versions of "security, stability, and identity."[57]

One suggested way for attaining "customized security" is to think of one's life as a "portfolio" of various assets. A gig portfolio can even be organized into different "buckets,"[58] such as different professional domains. One of the books refers to this strategy as "slashing":[59]

> A slasher is someone who does more than one thing to make a living: for example, an artist who also blogs and runs a catering business is an artist/blogger/caterer. The slash designates a separation between different careers or revenue streams that are distinct though often mutually reinforcing.[60]

The ability to "pick and choose"⁶¹ various "side hustles"⁶² that suit to one's portfolio is seen as pivotal for curating a set of gigs that carries a "higher sense of purpose."⁶³ Not all of the "activities" even have to generate income. The spectrum of gigs may include "some for money, some for interest, some for pleasure, some for a cause."⁶⁴ Certainly, gigging for free can be understood as a way of trying to achieve a paid-for gig later,⁶⁵ but what is at play here is a more fundamental reworking of the boundary between work and *not-work*. All of life's activities, even the "downtime" such as holidays and sabbaticals, can be conceived as a harmonious unity that expresses one's lifestyle design. Essentially, the notion of *life as a portfolio* manifests a turning of tables where *working life* (as a delimited sphere) is replaced by "*life-ing work*":

> Suddenly, your entire life isn't orbiting around your career: instead your career is playing second fiddle to your life.⁶⁶

Communicativeness: The Burden of Being Constantly Connected

While the imagery that the gig economy guidebooks conjure promises a getaway from the dull world of work to a more diverse and inspiring one, the books are still candid in explaining that starting to freelance may increase the amount of tedious management tasks in comparison to ordinary wage labor. The books discuss several duties such as bidding, billing, and communication with the clients. Even if the time used for communication is seen as being "away" from the actual value-generating work, its significance cannot be underestimated because building reputation and a positive brand, the books argue, is critical for a successful gigger. Thus, extra attention has to be paid, for example, to reacting appropriately to negative online reviews.⁶⁷ This requires certain mental capabilities (such as temper and self-restraint) but also concrete examples of how to act consistently in unpredictable circumstances.

As the idealized gigger is a person who continuously juggles several projects at the same time, the amount of communicative work can grow into a considerable burden. For this reason, the guidebooks offer hints on how to rationalize the communicative chores and minimize the amount of time that they take. For example, one of the books addresses the strain from communication by providing a set of 48 concise e-mail templates to be used in various situations when communicating with the clients. For instance, if there is a "dispute or conflict" to be settled, one can refer to template #27:

> I am so sorry that I may have misunderstood the [situation/issue/message/requirement]. According to [. . .], my understanding is [. . .]. At this point, we have the options to [. . .] or [. . .]. Would you please let me know which option you prefer? I value our working relationship and would like to resolve this to your satisfaction.⁶⁸

What would be the reasons to provide the reader with such pre-made e-mail templates? First of all, as the gig workers' community and the books' expected audience is global, the command of English (the assumed lingua franca) varies substantially. Secondly, there is a cultural expectation that the working etiquette in the gig economy is less formal than in the old corporate setting, so choosing the right tone (or salutations, sign-offs, etc.) of messaging is critical. Thirdly, the desire for templates written by someone else illustrates the difficulties that the *emotional and affective labor*[69] of gigging may involve—as well as the bare amount of time required for handling e-mails in the contemporary work economies. The growing complexity of communication and other instances of "meta-work" is an inevitable trade-off for choosing self-employment.

Gig workers are also expected to have good people skills and to be able to build networks, trust, and reputation—with both clients and other freelancers.[70] To achieve this, they have to be "constantly connected,"[71] "build relationships and connections,"[72] and connect to a "large pool of people who offer similar and complementary services."[73] This allows the giggers to smoothly delegate extra work to colleagues when a requested gig does not fit into their schedule or expertise.

Prudence: Nurturing Self-Control

> If you're going to freelance, then you need to be disciplined.[74]

A successful gigger requires *prudence*: a systematic and organized effort of managing one's life as a business. Organization researcher Thomas Lopdrup-Hjorth and his colleagues make an insightful distinction within the concept of "self-management" between two related practices: managing *by yourself* and managing *your own self*.[75] Whereas the former has to do with the capabilities to take up the concrete managerial tasks of organizing and monitoring one's work process, the latter is more about cultivating one's personality. Both aspects are present in the analyzed guidebooks: managing one's gigs as a quotidian chore of self-employment but also as a tedious challenge of training oneself to be more disciplined.

Two themes in the texts stand out in the context of prudence: time management and money management. The genre of pop-management bears a close resemblance to one of the popular sections of the electronic bookstores: the "productivity" literature that promises to boost job performance by assisting in reworking one's time-use patterns at work.[76] The narrative of the time management problems is prevalent in the gig economy guidebooks.[77] We are buried with all sorts of new communication technologies, the story goes, but our working cultures are not up to par to answer the challenges that the digital tools pose to us. The "always on" quality of e-mail and instant messaging has especially made it difficult to insulate blocks of time for work that requires full attention. Thus, the giggers have to learn "bit literacy"[78] to avoid the disfigurement of productive working time.

The texts compare time management to bodybuilding—developing "mental muscles" to support the effort of concentrating to the present moment and to the things that one can affect, and vice versa, letting go of the things that cannot be changed.[79] This "athletic"[80] perspective links the concrete techniques of time management (such as *pomodoro*, *maker's schedule*, and *time blocking*) to a broader ambition of "personal mastery"[81] that spans from mental focus to physical well-being and emotional "toughness."[82] In essence, what this toughness stands for is a never-ending stoic endeavor of protecting oneself from uncontrollable forces and establishing a self-reliant way of life that stands firmly on its self-established ground:[83]

> The term "Mental Toughness" may give the initial feeling of rigidity or lack of emotion but consider it more akin to a well-conditioned muscle; one that can easily handle various amounts of pressure, weight and strain with grace and ease. Mental toughness is essential for staying grounded while dealing with the potentially massive chaos that you will no doubt encounter in doing business. People will say one thing and do another. They may flat out betray you. You must remain emotionally neutral and take actions towards the outcomes you want.[84]

In addition to time management, the topic of personal finances is also familiar from the self-help bookshelves. Financial independence to be achieved by building streams of "passive income"[85] has become a popular utopia that resonates with the millennial work ethics and the overworking white-collar middle class's sentiments.[86] The texts argue that the shift to gig-based self-employment requires a radical change in how we consider our financial dependence and objectives.[87] In effect, the gig economy

> is also disrupting how we live. Our traditional highly leveraged, high-fixed-cost lifestyle won't work as well in an economy of variable work and income[.][88]

Because working in the gig economy leads to fluctuating monthly income, giggers are advised to monitor their expenses carefully and minimize their financial commitments. The impasse of a "high-fixed cost lifestyle" is exemplified by mortgage as a financial instrument that anchors "a human to keep on the treadmill forever."[89] Instead of submitting to permanent indebtedness,[90] the gig worker is supposed to commence a "personal financial revolution" which would lead to a life "without the debt, fixed costs, and physical ownership of so much stuff."[91]

Conclusions

In the imagery of transforming work portrayed by the gig economy guidebooks, there is a striking *paradox of freedom*. On the one hand, the shift towards more flexible forms of work is represented as an unprecedented opportunity for breaking away from the dullness and alienation of wage labor. On the other hand, the very same transformation imposes ever-heavier expectations of self-management that are not confined to a separate time and place of "work" but instead seek to occupy the whole way of life. Pop-management literature, as a particular cultural form, reflects a similar double bind: it promises to give advice on how to cope with and thrive in the new circumstances but ends up operating as a forceful tool of self-discipline, as a guide to pushing one's limits further and preparing oneself to live up to impossible demands.

In the analysis, the expectations for a successful gigger were examined through the categories of *entrepreneurialism*, *self-development*, *malleability*, *prudence*, and *communicativeness*. These five traits are not entirely harmonious but also bear intriguing tensions. For example, the creative, spontaneous, and even anarchic spirit of *entrepreneurialism* has some friction with the extreme *prudence* and decisiveness required for "dealing with the potentially massive chaos."[92] Similarly, there is some discordance between the demand to find one's own thing in which to excel and outcompete others (*self-development*) but also to be continuously prepared to leave everything behind and to invent a new professional identity (*malleability*).

Even more generally, the idealization of gig work portrays a curious mishmash of seemingly opposing orientations. On the one hand, there is a pursuit of *anti-work*:[93] to "abandon the 1950s ideal of a 9–5 job,"[94] to get away from the frustrating bureaucracy of corporate culture, to focus on things that "truly matter," and ultimately, to substitute "life" for "work." On the other hand, there is a tendency of *submerging life into work*: a scheme where one's "lifestyle business"[95] is readily allowed to occupy the whole space and time of living, where there is no place or time to hide from work, and where the quest for new business opportunities goes as far as to "monetizing even the most basic belongings, skills, [and] abilities."[96]

"How does one resist what appears to be life itself?" ponder Carl Cederström and Peter Fleming, attempting to trace the evolution of a *biocratic* mode of management in which the very entanglement of life and work "creates conditions ripe for self-entrapment."[97] This question is crucial in critically unmasking the often-glorifying descriptions of gig work. Where are the moments of resistance, or even the more prosaic situations to complain about workload or ill-tempered clients? How to "turn off" work, if the boss equates to yourself, workplace equates to home, and work equates to life?[98]

Cederström and Fleming suggest that we should invest ourselves in the process of "separating life from that which has now colonized it" (that is, work).[99] Even with the sporadic warnings about the potential burnouts and other pitfalls, the gig economy guidebooks point to an almost opposite direction. Whether looking at the tendencies of anti-work or the ones of submerging oneself into work, the books effectively dismiss the need to draw any boundaries or to resist transforming one's life into a commercial brand. In the emancipatory promise that the books paint, the only way to liberate oneself from work is—paradoxically—to fully submit oneself to work.

Gig economy guidebooks unhesitatingly celebrate an economy that surely is lucrative for a part of the high-skilled workers in the technology industry while simultaneously being extractive, onerous, and even immiserating for significant parts of its workforce. The guidebooks are not only descriptive accounts of a new working regime but also management technologies *as such*. In coaching the prospective gig worker, they become disciplinary tools that coordinate work like the assembly line, the factory bell, or the timecard did in the era of industrial production.[100] They operate as *technologies of the self*:[101] tools of self-education and self-cultivation in an era where this very "self" has become the core of economic activity. As one of the authors proclaim, "[s]ooner or later, most people are going to have to learn to be their own bosses"[102]—and guidebooks are a part of this process.

The ways in which the gig economy is portrayed as liberation from wage labor reminds of an affective structure that Lauren Berlant calls *cruel optimism*: it is an arrangement in which "something that you desire is actually an obstacle to your flourishing."[103] A person caught in precarious low-wage gigging is deemed *personally* responsible for the lack of success, as the books very outspokenly express that thriving in the gig economy is first and foremost about "picking oneself"[104]—a shift in the individual's attitudes rather than in the structural factors that sustain the uneven playing field. On the contrary, the books are more tight-lipped about what happens to those who have not become "prolific artists"[105] of the gig economy but would instead enjoy simpler forms of employment and life. Thus, in idealizing a certain mode of individual success and in downplaying its more-than-individual dependencies, there is a risk of *self-help* becoming *self-blame*.

Notes

1. John Frazer, "How the Gig Economy Is Reshaping Careers for the Next Generation," *Forbes*, February 15, 2019, www.forbes.com/sites/johnfrazer1/2019/02/15/how-the-gig-economy-is-reshaping-careers-for-the-next-generation/; Katy Steinmetz, "Exclusive: See How Big the Gig Economy Really Is," *Time*, January 6, 2016, http://time.com/4169532/sharing-economy-poll/; David Storey, Tony Steadman, and Charles Davis, "How the Gig Economy Is Changing the Workforce," *EY Global*, November 20, 2018, www.ey.com/en_gl/tax/how-the-gig-economy-is-changing-the-workforce.
2. Dick Kuiper, *Gig Economy: The Good, The Bad and the Ugly* (Self-published—Distributed by Amazon, 2018), location 136.
3. "Contingent and alternative" is a category used, for example, by the U.S. Bureau of Labor Statistics. See Bureau of Labor Statistics, "Contingent and Alternative Employment Arrangements Summary," Bureau of Labor Statistics, June 7, 2018, www.bls.gov/news.release/conemp.nr0.htm. Other sources refer to "atypical work," a term that symptomatically defines new work arrangements in opposition to the "standard," that is, full-time, regular, and open-ended employment. See Eurofound, "Atypical Work," *Eurofound*, November 24, 2017, www.eurofound.europa.eu/observatories/eurwork/industrial-relations-dictionary/atypical-work.
4. Raymond Williams, *Marxism and Literature* (Oxford: Oxford University Press, 1977).
5. For example, Peter Fleming, *Authenticity and the Cultural Politics of Work: New Forms of Informal Control* (Oxford: Oxford University Press, 2009); Melissa Gregg, *Work's*

Intimacy (Cambridge: Polity Press, 2011); Andrew Ross, *Nice Work If You Can Get It: Life and Labor in Precarious Times* (New York: New York University Press, 2009).
6. In the library catalog *WorldCat* (www.worldcat.org), the search phrase "gig economy" results in only 0–3 books per year before 2016, whereas for 2017–2018 there are already circa 90 books per year published on the topic.
7. For example, Norman Fairclough and Ruth Wodak, "Critical Discourse Analysis," in *Discourse and Social Interaction*, ed. Teun A. van Dijk (London: Sage, 1997), 103–36; Marianne Jørgensen and Louise Phillips, "Critical Discourse Analysis," in *Discourse Analysis as Theory and Method*, by Marianne Jørgensen and Louise Phillips (London: Sage, 2002), 60–95, https://doi.org/10.4135/9781849208871; Teun A. van Dijk, "Critical Discourse Analysis," in *The Handbook of Discourse Analysis*, ed. Deborah Tannen, Heidi E. Hamilton, and Deborah Schriffin (New York: John Wiley & Sons, Ltd, 2015), 466–85, https://doi.org/10.1002/9781118584194.ch22.
8. Carl Cederström and Peter Fleming, *Dead Man Working* (Winchester: Zero Books, 2012).
9. Similarly, see Andrew Ross, *No-Collar: The Humane Workplace and Its Hidden Costs*, paperback ed. (Philadelphia, PA: Temple University Press, 2004).
10. Cederström and Fleming, *Dead Man Working*, 21.
11. Tom Peters, *Liberation Management: Necessary Disorganization for the Nanosecond Nineties* (New York: Alfred A. Knopf, 1992).
12. See, for example, Brian M. Carney and Isaac Getz, *Freedom, Inc.: How Corporate Liberation Unleashes Employee Potential and Business Performance*, 2nd ed. (New York: Somme Valley House, 2016); Frederic Laloux, *Reinventing Organizations: A Guide to Creating Organizations Inspired by the Next Stage in Human Consciousness* (Brussels: Nelson Parker, 2014).
13. For self-help as a mode of self-governance, see, for example, Eva Illouz, *Saving the Modern Soul: Therapy, Emotions, and the Culture of Self-Help*, First edition (Berkeley: University of California Press, 2008); Daniel Nehring et al., *Transnational Popular Psychology and the Global Self-Help Industry: The Politics of Contemporary Social Change* (Houndmills, Basingstoke: Palgrave Macmillan, 2016); Heidi Marie Rimke, "Governing Citizens Through Self-Help Literature," *Cultural Studies* 14, no. 1 (January 2000): 61–78, https://doi.org/10.1080/095023800334986.
14. David Allen, *Getting Things Done: The Art of Stress-Free Productivity* (New York: Viking, 2001).
15. Thomas Oppong, *Working in the Gig Economy: How to Thrive and Succeed When You Choose to Work for Yourself* (London: Kogan Page Limited, 2018), location 1034.
16. Adam Sinicki, *Thriving in the Gig Economy: Freelancing Online for Tech Professionals and Entrepreneurs* (New York: Apress, 2019), location 2789.
17. Julian Haber, *Gigonomics: A Field Guide for Freelancers in the Gig Economy* (Self-published—Distributed by Amazon, 2018), location 373.
18. Carles Muntaner, "Digital Platforms, Gig Economy, Precarious Employment, and the Invisible Hand of Social Class," *International Journal of Health Services* 48, no. 4 (October 1, 2018): 597–600, https://doi.org/10.1177/0020731418807413; Juliet Webster, "Microworkers of the Gig Economy: Separate and Precarious," *New Labor Forum* 25, no. 3 (September 1, 2016): 56–64, https://doi.org/10.1177/1095796016661511; Austin Zwick, "Welcome to the Gig Economy: Neoliberal Industrial Relations and the Case of Uber," *GeoJournal* 83, no. 4 (August 1, 2018): 679–91, https://doi.org/10.1007/s10708-017-9793-8.
19. Valerio De Stefano, "The Rise of the Just-in-Time Workforce: On-Demand Work, Crowdwork, and Labor Protection in the Gig-Economy," *Comparative Labor Law & Policy Journal* 37 (2016): 471–504; Adrián Todolí-Signes, "The 'Gig Economy': Employee, Self-Employed or the Need for a Special Employment Regulation?" *Transfer: European Review of Labour and Research* 23, no. 2 (May 1, 2017): 193–205, https://doi.org/10.1177/1024258917701381.

20. Gerald Friedman, "Workers without Employers: Shadow Corporations and the Rise of the Gig Economy," *Review of Keynesian Economics* 2, no. 2 (April 1, 2014): 171–88, https://doi.org/10.4337/roke.2014.02.03.
21. Mark Graham, Isis Hjorth, and Vili Lehdonvirta, "Digital Labour and Development: Impacts of Global Digital Labour Platforms and the Gig Economy on Worker Livelihoods," *Transfer: European Review of Labour and Research* 23, no. 2 (May 1, 2017): 135–62, https://doi.org/10.1177/1024258916687250.
22. Leslie Regan Shade, "Hop to It in the Gig Economy: The Sharing Economy and Neo-Liberal Feminism," *International Journal of Media & Cultural Politics* 14, no. 1 (March 2018): 35–54, https://doi.org/10.1386/macp.14.1.35_1.
23. James DeCicco, *Master the Gig Economy: How a Next Generation Entrepreneur Builds Wealth* (Scotts Valley, CA: CreateSpace, 2018), location 471.
24. Mark Magnacca and gigCMO Team, *The Gig Economy: Things You Should Know to Make Your Business Grow* (London: gigCMO , 2018), location 485.
25. Olga Mizrahi, *The Gig Is Up: Thrive in the Gig Economy, Where Old Jobs Are Obsolete and Freelancing Is the Future* (Austin, TX: Greenleaf Book Group Press, 2018), location 101.
26. DeCicco, *Master the Gig Economy*, location 424.
27. Kuiper, *Gig Economy: The Good, The Bad and the Ugly*, location 246.
28. V. V. Cam, *Because Money Matters: How to Earn More Money as a Freelancer in a Gig Economy* (Self-published—Distributed by Amazon, 2018), location 210.
29. Richard Sennett, *The Corrosion of Character: The Personal Consequences of Work in the New Capitalism* (New York: W. W. Norton & Company, 1998), 47–48.
30. Diane Mulcahy, *The Gig Economy: The Complete Guide to Getting Better Work, Taking More Time Off, and Financing the Life You Want!* (New York: AMACOM, 2016), location 2233.
31. Oppong, *Working in the Gig Economy: How to Thrive and Succeed When You Choose to Work for Yourself*, location 981.
32. Magnacca and gigCMO Team, *The Gig Economy: Things You Should Know to Make Your Business Grow*, location 355.
33. Haber, *Gigonomics: A Field Guide for Freelancers in the Gig Economy*, location 1340.
34. Marion McGovern, *Thriving in the Gig Economy: How to Capitalize and Compete in the New World of Work* (Wayne, NJ: Career Press, 2017).
35. Mulcahy, *The Gig Economy: The Complete Guide to Getting Better Work, Taking More Time Off, and Financing the Life You Want!*, location 414.
36. Mizrahi, *The Gig Is Up: Thrive in the Gig Economy, Where Old Jobs Are Obsolete and Freelancing Is the Future*, location 772.
37. DeCicco, *Master the Gig Economy: How a Next Generation Entrepreneur Builds Wealth*, location 471.
38. DeCicco, *Master the Gig Economy: How a Next Generation Entrepreneur Builds Wealth*, location 433.
39. Haber, *Gigonomics: A Field Guide for Freelancers in the Gig Economy*, location 481.
40. Haber, *Gigonomics: A Field Guide for Freelancers in the Gig Economy*, location 485.
41. Haber, *Gigonomics: A Field Guide for Freelancers in the Gig Economy*, location 482.
42. Ibid.; Miya Tokumitsu, *Do What You Love: And Other Lies About Success and Happiness* (New York: Regan Arts., 2015).
43. Mizrahi, *The Gig Is Up: Thrive in the Gig Economy, Where Old Jobs Are Obsolete and Freelancing Is the Future*, location 517.
44. Magnacca and gigCMO Team, *The Gig Economy: Things You Should Know to Make Your Business Grow*, location 218.
45. Magnacca and gigCMO Team, *The Gig Economy: Things You Should Know to Make Your Business Grow*, location 526.
46. DeCicco, *Master the Gig Economy: How a Next Generation Entrepreneur Builds Wealth*, location 653.

47. Cam, *Because Money Matters: How to Earn More Money as a Freelancer in a Gig Economy*, location 884; from a checklist with the title "Self-Assessment: Do I Have What It Takes?"
48. Dorie Clark, *Reinventing You: Define Your Brand, Imagine Your Future* (Boston, MA: Harvard Business Review Press, 2013).
49. Cited in Mulcahy, *The Gig Economy: The Complete Guide to Getting Better Work, Taking More Time Off, and Financing the Life You Want!*, location 708.
50. Haber, *Gigonomics: A Field Guide for Freelancers in the Gig Economy*, location 547.
51. Sinicki, *Thriving in the Gig Economy: Freelancing Online for Tech Professionals and Entrepreneurs*.
52. Michael J. Piore and Charles F. Sabel, *The Second Industrial Divide: Possibilities for Prosperity* (New York: Basic Books, 1984).
53. DeCicco, *Master the Gig Economy: How a Next Generation Entrepreneur Builds Wealth*, location 478.
54. Sennett, *The Corrosion of Character*.
55. Catherine Casey, *Work, Self and Society: After Industrialism* (New York: Routledge, 1995).
56. Mulcahy, *The Gig Economy: The Complete Guide to Getting Better Work, Taking More Time Off, and Financing the Life You Want!*, location 155.
57. Mulcahy, *The Gig Economy: The Complete Guide to Getting Better Work, Taking More Time Off, and Financing the Life You Want!*, location 434.
58. Mulcahy, *The Gig Economy: The Complete Guide to Getting Better Work, Taking More Time Off, and Financing the Life You Want!*, location 544.
59. Haber, *Gigonomics: A Field Guide for Freelancers in the Gig Economy*, location 2310.
60. Haber, *Gigonomics: A Field Guide for Freelancers in the Gig Economy*, location 149–63.
61. Sinicki, *Thriving in the Gig Economy: Freelancing Online for Tech Professionals and Entrepreneurs*, locations 150, 178, 180, 1414, 3026, 3335, 3528, 3916.
62. Elana Varon, *The Ultimate Side Hustle Book: 450 Moneymaking Ideas for the Gig Economy* (New York: Adams Media, 2018); Sinicki, *Thriving in the Gig Economy: Freelancing Online for Tech Professionals and Entrepreneurs*, location 3854; DeCicco, *Master the Gig Economy: How a Next Generation Entrepreneur Builds Wealth (2018)*, location 439.
63. Magnacca and gigCMO Team, *The Gig Economy: Things You Should Know to Make Your Business Grow*, location 422.
64. Mulcahy, *The Gig Economy: The Complete Guide to Getting Better Work, Taking More Time Off, and Financing the Life You Want!*, location 460.
65. Leslie Regan Shade and Jenna Jacobson, "Hungry for the Job: Gender, Unpaid Internships, and the Creative Industries," *The Sociological Review* 63 (May 2015): 188–205, https://doi.org/10.1111/1467-954X.12249.
66. Sinicki, *Thriving in the Gig Economy: Freelancing Online for Tech Professionals and Entrepreneurs*, location 2789.
67. Alison Hearn, "Structuring Feeling: Web 2.0, Online Ranking and Rating, and the Digital 'Reputation' Economy," *Ephemera: Theory & Politics in Organization* 10, no. 3–4 (2010): 421–38.
68. Cam, *Because Money Matters: How to Earn More Money as a Freelancer in a Gig Economy*, location 1516.
69. Emma Dowling, Rodrigo Nunes, and Ben Trott, "Immaterial and Affective Labour: Explored," *Ephemera: Theory & Politics in Organization* 7, no. 1 (2007): 1–7; Silvia Federici, "On Affective Labor," in *Cognitive Capitalism, Education, and Digital Labor*, ed. Michael Peters and Ergin Bulut (New York: Peter Lang, 2011), 57–74; Arlie Russell Hochschild, *The Managed Heart: Commercialization of Human Feeling* (Berkeley [etc.]: University of California Press, 1983).
70. Piran van Dam, *Freelancing in the Gig Economy: The Practical, Fact-Based Guide to Launching Your Career by Understanding the New Rules of the Game* (Self-published— Distributed by Amazon, 2017), location 254.

71. Morissa Schwartz, *The Gig Economy: Our Road to Financial Freedom* (Self-published—Distributed by Amazon, 2016), location 162.
72. Cam, *Because Money Matters: How to Earn More Money as a Freelancer in a Gig Economy*, location 895.
73. Haber, *Gigonomics: A Field Guide for Freelancers in the Gig Economy*, location 2352.
74. Sinicki, *Thriving in the Gig Economy: Freelancing Online for Tech Professionals and Entrepreneurs*, location 224.
75. Thomas Lopdrup-Hjorth et al., "Governing Work Through Self-Management," *Ephemera: Theory & Politics in Organization* 11, no. 2 (2011): 97–104.
76. Melissa Gregg, *Counterproductive: Time Management in the Knowledge Economy* (Durham, NC: Duke University Press, 2018).
77. See Judy Wajcman, *Pressed for Time: The Acceleration of Life in Digital Capitalism*, 2015.
78. Mark Hurst, *Bit Literacy: Productivity in the Age of Information and E-mail Overload* (New York: Good Experience Press, 2007).
79. Haber, *Gigonomics: A Field Guide for Freelancers in the Gig Economy*, locations 898–912.
80. Michel Foucault, *The Hermeneutics of the Subject: Lectures at the Collège de France, 1981–1982*, ed. Frédéric Gros, trans. Graham Burchell (New York: Picador, 2005), 231; Gregg, *Counterproductive*, 53–77.
81. DeCicco, *Master the Gig Economy: How a Next Generation Entrepreneur Builds Wealth*, locations 876–993.
82. DeCicco, *Master the Gig Economy: How a Next Generation Entrepreneur Builds Wealth*, location 993; Carl Cederström and André Spicer, *The Wellness Syndrome* (Cambridge: Polity Press, 2015).
83. Similarly, see Foucault, *The Hermeneutics of the Subject*, 236.
84. DeCicco, *Master the Gig Economy: How a Next Generation Entrepreneur Builds Wealth*, location 980.
85. Sinicki, *Thriving in the Gig Economy: Freelancing Online for Tech Professionals and Entrepreneurs*, locations 2845, 3854; DeCicco, *Master the Gig Economy: How a Next Generation Entrepreneur Builds Wealth*, location 408.
86. Daniel Friedman, "Resisting the Lure of the Paycheck: Freedom and Dependence in Financial Self-Help," *Foucault Studies*, no. 18 (2014): 90–112.
87. Mulcahy, *The Gig Economy: The Complete Guide to Getting Better Work, Taking More Time Off, and Financing the Life You Want!*, location 1826; Kuiper, *Gig Economy: The Good, The Bad and the Ugly*, location 1452; Haber, *Gigonomics: A Field Guide for Freelancers in the Gig Economy*, location 119.
88. Mulcahy, *The Gig Economy: The Complete Guide to Getting Better Work, Taking More Time Off, and Financing the Life You Want!*, location 225.
89. DeCicco, *Master the Gig Economy: How a Next Generation Entrepreneur Builds Wealth*, location 319.
90. Maurizio Lazzarato, *The Making of the Indebted Man: An Essay on the Neoliberal Condition*, Semiotext(e) Intervention Series 13 (Los Angeles, CA: Semiotext(e), 2012).
91. Mulcahy, *The Gig Economy: The Complete Guide to Getting Better Work, Taking More Time Off, and Financing the Life You Want!*, locations 2046, 2249.
92. DeCicco, *Master the Gig Economy: How a Next Generation Entrepreneur Builds Wealth*, location 985.
93. Kathi Weeks, *The Problem With Work: Feminism, Marxism, Antiwork Politics, and Postwork Imaginaries* (Durham, NC: Duke University Press, 2011).
94. Schwartz, *The Gig Economy: Our Road to Financial Freedom*, location 74.
95. Sinicki, *Thriving in the Gig Economy: Freelancing Online for Tech Professionals and Entrepreneurs*, location 2789.
96. Varon, *The Ultimate Side Hustle Book: 450 Moneymaking Ideas for the Gig Economy*, location 67.
97. Cederström and Fleming, *Dead Man Working*, 14, 68.

98. Ibid., 13.
99. Ibid., 72.
100. Gilles Deleuze, "Postscript on the Societies of Control," *October* 59 (Winter 1992): 3–7.
101. Michel Foucault, *Technologies of the Self: A Seminar With Michel Foucault*, ed. Luther H. Martin, Huck Gutman, and Patrick H. Hutton (Amherst: University of Massachusetts Press, 1988).
102. Mizrahi, *The Gig Is Up: Thrive in the Gig Economy, Where Old Jobs Are Obsolete and Freelancing Is the Future*, location 501.
103. Lauren Berlant, *Cruel Optimism* (Durham, NC: Duke University Press, 2011), 1.
104. Mizrahi, *The Gig Is Up: Thrive in the Gig Economy, Where Old Jobs Are Obsolete and Freelancing Is the Future*, location 580; referring to Seth Godin, "Reject the Tyranny of Being Picked: Pick Yourself," *Seth's Blog* (blog), March 21, 2011, https://seths.blog/2011/03/reject-the-tyranny-of-being-picked-pick-yourself/.
105. DeCicco, *Master the Gig Economy: How a Next Generation Entrepreneur Builds Wealth*, location 222.

6

"UBER FOR RADIO?"

Professionalism and Production Cultures in Podcasting

John L. Sullivan

In *Gigged*, Sarah Kessler (2018) explores the explosion in Silicon Valley startups beginning in 2013, all of them hoping to reproduce the success of the ride-sharing service Uber. Describing themselves as "Uber for X," these entrepreneurs offered a vision of profitable companies built atop legions of contingent workers, providing what Kuehn and Corrigan (2013) have termed "hope labor." Following the runaway success of *Serial* in 2014, podcasting attracted similar entrepreneurial fervor. For example, well-resourced public radio station WNYC started its own podcasting division (Sisario 2015), and traditional corporate media giant E.W. Scripps made significant investments in the medium, spending $10 million to purchase Midroll—one of the largest podcast-centered advertising firms—as well as $4.5 million for Stitcher, a podcast consumption app widely available on mobile platforms and installed in many new cars (Perlberg 2016). These new corporate players have also altered the expectations for podcasting by grafting commercial-style production values, audio quality, content genres, methods, and monetization structures onto the medium.

While podcasting was once synonymous with an informal, amateur ethos, it is increasingly being identified as a potential career for amateur cultural producers. Underlying these shifts in labor practice is the notion of *professionalism* (Evetts 2003). Professionalism provides a set of principles that allow a subset of individuals to organize and understand their labor and to distinguish their labor from amateurs (often by creating skill barriers to entry). While the professionalization of amateurs has been celebrated by some as a democratization of cultural production (Bruns 2008; Jenkins, Ford, and Green 2013; Shirky 2008), critical scholars have scrutinized a new regime that commodifies volunteer labor while offering few opportunities for those individuals to become part of the professional class (Andrejevic 2009; Duffy 2017; Kuehn and Corrigan 2013; Ross 2009; Scholz 2016; Terranova 2000).

In this chapter, I explore labor shifts in online cultural production by examining emerging production cultures in podcasting. Specifically, I analyze the discourses of professionalism in two influential, well-known "how to" podcasts, *School of Podcasting* with Dave Jackson and *The Audacity to Podcast* with Daniel J. Lewis. These two podcasts are well known to the podcasting community and have each won the People's Choice Award for "Best Technology Podcast": *The Audacity to Podcast* in 2012, and *School of Podcasting* in 2017 (The People's Choice Podcast Awards 2018). These podcasts are often recommended to new podcasters who are looking for advice on how to start and manage a podcast.

In these podcasts, Jackson and Lewis act as ersatz mentors to aspiring podcasters, offering advice about technology, show preparation, interviewing style, and audience maximization. The advice in these podcasts goes beyond a simple "how to," however. Embedded within these podcasts is a professional work ethos that guides cultural labor in a gig economy. This ethos is one of self-actualization and self-fulfillment, both of which can be achieved through freelance work. In situating podcasting as a viable alternative career, however, these "how to" programs also traffic in myths about the power of authenticity and meritocracy in a media landscape that is being reshaped by commercial and corporate interests. The gig economy relies on the bedrock principle of delayed gratification when it comes to cultural labor; that the long hours and tedious unpaid work required to cultivate skills will ultimately be recognized and financially rewarded by corporate producers. In other words, the gig economy is built upon the ethos of *meritocracy*, or the belief that market forces—often assessed and expressed via algorithmic formulas—will properly recognize and incentivize online and offline labor. These "how to" podcasts demonstrate the inherent contradictions underlying the boom in digital cultural labor.

Podcasting and the Formalization of User-Generated Content

Podcasting is "a technology used to distribute, receive, and listen, on-demand, to sound content produced by traditional editors such as radio, publishing houses, journalists, and educational institutions . . . as well as content created by independent radio producers, artists, and radio amateurs" (Bonini 2015, 21). Podcasting emerged at a time of popular euphoria surrounding the affordances of Web 2.0. Given its relatively low barriers to entry (a computer and a cheap microphone), serialized online audio broadcasting became a popular form of amateur media in the early 2000s, though its existence was somewhat overshadowed by the popular fascination with blogging and, later, by the advent of video sharing via YouTube (which launched in 2005 and was purchased by Google in 2006), and audio streaming (Pandora launched its music streaming service in 2005). Nevertheless, podcasting shared a great deal in common with other forms of user-generated content in that it ignited a culture of participatory creativity online (Jenkins 2006; Lobato, Thomas, and Hunter 2012).

Scholars excitedly cataloged the cultural shift enabled by new content-sharing platforms online, arguing that online digital distribution had effectively leveled the playing field between media corporations and everyday citizens, allowing for a more democratic, "grass roots" economy (Freedman 2012). Shirky (2008), for example, has argued that we are witnessing the "mass amateurization" of cultural production. Benkler (2006) pushed this claim even further, arguing that human beings are experiencing a historical tipping point of engaged, democratic information access thanks to networked computing.

This utopian enthusiasm surrounding user-generated content, along with the surge in gig economy freelancing, has begun shifting the terms of labor for amateur podcasters. Amateur, online media producers are developing professional practices found in traditional media, and some are even abandoning their existing occupations to rely on their online activities for financial support. In fact, the podcasting scene today is looking less like a small backwater for amateur content and more and more like a commercial media industry. For example, well-resourced public radio stations like New York City's WNYC have started their own podcasting divisions (Sisario 2015), and advertising firms like Midroll have specialized in bundling popular podcasts for sale to advertisers. Recently, audio streaming giant Spotify stunned the podcasting community by purchasing the startup podcast production company Gimlet Media for $230 million, followed closely by its acquisition of Anchor.fm, the fastest-growing service for amateur-created podcast content (Kafka 2019). Large online platforms like Apple Podcasts, Spotify, and iHeartMedia have also announced plans to bankroll and promote "premium" podcasts that will attract large audiences and substantial advertising revenue while centralizing the role of these platforms for the medium (Sullivan 2019).

The entrepreneurial energy surrounding podcasting is fueling what scholars call *formalization*. Formalization describes the process by which "media systems become progressively more rationalized, consolidated and financially transparent" (Lobato and Thomas 2015, 27). Podcasting is currently in the process of formalization, both from the top down and from the bottom up. First, formalization is occurring "top down" via the expansion of existing public and commercial broadcasters expanding into podcasting, both as a form of online marketing and to create original content. Legacy and startup media firms are also creating "networks" of podcasts (such as Gimlet, HowStuffWorks, Radiotopia, and others) that act much like traditional networks: They curate content and act as scouts for new podcast talent (Heeremans 2018). These new corporate players also bring with them commercial-style production values, audio quality, content genres, methods, and monetization structures. Second, formalization is proceeding from the "bottom up" via the creation and (in some cases) institutionalization of production practices and communities around podcasting. Indeed, podcasting has become not just a hobby activity, but also a potential career for millions of disaffected creative professionals in the gig economy.

Production Cultures in Podcasting: Produsers, Pro-Ams, and Professionals

My focus in this chapter is specifically on the bottom-up process of podcasting formalization; specifically, the emergence of production cultures most commonly found in legacy forms of commercial media. What was once a bastion of "do-it-yourself" production ethos has now diversified into a constellation of new professional roles, including editors, advertisers, networks, technology companies, support software vendors, and a host of other ancillary services. Podcaster personalities like Leo Laporte, Marc Maron, Alex Blumberg, and others have served as role models for commercial success in the medium. This is having some recursive effects on independent, or "indie," podcasters by informing their own production practices.

The process underlying these shifts in labor practice is *professionalism* (or professionalization), which indicates the ongoing, emergent process of introducing professionalism into a given community of workers or creators. Sociologists have long been fascinated by professions and their role in organizing labor. One early and influential conceptualization of professionalism characterized it as a means for social communities to maintain a normative social order within capitalist economies (Parsons 1951). This view came under criticism in the 1970s and 1980s, with scholars arguing that professionalism represented an ideology that protected "powerful, privileged, self-interested monopolies" (Evetts 2003, 401). As either normative value system or ideological system, it is clear that professionalism provides a set of principles that allow a subset of individuals to organize and understand their labor in a particular way. Professionalism can also serve to create a "monopoly of competence legitimized by officially sanctioned 'expertise', and a monopoly of credibility with the public" (Larson 1977, 37). In this way, professions can be understood broadly as "the knowledge-based category of occupations which usually follow a period of tertiary education and vocational training and experience" (Evetts 2003, 397).

The rise of the gig economy—whereby amateur labor is decoupled from traditional institutional structures and managed remotely via apps or algorithms—has challenged traditional notions of professions. This shift has called into question traditional distinctions between "consumer" and "laborer." Media scholars have sought to understand the particular nature of online cultural production work and the unique collaborative affordances offered by online technologies. Bruns (2006, 2008) coined the term "produser" to describe this form of user-led content production and collaborative engagement, suggesting that it could provide a meaningful alternative to commercial media. Leadbeater and Miller (2004, 20) have described some of these amateur media creators as "pro-ams," or media creators who

> pursue an activity as an amateur, mainly for the love of it, but [who] set a professional standard. Pro-Ams are unlikely to earn more than a small

portion of their income from their pastime but they pursue it with the dedication and commitment associated with a professional.

While the professionalization of amateurs has been celebrated as a form of democratization of cultural production, other scholars have critically scrutinized a new cultural production system that commodifies the volunteer labor with few opportunities for those individuals to become part of the professional class (Andrejevic 2009; Duffy 2015; Duffy and Pruchniewska 2017; Kuehn and Corrigan 2013; Ross 2009; Terranova 2000).

Studying Production Cultures and Professionalism in Podcasting

Podcasting has traditionally attracted a small but dedicated cadre of amateur (mostly white male) producers (Markman 2012), but the explosion of its popularization since 2014 has brought a larger and more diverse group of producers into the medium (Florini 2015). As the formalization of podcasting has progressed, cultures of podcast production have begun to flourish online. Indie podcasters congregate on Facebook groups, via Twitter handles, and at conferences dedicated to the medium such as PodFest, Third Coast International Audio Festival, and Podcast Movement (Sullivan 2018). Podcasters monitor each other's work as well, particularly shows like the "how to" podcasts investigated in this chapter, to exchange tips on audio equipment, show management, marketing, and monetization. This type of "self-theorizing" ranges from talk about production practices to the types of professional talk among legacy media workers. Just as Caldwell (2008) found within the movie industry, the industry-related talk and industrial narratives among podcast practitioners are similarly instrumental in creating a sense of what podcasting is all about. Scholars have uncovered similar cultures of production, for example, among YouTubers (Burgess and Green 2009) and fashion bloggers (Duffy 2015, 2017).

Examining the discourse between and among these production cultures can illuminate some of the concerns, struggles, and values that shape individuals' understanding of the medium and their own labor. What types of production practices are most valued among these production communities, and what practices are to be avoided? How is the concept of "professionalism" understood by pro-ams and "prolancer" podcast producers? Toward what goals should indie podcasters strive in the rapidly formalizing landscape of podcasting? Lastly, what value systems or ethos should guide the production of podcasts?

As a medium freely distributed online, podcasting does not have an institutionalized structure for establishing social and professional norms, as do other legacy industries like broadcast radio or television. The trade press typically fulfills this function in those industries (Corrigan 2018). In contrast, podcasting mobilizes online forums such as Facebook groups and podcasts themselves, where amateur and self-employed podcasters exchange narratives about their production practices. Through these informal mechanisms, professional and social norms are discussed and perpetuated. This analysis of "podcasts about podcasting" can be understood as "listening in" to industrial discourses among practitioners of a craft (Corrigan 2018). On the one hand, these discourses constitute a collection of "best practices" for podcasters, helping them to navigate the logistics of recording, editing, distributing, marketing, and monetizing podcasting. On the other hand, these discourses also work to socialize podcasters by employing assumptions about work ethics, expectations for success, and developing standards for audio quality, among other things. Thus, these discourses play a constitutive role in building a professional ethos around the cultural practice of podcasting.

To explore production discourses in podcasting, I look specifically at two popular, long-running weekly podcasts, *School of Podcasting*, hosted by Dave Jackson (launched in 2005), and *The Audacity to Podcast*, hosted by Daniel J. Lewis (launched in 2010). To obtain a representative sample from across the history of each show (*School of Podcasting* has recorded 630 episodes, and *The Audacity to Podcast* has 333 episodes), 20 episodes of each podcast were selected randomly for analysis. Each show's first episode was also included in the analysis, as well as an episode of *School of Podcasting* when Dave Jackson interviewed Daniel J. Lewis. Every show in the sample was downloaded and transcribed for analysis using Quirkos qualitative data software.

The Discourse of Entrepreneurism and Professional Standards

The ostensible aim of both *School of Podcasting* and *The Audacity to Podcast* is to provide training for amateurs to assist them in creating, recording, and distributing, marketing, and monetizing their podcasts. Although blogging and podcasting have similar roots as a vibrant source for amateur, alternative media, the complexities of recording and editing sound, including the extra equipment (and associated costs) required to do this work, create technical barriers to entry for new podcasters. This creates a niche for shows like *School of Podcasting* and *The Audacity to Podcast*, both of which advertise themselves as new user-friendly guides to the world of podcasting. One of the chief aspects of professionalism is "the creation of a training credential that becomes a prerequisite for entering a labor market and performing a defined set of tasks" (Freidson 2001, 84) Jackson and Lewis position themselves as guardians of the complex world of podcasting by offering practical advice in the form of self-referential narratives about their own podcasting successes and failures. There were three main modes of professional discourse throughout the programs in this sample: (1) technical advice about production and distribution practices, including monetization strategies; (2) community building as a form of audience maximization; and (3) self-actualization, authenticity, and passion as the drivers to gig labor success.

1. Production and Marketing Advice: Professionalizing Audio Quality and Perfecting Sound

Throughout the episodes included in this sample, the primary topic of conversation was on the "best practices" for some of the technical aspects of launching a podcast, including recording and editing audio files, locating a web hosting service to store the audio files, managing the RSS feed, and making sure that the podcast is correctly listed in large directories such as Apple Podcasts, Google Podcasts, and Spotify, among others.

Although each podcast featured hundreds of episodes about specific tips, tricks, and "don'ts" regarding podcasting, Jackson and Lewis both argued consistently that the skill barriers to the medium were low. In one episode where Lewis describes the type of microphone and recording equipment he uses to record his show, for example, he made it clear that "If you want to start out podcasting, please don't let all of this high tech expensive equipment and all of these dollar signs intimidate you." When it came to questions of audio quality in the recording and editing process, Lewis eschewed the kind of perfectionism that defines commercial radio, noting:

> I'm not that worried about audio. I think your audio quality should be as good as you can get, but I've always realized that I'm the kind of person that can just never be happy with my audio, so I don't go that crazy with it.
> *(Daniel J. Lewis, January 10, 2010)*

Similarly, Jackson's podcast emphasized the conversational breeziness of podcast audio, noting that it required little in the way of extra time or effort, making it ideal as a hobby or "side hustle" in addition to a full-time job. When talking about the time necessary to launch and maintain a weekly podcast, Dave Jackson scoffed when reading one listener's email about how much time it takes to prepare for their podcast:

> Here's somebody that's saying, "Look, it takes me 14 hours to do two shows." And again, for me, that's insane. . . . To me you shouldn't be spending more than six hours [per week] to actually put out the podcast, record it, things like that.

Despite the assurances from Jackson and Lewis that podcasting did not require a good deal of money or upfront time commitment in order to succeed, their recommendations for podcasters about best practices—couched in narratives about their own failure or those of others—offered up a conflicting set of precepts for a "quality" podcast. For example, both hosts spoke disparagingly about free web hosting services. Web hosting is necessary for podcasters to create a webpage for the show, store the audio files, and maintain the RSS feed (which allows the podcast to be distributed). Dave Jackson remarked in in a 2012 episode, "I would never do something [like that] for *The School of Podcasting*." The clear implication here is, of course, that free web hosting is inadequate and reflects poorly on the podcaster. Similarly, in an episode of *The Audacity to Podcast*, Daniel J. Lewis reflects on some of his own early mistakes as a podcaster, noting:

> I also wasn't willing to invest money and maybe you can answer this question because I can't. What is it with podcasting that many people approached podcasting as a hobby? . . . This is one of my mistakes. I wasn't willing to invest money in my podcast. I wanted to do everything for free.
> *(Daniel J. Lewis, November 11, 2013)*

In a 2010 episode, Lewis linked non-free web hosting to a sense of professionalism for podcasters. Exhorting his listeners to spend money on their own unique domain name (like "lewis.com"), he stated,

> What's important about this is it just sounds so much more professional. Again, going back to branding, going back to having your own domain in the first place, is would trust someone more if they say, "Visit my podcast dot com." Or if they say, "Visit my podcast dot podbeam dot freepodcast dot com slash user?"

Similar to Jackson, the "mistake" of early podcasting is to find free services to host and distribute audio content.

Both hosts also dispensed advice on techniques for interviewing and speaking on air. For example, Jackson critiqued several podcasts for featuring dull interviews with guests, including one of his early podcasts. He noted that there's "nothing less fun than interviewing somebody with a bunch of 'yup' and 'nope' answers." Citing his own mistakes as an amateur podcaster in 2013, Lewis noted,

> another mistake I made was I didn't schedule my time for my podcast. . . . I started in 2007 and by 2009 I had only released nine complete episodes. Two years, nine episodes: That's fewer than one episode per month! I had a problem and that was, I was procrastinating.

Here Lewis argues that scheduled regularity and a strong work ethic are necessary for podcasts to be successful. Jackson offered similar recommendations for the regularization of output, noting that audiences are expecting content on a regular basis.

This level of commitment extends to the crafting of each episode as well. Speaking in his debut episode, Lewis remarked, "You need to be professional. You need to have your thoughts organized." Similar to the social media entrepreneurs discussed by Duffy (2017), these podcast mentors emphasized the necessity of being consistent with creative output in order to regularize content production and cultivate an audience base. There is a contradiction at the heart of these podcasts, however: While they celebrate the openness of the medium and the freedom of amateurs to create new cultural content, they caution listeners against seeming "unprofessional" by eschewing time commitments, money, organization, and specific interview styles.

Additionally, Jackson and Lewis outlined specific strategies for monetizing podcast content, often offering their own shows as exemplars for successful monetization. Jackson, for example, offered "premium content" on a password-protected segment of his website for listeners who paid a monthly subscription fee. Lewis noted that this was a potentially successful model for monetization, but that the

> model of premium stuff is a bit difficult because you have to have content that's in high enough demand . . . Someone else said it to me today, is that "content wants to be free," and we want content for free. So, it's very difficult if you're going to charge for content.

Lewis noted that some podcasters also rely on listener donations as well. Both hosts suggested that advertising sponsorships or affiliate links—whereby listeners could use a special code with an online retailer to obtain a discount—were more likely to be effective for amateur podcasters. Jackson noted that advertisers would expect to see metrics in order to "prove to the advertiser that that traffic came from you so that when it comes time to renew that advertiser, you can say, 'Well look, in a month time I brought you a 120 clicks. You said that 30 people bought our product' et cetera." Monetizing podcast content through branded merchandise such as T-shirts and cups were also mentioned as a possible method of monetization.

This production and marketing advice dispensed by Lewis and Jackson thus emphasized several key points: First, that podcasts had relatively low barriers to entry, but for those wanting to produce "professional" quality shows, upfront investment was a necessity. Second, both hosts outlined specific production strategies, such as purchasing specific equipment, speaking technique, interview styles, and regularizing new production as a means for success. Third, these hosts introduced monetization as a key goal for podcasters and outlined several strategies to extract value from listeners, through either subscriptions, donations, advertising sponsorship, or merchandising.

2. Building Communities, Not Audiences: Podcasting as Affective Labor

The podcasting advice outlined earlier often contrasted with other discourses that emphasized the unique aspects of podcasting labor as an engaging, interactive experience for both hosts and audiences. Both Lewis and Jackson mobilized terms often associated with nonprofit media, such as "providing a service" for the audience or fostering a sense of "community" via podcast production. Part of the "service" that is expected of podcasters, they noted, is to create a *personal and emotional connection* with listeners while simultaneously commodifying those listeners by connecting them to advertisers via personal "host read" ad copy. As mentioned previously, both hosts identified monetization as a central goal of successful podcasting. David Jackson framed this need rather baldly in a 2006 episode, stating, "What does the podcaster want? He wants listeners. Okay?" The key to this, however, was identified as building "relationships" with audiences and creating forms of organic "community" around the podcast. Both hosts argued that successful podcasters were able to expand their audience base by connecting to their listeners on a personal and emotional level. On top of the technical and entrepreneurial savvy, then, podcasting was associated with a type of affective labor that defines other types of Web 2.0 production as well (Andrejevic 2011; Duffy 2015; Gregg 2009).

Notwithstanding the professional advice about audio quality and monetization, both Jackson and Lewis argued that podcasting labor should be motivated by the desire to give something to others rather than crass, commercial imperatives. The message here was that a podcaster should "be a giver, not a taker." As Jackson stated in an early episode, "Behind the scenes, I really just want to help people. I mean, it sounds kind of cheesy, but that's really a lot of the motivation behind it." This altruistic goal was echoed by Lewis, who argued podcasters should be motivated by a desire to help others and to create a lasting personal connection. Speaking about another podcast he hosts that features TV show reviews, Lewis expanded upon this theme of selfless giving:

> It's not about us telling our stories. It's about making people smile and laugh and lifting their moods during a rough day . . . It's about sharing passions together. . . [audiences] can join our community, listen to our podcast, and they feel like they're one of us and they enjoy chatting with us.
> (Daniel J. Lewis, November 11, 2013)

Both hosts argued that the motivation for podcasting came from this desire to provide support, entertainment, or respite to listeners. As Lewis notes earlier, the ethos of podcasting is about giving away labor for free out of a desire and commitment to change others' lives for the better. Given the urgings of both hosts to pursue professionalism in podcast production, this public service-oriented discourse rests uncomfortably alongside the goals of audience monetization. The two were linked, however, in one important way: The putative reward for such efforts was a sense of personal satisfaction that would inevitably lead to more listeners and—by extension—expanded opportunities for monetization.

Both podcasts linked this notion of affective labor to the interactions between the podcaster and the audience by repeatedly invoking the concept of "community." Successful podcasters were able to expand their audience by creating and carefully nurturing a community of listeners and responding to their desires. While podcasting audiences are typically the ones who listen to media content, Jackson and Lewis urged podcasters to carefully listen to their audiences to show them that they "care" about those audiences and their needs. For example, in a 2013 episode, Jackson played a voicemail from another podcaster who had conducted a survey of her listeners in order to determine the types of topics she should cover in her show. Jackson was enthusiastic about this approach, noting approvingly, "She listened to her audience and in the same way that people trust you because you're the expert, you trust your audience, right, because you're pals, you're buds." Lewis was similarly enthusiastic about fortifying personal connections to listeners, describing the interaction between podcaster and audience as a "relationship" that required careful nurturing. Instead of pursuing large numbers of downloads necessary for successful monetization, Lewis stressed that quality was more important than quantity, noting:

> Make this about relationships, not just numbers . . . All of the tips I'm going to present to you today are related to relationships, connecting with people, not just trying to make another notch in your belt for RSS subscribers, but connecting with people. A relationship is far more beneficial to both of you in the relationship than just an extra subscriber, because a relationship has potential to go a whole lot farther in life.
>
> *(Daniel J. Lewis, October 24, 2011)*

One way to develop those relationships, argued Lewis, was to live broadcast the recording of the podcast so that podcasters could engage with listeners simultaneously. Lewis noted in a 2010 episode that he was familiar with several repeat listeners in his chat room and was used to

> calling my listeners by name. In the chat room right now, we've got Chuck, we've got Kay, we've got Faye, we've got Kylie Mac, we've got Ray was in here earlier . . . I love that I know things about my listeners, and know what they're doing, and even consider them friends.

The foregrounding of this type of intensive relationship-building labor is similar to what scholars have found in other forms of online gig labor. In interviews with self-employed female bloggers, for example, Duffy and Pruchniewska (2017) found that these entrepreneurs felt compelled to present themselves continually on social media in ways that reinforced traditional notions of femininity. Specifically, their interviewees felt a need engage in "soft self-promotion" to brand themselves through constant online interactions with their audience. These social media entrepreneurs found it increasingly challenging to maintain these relationships with their audience, leading to stress and burnout (Duffy 2017). Similarly, both Lewis and Jackson argue that podcasting is less about building audience size than it is about reaching listeners by creating deeply emotional attachments to them in order to share ideas and to build an online community. These podcasts make it clear, however, that it is the responsibility of the podcaster to expend this emotional labor to ensure continued audience growth.

3. *The Passionate Podcaster: Narratives of Authenticity and Self-Actualization Through Podcasting Labor*

There is a contradiction at the heart of these "how to" podcasts. On the one hand, as outlined previously, much of the content of these podcasts consists of practical advice on both the technical and entrepreneurial aspects of podcasting. At the same time, however, woven throughout these narratives is an underlying ethos of self-actualization or self-fulfillment that is strongly linked to freelance online cultural labor. Throughout the episodes sampled for this project, Jackson and Lewis strongly emphasized the necessity for successful podcasters to approach their craft with "passion" and "dedication" rather than to achieve high download numbers or to earn money from advertising. The key to podcasting success, according to these "how to" gurus, is to display your authentic, true personality in order to capture the audience's attention, imagination, and trust.

For example, in his debut episode, Daniel J. Lewis outlined the three core ingredients to a successful podcast: "P-O-D. Passion, organization, and dialogue. Passion is what is the most important thing for you to have in podcasting. If you are not passionate about what you're podcasting, then why are you podcasting?" As Lewis makes clear throughout his show, the motivation to create new content must come from an individual's inner drive and inspiration, regardless of whether the amateur podcaster has the skill or the equipment. The end result of this enthusiasm for your podcast subject matter was essentially the same for both hosts: It was to generate enthusiasm and a larger audience because, according to Lewis, "that passion is what will make people want to listen to you." Jackson similarly extolled the virtues of honesty in podcasting as the means for connecting most powerfully with listeners. He emphasized the importance of "being honest with yourself in terms of, 'This is what I want to talk about; this is what I love,' and find your voice. Be your voice."

Notions of authenticity were closely connected to ideals about the self-actualization that can come from gig labor. Both hosts spoke enthusiastically about "achieving the dream" of pursuing podcasting as an alternative to waged labor. As Lewis remarked, "be intentional about the things that you do, then someday, podcasting can help you achieve your dream, too. Whether it's a dream job, a dream position, a dream whatever, podcasting can help you get there." At times ignoring his own advice, Jackson argued that podcasting allowed individuals to free themselves from commercial conventions of audio production. In a 2007 episode, for example, he expressed his delight at having the creative freedom to decide upon the length of his show from one episode to the next:

> I'm less anxious for material. Every week, I'm going, "You know what? If you just do a half an hour, that's okay. No one is saying you have to do 45 minutes or 55 minutes or whatever." There's no rule. That's what's so lovely about this format, is that if for some reason I only have, heck, even 20 minutes or a half hour of material, it's okay.
> (Dave Jackson, September 17, 2007)

Lewis also contrasted podcasting labor with the more regimented, more constricted confines of wage labor. Over the first several years of his program, Lewis produced his show on weekends and evenings, all the while expressing his desire to pursue podcasting as a full-time occupation. He noted in 2012:

> I had always loved this idea of being a freelancer, and I was getting to know more entrepreneurs and self-employed people, and I thought this idea was really neat because of the flexibility, because of the ability to pursue the passions that these people have, and it was really what I wanted to do.

While Lewis chronicles his transition to podcasting several years later in his show, he offers some cautions to would-be podcast entrepreneurs looking to make a similar transition:

> You want to quit your job, you want to podcast full time and make all of your money just podcasting. I'll tell you what, it's very hard to do and most of the podcasters who are making lots of money from podcasting aren't making that lots of money from just their podcast. Their podcast is a part, but their podcast is a springboard to something else making them money.
> (Daniel J. Lewis, July 1, 2013)

Jackson's and Lewis's orientation to the professionalization of podcasting emerges as both complex and contradictory. On the one hand, both hosts emphasize the creative freedoms and enhanced autonomy that is enabled through gig labor. On the other hand, they argue that successful freelance podcasting is dependent on the willingness of amateurs to project an indelible sense of authenticity to their audience and to carefully nurture that audience through extensive outreach, relationship maintenance, and affective labor.

Discussion: Podcasting, Professionalism, and the Contradictions of Gig Labor

Podcasting is undergoing rapid formalization thanks to the entry of corporate media interests and an increased desire to seek profit by regularizing and standardizing the media. One major consequence of formalization in podcasting is the introduction of professionalism, or the development of standardized rules and routines that are meant to distinguish labor that is informed by the development of specialized skills and a particular orientation toward cultural labor. As I have explored in this chapter, two prominent "how to" podcasts—*School of Podcasting* and *The Audacity to Podcast*—actively construct a particular view of podcasting as an emergent, commercially viable industry that can serve as a full-time occupation for entrepreneurial amateurs. In these podcasts, hosts Jackson and Lewis argue that specific professional practices are key to success, such as the purchase and use of specific types of audio recording equipment, regularized production schedules, and reliance on advertising sponsorship and other monetization strategies. The hosts of these podcasts develop a specific image of the successful podcaster as a profit-driven professional. These discourses are extended via Jackson's and Lewis's own self-branding as experts in the field. These two podcasts construct the notion of professionalism in two key ways. First, they dispense forms of knowledge that are important for the professionalization process, including technical knowledge about audio production, editing, and web hosting, among many other topics. Second, these hosts create an ethos of professionalism by offering praise for adopting standardized production techniques and by offering self-deprecating critiques of their own failures in this regard.

Podcasting production sits at an important nexus point between low- and high-skilled digital labor. Unlike "clickworkers" who perform micro-tasks for large platform-based web services like ClickRabbit, Fiverr, Amazon Turk, and ClickWorker (Casilli 2017; Scholz 2016), amateur podcasting involves the development of technical skills in audio recording, editing, and distribution. It is also accompanied by more creative autonomy than other forms of gig labor (such as ridesharing or grocery delivery, for example) in the sense that amateur labor is not specifically driven by algorithmic requirements or time constraints. Indeed, as outlined in these two "how to" podcasts, the promise of labor autonomy associated with podcast freelancing emerges as the cornerstone of their evangelism about the merits of the medium for amateur cultural production. At the heart of this discourse of professionalism is a powerful and seductive message of meritocracy: that amateur podcasters can successfully compete with established industry players thanks to the absence of industry gatekeepers, if they have the will to learn the skills and make shrewd choices about forms of production and distribution.

Yet amidst all of the highly detailed, technical advice, Jackson's and Lewis's consistent message is that skills acquisition is only one part of the recipe for success. Indeed, as they emphasize, the innate precarity of gig labor can only be surmounted by being one's authentic, passionate self with their audience. On this point, Jackson and Lewis invoke an "imagined audience" that requires a level of ongoing emotional engagement in order to build an economically sustainable business. The affective labor described here has two components. First, it involves a particular type of self-branding that portrays one's self as unique and authentic by effectively stage-managing one's online presence on social media to cultivate new audiences. This emphasis on affective investment as a cornerstone of online labor has been found among other forms of gig labor such as social media marketing (Duffy and Pooley 2017; Scolere, Pruchniewska, and Duffy 2018), blogging (Duffy 2017; Duffy and Pruchniewska 2017), and even amateur online pornography (Paasonen 2010). The second aspect of this affective labor involves a constant maintenance of the podcaster-audience relationship by incorporating listener feedback, suggestions, and their voices into the podcast itself. This type of "relational labor," as Baym (2015) has noted, refers to these continued efforts to "build social relationships that foster paid work." These forms of relational labor are largely invisible, yet are noted as the key for entrepreneurial success. As Terranova (2000, 38) notes, unwaged digital labor involves both technical skills as well as self-taught "forms of labour we do not immediately recognise as such: chat, real-life stories, mailing lists, amateur newsletters, and so on." The internalization of this ethos of self-actualization through skills-based professionalism and relational labor are the two pillars supporting notions of meritocracy in amateur podcasting.

In conclusion, these two "how to" podcasts offer a glimpse into how the inherent contradictions of the gig economy—freedom from wage labor on the one hand and precarity on the other hand—are discursively maintained. While they differ greatly in style, both *School of Podcasting* and *The Audacity to Podcast* construct podcasting as a profession by emphasizing specific production and distribution practices, by stressing the goal of audience maximization and monetization, and by embracing an entrepreneurial ethos. At the same time, hosts Jackson and Lewis advance familiar tropes of online gig labor by exhorting their listeners to cultivate and actively manage their relationships with audiences via forms of affective labor. At the core of these podcasts is an implicit message of meritocracy: If amateurs are willing to learn the skills, follow the advice, and invest the necessary time and capital, they will achieve economic viability. Given the stiff headwinds of a rapidly formalizing podcasting market, this call to take on "hope labor" (Kuehn and Corrigan 2013) ultimately obscures the more grim economic realities facing online digital workers.

7

GOOD PEOPLE "BELONG ANYWHERE"

Airbnb's Emerging Neofascism

Brian Dolber and Christina Ceisel

At a 2015 conference in Paris, Airbnb CEO Brian Chesky told the origin story of his prominent "homesharing" app. The company, which offers access to approximately five million lodging options in 81,000 cities, began when he and his roommate, Joe Gebbia, could not pay the rent on their San Francisco apartment. In order to make ends meet, they offered air mattresses to strangers in their apartment. Emphasizing the conviviality of hosting, Chesky recalled their first three guests who became lifelong friends. Insisting that the host community is misunderstood by those who would place regulations and restrictions on short-term rentals, Chesky declared, "They are looking at us and they see spaces and they see houses." Then, gesturing towards the audience, he added, "And what they miss is it's not about our spaces, it's actually about you, it's about me, it's about the hosts themselves."[1]

This narrative, where entrepreneurship builds community, is emblematic of how Silicon Valley firms defend themselves against public criticism. Silicon Valley has long wrapped itself in a utopian ideal: the counterculture would be built through, rather than against, corporate capitalism. This "Californian ideology" drew together the hippie bohemianism of the New Left and the bourgeois Reaganism of the New Right, connecting liberal cultural attitudes to entrepreneurial individualism.[2] We argue that Airbnb's business model serves as a transition point between this neoliberal ideal and a new neofascist formation.[3] This chapter outlines key aspects of Airbnb's economic and rhetorical strategies that position them as such.

Unpacking this argument means first recognizing tech companies as a key force within what Nancy Fraser terms the progressive neoliberal hegemonic bloc. This bloc linked together two seemingly oppositional political fractions: "mainstream liberal currents of the new social movements (feminism, anti-racism, multiculturalism, environmentalism, and LGBTQ rights)" with "the most dynamic, high-end 'symbolic' and financial sectors of the U.S. economy (Wall Street, Silicon Valley, and Hollywood)." The supporting ideology argued that inequality could be addressed without interfering in markets or challenging capitalism. By adopting an inclusive politics of recognition, corporate players within the progressive neoliberal bloc positioned themselves as partners in the struggle for justice.[4] When the global financial crisis of 2008 fractured faith in the neoliberal project, a new crop of entrepreneurs and investors promised that digital technologies continued to offer possibilities for democratization and economic growth.

The gig economy emerged in this context. New "start-up" platforms—like Airbnb, founded barely two months before Wall Street's meltdown—encouraged speculative investment in a destabilized economy. At the same time, platforms promised opportunities for entrepreneurship, offering hope to professionals and small business owners who feared proletarianization.

Now, one decade later, the future of the neoliberal project is in question. We characterize this moment as an interregnum, a historical moment with no clear hegemonic authority. Most strikingly, reactionary populism offers an alternative to the neoliberal order, from the US to the UK, from Duterte's Philippines to Bolsonaro's Brazil. As Fraser puts it, reactionary populism "combines a hyper-reactionary politics of recognition with a populist politics of distribution: in effect, the wall on the Mexican border plus large-scale infrastructure spending." In other words, reactionary populists believe the state should provide economic security as a privilege for those who can claim a primordial belonging to the nation.[5]

The tensions between progressive neoliberalism and reactionary populism became clear to us when, just weeks before Trump's inauguration, we, the authors, tried to earn some extra money as Airbnb hosts while traveling during the 2016–17 winter holiday. We had agreed to rent out our two-bedroom apartment in a largely Latinx, gentrifying neighborhood in Los Angeles to a middle-aged white couple from Arizona planning to attend the Rose Bowl Parade. Upon their arrival, we received notification that they wanted to cancel their reservation. They noted that although our apartment was lovely, the presence of "food trucks" (in our neighborhood, these serve tacos, burritos, and tortas) and "people on the stoop" was enough to force them to find alternative accommodations on New Year's Eve.

That our neighborhood was read as "unsafe" reveals white supremacist values of racial segregation and xenophobia. The guests' reaction to signs of Chicanx people and culture highlight the inability of progressive neoliberalism to achieve its professed desire for multiculturalism through market and brand initiatives. Struck by these contradictions, we began exploring how Airbnb navigates the political terrain at this conjuncture.

Inspired by approaches advanced by Stuart Hall, we offer a materialist account of how Airbnb's neofascist discourses and practices have been produced, as well as how they have garnered "material force."[6] In other words, we examine the strategic practices of Airbnb, and organizations challenging Airbnb, in order to show how the discourses employed do the work of making new political realities. Paying particular attention to the political fights over homesharing in the City of Los Angeles—the center of Airbnb's second largest market in the US and the site of one of the nation's largest real estate bubbles—we employ a qualitative and historical mixed-methods approach. We draw on participant observation at Airbnb events, textual analysis of corporate websites, and discourse analysis of transcripts of municipal hearings. In addition, we draw on our experiential knowledge of the subject—we are frequent Airbnb guests and have been occasional hosts. One of us attended and spoke at hearings regarding short-term rental policy in Los Angeles in the capacity of being paid staff at Unite Here Local 11, the hotel workers' union.

Our argument is threefold. First, we argue that Airbnb's brand strategy presents Airbnb as aspirational and cosmopolitan. Central to this is the construction of a brand community rooted in progressive neoliberal values that obfuscates host's labor while encouraging conformity to brand expectations. Second, we focus on Airbnb's political strategy. Through Airbnb Citizen, the brand community is mobilized as a political force within the struggle over the right to the city, to defend the interests of Airbnb against regulatory efforts aimed at curbing housing inequities.

Third, we argue that through these processes, Airbnb forges a politically active, petty bourgeois class, undermining the inclusive, progressive neoliberal vision of the brand. We demonstrate this by analyzing Airbnb hosts' testimony at municipal regulatory meetings in Los Angeles. By forging a unified petty bourgeoisie in these settings, where they stare down labor unions and housing advocates while donning a populist mask, the case of Airbnb highlights how the gig economy may signify a transition between neoliberal and neofascist social formations.

In mobilizing petty bourgeois homeowners to political action at a conjunctural moment, we argue that Airbnb enables the formation of what Nancy Fraser would term a reactionary populist bloc. Still, our conjuncture sees emerging possibilities for a multiracial, progressive populism that may challenge the inequities wrought by progressive neoliberalism. Charting this process is necessary in order to develop strategies for radical intervention.

Airbnb's Brand Strategy: "Belong Anywhere"

Airbnb's promotional discourse constructs a progressive neoliberal myth, wherein hosts and guests are part of a global yet intimate creative community free of exploitation. Expanding on its origin myth, Airbnb launched a 2013 branding campaign under the slogan "Belong Anywhere." This campaign illustrated the brand community's adherence to the belief that a progressive, inclusive, cosmopolitan ethos may be realized through a particular mode of travel. Their logo, the Bélo, was meant to be "a community symbol that can be expressed differently by each community member and in every listing—it is not bound by language, culture or location. It is one that accepts we are all different, one to wear with pride."[7]

At the 2016 Airbnb Open in Los Angeles, Airbnb expanded this brand narrative, unveiling their new slogan, "Don't Just Go There, Live There." Chris Lehane, Head of Global Policy and Public Affairs, positioned the endeavor in one panel as a means to "further the economic exchange" as Airbnb continues its mission to "democratize travel."[8] Dovetailing with the launch of "Airbnb Experiences," which allow travelers to interface with artists, musicians, chefs, outdoor enthusiasts, and "locals" at preferred bars and restaurants, Airbnb executives and a self-proclaimed "experience therapist" discussed how people stopped caring about material things and now "collect" experiences.[9] These narratives stood in stark contrast to the political realities of the prior week, which saw the election of Donald Trump. Luminaries of progressive neoliberal culture—tech scions, celebrities, and lifestyle gurus—repeatedly offered the brand's cosmopolitan fantasy as the antidote to Trump's reactionary populism.

The notion that hosting allows hosts to remain in their homes, sustain their own businesses, and engage in creative endeavors is central to Airbnb's argument that they serve progressive ends. Thus, the company claims to provide a ladder to success, preventing petty bourgeois hosts' proletarianization. While boosters tend to see this as a win-win for hosts and investors alike, the majority of Airbnb's revenue comes not from "homesharing" but from unoccupied housing stock that is more profitable for its owners to operate as hotels. For example, in July 2015, while most on-site, space-sharing hosts in the Los Angeles market accounted for 35 percent of all listed properties, they accounted for only 11 percent of Airbnb's revenue. However, leasing companies that constituted only 6 percent of listing agents generated 35 percent of Airbnb's revenue. When single lessors were included, this accounted for 48 percent of the listing agents, but 89 percent of Airbnb's revenue.[10] Thus, those who rely on hosting income to pay rent or mortgage tend to earn less revenue themselves, producing less value for the company.

Host workshops and corporate communications mask how Airbnb generates the majority of its revenue. As the number of listings, the number of guest arrivals, and the average rents have all grown dramatically in recent years, hosts earned a gross rental income of approximately $30.4 billion in 2018. From this, Airbnb generated a projected $3.8 billion in revenues, leading *Forbes* to dub it "a rare, profitable unicorn" in contrast to other gig titans, such as Uber, which has yet to show profits.[11]

Although hosting is framed in entrepreneurial terms, it does not typically provide enough income to be an individual's sole job. The average property gross is only six thousand dollars in revenue annually. Low host compensation stems from Airbnb consistently taking between 3 and 23 percent of each booking. Thus, Airbnb's $3.8 billion in profits in 2018 came from real estate that it did not own and labor that it did not compensate.

This does not mean that on-site, space-sharing hosts are not of value to the company. They do the important ideological work of validating Airbnb's brand.[12] This produces a tension between the company's economic imperatives and its professed commitment to building an inclusive and authentic community. In order to reconcile these tensions, Airbnb works to homogenize the homesharing experience, encouraging hosts to bring properties in line with the brand. Airbnb created its Hospitality Lab in Dublin in 2013, where it trains hosts on nine key standards.[13] The next year, the company launched a portal dedicated to business travel, allowing for third-person booking, as well as filtering for residences with the amenities one might expect at a business hotel—work station, Internet, iron. In 2017 Airbnb challenged the luxury hotel market, announcing that they would add a "premium service" featuring hosts who had been personally vetted by inspectors.[14]

By emphasizing aesthetics and partnerships with high-end retailers, Airbnb hosts are encouraged to reconfigure their homes as petty bourgeois spaces, reassuring guests and hosts that they are members of the same (perhaps aspirational) class. In March of 2016 one of us attended a champagne meet-and-greet at the Jonathan Adler store on Melrose Avenue in affluent, gay-friendly West Hollywood. In order to attract more upscale guests, hosts were offered 20% off everything in the store, with the option of having a complimentary in-home consultation. In the store, displays noted the importance of lighting, how scent can elevate one's mood, and other ways we can increase our host ratings. Thus, Airbnb's costly cultural exclusivity squeezes out lower value hosts with less space to offer and fewer resources to put into meeting Airbnb's best practices.

In addition, the company reinforces racial segregation and gentrification of US housing markets. While Chesky states on the company website that central to Airbnb's mission is "the idea that people are fundamentally good and every community is a place where you can belong," Airbnb has exacerbated housing inequities experienced by Latinx and African American communities since the 2008 crisis.[15] A 2018 McGill University study reported that white neighborhoods make more money through Airbnb than non-white neighborhoods. Significantly, black neighborhoods being gentrified have the most Airbnb use, but revenue disproportionately goes to new white residents and speculators. For example, in the Stuyvesant Heights neighborhood in Brooklyn, there was a 1012% disparity between white and non-white Airbnb hosts. The neighborhood itself is 7.4% white and 89.7% black. The study concludes that neighborhood disruption was twelve times more likely to affect black residents, while economic benefits are four times more likely to go to a white host.[16]

These dynamics have encouraged discrimination against Airbnb guests as well. The *New York Times* reported in 2016 on a wave of Airbnb hosts canceling reservations of guests of color. One Harvard Business School study argued that the Airbnb platform enabled discrimination among hosts, as guests with distinctly African American names were less likely to be accepted for stays. In other instances, neighbors called police upon seeing African American guests entering short term rental properties, leading to the trending hashtag #AirbnbWhileBlack.[17]

In response to the controversy, Chesky proclaimed discrimination to be "the greatest challenge we face as a company," because it "cuts to the core of who we are and the values that we stand for."[18] The company has relied on relationships with Democratic and liberal leaders to jump over such public relations hurdles. At the 2016 Open, former Attorney General Eric Holder described his anti-discrimination efforts with the company as an "extension of his work at the Justice Department," while assuring that the company ultimately offers a way to "bridge cultural divides."[19] Airbnb hired Laura Murphy, the former head of the ACLU's Washington Legislative Office, to manage the controversy. She pushed for a technological fix by privileging hosts who allow "instant booking," where properties are assumed to be available at all times, in search results.[20]

Instant booking poses challenges for hosts who live on site, or who make their home available only when they may be out of town. Instead, it privileges large-scale property holders running their property as a professional operation. Thus, the solution to discrimination on the platform inadvertently privileged wealthy, white hosts. Here we see the failure of market-based approaches to remedy racism, as they fail to address core issues on the one hand and reproduce modes of racial exclusion on the other. By focusing on individualized acts of discrimination, Airbnb not only overlooks how it perpetuates structural racism; it also affirms the notion that hosting is an individual effort not a social relation.

The Airbnb community's systematic marginalization of people of color is a product of the company's branding decisions. Airbnb promotes the notion that criticizing the company for such marginalization—and proposing regulations to address them—constitutes an attack on the Airbnb "community" as a whole, including hosts. In order to combat such regulations, Airbnb has developed a program, Airbnb Citizen, which mobilizes petty bourgeois hosts towards political action in order to protect corporate interests.

Airbnb's Political Strategy: Hosts as "Citizens"

As part of the response to charges of discrimination on the platform, Airbnb developed the "Airbnb Citizen" program. The program highlights efforts the company makes to build an inclusive community, while also organizing hosts, guests, and community members to advocate for Airbnb's political goals. Airbnb Citizen reflects neoliberal and neofascist tendencies in mobilizing consumers in its interests. The company draws on progressive neoliberal tropes of creativity and multiculturalism to link together a petty bourgeois class to fight for the "right to the city" at the expense of working-class people of color. According to Airbnb Citizen, homesharing is an approach to "unlocking economic opportunity," "investing in cities," "boosting small business," and "reflecting new priorities" such as climate change. The program organizes hosts as members of an aggrieved class in the wake of the 2008 financial crisis. "Home sharing provides much needed extra income for middle-class families set back by the Great Recession, seniors living on fixed incomes, and growing ranks of part-time and freelance workers."[21] Thus, municipal regulations that might limit homesharing are a threat to the "good people" of the Airbnb brand community.

By helping to structure an aggrieved petty bourgeoisie, Airbnb Citizen frames the struggle over the right to the city as one over resources, and as David Harvey suggests, casts it as a contest over the power to shape urban environments. As real estate and development have become increasingly entwined with the financial sector, policies have tended to serve the interests of developers and transnational capital while urban neighborhoods and communities experience dispossession and displacement.[22] These dynamics undermine "the relative mutual toleration, the 'convivial culture' of mixity" so central to urban life.[23] Airbnb Citizen points to fissures in progressive neoliberal urban politics, as a new coalition is formed to protect against alleged harms done by unfair regulations supported by Democratic politicians, powerful trade unions, major hotel chains, and financial elites.

Through text-based and video narratives, Airbnb Citizen calls upon hosts to combat municipal homesharing regulations that threaten profits. Airbnb Citizen repeatedly represents cities where such battles are tense through dedicated weekly series. For example, the "Los Angeles Spotlight series" shows how "Angelenos have democratized travel by turning their largest expense—their homes—into an asset to earn extra income, allowing travelers to live like locals and generate economic activity across the city."[24]

The personal narratives in the Spotlight series assume one of three generic forms. Each of these praises Airbnb, in one way or another, for contributing to the lives and livelihoods of deserving representatives of the petty bourgeoisie. In the first, hosting improves the hosts' quality of life by being part of the Airbnb community. In the second, hosting allows homeowners maintain their class status despite economic hardship. In the third, local small business owners who aren't directly affiliated with Airbnb praise the company for adding to their customer base. While these all draw on progressive neoliberal myths, taken together, they do the work of class formation, constructing an imagined community of various components of the petty bourgeoisie, and mobilizing them towards unified action in the struggle for the right to the city.

In the first genre, Airbnb Citizen showcases how hosting has improved the lives of the hosts. In many of these examples, the hosts are people of color, reflecting the brand's progressive neoliberal ethos while erasing the harm the company does to communities of color. One such "spotlight" features the couple James and Inja Yates, who have been married for 53 years. James, who is African American, and Inja, who is Korean, started the Soul 2 Seoul scholarship fund to assist mixed-race students of African American and Asian ancestry. Through hosting, they have been able to expand the scholarship. As students and former guests have become family, Airbnb provides James and Inja not only a source of income, but also personal fulfillment.

Building on Airbnb's brand identity as a "community," hosts describe guests as extended family members and lifelong friends. Hosting is not labor—there is no discussion of doing dishes, laundry, house cleaning, or having to pay for such services—but a natural expression of their true self. While they communicate security in their middle-class position, Airbnb allows them to go above and beyond as philanthropists. Further, this community reflects the values of progressive neoliberalism, as the revenue generated provides the basis for privately funded solutions to promote education and multiculturalism.

The second genre highlights hosts who, without Airbnb, might have otherwise fallen down the socioeconomic ladder. For example, Andrea, "a silver-haired mother of two" in West Hollywood, "rents out her master bedroom and relies on the extra income to stay in her home." Here again, Airbnb mobilizes progressive neoliberalism, suggesting the company has been a force for economic stability while connecting to the larger creative economy. Rather than placing blame on the economic conditions that have placed Andrea in a precarious financial position, the narrative here focuses on how municipal regulations threaten her livelihood. She proclaims, "If they [install a cap], that would be the difference between me living in my apartment and living in my car."[25] Such a move, then, would violate the petty bourgeois assumption that their class interests (perhaps, above all others) should be of central concern to policymakers.

In the third Spotlight genre, local business owners share personal stories of struggle, emphasize the community-oriented nature of their business, and praise the customers that Airbnb brings. One such narrative features Willy, owner of Vicious Dogs, a hot dog shop in North Hollywood. Willy maps Airbnb's business model onto the national myth that "America is the land of opportunity." Echoing middle-class anxieties, he adds, "and for a while, we were drifting away from that. But now, thanks to these new companies like Airbnb, people are able to benefit from things like travel in a way they never were before. Don't get in the way of that." Although Willy proclaims that he "loves a level playing field," he does not see large companies as an obstacle to achieving that. "I'm glad there are companies looking out for the little guy," he says. "Because really, in the end, we're all just little guys trying to make it. And Airbnb gives people a chance to do just that."[26] By philanthropists and struggling home- and small business owners—as Chesky would put it, "good people"—the Spotlight videos invoke both progressive neoliberal and populist discourses to link together a petty bourgeois coalition.

In order to advance a political agenda, Airbnb Citizen launched its "homesharing clubs" in 2015 to institutionalize the alliances reflected in the Spotlight narratives. At the 2016 event in Los Angeles, the company claimed there to be 109 across the world. These clubs enable the exchange of best practices and facilitate connections between guest and other hosts. Primarily, however, they are advocacy groups, extending the brand community into an explicitly political realm.

Homesharing clubs reflect the desire that Marx attributed to the petty bourgeoisie—they "would like the whole of society to become petty-bourgeois."[27] They do this by insisting that they are not simply an extension of, but a replacement for, labor unions. At the 2016 Open, Chris Lehane explained, "the clubs are the next iteration of people organizing themselves to represent themselves, advocate for themselves." According to Lehane, they demonstrate "the evolution of organizing," which has moved from guilds to unions to clubs. These were represented visually on a PowerPoint slide by images of craftspeople, striking workers, and groups of middle-class people.[28]

Airbnb's suggestion that unions are no longer necessary in the 21st-century economy minimizes how the company has exacerbated inequities that have been levied by labor and tenant organizations in an ongoing battle over "the right to the city." For example, under the coalition name "Keep Neighborhoods First," Unite Here Local 11, which represents hotel workers in Los Angeles and Orange Counties, housing organizations such as Strategic Actions for a Just Economy (SAJE), and hotel industry trade associations launched a campaign calling for a municipal ordinance aimed at reigning in the impact of short-term rentals on Los Angeles' tight rental market, rapid gentrification, and increased homelessness.[29] While Airbnb touted their slogan "Don't Just Go There, Live There," at the 2016 Open, Keep Neighborhoods First argued that Airbnb was preventing many Angelenos from living in their own communities.

Exposing progressive neoliberalism's contradictions, Airbnb has cultivated a populist politics, where reactionary hosts argue for unrestricted economic freedoms regardless of their impact on working-class communities of color. These dynamics play out in real time at hearings regarding municipal homesharing ordinances. Airbnb Citizen organizes hosts to argue for policies that favor them, in opposition to working-class people of color and at their expense.

Hosts, Workers, and the Right to the City

This forging of a brand community and political bloc can be best understood as an emerging neofascist formation borne of neoliberalism's contradictions. This is nowhere more evident than in the public debates over municipal homesharing regulations. Between 2015 and 2018, meetings of the Los Angeles Planning Commission and the Los Angeles City Council's Planning and Land Use Management committee became battlegrounds in the "right to the city." Hosts, mobilized through Airbnb Citizen, faced off against members of labor unions and representatives of housing organizations who were in favor of implementing restrictions. Overlooking how they were serving the interests of a $30 billion corporation, hosts called for neoliberal "deregulation" that would benefit Airbnb. In the name of entrepreneurialism, they appeal to the government to intervene on behalf of their own petty bourgeois class interests. Thus, these hearings became sites of emerging neofascism, as hosts became petty bourgeois political actors, working in alliance with a major corporation, in direct opposition to working-class interests.

In December 2018, the battle culminated in the passage of light regulations on Airbnb hosts to ameliorate impact on the housing market. As of July 2019, homesharers in Los Angeles must register with the city and pay an annual fee of $89. Hosts are to be restricted to operating one homeshare at a time and cannot rent the property for more than 120 days per calendar year, although they may apply for an extended permit. In addition, hosts may not rent out rent-stabilized units, and renters may not host on properties without the explicit written permission of their landlords.[30]

The statements we analyze in this section were made at the April 10, 2018, meeting of the Planning and Land Use Management Committee.[31] As one of us had attended several other hearings as staff of Unite Here Local 11, we know they are typical of the arguments that hosts often made. They suggest the mobilization of a petty bourgeoisie around a reactionary populist politics. First, hosts paint themselves as deserving citizens, erasing the challenges faced by working-class proponents of homesharing regulation. Second, they negate the elite power of gig companies by suggesting that they represent petty bourgeois interests. Third, they suggest that government regulations would harm them while only serving elites.

Hosts often highlight their economic precarity but argue that it is no fault of their own. To demonstrate their deservedness, they emphasize that they are "good people" with families. For example, Eric, a former real estate agent who had been "flipping homes," bought a triplex in 2007 "with my family and my mom and my brothers. And after the market went down I had to short sell the property." Eric continues to live in his home, as his landlord rents it back to him. Eric, in turn, makes a living renting it on Airbnb. Eric offers a redemption narrative, arguing, "We found a way to, you know, benefit. And, if you place a cap . . . we're going to have to find something else to do. That's going to be pretty tough." By "working on" Airbnb, Eric is able to continue living in his own home as market forces would otherwise push him out. But in advocating against the caps, he affirms the market's power. As he has been able "to benefit," he politically aligns with Airbnb and his landlord, in opposition to working-class organizations combating Airbnb's impacts on a renewed real estate bubble.

This sense of deservedness leads hosts to call on the state to intervene on their behalf, reflecting an emerging neofascist ideology. Angela, "a homeowner and single mom with two teenage kids," argues that her ability to pay her daughter's tuition at "the distinguished Notre Dame Academy high school" is "solely dependent on the fact that I'm able to rent out two spare rooms in my home through Airbnb." Angela believes that state action should be taken in order to offer her daughter the privileges of a private education because she has proven herself to be deserving—"She is 13 years old and worked very hard all year to be accepted into this school"—adhering to the petty bourgeois entrepreneurial ethos.

Another host highlighted his entrepreneurialism. Rob, a "22 year resident of Los Angeles" explained how he "flexed [his] entrepreneurial spirit and began independent consulting" five years ago. "I also flexed my entrepreneurial spirit by putting $4,000 into my apartment refurbishing it with a lot of elbow grease as well. Some things that the landlord would never do." Rob requests that the city not restrict hosting in "RSO units for tenants that reside in them," "not institute a cap that goes under 180 days," and "not require neighbors or landlords to sign off on—to require their permission." Rob's desire for city policy to meet his own personal convenience trumps public concerns about preserving affordable housing. Like Angela, his comments are consistent with Poulantzas' observation that the petty bourgeoisie expect the state to reflect their own interests.

The possibility that the City of Los Angeles would take other concerns into consideration elicits populist ire. As Mary Kate, a 50-year resident of Culver City, declared, "The sharing economy is upon us. We need to accept and embrace the change. Money aside, it's wrong to deny good people the opportunity to do what they want to do. Why deny good people the opportunity to be where they want to be?" In this scenario, "government intervention" would harm the ability of "good people" to compete in a free market. For these hosts, the risk of not being able to operate their homesharing business would be the loss of their middle-class status.

By positioning themselves as being in a David-Goliath fight with a rigged market, hosts mask the extensive lobbying work done by Airbnb. Thus, their comments ultimately fail to challenge corporate power; in fact, Mary Kate naturalizes her views as part of the "accelerating world." Furthering this logic, Mary Kate likens Airbnb hosts to other gig workers. She asks, "should we try to limit the number of days people are allowed to Uber so we can force people into taxis? No." Thus, hosts position gig workers as an emerging class of entrepreneurs threatened by entrenched power. Hotels and taxis are not only of the past; they use their power to hinder progress while limiting opportunities for the deserving middle class.

Speaking as entrepreneurial subjects, hosts erase the ways their labor undercuts union-led standards in the hospitality industry. As Anna, a member of Unite Here Local 11, testified,

> I'm here today to ask you to pass the short-term renter ordinance as soon as possible. I think this ordinance is very important, because it affects the hospitality industry standards. I work hard every day to give an outstanding service to my guests. When people buy apartment buildings and turn them into hotels, it hurts me and the standard that we fought for many years. That standard is for our guests, but it's also for the quality of our lives and our families.

The deserving nature of the Airbnb brand community provides a rhetorical resource that hosts, and ultimately Airbnb, can use to dismiss union concerns, echoing Lehane's declaration that homesharing clubs are the next generation of labor unions. For Airbnb, the deserving workers are actually entrepreneurial, small business owners. Thus, actual unions are cast not only as vestige of the past but also as providing cover for the larger hotel industry. Such allegations were made repeatedly by hosts at the May 2016 hearing before Planning Department staff, enabling petty bourgeois hosts to dismiss the claims made by the working-class—largely female, immigrant, and of color—members of Local 11 as a ruse to protect elite interests.

Given this anti-labor context, Local 11 focuses its critique of Airbnb on its contribution to Los Angeles' housing crisis. Declaring "Today we need to end this growing displacement," Kurt Petersen, co-president of Local 11, told the council,

> Workers have fought for living wages, safer [conditions], respect on the job. Now we fight for fair housing practices, the ability to live where we work and not have our homes snatched out from under us only to be turned into short-term rentals by owners and landlords who are putting profits before people.

Thus, Petersen positions Unite Here members as part of a working class exploited on multiple and growing fronts. Petersen demands the right of working people to be heard and represented within public decision-making, based on their contributions to the community. In this way, he locates the struggle for worker power within the larger battle over the right to the city, a contest that sits at the nexus of power and the politics of space.

Local 11 member narratives underscore the vastly different stakes faced by Los Angeles' working class (predominantly of color) and its petty bourgeoisie (predominately white). In contrast to the need for extra money to afford private school tuition or being prevented from having to sell their home, hotel workers point to the hardships they face in finding affordable and secure housing and connect them to Airbnb's inflationary impact on the real estate bubble. Carla, a single parent, notes that she and her five children "have been forced into homelessness" even though she has "a good union job, because there are not enough affordable places in the neighborhood." Echoing Petersen's statement, she suggests that the housing crisis is perhaps a greater concern to workers than their wages. In fact, Carla recognizes herself as relatively privileged because of her "good union job." Thus, she is able to speak for the workers in her sector who are directly impacted by Airbnb and articulates the precarious existence that characterizes contemporary proletarian life.

> Because of this issue I have to live with my parents and share one-bedroom apartment and have virtually no privacy. And after coming home from a long day of cleaning rooms, I'm exhausted. I'm not even able to lie on the

bed or have a place to rest my head on. It's becoming a bigger barrier for my family and I. And everyone in my community. I grew up in this area and I deserve to have a place to live, a bed to sleep on, and this is why I'm here to urge you to pass the ordinance.

Petersen's and Carla's testimonies reveal that what is really at stake is far greater than the ability to negotiate wages and benefits; it is the ability to belong, not anywhere, but at home.

While members of the Airbnb brand community proclaim their desire to belong anywhere, workers in Los Angeles—and globally—resist the growing sense that they belong nowhere. The irony of progressive neoliberalism is that it promotes a politics of place that welcomes strangers as family while displacing neighbors within their own communities. The precariat's displacement is a result of capital's demand for constant growth against the pressures of stagnation, leading to rapacious rent-seeking and gentrification. The complex politics of place that generate the convivial culture of the city are threatened by a politics that amplifies the historical inequities of redlining practices as access to the economic benefits of homesharing are reserved for the elite.

Airbnb contributes to the housing crisis by inflating real estate prices, while doing the ideological work to justify this process and the political work to ensure its continuance. Through its "brand community," the ideologies, institutions, rhetorics, and signifiers of progressive neoliberalism speak to widespread desires for belonging that seem increasingly elusive. In so doing, Airbnb produces a petty bourgeoisie that is ready to defend the interests of big capital against the concerns of workers facing displacement.

Conclusion: From "Good People" to Solidarity

Since the 2008 financial crash, the gig economy has reframed atomized labor as entrepreneurship, transforming low-wage workers into petty bourgeois subjects. While orthodox Marxists typically characterized the petty bourgeoisie as artisans and small-scale owner-operators, Nicos Poulantzas argued in the 1970s that capital in its monopoly stage necessitates a new stratum of the petty bourgeoisie, "non-productive salaried employees" involved in the circulation of capital. These individuals help realize surplus value in commerce, banking, insurance, sales departments, and advertising. Although different fractions of the petty bourgeoisie occupy different economic positions, they adapt both bourgeois and proletarian ideology to their own aspirations.[32] Poulantzas notes that the petty bourgeoisie share in their economic frustrations, in their desire for true meritocracy, and in their belief that the state should reflect their values.[33]

The convergence of various class positions and identities during the neoliberal era have made such class distinctions even more complex. The centrality of finance and digital technologies in circulating value and engendering "flexibility" during the last decades has produced a "creative class" who are awarded high social capital while often facing precarious economic conditions. While the making of a unified petty bourgeois class will not inevitably lead to neofascism, the ways in which the gig economy renders labor invisible by elevating entrepreneurialism enables the annihilation of a working class that might offer a radical alternative.

Through discourses of "entrepreneurship" and "community," Airbnb positions itself to petty bourgeois hosts as a means to survive and even thrive amidst precarity and social isolation. While low-wage gig workers such as rideshare drivers and delivery workers, who require access only to a car or bicycle, often understand these promises as hollow and resist job and wage-degrading practices through collective action, Airbnb hosts, who either own or have access to real estate, occupy a privileged position within the gig economy.

While corporations have long worked to gain favorable regulations by appealing to the middle class through astroturf campaigns, Airbnb's efforts are distinct. They encourage hosts to see themselves as small business owners, denying their productive role. This process entails not merely the promotion of "false consciousness"; rather, it creates real political alliances at a conjunctural moment. With the ideological and financial support of Airbnb, petty bourgeois hosts defend their material interests against workers of color, helping to preserve a larger structure of corporate capitalism.

Airbnb's role in the struggles for the "right to the city" are most troubling when understood within historical context. Writing at neoliberalism's dawn, Poulantzas noted that fascism emerged during a transitional phase in the 20th century as monopoly capital relied on state power to secure hegemony. He cautioned, however, "the fascist phenomenon is by no means restricted to [the interwar era], as "the political crises to which fascism corresponds . . . may well occur in other periods too."[34] Now, as neoliberalism is challenged, we find ourselves amidst another political crisis heightened by the COVID-19 pandemic.

The point here is not that Airbnb is a fascist organization. Poulantzas notes that fascist parties broker alliances between the elite and the petty bourgeoisie, rather than being under direct bourgeois control.[35] Thus, Airbnb's maintenance of a "brand community" suggests the persistence of neoliberal formations, while contradictions within it and within progressive neoliberalism itself work to produce an ideology that may, in turn, provide the basis for a neofascist movement.

Further, we do not mean to suggest that Airbnb hosts themselves are fascists, either in the expression of their views or by virtue of their class position. Petty bourgeois ideology is rife with contradictions that might be mobilized in a variety of directions. Indeed, many of the stories that hosts tell, particularly those that reflect a fear of losing one's home or economic security, are cause for alarm and deserve political responses. But if fascism, or some post-neoliberal variant of it, is to emerge, it will be as a ruling coalition, a historical bloc that fuses together disparate and contradictory interests. Undoubtedly, this will include some "good people."

In identifying the contradictions, there is cause for optimism. Nancy Fraser argues that "progressive populism," which "[combines] egalitarian redistribution with nonhierarchical recognition . . . has at least a fighting chance of uniting the whole working class."[36] The efforts of Unite Here Local 11 and the Keep Neighborhoods First coalition reflect this. By connecting the concerns of workers to the concerns of renters, they demonstrate how the contemporary working class is exploited on multiple fronts, particularly in urban communities of color. Fraser continues, "[progressive populism] could position that class, understood expansively, as the leading force in an alliance that also includes substantial segments of youth, the middle class, and the professional-managerial stratum."[37]

Unite Here Local 11 and the Keep Neighborhoods First coalition may indeed be organizing this progressive populist force. While regulations on short-term rentals may ameliorate some of Airbnb's harmful impact, such campaigns do little to advance a larger political agenda. In order to harness political power, working-class communities impacted by Airbnb must develop strategies that go beyond restricting hosts. By working towards a progressive populist vision, organizers might help hosts see themselves as exploited workers who are converting their primary asset—their home—into a site of accumulation for a $38 billion corporation.

Notes

1. "Hosts Are Heroes—Brian Chesky," *YouTube,* November 15, 2015, accessed February 23, 2019, www.youtube.com/watch?v=Bor-OyjULnM.
2. Richard Barbrook and Andy Cameron, "The Californian Ideology," *Mute,* September 1, 1995, accessed March 10, 2019, www.metamute.org/editorial/articles/californian-ideology.
3. By neoliberalism, we refer to the economic ideological project, dominant since the 1970s, to make markets sovereign at the expense of worker and citizen power. By neofascism, we refer to emergent trends that critique neoliberalism's close relationship to global monopoly capital, and the culture it produces, by harkening back to the fascism of the 1920s and 1930s through appeals to nationalism, racism, and patriarchy.
4. Nancy Fraser, "From Progressive Neoliberalism to Trump—and Beyond," *American Affairs Journal* I, no. 4 (2017), accessed October 27, 2018, https://americanaffairsjournal.org/2017/11/progressive-neoliberalism-trump-beyond/.
5. Ibid.
6. Stuart Hall, "The Problem of Ideology: Marxism Without Guarantees," *Journal of Communication Inquiry* 10, no. 2 (1986).
7. Design Studio, accessed March 10, 2019, https://design.studio/work/airbnb.
8. Chris Lehane, "The Making of a Movement for Home Sharing," Presentation, *Airbnb Open,* Los Angeles, CA, November 18, 2016.
9. Pamela Adams, Nicki Clark, Mike Curtis, Alex Schleifer, and Joe Zadeh, "Beyond the Home: The Future of Airbnb," Presentation, *Airbnb Open*, Los Angeles, CA, November 18, 2016.
10. Los Angeles Alliance for a New Economy, "Airbnb, Rising Rent and the Housing Crisis in Los Angeles," March 2015, accessed February 23, 2019, www.laane.org/wp-content/uploads/2015/03/AirBnB-Final.pdf.

11. Trefis Team, "As a Rare Profitable Unicorn, Airbnb Appears to Be Worth $38 Billion," *Forbes*, May 11, 2018, accessed February 23, 2019, www.forbes.com/sites/greatspeculations/2018/05/11/as-a-rare-profitable-unicorn-airbnb-appears-to-be-worth-at-least-38-billion/#2d991a642741.
12. Accessed March 7, 2019, www.airbnb.com/diversity.
13. Ken Yeung, "With 8.5m Guests, Airbnb Seeks to Build a More Uniform Customer Experience via Its Hospitality Lab," *The Next Web*, September 17, 2013, accessed March 10, 2019, https://thenextweb.com/insider/2013/09/17/with-8-5m-guests-clity-lab/.

    Austin Carr, "Inside Airbnb's Grand Hotel Plans," *Fast Company*, March 17, 2014, accessed March 10, 2019, www.fastcompany.com/3027107/punk-meet-rock-airbnb-brian-chesky-chip-conley.
14. Rob LeFebvre, "Airbnb to Target Wealthy Customers Who Prefer Luxury Hotels," *Endgadet*, June 22, 2017, accessed March 10, 2019, www.engadget.com/2017/06/22/airbnb-luxury-option/.
15. Jillian Báez and Mari Castañeda, "Two Sides of the Same Story: Media Narratives of Latinos and the Subprime Mortgage Crisis," *Critical Studies in Media Communication* 31, no. 1: 27–41.
16. David Wachsmuth, David Chaney, Danielle Kerrigan, Andrea Shillolo, and Robin Basalaev-Binder, "The High Cost of Short-Term Rentals in New York City," Urban Politics and Governance Research Group, McGill University, https://mcgill.ca/newsroom/files/newsroom/channels/attach/airbnb-report.pdf.
17. Elaine Glusac, "As Airbnb Grows, So Do Claims of Discrimination," *The New York Times*, September 26, 2016, www.nytimes.com/2016/06/26/travel/airbnb-discrimination-lawsuit.html.

    Benjamin Edelman, Michael Luca, and Dan Svirsky, "Racial Discrimination in the Sharing Economy: Evidence from a Field Experiment," *American Economic Journal: Applied Economics* 9, no. 2 (2017): 1–22, https://doi.org/10.1257/app.20160213.
18. Alex Fitzpatrick, "Airbnb CEO: 'Bias and Discrimination Have No Place Here," *Time*, September 8, 2016, http://time.com/4484113/airbnb-ceo-brian-chesky-anti-discrimination-racism/.
19. Eric Holder Jr, Belinda Johnson, David King, Johnica Reed Hawkins, Kharima Richards, Margaret Richardson, "Universal Belonging," Presentation, *Airbnb Open*, November 17, 2016.
20. Glusac, "As Airbnb Grows."
21. Airbnb Citizen, "About Airbnb," accessed March 10, 2019, www.airbnbcitizen.com/about-airbnb/.
22. David Harvey, "The Right to the City," *New Left Review* 53 (2008): 23–40.
23. Doreen Massey, *World City* (Cambridge: Polity Press, 2007), 71–72, cites Paul Gilroy, *After Empire: Melancholia or Convivial Culture?* (London: Routledge, 2004).
24. Airbnb Citizen, "LA Spotlight: Owner of O&M Leather Talks Passion, Innovation, and Home Sharing," accessed March 10, 2019, www.airbnbcitizen.com/stories/la-spotlight-om-leather/.
25. Airbnb Citizen, "Meet Andrea: Airbnb Host in West Hollywood," December 12, 2017, accessed February 23, 2019, www.airbnbcitizen.com/stories/west-hollywood-spotlight-andrea/.
26. "Meet Willy Fedail, the Man Behind North Hollywood's Vicious Dogs," July 25, 2017, accessed February 23, 2019, www.airbnbcitizen.com/stories/meet-willy-fedail-the-man-behind-north-hollywoods-vicious-dogs/.
27. Nicos Poulantzas, *Fascism and Dictatorship: The Third International and the Problem of Fascism* (New York: Verso Books, 2018), 241.
28. Lehane, "The Making of a Movement for Home Sharing."
29. Accessed February 17, 2019, www.keepneighborhoodsfirst.org/airbnb_open_press_conference.

30. City News Service, "After Three Years of Debate, LA Approves Airbnb Rules," December 11, 2018, accessed March 10, 2019, www.nbclosangeles.com/news/local/Airbnb-Home-Sharing-Los-Angeles-Rules-Travel-Homes-Housing-502458851.html.
31. Transcript of the Meeting of the Los Angeles City Council, Planning and Land Use Management Committee, April 10, 2018, accessed February 23, 2019, http://lacity.granicus.com/TranscriptViewer.php?view_id=46&clip_id=17856.
32. Poulantzas, *Fascism and Dictatorship*, 239; 241.
33. Ibid., 237–46.
34. Ibid., 53.
35. Ibid., 83–8.
36. Fraser, "From Progressive Neoliberalism to Trump—and Beyond," para. 35.
37. Ibid., para. 36.

8

'UBER' UNIVERSITY AND LABOR RECOMPOSITION

Struggling Notes on (Dis)organized Academia

Marco Briziarelli and Susana Martínez Guillem

The profound repercussions of the most recent economic crisis in the West have brought a proliferation of studies focused on workers' lived experiences in relation to neoliberal structuring dynamics. This strand of research also increasingly calls for a thorough critique of academic labor.[1] In line with this literature, we point to the dramatic tendency towards casualization and precariousness, the intensification and extensification of work, surveillance, and audit culture that characterizes contemporary academic labor.

In this chapter, we map the relationship between these conditions and our research and teaching practices, as well as the impact of these practices on our students' learning conditions. Focusing on the role that ideologies about language and communication play in mediating our understandings of who we are/should be as workers, we show how the critique of academic labor can benefit from a political-economic perspective on its digital labor components. By examining dominant institutional discourses and pedagogical practices, we uncover how the structural and everyday dynamics associated with online teaching adhere to an ideology of "connectivity/connectedness"[2] sustained by reducing communication to its economically productive aspects.[3] Such a move systematically fetishizes our labor, reducing it to a disembodied transmission of information while contributing to an increasingly precarious and unequal 'Uberized' working environment.

Our rhetorical intervention, first, explicitly connects the current working conditions in academia to the general process of neoliberalization; second, illustrates how online education platforms (widely known as learning management systems, such as Blackboard or Canvas) mediate important aspects of the academic labor process; and third, reflects on how these dynamics make faculty unionizing both urgent and particularly challenging.

Neoliberal Developments: Capitalism and the Emergence of Uber University

Before we examine concrete teaching and learning practices, it is important to historically connect the decomposition[4] of academic labor to the general process of neoliberalization.

Recognizing the importance of preserving the Humboldtian normative model of the university,[5] our critique of capitalism's co-development with higher education explicitly means to avoid a simplistic discourse denouncing the regimentation and commodification of an otherwise idealized notion of the scholar.[6] We detect a pressing need to 'depurate' the understanding of higher education from its idealization as a platonic/idealist imagery of *akademia*, supposedly propelled by vocation and "creative inspirational work"[7] While those idealizations help constitute faculty's self-understanding and professional identity,[8] and provide a way to cope with general societal expectations,[9] we assume the integration of higher education into the capitalist mode of production to be a given fact.[10]

The historical conditions for such neoliberal transition slowly but steadily crystallized with the early interaction between capitalism and higher education, as the post–World War II context witnessed a shift away from public funding[11] and the general trend towards "accumulation by dispossession."[12] As Karl Polanyi describes it, the expansion of capital's presence in higher education implied a broader cognitive shift, which framed educational knowledge as a commodity/object.[13] This objectification meant the preponderance of commensurability and standardization principles, allowing for the quantification costs and outcomes of education as an economic enterprise.

Higher education, therefore, did not simply experience capitalist expansion as a passive 'victim.' Rather, the co-development between capital and particular scholastic traditions such as structural functionalism, for example, suggests how the academy actively contributed to create an empiricist ideology that transformed fluid processes into quantifiable 'objective' products. Thus, while capitalist needs shaped the university, the university 'academized' capital, as capital appropriated ideologies and techno-knowledge that originally emerged in academia. Silicon Valley's technological utopianism, linking venture capitalism and computer science, constitutes a particularly telling example.

Several scholars have acknowledged the process of privatization and the permeation of corporate logic into higher education. Notions such as 'McDonaldization,' 'academic capitalism,' and 'corporate university'[14] describe a trend that started in the 1990s and gradually increased with the multiple economic downturns that brought funding cuts in public education, together with the infusion of private capital. While those studies pointed towards the casualization and Taylorization of academic labor, we use here 'Uberization' to try to understand how academic labor moved into the sphere of the gig economy. Concisely, 'gig economy' refers to the restructuring brought by digital technologies towards a general casualization of working, which becomes on-demand and freelancing, thus reflecting the transition from Fordist to post-Fordist labor organization and value extraction.[15]

The tendency towards Uberization[16] not only exacerbates characteristics already implied by the so-called McDonaldization, but it also sheds light on a new, complex post-Fordist labor process that implies precarity, digitalization via the massive incorporation of information and communications technologies (ICTs), and the increasing propensity to displace the 'business risk and costs' of education to faculty. Additional post-Fordist features include the tension between a structure of power that controls our labor and the process of subjectification of academicians. We, subjectivities shaped by our academic labor, thus operate as self-employed, self-activated, and self-exploited; self-outsourced, freelancing, and (partially) assessing our own performance. Such a subjectification process is significantly implemented by digital and mobile technologies.[17]

Lorenz provides a useful framework of continuity between Fordism and post-Fordism, understood as shifting "its focus from rights to 'risks.'"[18] In the context of academic labor, this transfer of risks and costs to faculty means that we are no longer solely seen as producers of academic commodities, but also responsible for commercializing them, and thus subject to last-minute reappointments or terminations if a particular product does not 'sell' well—in other words, low enrollment. Thus, *de facto* the transfer of risks and costs erodes the material base of the right to academic freedom. As Giroux points out, many faculty are now expected to be "social entrepreneurs" and enjoy it.[19]

The Contradictory Constitution of Academic Labor

To better understand such an Uberized condition, it is useful to consider labor process theory,[20] looking at how labor is contradictorily constituted. In our specific case, we concentrate on its 'digital' and 'free' aspects. First, by digital, we do not simply refer to the introduction of digital technology within the academic context, but also to how such technology both reflects and affects changes in the way labor is arranged and value is extracted. Because capital increasingly relies on cognitive/linguistic and knowledge labor, its capability to interact with higher education has significantly increased, making it a crucial sector for post-Fordist accumulation.[21] As Allmer points out, the process of integration and interaction of universities with post-Fordist capital "had an effect on the working conditions, practices and relations of subjects."[22]

Such integration also helped produce a paradoxical environment where a strong trajectory towards further levels of commodification (exemplified by the growing prominence of online education) stands side by side with a renewed sense of social justice characterized by anti-racist, feminist, and decolonial sensibilities.[23] As we will discuss later on, it is from such a contradictory development that some positive conditions for organization may emerge.

Many of us also experience academic labor as limitless, precarious, and ambivalently 'free'—in the twofold sense of unpaid and voluntary.[24] On the one hand, free means unpaid, because Uberization implies a significant offsetting of production costs from the employer to the employee. In our experience, this is exemplified by the costs of producing and reproducing scholarship. For instance, while in our research-intensive type of job contract and tenure and promotion conditions, there are expectations to attend multiple academic conferences per year; the university hardly provides enough funds to pay for the expenses of a single national conference. *De facto*, such lack of funding places faculty in the material and psychological condition of precarity.

Free also means voluntary, at least to a degree, because our reasons to work derive from a varying *ratio* of compelling necessities and genuine motivation. Reflecting the Marxian distinction between work and labor, functioning as an academic laborer in 'Uber University' implies both *free work* as an unconstrained, voluntary, and creative product that can even dis-alienate through its personal creative aspects, and also *free labor* as unpaid and unregulated productive services.[25]

In this context, studies have drawn on participant observation and interviews to show faculty's increasing difficulties in coping with job responsibilities that constantly blur the lines between working time and spare time, public/working space and private space.[26] While producing scholarship often requires tasks to be performed outside of academic walls (e.g., fieldwork, *in vivo* approaches, empirical engagements with phenomena), digital and mobile technologies have served to 'domesticate' our profession as scholarly writing and administrative tasks are performed from home.[27] Domestication here refers both to more flexibility and more informality in terms of the level of hours and engagement, as well as to domesticated subjects that steadily activate on a 'project by project' basis—a defining characteristic of the 'gig' economy.

Internalizing domestication frequently leads us to moralize those voluntary and gratuitous services as part of a 'gift economy' logic. In our university, this is epitomized by the constant administration appeals to our status as a "minority serving" institution, effectively placing us in the terrain for free labor by linking our job to a vocation, as well as to abstract notions of 'social justice,' 'democratization of education,' or 'community engagement.' For example, in our personal experiences, current trends of low student enrollments translate into proposals to 'freely' recruit prospective students from high school communities who cannot afford to visit our department. This creates a dangerous ambivalence, combining the genuine vocational and community engagement values of 'reaching out' with the corporate interests of an institution that receives much of its revenues from tuition fees.

Despite internalized ideologies about academia, the reality is that Uber Universities place us into a hard condition of precarity. First, this happens in terms of objective labor relations and contractual insecurity. According to a recent American Association of University Professors report, more than 40% of current faculty positions in the US are part time, and over 70% are non-tenure-track positions, including mostly lecturers and part-time instructors.[28] Second, faculty internalize such precarity due to their incapacity to meet expectations attached to present employment and future employability. Consequently, precarious academic labor leads to 'free' and even self-funded academic labor, since most academics must rely on their own resources to reproduce the expected conditions of employment and employability. These broad discursive formations connect with more specific discursive practices that domesticate our labor. As we demonstrate in the next section, communication ideologies that shape online education signal the emergence of gig labor in Uber academia.

The Pitfalls of Connectivity and Connectedness in Online Learning Discourse

In this section, we examine the structure and dominant discourses around online education, as well the 'learning management system' that supports our online teaching and shapes the kinds of interactions that (do not) take place with our students. We focus on two united but distinct processes of fetishism enabled by communicative idea(l)s of connectivity and connectedness. We argue that these processes foster, first, the mass production and consumption of our labor, and second, the systematic erasure of the "unruly bodies" of both students and faculty.[29]

Online Teaching as Transmission of Information

Reflecting on the general process of digitalization pushed by current capitalism, van Dijck uses the term "connectivity" to describe a condition conducive to the monetization of users' networks and intermediary capitalist platforms. "Connectivity" consists of "automated forms of connections that are engineered and manipulated" and have quickly "developed into valuable revenue." "Connectedness," however, describes a normative principle operating in the social, which capitalizes on a rhetoric of relationality and communicability that can potentially "disassemble platforms and reassemble sociality."[30] Connectedness reflects that particular utopic thrust, which consistently accompanies the emergence and introduction of new technologies,[31] and that speaks to the genuine hopes about how digital technology can significantly improve our lives. However, the uncovering of power relations of this allegedly neutral online environment reveals a profound asymmetry between the two components. Such unevenness advances overall fetishistic processes.

Crucially, connectivity and connectedness represent two competing ideologies of mediated communication.[32] Connectivity tends to naturalize communication as a transmission instrument, a logistical resource that succeeds when useful information is transported from point/speaker 'A' to point/speaker 'B'; connectedness, on the other hand, conveys an idea and practice of communication as a constant enactment of communal rituals of social integration, which is aimed at the production and reproduction of a community united by shared meanings and values.

In the case of online teaching, knowledge is fetishized via the ideological subsumption of connectedness under connectivity, which facilitates movement from knowledge-process to knowledge objectified as a product. This happens when online classes are generated out of a conversion from a face-to-face format, transforming social relations among people (i.e., instructor and students) into social relations between modules and their associated interfaces—recorded lectures, posts, assignments, and grades. As a result, co-constructed lived experiences are dematerialized and then substantiated in colorful images on online learning management systems (LMS) such as Blackboard or Canvas. The greatest functionality of fetishism in this context is the crystallization, parceling, and platformization of analogic relations into digital ones.

Thus, in the different courses that we have taught online, the pedagogical relationship with students has been almost entirely reduced to technical questions of connectivity—problems accessing the reading/viewing material, uploading assignments, or finding a grade, for example. Our occupation almost exclusively turns into providing some kind of IT support to the class, as well as being the 'arbitrator' of a course that *de facto* operates as a board game, that is, made by points to be earned and lost according to a given set of rules called 'syllabus.' Fetishism transforms the interactive and exploratory aspects of learning into a highly strategic game of resource management—of time, points, and content.

Online Teaching as Disembodied 'Prosumption'

When examining public discourses around online teaching, we can observe how the idea(l) of connectedness promotes these practices as part of an effort to democratize higher education. Online courses are linked to a rhetoric of giving access to people who would not be able to obtain a college degree otherwise, due to geographic and/or 'work-life balance' constraints. However, a closer look at how this kind of educational 'product' is typically marketed reveals that 'democratization' is far from the driving goal for universities. Rather, the goal is to maximize the profits of consumption while minimizing the costs of production. In our institution's website, for example, prospective online graduate students are interpellated with statements like: "The power to choose when and where learning takes place makes the other sacrifices for grad school much more bearable and its payoff—financial or otherwise—sweeter" and "There's a reason why online grad school is so popular among international students, too: there are no visa issues."

There is no attempt to expand connectedness in order to "disassemble platforms and reassemble sociality."[33] Rather, the way society is already unequally assembled—with, for example, racialized foreign students banned from obtaining visas, or working-class students having to make 'financial sacrifices'—is the basis on which to build an online presence and help students enhance their 'human capital.' Being empowered, for students, is framed as 'choosing' when and where to connect, but these 'choices' always take place within the restrictions that shape available connectivity. In this realm, connectedness is subsumed under connectivity through the powerful discourse of efficiency, choice, and control.

Moreover, our brief survey of the predominant discourses on online education promotion also reveals how the ideological components of post-Fordist labor penetrate the ideal worker profile of higher education students. University of Illinois Online programs list arguments such as "Flexible schedule and environment," and "Self-discipline and responsibility." Purdue mentions "balancing job with education," "individualized learning style," "de-localized learning" and "flexibility." Minnesota State describes successful learners as having "effective and appropriate communication skills," "technical skills," or "motivation and independence."[34] Thus, students' ideological socialization as post-Fordist subjects begins *even before* entering the labor environment, (re)creating a social logic of ICT connectivity, self-reliance, and self-activation.

Digital Borders as Embodied/Physical Barriers

The promotion examples discussed in the preceding paragraph also show how the annihilation of time and space constraints previously mentioned also reverses itself. Here, universities enthusiastically abolish digital borders, only to reinforce physical ones, as 'undesirable' international students *de facto* do not receive the visa that would allow them to be legitimately present on campus, and in-state, 'non-traditional' students are not incentivized to occupy these spaces either. This potential disappearance of marked bodies from educational spaces risks exacerbating their social invisibility. Thus, the connectivity/connectedness tension resurfaces. The technologically driven platform aspires to emancipation, while capitalizing on prospective online students' marginal(ized) social position, rather than aiding in its eradication.

In the idealized virtual world, as Giroux observed, a divide begins to materialize as 'traditional' (i.e., normative) students are offered the richer experience of social interaction, cooperative critical thinking, and problem-solving and the potential to forge a collective identity, and those who do not fit into the racial, class, gender, or ability 'norm' are relegated to low-investment, low-cost—for the university—education.[35] Thus, when put at the service of a 'gig' economy, distance education runs the risk of becoming "a conduit through which unruly bodies are channeled, leaving neoliberal structures uninterrupted."[36] Ultimately, through the potential segregation of alternative ideas, people, and practices into online spaces, 'accessible,' 'flexible,' and supposedly democratizing online education, paradoxically, capitalizes on and exacerbates pre-existing inequalities.

The prospective picture is one where digital education is rapidly becoming the 'second-class' education. The online student population, while bearing the weight of structural inequalities that often translates into a need for more institutional and informal support and networking, are left with no easy access to the physical facilities where such support mostly happens—on-campus organizations, libraries, or informal, face-to-face mentoring. In spite of this, they are expected to perform as 'super-students' and "do it all," which often means "juggling multiple responsibilities"—including full-time jobs or family-related duties—that may leave little or no time for thoughtful engagement with course materials, all in the name of "flexibility."

Similar processes can be observed among faculty. The naturalization of a transmission model of communication documented earlier significantly impairs our operational environment, as well as our self-understanding of who we are/must be as workers. Contextualizing online education within the enterprise of knowledge production, we see that both instructors and students have become prosumers: 'producers' and 'consumers' of knowledge.[37]

While online education exponentially expands a course's reach and potential 'consumers,' it also reduces the amount of paid labor that educators put into developing a particular class. Once created, the same 'shell'—a term that powerfully summons the impoverishing implications of the fetishist process—can be easily recycled by any instructor over and over again.[38] Faculty are transformed into "mere producers of marketable instructional commodities" that they may or may not themselves 'deliver.' Such "standardization" and "rationalization of course materials" thus contributes to deskilling, disqualifying and—why not say it—demotivating the workforce.[39]

In our department, for example, online courses have increased in the last years by 35%, while tenured faculty has decreased by roughly 30%.[40] Most online teaching is thus carried by non-tenure-track faculty, part-time instructors, and graduate students. Even though these bodies are hardly visible,[41] this is also a gendered and raced phenomenon, since women of color are overrepresented in contingent appointments. Perhaps most interestingly, teaching online has also become a viable option for the remaining tenure-track faculty, who have seen their purchasing power progressively diminished and are resorting to a teaching overload to compensate for this loss or to finance their 'free' research duties. Paradoxically then, the production of capital in a "teaching factory" is completed, with online instructors' labor supporting a system that is responsible for our precarity.

Dis/Organized Academia: Creating a 'Collective Speech'

While the picture painted is grim, for better or worse it is destined to change. After all, the whole idea of contextualizing academic labor within the gig economy consists of acknowledging the profound changes the field is currently experiencing. As disempowering as our conditions may seem, they can actually lead to stronger, longer, and more effective struggles.

Thus, 'gig academia' may be normalizing precarity enough to achieve something that, in recent decades, has been little more than a utopia in the United

States: the resurgence of labor unions or possibly a labor path to implement the democratic ideal behind the Humboldtian ideal.[42] The most recent Pew Research survey available at this time shows 55% of Americans have a positive view of unions, with a remarkable 40% of Republicans sharing this view.[43] In educational contexts, the last few years have witnessed a sort of momentum, with new unions being formed by Harvard and Yale graduate students, faculty unionizing in states like Oregon, Michigan, Illinois, and New York, and last but not least, successful teacher strikes in West Virginia, Oklahoma, and Arizona. Unionizing efforts are also emerging in other, highly precarized realms of the gig economy. The logistics and transportation sectors in many Western countries, for example, are witnessing the growing relevance of self-organized unions.[44]

While we are aware that these dynamics are not universal,[45] the Uberization of the university makes organizing more *exigent* than ever, in the sense of both necessary and difficult. First of all, why is it difficult? Drawing on Alquati's reflections on the dialectics of technical decomposition and political composition of labor, we argue that the main reason is that capital tries to decompose us as a collective, thus producing obstacles to organizing.[46] In the context of gig academia, the changes we sketched throughout this chapter point towards the political potential of the 'cybertariat.' The cybertariat is a political subject and a site of struggle where the "impacts of systemic casualization, the intensification of work, cultures of audit, surveillance and performance management, alongside both entrenched and newer inequalities"[47] are made visible and heard as collective issues. Thus, acknowledging the increasingly common ways in which our labor is decomposed—by the increased spatial, structural, and ideological distance that separates academic workers—can be a first, strong step towards effective recomposition.

The structural constraints that surround organizing in the US make this particularly challenging. Legal scholars note that collective bargaining, when allowed, typically happens at the "enterprise level," rather than across a whole sector.[48] This means that negotiations affect working conditions within an individual company—or institution—and not the conditions of all workers in an industry, regardless of whether they are unionized. Enterprise-level bargaining thus discourages broad alliances beyond a specific workplace or what, according to Alquati would signal a "horizontal integration," a recomposition of different professions that aspires to sector composition rather than just labor collectives within one profession.[49] Such a procedure also incentivizes aggressive corporate or institutional campaigns against unions and their members, since managers and administrators see a direct correlation between a union and the possibility of having to negotiate wages and/or benefits.

In our own organizing experience with the United Academic of University of New Mexico (UA-UNM), this expectation translated into self-imposed clandestinity during most of the organizing process, paradoxically atomizing workers into one-on-one, private conversations, rather than presenting a common, widely supported, public project from the beginning. These strategies risk symbolically situating unions as an outside, self-serving, subversive element of the university structure, rather than a natural component of it—not only for administrators, but also for faculty. Such framing diminishes the potential for strong, broad alliances among faculty, making the recomposition process slow, fragmented, and often frustrating.

Despite these limitations, we may still develop vertical alliances that acknowledge the different experiences of different kinds of faculty, as well as other kinds of labor on which faculty depend to do their job—clerical, technical, manual.[50] Such a recomposition may also include those we are supposed to serve—our students and the larger community. The strong vocational element inserted into our job description, together with the proliferation of university 'brands' that ideally speak to all those affiliated with a higher education institution, can aid in presenting faculty demands based not on self-interest, but on community needs. Here we can learn from the recent teacher strikes by incorporating those with whom we share the workspace, as well as our students, into a view of organizing as means to guarantee that the university fully delivers on its mission.

One way to acknowledge that our shared anxieties as precarious workers are systemic is to proactively affirm "slow scholarship" as a mode of knowledge production that acts not only on time, but also on power structures.[51] Slow scholarship means claiming more time to prepare and teach our undergraduate courses and our graduate seminars, to collaborate with common/public initiatives, and to process and help our students process what we read and do, all as "part of the struggle for accessible higher education and for the decolonization of knowledge, in which experimentation, creativity, different epistemologies, and dissidence are all valued and encouraged."[52] In this sense, 'slowing things down' may provide an opportunity for recomposition that can help consolidate a diverse but collective identity.

Normalizing slowing down can also be part of an organizing strategy that acknowledges and acts upon the fact that, even within the cybertariat, there are important lines of division, starting with the increasing segregation of women and people of color into online teaching. An effective movement thus needs to recognize that, for some of us, *there is no other way* but to go slow, whether this means working in English as a foreign language on a regular basis, or coping with the prevalent sexism, ableism, and racism in academia that exacerbates our own and others' surveillance and forces people of color to over-prepare for lectures, conference presentations, or even supposedly 'easy' service tasks.[53]

Ultimately, slow scholarship can be put at the service of literally making space for other(ed) bodies in the context of Uber universities. We must ensure that institutional strategies, even when they are developed in the name of 'diversity,' do not exacerbate the 'gig academia' logic, and we must refuse individual-based psychologization of responses to a toxic academic environment. This means, for example, shifting the focus away from individual behaviors that concentrate on achieving 'work-life balance' and other forms of self-management and self-care as the remedy to the problems of overwhelm. It means actually joining and uniting faculty in the struggle for a "different organization of learning, teaching, writing, and working."[54]

A Concluding Note: Platforms of Capital and Platforms of Struggle

We have examined the conditions of academic labor in relation to the general capitalist developments and their tendency towards an Uberized gig-economy academia. We have defined ours as a rhetorical intervention advocating for a materialist look at our profession, with the aim of debunking idealized notions of the academic profession while problematizing the typical rapprochements against an academia that, allegedly, does not engage enough with civil society.[55]

We thus try to reinterpret the world before trying to change it, arguing that such engagement should start with an inquiry about our own condition as laborers and the purpose of the university as a whole. Accordingly, we invoked unionization as a tentative answer to the dilemma of being involved with the general issues of social justice and defending the working rights of a particular sector.[56] Especially when such sector's identity relies so much on vocation, 'gift economy,' and free labor, and when "the costs and risks of research have thereby been socialized, while the benefits of innovation privatized."[57] Precarity, from this perspective, constitutes an opportunity to intervene in common sense, building the necessary "chains of equivalence"[58] among all the different forms of work that make up a university so that we can unite in solidarity and demand decent working conditions for all.

Second, our rhetorical intervention also problematizes recurrent narratives on (media) technology and education, which cannot be celebrated as unreflective progress or undisputed disruption. We used the tension of connectivity and connectedness to expound our dialectical understanding of digital technology in higher education. Thus, we would argue that what makes online teaching/learning problematic is not online platforms *per se*, but the relations of production in which such educational processes take place.

Online teaching is here to stay, and its educational use-value cannot be simply superimposed to its exchange value. However, if we cannot reject it, we can rework it, changing its meaning and associated practices to delink them from the most dysfunctional facets of the gig economy, organizing to change the conditions in which (online) teaching happens, and ultimately joining the broader struggle against capitalism.

Notes

1. Kathleen McConnell, "Labored Speech: Reconsidering How Communication Studies Works," *Review of Communication* 18 (2) (2018): 67–84, https://doi.org/10.1080/15358593.2018.
2. Jose van Dijk, *The Culture of Connectivity. A Critical History of Social Media* (Oxford: Oxford University Press, 2013).
3. Catherine McKercher and Vincent Mosco, *Knowledge Workers in the Information Society* (Lanham: Lexington Books, 2007).

4. Romano Alquati, *Organic Composition of Capital and Labor-Power at Olivetti* (1961), www.viewpointmag.com/2013/09/27/organic-composition-of-capital-and-labor-power-at-olivetti-1961/.
5. L. Roger Geiger, *Knowledge and Money, Research. Universities and the Paradox of the Marketplace* (Palo Alto: Stanford University Press, 2004).
6. Lisa Lucas, *The Research Game in Academic Life* (Maidenhead: McGraw-Hill International, 2006).
7. David Harvie, "Value Production and Struggle in the Classroom: Teachers Within, Against and Beyond Capital," *Capital & Class* 30, no. 1 (2006): 1–32.
8. Sue Clegg, "Academic Identities Under Threat?" *British Educational Research Journal* 34, no. 3 (2008): 329–45.
9. Nick Butler and Sverre Spoelstra, "The Regime of Excellence and the Erosion of Ethos in Critical Management Studies," *British Journal of Management* 25, no. 3 (2014): 538–50, https://doi.org/10.1111/1467-8551.12053.
10. Gary Rhoades and Sheyla Slaughter, *Academic Capitalism and the New Economy: Markets, State, and Higher Education* (Baltimore: JHU Press, 2004).
11. Harry A. Giroux, "Neoliberalism, Corporate Culture, and the Promise of Higher Education: The University as a Democratic Public Sphere," *Harvard Educational Review* 72, no. 4 (2002): 425–64.
12. David Harvey, *The Enigma of Capital and the Crises of Capitalism* (London: Profile Books, 2007).
13. Karl Polanyi, *The Great Transformation: The Political and Economic Origins of Our Time* (Boston, MA: Beacon Press, 2001).
14. George Ritzer, *The McDonaldization of Society* (Thousand Oaks, CA: Pine Forge Press, 2004); Sheila Slaughter and Larry Leslie, *Academic Capitalism: Politics, Policies, and the Entrepreneurial University* (2003), http://lst-iiep.iiep-unesco.org/cgi-bin/wwwi32.exe/[in=epidoc1.in]/?t2000=010922/(100); Giroux, "Neoliberalism, Corporate Culture, and the Promise of Higher Education," 2002.
15. Nick Srnicek, *Platform Capitalism* (Cambridge and Malden, MA: Polity Press, 2017).
16. Trebor Scholz, *Uberworked and Underpaid: How Workers Are Disrupting the Digital Economy* (Cambridge: Polity Press, 2016).
17. Nick Dyer-Witheford, "Cognitive Capitalism and the Contested Campus," in *Engineering Culture: On the Author as (Digital) Producer*, ed. Geoff Cox and Joasia Krysa (New York: Autonomedia, 2005), 71–93.
18. Chris Lorenz, "If You're So Smart, Why Are You Under Surveillance? Universities, Neoliberalism, and New Public Management," *Critical Inquiry* 38, no. 3 (2013): 599–629, 602.
19. Giroux, "Neoliberalism, Corporate Culture, and the Promise of Higher Education," 2002.
20. Harry Braverman, *Labor and Monopoly Capital: The Degradation of Work in the Twentieth Century* (New York: Monthly Review Press, 1974).
21. Dyer-Witheford, "Cognitive Capitalism and the Contested Campus."
22. Thomas Allmer, "Precarious, Always-On and Flexible: A Case Study of Academics as Information Workers," *European Journal of Communication* 33, no. 4 (2018): 381–95, 382.
23. Gabriella Gutiérrez y Muhs, Flores Niehmann, Yolanda González, and Angela Harris, eds., *Presumed Incompetent: The Intersections of Race and Class for Women in Academia* (Boulder: University of Colorado Press, 2012).
24. Tiziana Terranova, "Free Labour," in *Digital Labour: The Internet as Playground and Factory*, ed. T. Scholz (New York: Routledge, 2013), 33–57.
25. Ibid.
26. Andrew Ross, *Nice Work If You Can Get It: Life and Labor in Precarious Times* (New York: New York University Press, 2009).
27. Sergio Bologna and Andrea Fumagalli, *Il lavoro autonomo di seconda generazione. Scenari del postfordismo in Italia* (Milano: Feltrinelli, 1997).

28. American Associations of University Professors (AAUP), "Visualizing Change: The Annual Report on the Economic Status of the Profession, 2016–17," *aaup.com* (2017), www.aaup.org/file/FCS_2016-17.pdf.
29. Kristin Smith and Jeffrey Donna, "Critical Pedagogies in the Neoliberal University: What Happens When They Go Digital?" Special Issue: *Critical Geographies of Education* 57, no. 3 (2013): 372–80.
30. Van Dijk, *The Culture of Connectivity*, 4, 12, 24.
31. Vincent Mosco, *The Digital Sublime: Myth, Power and Cyberspace* (Cambridge, MA: MIT Press, 2004).
32. James Carey, *Communication as Culture. Essays on Media and Society* (Boston: Unwin Hyman, 1989).
33. van Dijk, *The Culture of Connectivity*, 24.
34. https://online.illinois.edu/; https://online.purdue.edu/; www.minnstate.edu/online/.
35. Giroux, "Neoliberalism, Corporate Culture, and the Promise of Higher Education."
36. Smith and Donna, "Critical Pedagogies in the Neoliberal University," 370.
37. Szymusiak Tomasz, *Prosumer—Prosumption—Prosumerism* (Düsseldorf: OmniScriptum GmbH & Co. KG, 2015).
38. T. Allmer, "Academic Labour, Digital Media and Capitalism," *Critical Sociology* 45, no. 4–5 (2019): 599–615, https://doi.org/10.1177/0896920517735669.
39. Giroux, "Neoliberalism, Corporate Culture, and the Promise of Higher Education," 448.
40. In the aftermath of the COVID-19 pandemic restriction measures and as in most institutions, 99% of courses moved online. See Chrysi Rapanta, Luca Botturi, Peter Goodyear, et al., "Online University Teaching During and After the Covid-19 Crisis: Refocusing Teacher Presence and Learning Activity," *Postdigital Science Education* 2 (2020): 923–45, https://doi.org/10.1007/s42438-020-00155-y.
41. Patti Duncan, "Hot Commodities, Cheap Labor: Women of Color in the Academy," *Frontiers: A Journal of Women Studies* 35, no. 3 (2014): 39–63.
42. Stephen Stolzoff, "One Thing Millennials Haven't Killed: Labor Unions," *qz.com* (2018), accessed July 5, 2019, https://qz.com/work/1399288/labor-unions-are-on-the-rise-for-people-under-age-35/.
43. Richard L. Trumka, "Can Organized Labor Come Back?" *Yale Insights* (2018), accessed July 5, 2019, https://insights.som.yale.edu/insights/can-organized-labor-come-back. Pauline van Mourik Broekman, Gary Hall, Ted Beyfield, Shaun Hides, and Simon Worthington, *Open Education: A Study in Disruption (Disruptions)* (New York: Rowman and Littlefield, 2015).
44. Marco Briziarelli, "Spatial Politics in the Digital Realm: Or the Productive Tension Between Logistics and Precarity," *Cultural Studies*, no. 4 (2018): 1–19.
45. Ana Alakovska and Rosalind Gill, "De-Westernizing Creative Labour Studies: The Informality of Creative Work From an Ex-Centric Perspective," *International Journal of Cultural Studies* 22, no. 2 (2019): 195–212.
46. Alquati, *Organic Composition of Capital and Labor-Power at Olivetti*.
47. R. Gill and N. Donaghue, "Resilience, Apps and Reluctant Individualism: Technologies of Self in the Neoliberal Academy," *Women's Studies International Forum* 54 (2016): 91–99, https://doi.org/10.1016/j.wsif.2015.06.016.
48. Dylan Matthews, "Europe Could Have the Secret to Saving American Unions," *Vox.com*, 2017, accessed July 5 2019, www.vox.com/policy-and-politics/2017/4/17/15290674/union-labor-movement-europe-bargaining-fight-15-ghent.
49. Alquati, *Organic Composition of Capital and Labor-Power at Olivetti*.
50. Almer, "Academic Labour, Digital Media and Capitalism".
51. Alison Mountz, Anne Bonds, Becky Mansfield, Jenna Loyd, Jennifer Hyndman, Margaret Walton-Roberts, Ranu Basu, Risa Whitson, Roberta Hawkins, Trina Hamilton, and Winifred Curran, "For Slow Scholarship: A Feminist Politics of Resistance Through Collective Action in the Neoliberal University," *ACME: An International*

Journal for Critical Geographies 14, no. 4 (2015): 1235–59, accessed July 5, 2019, www.acme-journal.org/index.php/acme/article/view/1058.
52. Ibid.
53. Michelle A. Holling, "*You Intimidate Me* as a Microaggressive Controlling Image to Discipline Womyn of Color Faculty," *Southern Communication Journal* 84, no. 2 (2018): 99–112, https://doi.org/10.1080/1041794X.2018.1511748.
54. Mountz et al., "For Slow Scholarship," 1248.
55. Dip Koomar and Aziz Choudry, *Learning From the Ground Up: Global Perspectives on Social Movements and Knowledge Production* (Berlin: Springer, 2010).
56. Dyer-Witheford, "Cognitive Capitalism and the Contested Campus," 76.
57. Ernesto Laclau and Chantal Mouffe, *Hegemony and Socialist Strategy* (London: Verso, 1985).
58. Ibid.

IV
Media
Negotiating the Gig Economy

9
"¿QUÉ HAY DETRÁS DE TODO?"
Opacity, Precarity, and the Unwaged Labor of Latina Audiobook Narrators

Ruth L. Nuñez

Introduction

The world of audiobooks represents a generative site for informing our understanding of how the future of digitally mediated creative work is being structured within the gig economy, by whom, and to what effects and affects. I come to this research as a Screen Actors Guild-American Federation of Television and Radio Artists (SAG-AFTRA) union member and audiobook narrator;[1] someone who brings the text to the audiosphere via her voice, her creativity, and the skill with which to connect with her audience on an emotional level.[2] I began narrating audiobooks following my work on a project that received a Grammy nomination for "Best Spoken Word Album" in 2012. At the wrap party for the project, I was approached by audiobook producers. I thought of this job, as many gig workers are encouraged to see their labor, as an occasional source of additional income. Neither the pay rate nor the opportunities to work were significant enough for me to consider it otherwise. Yet, as a book lover, I figured, "Why not get paid to read books from time to time?" After experiencing a series of workplace frictions, however, I paused and took a closer look. Realizing that what I considered to be a 'side job' is actually a key component to a growing global multibillion-dollar industry, I understood that the media's celebratory discourses did not align with what I was experiencing at work.

Audiobook narration is being structured as a form of precarious labor within today's gig economy, and the audiobook ecosystem is opaque by design. News stories contribute to this obfuscation by keeping our focus on the overall financial strength of this industry. They tell us that US audiobook sales were estimated at $2.1 billion in 2016,[3] sales increased to $2.5 billion in 2017,[4] and the trend continued in 2018 with another 22.7% increase to over $3 billion.[5] Far from being a sideline of the publishing industry, audiobooks have been its "fastest-growing format,"[6] helping to offset declines in frontlist and e-book sales for years.[7] Yet, it seems that it is the publishers and retailers who benefit from what some refer to as the audiobook revolution, not the performers themselves who bring the books to life.

This disparity is significant given that SAG-AFTRA defines audiobooks as "audio recordings of published texts performed by professional narrators."[8] SAG-AFTRA's definition identifies three key components to an audiobook and their corresponding labor areas: the text/author, the recording of audio/engineer, and the performance of the text/narrator. It makes no demands, however, that these narrators' compensation be commensurate to their contributions, a fact that both the industry members and a mostly laudatory media generally fail to acknowledge.

In order to look beyond the surface of these celebratory market discourses and not be mystified by their neoliberal framings, I interrogate what the audiobook industry's perspective elides about the labor process, where value is created.[9] By recalibrating and expanding the focus to issues of labor, both visible and invisible, I bring workers and their labor conditions to light. In particular, I focus on the experiences of US Latina audiobook narrators because their perspectives offer us the opportunity to detangle the racial and gendered registers of this digital labor environment. And, today, when any analysis of digital media structures necessitates a transnational lens, the views of US Latinas are key because they bring transnational and intersectional lenses to their self-reflexive views as creative workers. Plus, while they are one of the most under- and misrepresented communities in legacy media (relative to their numbers in the US),[10] Latinas are an important and growing segment of the audiobook labor force.[11]

To bring their voices to the forefront, I employ a Chicana/Latina feminist methodology and engage in *pláticas* (culturally relevant, in-depth, open-ended interviews) because this method allows workers the space to explain in their own words what this growing commercial ecosystem looks—and feels—like from their perspectives. Examining audiobook narration from the intersection of Chicana/Latina feminism and labor demonstrates how opacity and precarity enable abusive labor practices in digital arenas and how this precarity is unevenly distributed. *Pláticas* with three Latina narrators help illuminate the ways in which gig economy labor structures have been woven into media industry production processes. They also point to a link between the intersectional marginalization of US Latinas in traditional media and their exacerbated exploitation in digital environments.

The insights from this work may help support union organizing efforts by encouraging an expanded understanding of digital era concerns. Ultimately, I argue that we must demand transparency of gig economy labor structures and reimagine more inclusive worker-centered alternatives.

Historical Context and Situating the Current Boom

The contemporary moment has seen audiobooks move firmly into the mainstream commercial market, such that their sale and consumption can even be considered a 'boom'. The Audio Publishers Association (APA) tracks the audiobook's US trajectory by primarily highlighting technological developments.[12] In 1997, Audible debuted the first digital audio player; in 2003, "Audible's deal with Apple," which made audiobooks available on iTunes, increased public awareness and access to digital audiobooks. From 2003 to 2004, CDs replaced cassettes as the preferred format. In 2005, "Preloaded Digital Players . . . were created." The APA ended their trajectory in 2008 when "digital downloads surpassed CDs as the most popular audiobook format." It is worth noting that 2008 was also the year that Amazon purchased Audible for $300 million.[13]

The beginning of today's digital boom can be traced to 2011 when Amazon's Audible launched its Audiobook Creation Exchange (ACX) digital platform, ushering in fundamental changes in audiobook production.[14] ACX is a digital "marketplace" where creatives and rights holders can connect to produce audiobooks. This platform, and others like it, theoretically open up the playing field to a global workforce. The result, the ACX site states, is that "more audiobooks will be made."[15] Audiobook audiences are concurrently growing. Recent APA studies have found that, in 2019, "50% of Americans have listened to an audiobook,"[16] and that "the multiple ways audiobook listeners can digitally access their content are helping them carve out more time to listen."[17] Digital devices such as smart phones, smart speakers, and the ubiquity of Wi-Fi have made these downloadable productions more widely available and accessible than previous formats.

From the industry's perspective, new technologies have simply been meeting evolving consumer needs. As the *Wall Street Journal* reported in 2016, "Smartphones and multitasking have stoked an explosion in audiobooks. . . . Downloadable audiobooks are about half the price of the CD version and can be even cheaper through a subscription service."[18] These facts translate to strong sales figures. Chris Lynch, co-chair of the APA's Research Committee and president and publisher of Simon & Schuster Audio, summarizes, "More audiobooks are being produced and more people are listening than ever."[19]

However, a narrow market perspective gives us an incomplete understanding of the audiobook boom. We must expand our focus to consider the humans who are doing the labor and their labor conditions. Engaging with Marx's labor theory of value, it is important to examine to what degree today's increased production and lower prices are possible because of an imbalanced pay structure, in which the total amount of labor and labor time that narrators contribute to the final audiobook remains out of view and unwaged. We must interrogate who benefits and who loses when our attention is kept away from labor concerns.

As stated, this study looks into labor issues by engaging with Latinidad, because Latina talent is a growing segment of this labor force and because of its deeply rooted transnational registers. As Arlene Dávila tells us, US Latinx media has

> historically been the product of transnational processes... [this] means analyzing at least two industries: one with roots in Latin America and the other with roots in Hollywood... linked to at least three distinct language media worlds in Spanish, in English, and in Portuguese (translated into Spanish).[20]

Such is the case in this context. According to a SAG-AFTRA "Taller de Audiolibros" 2019 workshop, 2018 marked the fourth year in a row with a 20% global increase in audiobook production. Production in the Spanish language market has been particularly rapid, at 33% in 2018. This increase speaks to both a production gap and (foreseeable) demand given that, in 2019, Spanish was second in number of native speakers and third in total language speakers worldwide.[21] The Cervantes Institute 2019 report states that, in the world of books, Spanish is a "language of translation."[22] Globally, it is the sixth language *from* and the third *to* which translations are made. Latina audiobook narrators' potential audiences, therefore, are substantial, given that they contribute their creative work and cultural knowledge to both English- and Spanish-language markets (if not more).

The potential US Latinx market alone is significant: The Latino Media Gap found that "If US Latinos constituted a nation, it would be the 14th largest economy in the world."[23] Today, 18.3% of the US population are Latinx with 13.5% (about 41.5 million) who speak Spanish at home, which does not mean we speak Spanish exclusively.[24] As Jillian Báez finds, "Overall Latina/o audiences appear to oscillate between English-language and Spanish-language media, albeit to different degrees depending on language competency, generation, and class."[25] In other words, Latinx media consumption is dynamic and hybrid.

Nonetheless, when it comes to legacy media targeted at US Latinx audiences, producers continue to marginalize us via problematic portrayals, which include essentializing ideas about race, ethnicity, culture, and linguistic practices. The impacts of these representational decisions are significant. As Báez additionally tells us, "media become the gauge for Latina audiences to measure their status in the United States."[26] It is via media as cultural artifacts that Latinas assess their cultural citizenship; a conceptualizing of citizenship as belonging that extends beyond legal status to include both material and symbolic forms of citizenship.[27] Similarly, Latina media professionals gauge where we stand in our industry's (and the national) imaginary via the quantity and types of characters we are asked to portray. As traditional media fails us, US Latinas turn to digital arenas, like the audiobook industry, to look for additional and more creatively fulfilling labor opportunities. Unsurprisingly, labor protections are not keeping pace in the digital sphere, which increases Latinas', and other marginalized communities', exposure to precarious labor conditions.

Methodology and Method

I engage with Chicana/Latina feminism as my epistemological, methodological, and theoretical framework because this approach centralizes the lives of Latinas and prevents them from being hidden and folded into traditional patriarchal [Latino] and liberal feminist [White female] scholarship.[28] Such an approach to understanding digital labor builds on Sarah T. Roberts's groundbreaking work on commercial content moderation, where she identifies a legion of unseen laborers and brings their working conditions out of the shadows. These perspectives are informed by the ways in which labor—and particularly labor in the information and communications technologies industries (ICT)—is racialized and gendered. Roberts points to Mar Hicks' work as an example of research that reveals how "the histories of technological developments have been subject to structural exclusion of women," and to Venus Green and Melissa Villa-Nicholas, whose works look into the "systemic racial and gender discrimination. . . [that] adversely impacted the burgeoning Black and Latina workforce from meaningful long-term careers" in ICT.[29] Safiya Noble's Black feminist approach to studying Google search further demonstrates how analytical frameworks that center intersections between race and gender offer fruitful ways of understanding digital economies and processes.[30]

Building on this trajectory, I ask what new insights we might gain by analyzing the audiobook ecosystem from the intersection of Chicana/Latina feminism and labor. A Chicana/Latina feminist framework is a critical lens that shifts the focus to people by listening to and honoring their voices and challenging dominant market discourses. It is an intersectional approach that affords the opportunity to interrogate what might seem 'natural' or 'normal' from a dominant lens. It provides us with a toolkit for understanding how precarity might be distributed along racial, gendered, and linguistic lines. As Dolores Delgado Bernal tells us, "a Chicana feminist epistemology . . . becomes a means to resist epistemological racism . . . and to recover untold histories."[31] This approach helps us to unpack the experiences of Latinas in this context and to explain the disparities in labor opportunities and conditions. I also engage in Latinidad as a political move to participate in inscribing Latinas into this history.

The method that I employ is *pláticas*, a culturally relevant interview approach that "aligns with the strong feminist tradition of theorizing from the brown body."[32] *Pláticas* push back against "politics of exclusion"[33] by foregrounding the experiences of US Latinas. They support a Latina feminist commitment to reciprocity. *Pláticas* are not clinical and extractive, but instead ensure that the conversations be a space for open dialog and mutual sharing between researcher and research collaborators, thus contributing to a decolonization of the research process.[34]

I used convenience sampling to identify my collaborators. My inclusion criteria were that they be self-identified Latinas who have worked as audiobook narrators whether under SAG-AFTRA contracts and/or on non-union audiobook projects. My aim was to gain an understanding of their experiences across union statuses. I chose women with differing degrees of narration experience and proximity to me: I had not met all of the women before this study. All three are bilingual (English-Spanish) seasoned professional actresses. The jobs discussed were produced via independent producers. This means that the work locations and conditions varied: from self-recorded sessions at home studios to recording with an engineer at a production house. Our *pláticas* took place between December 2018 and January 2019. Two of the *pláticas* took place in the women's homes and one was via Skype. With their permission, all of the sessions were audio-recorded. My goal was to not miss any nuance that could be lost during the fluidity of our conversations. Having these recordings for future reference and analysis also allowed me to be fully present as we conversed. I later transcribed the recordings and coded them for themes.

Pláticas: Audiobook Narration From Narrators' Points of View

The job of an audiobook narrator is to bring the author's work to the audiosphere via her voice while connecting with the audience on an emotional level. During our *pláticas*, Carmen, Jenny, Graciela, and I discussed the material and affective dimensions of our work and how we understand our labor and this ecosystem to be structured.[35] I have organized the insights from our *pláticas* into four overlapping themes: (1) employer immunity via opacity, (2) invisible, unrecognized, and uncompensated labor, (3) exacerbated exploitation, and (4) the affective impacts of precarious labor.

Employer Immunity via Opacity

During our *pláticas*, it became clear that audiobook employers engage with a series of strategies that infuse opacity into the system. This serves to obfuscate where the labor is taking place, who is laboring, and under what conditions. Three of the key intertwining strategies deployed are information asymmetry, imprecise contracts, and diminished talent representation. I will discuss each individually, but, collectively, these tactics help employers build immunity by yielding them uneven power and at times allowing abusive practices and the accumulation of capital without accountability for (and to) the humans doing the work.[36]

Information Asymmetry

Instances of information asymmetry emerged from the moment Carmen and I began our conversation. Though she is a seasoned actress, Carmen is new to audiobook narration. She recently recorded her first long-form work of nonfiction from her home studio. Her setup consists of a laptop, a mic, editing software, and an internet connection. We began by discussing how this job came about:

C: I had an audition process first. He [the producer] said he had a couple projects lined up. . . . He said that the client had selected my voice . . . so, I still didn't know . . . how long the project was or what the project was . . . I said, "What is the time commitment?" . . . "What are you looking for and I can tell you what my availability is?" . . . I remember him saying something like, "Oh, probably like four hours," like per weekend. . . . At the time that he told me that, I didn't know how long the chapters were or how many chapters there were or how long the textbook was. So, that's why I was, okay great: My weekends are free, and I can even do two full days on the weekend. . . . But, that was woefully underestimated because it doesn't take into account the research, the recording, the post, and the pickups.[37]

Lack of clarity permeated her experience. The producer gave Carmen a lot of different and contradictory time estimates, hindering her ability to assess the actual labor and labor time to which she was committing. He was also unclear about the length of the final audiobook. This is significant because audiobook narrators typically are paid per finished hour (pfh). This means that they are only paid for each hour of the final audiobook. So, absent this information, Carmen does not know how much she will be paid. She also worries that she will not be paid at all because there was no contract. The lack of a contract represented an additional form of information asymmetry; a tactic that further obfuscated the terms of their agreement. Instead, the gig was negotiated via email.

I would like to offer my own experience as another example of how information asymmetry has been deployed by an employer. I booked a job, but when I questioned the pay rate a series of events were activated. First, the producer did not respond to my query. Instead, I received an email from the company's casting department with an 'official' work offer, which was an even lower rate than the original offer. I responded by pointing out that the union's rate sheet supported my argument. At this point, the producer came back into the loop and told me that I was to be paid a lower rate because they have a "tier structure" and some of my previous jobs did not count as audiobooks.[38] I contacted my union and was advised that the producer's definition of audiobooks would likely prevail, so I could either take the job or decline the work. I refused the job. The company came back with a higher offer. However, it seems that this shift only happened because the author had a say on this project, and she had chosen my voice.

Carmen's and my experiences exemplify how information asymmetry or fuzzy information can be deployed as a tactic to control laborers while yielding uneven power in favor of employers. Fortunately, these experiences also provide a glimpse into the potential strength in solidarity building between two of the three key contributors to an audiobook: authors and narrators.[39] In my case, since the author had a say, my fungibility was decreased and my negotiating power increased. This insight matters because it can inform reimaginings of more worker-centered labor structures.

Imprecise Contracts

Current audiobook contracts tend to be imprecise, with the discretion unevenly yielded to the employer. Their main function, it seems, is to protect employers from liabilities; in my experience, except for pension and health contributions, these contracts offer no identifiable worker protections—no work time limits, overtime, late payment penalties, itemized fees for work beyond narration (e.g., engineering, editing, directing), pickup fees, residuals, or explicit protections against future uses of the narrators' work (e.g., for machine learning). Importantly, contracts typically clarify narrators' pfh pay rate as the "only and final amount" that they will be paid, which leaves their actual total labor contributed 'off the books.'[40] These moves bring Marx's concept of exploited surplus value, the concept via which he "intends to show that capitalism is a class society," into the conversation.[41] As Christian Fuchs explains, "Surplus labour time is all labour time that exceeds necessary labour time, remains unpaid, is appropriated for free by capitalists and is transformed into money profit. Surplus value is in substance the materialization of unpaid labour-time."[42]

Regardless of union status, audiobook contracts generally fail to include residuals, which serves to alienate narrators from their work.[43] This is an egregious move, since a platform's design puts it in a privileged position to easily and exactingly record the interactions between sellers and buyers. This means that tracking downloads should facilitate, rather than make more difficult, the establishment of a residual structure as common practice.[44] Contracts also neglect to include penalties to employers for late payments. All of this motivates the question: Who is looking out for narrators' best interests?

Diminished Talent Representation

Typically, one entity in the entertainment industry whose job is to look out for those best interests is a talent agent. Because agents represent several to hundreds of people ("talent," in industry parlance), they have a broader view of the playing field and can thus advise their clients on best practices and negotiate optimal contracts on their behalf. When this relationship is strong and healthy, artists can focus on their work with the assurance that their agent(s) (manager and/or entertainment attorney) will ensure they are treated and compensated fairly on each job. This is why it gave me pause when their notable absence came into focus during our *pláticas*. Carmen mentioned:

C: Years ago, I asked one of my voiceover agents about audiobooks . . . I think I asked her for any recommendations on training or workshops and/

or about doing an audiobook . . . she gave me recommendations and she also said, "It's a lot of work."

Her agent does not represent her in this arena. Jenny, an experienced narrator, also mentioned her agent's warnings:

J: . . . and let me tell you [my agent] I mean, anytime I bring up audiobooks is like, ". . . really? Are you . . . I mean it's an abuse. It's crazy. Why are you going to do it?"

Absent their agents' protections, talent shoulders the responsibility of self-representation. This can effectively weaken narrators' position as we attempt to navigate a sea of information asymmetries within an opaque ecosystem and, in many cases, without negotiating experience, business acumen, or a legal background.

Union representation is also crucial. A key characteristic of precarious labor is that unionizing, if not prohibited, is highly challenging. Admittedly, this is not exactly our case: When workplace frictions arise, union narrators have the option of turning to SAG-AFTRA. Our union represents approximately 160,000 actors, recording artists, singers, dancers, stunt performers, and other media professionals.[45] However, not all audiobook work is unionized. And, for underrepresented communities, like US Latinas, the lack of unionized and creatively substantial work opportunities in traditional media may affect their consenting to abusive labor conditions. Audiobook narration may not be precarious because of the lack of a union, but traditional media's exclusionary practices have an impact on the exploitation of marginalized talent in digital labor arenas.

Invisible, Unrecognized, and Uncompensated Labor

One of the reasons why talent agents may be disincentivized to support clients in audiobook production is due to its notoriously low pay rates.[46] Our *pláticas* revealed the myriad ways in which laborers are being overworked and underpaid. This is in line with Marx's understanding of capitalism. As Fuchs summarizes, "For Marx, capitalism is based on capitalists' permanent theft of unpaid labour from workers."[47]

Jenny is an audiobook veteran. She has worked in this arena since the mid-1990s and has transitioned with it across formats. Jenny shared that one of the ways in which the industry has changed is in the consolidation of labor without commensurate compensation. In the 1990s, for example, directors were included in the audiobook production process. Those roles have increasingly been eliminated and, today, it is either the engineer or the narrator herself who performs this role:

R: *Did you have a director for this [most recent job] too?*
J: Now, they're getting very . . . because the director is now the engineer. They figure that we, as actors are precious with our work, so [they know

you] want to do it the best that you can. So, in a sense, they figure, "we don't need a director, director."

Another example came into focus as Jenny described an experience with self-recording at a production studio:

R: *Why were you in there by yourself?*
J: . . . they make deals with authors that don't have that much money to get it done . . . so, it's . . . okay, so if we have it self-recorded . . . the actor will be the engineer . . . it's basically getting you to do double work. (pause) How about that? But, it sounds . . . you know, that's what happened with freelance, right? It sounds fantastic. But, it's like: Ok, you're your own boss and you can work 24 hours a day. And, you better. Because, otherwise, there will be somebody else who will do it and will probably get the job and we will never call you again.

Job consolidation without compensation is one of the ways in which precarity is built into this labor structure. Jenny's labor as engineer and director were not added to her contract. Rather than be compensated for her ability to manage so many aspects of the production process herself, her combination of skill sets was devalued, remaining contractually invisible. Jenny's comment points to key characteristics of precarious labor: Narrators 'get to freelance,' they are 'on call,' and the threat of 'fungibility' looms over their heads.

At the same time that jobs have been consolidated, pay rates have been decreased:

R: *So, let's talk about the compensation.*
J: Ha.
R: *What is that like for you?*
J: Okay, so going back; books on tape was like the wild, wild: I have six thousand dollars you take it, you don't. . . . Then, all of a sudden CDs come out . . . when your Walkman CD went to the MP3: total silence in the audiobook world. Because it was, "What technology are we going to use? Who is listening where?". . . . Then, it was, "Hey, we have struck a deal with the union." Oh, wow, you're back, what's going on?

This deal included the aforementioned 'pfh' pay rates.

J: . . . which, of course, was like, okay, so it takes many times three hours per finished hour, right? So, you're like, "this doesn't sound exactly right." Cause, it's . . . I'm not a partner in this. I'm just working per hour to get this done. So, it was kind of awkward, but, as I say, you're like, "I kind of like this book. I'll read it anyway" . . . The thing is, [a union job] pays pension and health, so I thought it was a better deal to do it through the union, you know? It's always a better deal, in the long run, for the actor. But, I was surprised. I said, "so what happened to the six thousand dollars? The flat deal?"

R: *That's a huge change. Because it's per finished hour and you can prep for however long it takes you to prep.*

J: Yeah, I mean, forget the work that you do, the prep. I'm talking . . . I was talking even in the studio it's taking you so much longer to record an hour . . . it's at least two hours per hour . . . depending on the difficulty of the thing, you know?

Jenny alludes to the general lack of transparency about budgets and budget allocation that permeates this ecosystem: What happened to the directors? "What happened to the six thousand dollars?" She also points out that the pfh rates do not account for the "difficulty of the thing."

For Carmen, the 'two hours of recording-to-one finished hour' average ratio that is accepted as industry-standard was an extreme underestimation. In addition to providing her home studio, she was expected to be researcher, editor, engineer, proofer, and director without commensurate guidance or compensation. During the production process, she had many questions, from how to approach research in this context, to what equipment to use, to how to label files, and how much post-production she was expected to do. The company provided no answers, which added to her labor time.

R: *How much work do you think, que le calculas más ó menos,*[48] *that it actually took, if you take all of it into consideration?*

C: Yes, so I was blindly working, and I wasn't tracking it. I started to track it, so I would see how long it really was taking and each chapter was different, but . . . you end up averaging 20 to 30 hours per chapter. . . . Yeah . . . I don't understand how the other readers were working.

This is an example of the type of abusive labor practices that are hidden when labor conditions are obfuscated. It also points to how narrators can be isolated and made invisible to each other, which impedes their ability to build solidarity, or to even do basic information sharing that might ease the way of getting the job done well and efficiently.

My *plática* with Graciela brought to light additional examples. Graciela recently entered the audiobook world. She works primarily in Spanish and, unlike Carmen and Jenny, she has never self-recorded; all of her jobs have been in studios with an engineer/director. She initially shared that she found that the lower pay rate was balanced out by a good working environment and flexible schedules, but returned to it later in the conversation:

G: Volviendo a lo de 'leerlos antes', aunque no lo estoy leyendo cien porciento, si invierto una buena cantidad de horas marcando el libro. Que no

> me pagan, obviamente . . . lo único que te pagan en el audiolibro es la hora producida . . . sería ideal que de alguna forma, lo que pagan, compensara un poco, esas horas que estás invirtiendo. // *Returning to how much you read them beforehand. While I don't read them one hundred percent, I do invest a good number of hours marking up the script. That is, obviously, not paid. The only thing they pay in audiobooks is per finished hour. . . . It would be ideal, if somehow folded into the pay, they would compensate some of that work that you are investing.*

While narrators approach their prep work as it best fits their needs, Graciela's approach is rather typical. Narrators do a skim-through read of the book. Then, they go through it again and invest a significant amount of time marking up the text. These include mark-ups to differentiate between characters, emotions, settings, tone, pronunciation, rhythm, and so on. Their effort is a combination of both technical skills and creative/acting labor.[49] As an audiobook producer stated at a Spanish-language SAG-AFTRA audiobook workshop:

> El trabajo del narrador es el trabajo más importante y más difícil . . . el candidato ideal para narrar, es un actor. // *The job of narrator is the most important and difficult job . . . the ideal candidate to narrate is an actor.*[50]

He went on to say that all good narrators are great actors, but not all great actors make good narrators. This underscores the combination of specialized skill sets needed to do this work well, far from the kind of haphazard gig economy labor that audiobook narration is increasingly treated as. Unfortunately, even while discursively celebrating narrators, employers find creative ways to not compensate them for the actual value they contribute to the final audiobook.

While frictions are not always present and not all employers seek unfair advantages, a systemic lack of transparency keeps narrators from effectively addressing abusive labor practices if and where they occur. As Graciela interrogates:

> G: Qué hay detrás de todo antes de que me llama [el productor] y me dice ven a grabarlo? // *What is behind everything before [the producer] calls and says come and record?*[51]

Graciela's question illustrates how opaque this ecosystem can be from a narrator's perspective.

Exacerbated Exploitation

Making a living as an audiobook narrator sounds very attractive. Among other incentives are the ability to work remotely and on flexible schedules. As Carmen stated:

> C: . . . it totally makes sense to me, as a woman in this industry, why there's that interest to do audiobooks . . . to be independent.

Graciela mentioned that audiobooks are a great, creatively fulfilling acting exercise:

G: A mí me gusta mucho hacer los audiolibros. Es muy pesado, te digo, pero me gusta hacerlos. Es un ejercicio actoral muy bueno. . . . Es tu voz y ya. Y la actuación que tú le das . . . por eso lo encuentro más retante . . . cuando regreso de un audiolibro llego con esa sensación de satisfacción y de que hice algo bueno. // *I really enjoy doing audiobooks. It's hard work, but I like doing them. It's a great acting exercise . . . . it's just your voice, and your acting. That's why I find it more challenging . . . when I do an audiobook I return with a sense of fulfillment and that I did something good.*

While Jenny also finds audiobooks creatively fulfilling, she concurrently points to this as a reason why Latinas may endure problematic labor conditions:

J: One of the reasons we go back to the audiobook, under the discrepancies and unfairness in terms of labor, is because it's a space where the content that we are asked to work with has the depth and complexity that we would like to see ourselves doing on screen . . . and we don't. [There], we get one-liners and, here, we get to tell the whole story.

Her comment surfaces a connection between the exclusionary structures of legacy media and the exploitation of labor in digital environments and how these may be distributed across racial and gender registers.

While the promise of creative fulfillment as a reason for entering this labor area may not be exclusive to Latinas, what these women's experiences bring to light is that exploitative practices are sustained and exacerbated when narrators enter this ecosystem from an already precarious condition. For example, regarding pay schedules, Jenny shared:

J: The actual pay of it comes, I think, it's thirty days or sixty? Yeah, thirty days after the book is . . . out . . . approved, done, no changes. Thirty days after a date you can't control.
Q: *So, you have no idea really [when you will get paid].*
J: You kind of don't. You have to just relax.
Q: *You have to relax. Viene cuando viene, no es gran cantidad de dinero.*[52]
J: Yeah, it's not. But, *ya sabes como es* with actors;[53] I mean, one residual check can save your life that month.

Actors might thus enter this arena from an already financially precarious situation, deeming them easier targets for exploitation. For Latinas, our intersectional axis of marginalization in Hollywood across race, gender, and linguistic lines may indeed exacerbate our exploitation in this space.

One way in which this is operationalized is by limiting Latina access to narration jobs via casting categories that include linguistic assumptions and conceptual hierarchies. In US media, whiteness and the English language are equated with Americanness and positioned as the aspirational norms; a problematic move that reifies a narrow, racially charged understanding of what it means to look and sound 'American.'[54] Within this context, Latinx communities are often equated with Spanish language (exclusively) or with an accent intended to mark them as 'other' than American. This limits the jobs for which Latinas are considered.

The Affective Impacts of Precarious Labor

What does exploitation feel like? The words Carmen, Jenny, and Graciela used to describe the negative affective impacts of their experiences include frustration, torture, horror, disrespect, heavy, and abuse. In describing her experience with self-recording, Jenny said:

J: Qué horror de experiencia. // *What a horror of an experience.*

Carmen shared:

C: [This project] it was like eight months of my life. . . . I'm not expecting anything. I just want to close this chapter and move on. . . . It was such a frustrating experience . . . the time I spent on this compared to payment . . . I've come to terms with myself that I basically worked for free.
. . .
R: *Did this turn you off from doing narration or is this still something that you would want to do 'under different circumstances', cómo tú dices?*[55]
C: It turns me off a little bit, but it turns me off because of the ongoing abuse that is happening . . . and what I mean by 'abuse,' I mean taking advantage of voice actors and not paying them for the amount of work that they are doing . . . it's, it's horrible. . . . And, there's more and more opportunity for people to work from home and to either supplement their income or do this full time, and that's great. But, people are taking advantage.
. . .
C: Not only not getting respect financially, I'd be interested to see the male/female ratio. I mention that because I felt disrespected. He [a proofreader] mansplained to me. . . . That kind of environment. . . . Not being treated like an equal. There's no way he would have talked to a male this way.

Carmen offers us a glimpse into gendered dimensions present within this ecosystem that necessitate further scrutiny. Finally, Graciela describes a "torturous" experience when a non-creative executive directed her over the phone for the first few days of a project:

G: Me paraba cada tercer palabra . . . fué una tortura verdadera el comienzo de ese libro. // *She'd stop me every third word. . . . The start of that book was truly torturous.*

Graciela shared that the executive slowed down the process and stunted creativity. It was not until after she left that Graciela and the engineer were able to really get to work.

Conclusion

By taking a glimpse into the complex commercial audiobook ecosystem from the intersection of Chicana/Latina feminism and labor, I illuminate intersectional spaces that may not have otherwise been considered via dominant lenses. In the process of our *pláticas*, the ways in which precarity and opacity are built into this system came into focus, as did the effects and affective impacts of this design. The insights from this research have broad implications beyond audiobooks. By pointing to instances in which gig economy logics are shaping labor structures and the future of creative labor beyond platforms and into sectors perhaps considered largely immune to such logics, I demonstrate how this ecosystem's obfuscation hinders our ability to interrogate the overall imbalance—or inversion—of the structure. This obfuscation serves to hide abusive labor practices and how these abuses might be distributed and further exacerbated along racial and gender lines. This research exemplifies why it is critical that we demand transparency in gig economy labor structures wherever they are found.

By centering the voices of US Latina audiobook narrators, this study highlights some of the ways in which race, ethnicity, gender, and language impact media professionals' experiences in digital environments. While the views of US Latina talent have historically been marginalized in legacy media, I argue that they are key to understanding the transnational and intersectional dimensions of creative digital labor structures. Latina insights are also crucial to supporting SAG-AFTRA's organizing efforts in this new digital era by helping to expand and reframe what labor issues are addressed, how they are understood, and what potential solutions are considered. This research listens to the voices of traditionally overlooked creative labor because without these women's perspectives our understandings of digital labor structures are skewed and incomplete.

Acknowledgments

A huge thank you to my academic advisor, Dr. Sarah T. Roberts, for your mentorship and constant support, the editors of this volume for your invaluable notes, and to you Latina audiobook narrators for collaborating on this work by sharing your knowledge.

Notes

1. "SAG-AFTRA represents approximately 160,000 performers and media professionals," www.sagaftra.org/membership-benefits.
2. SAG-AFTRA Audiobook workshop. February 13, 2019; Paul Alan Ruben, "Upping Your Performance Game While Recording Home Alone (now that you're really alone)," Audiofile presents Audiobook Narration webinar with Paul Alan Ruben, April 18, 2020, www.youtube.com/watch?v=IRYOvqYgrkc.
3. Jeffrey A. Trachtenberg, "Amazon Already Disrupted the Sale of Print Titles. Up Next: Audiobooks," *Wall Street Journal*, February 5, 2018, sec. Business, www.wsj.com/articles/readers-listen-up-amazon-wants-to-extend-its-dominance-in-audiobooks-1517832000.
4. John Maher, "Audiobook Revenue Jumped 22.7% in 2018," *PublishersWeekly.com*, accessed December 18, 2018, www.publishersweekly.com/pw/by-topic/industry-news/audio-books/article/77303-audiobook-revenue-jumped-22-7-in-2018.html.
5. Maher.
6. Jennifer Maloney, "The Fastest-Growing Format in Publishing: Audiobooks," *Wall Street Journal*, July 21, 2016, sec. Arts, www.wsj.com/articles/the-fastest-growing-format-in-publishing-audiobooks-1469139910.
7. Jim Millot, "For Publishers, 2018 Is Off to a Decent Start," *PublishersWeekly.com*, accessed December 18, 2018, www.publishersweekly.com/pw/by-topic/industry-news/publisher-news/article/76924-for-publishers-2018-is-off-to-a-decent-start.html.
8. SAG-AFTRA, "SAG-AFTRA: Audiobooks," 2018, www.sagaftra.org/audiobooks.
9. Christian Fuchs, *Digital Labour and Karl Marx* (New York: Routledge, 2014).45.
10. Frances Negrón-Muntaner, *The Latino Media Gap: A Report on the State of Latino in U.S. Media* (Columbia University, 2014, Online).
11. According to a SAG-AFTRA, "Taller de Audiolibros" workshop on February 13, 2019, 2018 marked the fourth year in a row that there was a 20% global increase in audiobook production and a 33% increase in the Spanish language arena.
12. APA, "A History of Audiobooks" (Audio Publishers Association), accessed March 9, 2018, www.audiopub.org/uploads/images/backgrounds/A-HISTORY-OF-AUDIOBOOKS.pdf.
13. Paul Franklin, "Amazon to Buy Audible for $300 Million," *Reuters*, January 31, 2008; Brad Stone, "Amazon to Buy Audiobook Seller for $300 Million," *New York Times*, February 1, 2008.
14. PT Editors, "Keeping Up With the New Demand for Audiobooks—Publishing Trends," *Publishing Trends*, August 1, 2011, www.publishingtrends.com/2011/08/keeping-up-with-the-new-demand-for-audiobooks-2/; "Audiobook Creation Exchange," in *Wikipedia*, May 29, 2019, https://en.wikipedia.org/w/index.php?title=Audiobook_Creation_Exchange&oldid=899386904.
15. ACX website: www.acx.com/help/about-acx/200484860.
16. It is not clear how they define 'Americans.'
17. APA, "New Survey Shows 50% of Americans Have Listened to an Audiobook" (New York, NY, April 24, 2019).
18. Maloney.
19. APA, "U.S. Publishers Report Nearly $1 Billion in Sales as Strong Industry Growth Continues" (New York, NY, July 17, 2019).
20. Arlene Davila, "Contemporary Latina/o Media: Introduction," 2, accessed August 27, 2020, www.jstor.org/stable/pdf/j.ctt9qfn6s.3.pdf?refreqid=excelsior%3Ade3932c151426448ffd7b27501b6c5ff; Dávila points to Yeidy M. Rivero, "Havana as a 1940s–1950s Latin American Media Capital," *Critical Studies in Media Communication* 26, no. 3 (August 2009): 289, https://doi.org/10.1080/15295030903015070.

21. David Fernández Vitores, "El Español Una Lengua Viva: Informe 2019" (Spain: Instituto Cervantes), 5, accessed August 26, 2020, www.cervantes.es/imagenes/File/espanol_lengua_viva_2019.pdf.
22. Ibid., 80.
23. Frances Negrón-Muntaner, *The Latino Media Gap*, 7.
24. US Census Bureau, "ACS Demographic and Housing Estimates," 2018, https://data.census.gov/cedsci/table?q=hispanics%20in%20US&tid=ACSDP1Y2018.DP05&hidePreview=false; US Census Bureau, "Languages Spoken at Home," Table ID: S1601, 2018, https://data.census.gov/cedsci/table?q=languages%20spoken%20at%20home&tid=ACSST1Y2018.S1601&hidePreview=false.
25. Jillian M. Báez, *In Search of Belonging: Latinas, Media, and Citizenship* (Urbana: University of Illinois Press, 2018), 10, https://doi.org/10.5406/j.ctt21h4z2j.
26. Ibid., 3.
27. Ibid., 33; Renato Rosaldo, "Cultural Citizenship in San Jose, California," *PoLAR: Political and Legal Anthropology Review* 17, no. 2 (1994): 57.
28. Dolores Delgado Bernal, "Using a Chicana Feminist Epistemology in Educational Research," *Harvard Educational Review* 68, no. 4 (December 1998): 4, https://doi.org/10.17763/haer.68.4.5wv1034973g22q48.
29. Sarah T. Roberts, *Behind the Screen: Content Moderation in the Shadows of Social Media* (New Haven: Yale University Press, 2019), 31; Marie Hicks, *Programmed Inequality: How Britain Discarded Women Technologists and Lost Its Edge in Computing*, ed. William Aspray, 1st ed. (Cambridge, MA: MIT Press, 2017); Venus Green, *Race on the Line: Gender, Labor, and Technology in the Bell System, 1880–1980* (Durham, NC: Duke University Press Books, 2001); Melissa Villa-Nicholas, "Ruptures in Telecommunications: Latina and Latino Information Workers in Southern California," *Aztlan: A Journal of Chicano Studies* 42, no. 1 (2017): 73–97.
30. Safiya Umoja Noble, *Algorithms of Oppression: How Search Engines Reinforce Racism* (New York: New York University Press, 2018).
31. Bernal, "Using a Chicana Feminist Epistemology in Educational Research," 2; James Joseph Scheurich and Michelle D. Young, "Coloring Epistemologies: Are Our Research Epistemologies Racially Biased?" *Educational Researcher* 26, no. 4 (May 1997): 4, https://doi.org/10.2307/1176879.
32. Cindy O. Fierro and Dolores Delgado Bernal, "Vamos a Platicar: The Contours of Pláticas as Chicana/Latina Feminist Methodology," *Chicana/Latina Studies* 15, no. 2 (2016): 116.
33. Alvina E. Quintana, "Book Review *The Decolonial Imaginary: Writing Chicanas Into History*. By Emma Pérez. Bloomington and Indianapolis: Indiana University Press, 1999. *Speaking Chicana: Voice, Power, and Identity*, ed. D. Letticia Galindo and María Dolores Gonzales. Tucson: University of Arizona Press, 1999. *Feminism on the Border: Chicana Gender Politics and Literature*. By Sonia Saldívar-Hull. Berkeley: University of California Press, 2000," *Signs: Journal of Women in Culture and Society* 28, no. 2 (January 2003): 724, https://doi.org/10.1086/342586.
34. Fierro and Delgado Bernal, "Vamos a Platicar: The Contours of Pláticas as Chicana/Latina Feminist Methodology."
35. All names are pseudonyms.
36. Sarah T. Roberts, "Digital Labor" (Doctoral seminar, UCLA, 2018).
37. Post means post-production or the stage that happens after the recording. This includes editing, labeling, etc. Pickups are any words, phrases, or sections that will need to be rerecorded.
38. This means that narrators who have worked on more than x number of audiobooks are paid a higher rate.
39. According to SAG-AFTRA's definition.
40. From contracts under which I have worked.

41. Fuchs, *Digital Labour and Karl Marx*, 54.
42. Ibid., 55.
43. Residuals are royalties that are typically paid to individuals involved in the making of a film, television show, or radio/voice project. For more information on residuals in the entertainment industry, see https://en.m.wikipedia.org/wiki/Residual_ (entertainment_industry).
44. ACX offers an either/or choice for narrators: pfh or a share in royalties.
45. www.sagaftra.org/about.
46. Compared to other unionized areas.
47. Fuchs, *Digital Labour and Karl Marx*, 34.
48. Translation: "that you calculate, more or less."
49. Lucy Bednar, "Audiobooks and the Reassertion of Orality: Walter J. Ong and Others Revisited," *CEA Critic* 73, no. 1 (2010): 78; SAG-AFTRA audiobook workshop. February 13, 2019.
50. SAG-AFTRA audiobook workshop. February 13, 2019. Translation is mine.
51. Translation is mine.
52. *It will come when it comes, it's not that much money.*
53. You know how it is with actors.
54. Also problematic is the US being equated with 'America.'
55. As you say?

10
LIQUID ASSETS

Camming and Cashing In on Desire in the Digital Age

Kavita Ilona Nayar

Introduction

Since the first adult webcam platforms emerged in 1996, thousands of workers have registered as cam models in a now multibillion-dollar industry that still somehow eludes mainstream attention.[1] Despite its low profile, "camming" has developed a reputation as the new frontier of adult entertainment because it satisfies desires for authenticity with live performances by "amateurs" (e.g., "real people" streaming video feeds), technological experimentation (e.g., use of teledildonics and virtual reality), social interaction, and community. The job of a cam model is essentially to interact with and entertain users by hanging out, playing games, dancing, stripping, performing sex acts, and exploring fetishes in shows performed for a group or individual. Because the imagined audience for camming is heterosexual cisgender males from the Global North, the industry caters to their presumed tastes, meaning it seeks young, conventionally attractive, native English-speaking, cisgender women to perform this work. In turn, many women in the US who fit the bill appreciate being courted by this industry. They leap at the opportunity of a work-from-home gig that promises fun, friends, flexibility, and easy money, having come of age in an era marked by the sex-positivity of popular feminism, tech-driven entrepreneurship, and the glamorization of side hustles.

But making a living as a cam model is often harder than workers first realize. As independent contractors searching for work on online platforms, they join a budding class of temporary, freelance workers with "entrepreneurial" spirits who have foregone dreams of a traditional job's security, benefits, and consistent paycheck in favor of a precarious lifestyle that enticingly dangles the possibility of autonomy. As digital workers, cam models stitch together a livable wage by performing "microtasks"[2] for tips and per-minute fees, routinely on multiple cam platforms, and supplementing this unreliable income by pursuing work in other adult industries such as photo, video, and panty selling; phone sex; and pornography. They face intense competition in an oversaturated field, do their own promotion and marketing to attract loyal customers, and receive a mere fraction of their profits after a platform takes its cut. With no formal hiring process, cam models are not even considered "1099" workers, unworthy of being paid until they reach a certain earnings threshold. Thus, countless models never receive a single payout.

Entering the gig economy is both a choice *and* necessity for many prospective workers. For instance, a 2016 survey found that workers who were low-income, racial minorities and not college-educated were more likely to consider gigs "essential" or "important" to their livelihood, suggesting social disparities help shape the popularity of these sociotechnical fields.[3] Self-reported reliance on gigs is concerning given digital labor studies that suggest industry rhetoric touting the benefits of "being your own boss" draws more American workers into precarious careers of freelancing and independent contracting, which exacerbate problems like financial insecurity that they sought to escape or solve.[4] While illuminating the discrepancies between workers' aspirations and their lived realities, extant research tends to center male-dominated industries, which leads to gender-biased claims.[5] Scholars have called for more intersectional feminist studies that consider how race, class, gender, sexuality, ability, and nationality, for instance, mediate workers' experiences and the gig economy's implications.[6]

Camming is a platform-mediated gig that foregrounds gender, sexuality, and social marginalization, which has been largely overlooked within digital labor and cultural production studies.[7] This oversight gives tacit consent to the continued marginalization of sex work. For example, the 2013 US Department of Justice investigation of banks known as "Operation Choke Point" explicitly targeted businesses at high risk for fraud and money laundering such as firearm dealers and payday lenders, but it also made banks skittish about dealing with sex workers, effectively shutting them off from essential economic resources. Similarly, on April 11, 2018, President Donald J. Trump signed into law the Allow States and Victims to Fight Online Sex Trafficking Act and the Stop Enabling Sex Traffickers Act, known as FOSTA-SESTA (Public Law 115–164), which amended Section 230 of the Communications Decency Act in order to increase the legal liability of third-party providers for the content on their platforms, presumably to regulate sex trafficking and child abuse. However, this legislation also pushed platforms to act more conservatively by instituting or acting on "morality clauses" that bar voluntary and legal sex workers from using their services.

In order to "un-exceptionalize" sex workers, this chapter explores camming as work worthy of inclusion in the academic and political imagination.[8] Just as scholarship has informed activism in car-share and care labor industries, sex workers benefit from research that dignifies and destigmatizes their experiences. As some of the most unprotected members of a burgeoning class of precarious workers, sex workers provide experiences, perspectives, imaginaries, and politics that help envision how to make all work more fair, humane, and gratifying. I inquire: What are the perceived benefits and drawbacks of this labor? How do platform conditions shape this labor? What does an intersectional feminist analysis of this labor reveal?

Drawing upon in-depth interviews with 24 US-based women conducted between June 2017 and April 2020, I argue that camming is an individualized strategy for managing systemic gender inequality under patriarchal capitalism. Adopting an intersectional feminist approach, I paid close attention to ambivalences in the social status of women I interviewed and variation in their experiences and perspectives. On the one hand, all interviewees identified as cisgender female, ranging in age from 18 to 54, with 27 being the median age. Two-thirds identified as white. The remaining third overwhelmingly identified as black, but also Latina, mixed, or Asian. In this respect, most interviewees were relatively privileged by their sexual orientation, race, and young age. On the other hand, privilege and oppression are not mutually exclusive. Two-thirds of interviewees lacked a bachelor's degree, most of whom were cisgender white. Many of these same interviewees juggled full-time camming with parenting and marriage, were taking college courses to improve their access to resources, and suffered from chronic health conditions that made it difficult to retain traditional employment. Their stories of overwhelming life circumstances and events, limited access to education, and disabilities reveal the sometimes subtle ways social status shapes understandings of gig work and what workers value and need.

Based on these interviews, I highlight both the possibilities and the constraints of this work for women in their positions. I argue that camming offers them significant economic, pragmatic, and symbolic benefits, bringing access to money, dignity, and pleasure that should not be dismissed. In recent years, workplace reform has risen in the ranks of liberal feminist concerns, bringing awareness to issues like sexual harassment, gendered pay gaps, and lack of paid parental leave and affordable childcare. Yet progress is uneven and slow, and many women have turned to the gig economy as a coping strategy, cam models included. Women entering this industry are looking for work that is lucrative, enjoyable, and, most of all, flexible. However, cam platforms are also designed, governed, and populated under patriarchal capitalism, limiting the possibilities of this work and introducing risks and concerns. I analyze these tensions not only to advocate for sex workers' rights, but also to explore what these contradictions can teach us about better advocating for the needs of gig workers at large.

Camming as Gendered Gig Work

For all of the techno-optimism surrounding the gig economy and echoed by many of its millions of workers, emerging research suggests this outlook masks a grim reality. The US Bureau of Labor Statistics defines a gig as "a single project or task for which a worker is hired, often through a digital marketplace, to work on demand,"[9] but scholars critique this definition as misleading because it frames platform companies as multi-sided markets, as "intermediaries" that merely facilitate transactions between buyers and sellers.[10] This rhetoric importantly obscures how many platforms dodge the label of "employer" whilst hiring contingent workers to perform low-paying service or manual labor, which allows these companies to save money and offload risks to workers by circumventing traditional labor law. They are not obligated to provide a minimum wage, work-related resources and support, safe working conditions, unemployment insurance, or benefits like health care, paid time off, and retirement savings plans.[11] In a digital economy, gigs are also globally distributed, which increases worker competition and cheapens their labor.[12] Thus, scholars almost unanimously agree the gig economy further erodes labor protections that have been vanishing for decades under neoliberal economic policies.

Platform-mediated labor also introduces new ways for old problems to haunt workers. Algorithms and other sociotechnical features of platforms reinforce yet obscure social inequalities by purportedly removing the element of human bias.[13] Platforms claim neutrality but create hierarchies by design.[14] According to legal scholars, this makes it harder to detect machinations of power and regulate discrimination using standards applied in other contexts. As more work and social life transitions onto platforms, datafication—the capture and monetization of user activity—adds new layers of value creation, labor exploitation, and surveillance, creating a web of undetected power.[15]

Still, much sex work scholarship downplays unanticipated outcomes and risks characteristic of platform-mediated labor, highlighting the benefits of added safety, control, and community of platforms to street workers and escorts. Such research importantly counters a dominant political narrative that conflates voluntary online sex work with sex trafficking and promotes policymaking antagonistic to all online sexual content and services. Though important to protecting sex workers' rights, these studies too often laud technology and gloss over the reification of power in sociotechnical systems.[16] However, recent studies, particularly on cam modeling, critique platform mediation in terms of risks to sex workers such as surveillance, privacy violations, harassment, and police targeting;[17] the intensity and implications of worker competition;[18] and the extraction of value from workers.[19]

Against this backdrop, workers still see desires for flexibility, independence, and control as guiding their choices to enter the gig economy, but they likely need this work to fill income gaps created by low or loss of wages, representing what Annette Bernhardt calls "the privatization of the safety net."[20] Just as dot-com era creative workers romanticized risk and uncertainty,[21] Web 2.0 gig workers are emboldened by the rhetoric of entrepreneurialism to see self-reliance as a *choice*, not capitulation to unsustainable conditions.[22] Many workers see themselves as motivated by an enterprising spirit to create multiple income streams, when it may also be an economic necessity,[23] demonstrating how habituation to uncertainty has become even more entrenched in workers' subjectivities. Needing to hold multiple jobs is not new, but its veneration as part of the aspirational identity of a digital entrepreneur with admirable "hustle" is problematic.

Of course, industry discourses do not hail all workers unanimously. Gig work is highly gendered, and women's inroads into the gig economy differ depending on their race, class, and appearance. Women with racial and/or class privilege are encouraged to identify as "girlbosses," self-employed entrepreneurs and creative workers trading in self-brands and attention as influencers, bloggers, and digital boutique owners. Their activities are romanticized and filtered through discourses of passion, pleasure, self-fulfillment, self-expression, friendship, fun, and community.[24] These discourses cohere in a neoliberal feminist ethos of empowerment and self-improvement, increasing women's affective investment in gigs tapping into these desires. Though valuable, feminist critiques of women's motivations sometimes downplay their agency and how intersectionality shapes experiences. Many women, especially women of color or those without college degrees who are more likely to work in low-wage service industries, choose gigs to escape the confines of a rigged system that undervalues them and ignores or derides their needs. For women already marginalized by their racial and class positions, the trade-off is not between a well-paying, reliable corporate job with benefits and a flexible gig without stable earnings and worker protections, but one between two insecure scenarios.[25] Sexuality scholars who situate camming and porn work in this nexus have importantly problematized prior feminist framing of women's desires for flexibility, control, and independence as inherently misguided or unfulfilled.[26]

By bringing the views and lives of sex workers into the conversation about social media and creative work, interesting potential alliances emerge. Nancy Baym's research on the relational labor required of musicians helps me conceptualize the added demands of newer forms of sex work like camming, which combine service work with content creation.[27] Baym writes, "these jobs raise enormous challenges around maintaining boundaries between personal and professional, paid and unpaid labor, and pleasure and exploitation," a statement one might assume was written about sex workers, and cam models in particular, if unaware of the context.[28] Like Baym's musicians, cam models enjoy their work whilst negotiating demands to be authentic, emotionally available, and in constant communication with users. They build self-brands, connect with fans, and participate in an attention economy as creative workers but are siloed by the stigma of sex work and what Sarah Banet-Weiser calls the "idealization of white femininity," which constructs a dichotomy between gendered work that is "empowering" and that which is "pathologized and considered immoral" and usually performed by marginalized women.[29] The isolation of research on stigmatized sexual content creation from other feminized social media professions suggests intersectional approaches are needed to unpack women's varied motivations for entering the gig economy and the stakes of gig labor for women beyond those whose visibility is most celebrated.

A Financial and Pragmatic Choice

Camming's low barriers to entry attracts those needing quick access to cash. With a computer, webcam, internet connection, and legal identification, it is easy and inexpensive to start camming, at least compared to the onerous process of securing traditional employment. Models lacking capital may work for a studio that provides resources, support, and a staged set in exchange for a percentage of their profits, a compromised arrangement that nevertheless appeals to cash-strapped models. Camming also does not require background checks, providing access to jobseekers with criminal records who may not be approved to work in other fields, including adult films and strip clubs. Ex-offenders are vulnerable to discriminatory hiring practices that reduce their chances at procuring steady income, leading to recidivism. The ease of entry to camming is a relief. Also unlike traditional jobs, being new works in a model's favor. Platforms privilege newness by using algorithmic rankings and search filters to increase a new model's visibility on a site and induce a surge of traffic into her room for a limited time. During this honeymoon period, money flows to models. Though this success is fleeting and misleading (models report a dip in traffic and tips when their "new" tag disappears), many models find this initial boost sets them up for future success by allowing them to find fans and their niche in the community.

Dissatisfied with the wages and workloads of other service industries, women turn to camming because it is more lucrative and time efficient. Between tips, per-minute fees for exclusive shows, and merchandise sales, models can end up averaging a higher hourly rate than they would from other work they are qualified to do. Josie,[30] for instance, worked at a coffee shop and was pursuing a career in film animation when she began camming. Already busy with unpaid internships expected of her as a creative aspirant, she cams because it saves time. In three to four hours of camming, she makes what it would take a week to make as a barista. Similarly, Alexa said camming gives her "more time, more freedom, and more financial stability to afford school again," an opinion shared by other interviewees who cam to pay off or avoid student debt. Women strip at clubs for similar reasons, and generally make more money in a single night, but their access and choice of venues is limited by their physical location and/or ability to travel. As remote online work, camming can be done from anywhere it is legally sanctioned.

Many women compare camming to feminized fields in which they also worked such as office administration, education, and healthcare, household, and childcare services, finding camming better rewards their skillsets. Penny, a former hospital worker, felt "underpaid, overworked, [and] under-appreciated" when she started camming part-time for extra money. She eventually quit, but skills she honed as a healthcare professional such as geniality, self-motivation, and time management were helpful for developing a fan base, increasing her earnings, and consistently producing content for multiple outlets. Disillusioned by the demands and low pay of care work, she describes camming as offering her a better quality of life and financial stability. She and her husband have used her camming income to take vacations, buy investment properties, and build savings. Others shared similar stories of drawing on skills gained in devalued economic sectors and finding greater monetary success as cam models. Considering sex work is socially devalued, it is puzzling that many cam models report earning more and feeling valued than they do in socially acceptable feminized professions. Some allude to what I call a "stigma bonus," the payoff of doing work that other women, fearing or sitting in judgment, are unwilling to do. Choosing this life is difficult but brings a sense of possibility given their alternatives.

Camming also feels more approachable and inclusive than do other adult industries. Stories about successful "non-nude" models circulate as industry lore, encouraging women to believe it is possible to cam without being naked or sexual on camera (none of my interviewees were non-nude). Models also appreciate the range of workers' bodily appearances. Abbie, a model in the "Big Beautiful Women" (BBW) niche, rejects the presumption that thinness or conventional beauty is required to cam. Still, she emphasizes the importance of self-awareness and avoiding false advertising when creating tags used to attract interested users that describe one's physical appearance. A thin woman, she argued, would perform just as poorly using a "BBW" tag as she would *not* using it. While valid, her point does not address potential differences between categories such as average number of users, money made, and treatment of workers. Similarly, the women of color I interviewed claimed industry-driven racial inequalities are less of a problem in camming than in other sex trades. Avery told me fans embraced her when she came out as a "fat black woman" after a decade of promoting herself using a "skinny white woman" persona as a phone sex operator. Josie, a Mexican-American model, even recommends models emphasize their ethnic differences to attract fans.

Race play, a fetish for roleplaying racial power dynamics typically requested of black female performers, is popular on cam platforms, suggesting a demand for diversity even if it reinforces white patriarchy. Some black female performers I interviewed refused to do race play out of self-respect, while others dismissed the potential for damage and used tactics to depersonalize the interaction, framing their thick skin as good business sense. Blair, for instance, retorted, "If you want to pay me to call me the n-word, go ahead! You could have done it for free." Either way, models felt they had a choice to refuse and still earn money. Commodifying and sexualizing cultural difference is a complex phenomenon that other scholars have addressed better than I can here.[31] Still, models' outlooks suggest the atmosphere created by the camming community promotes *feelings* of racial inclusion. This sensibility increases black performers' enjoyment of the work regardless of expectations to perform sexualized racial tropes and difficulties gaining traction on platforms like MyFreeCams, which cater to mainstream (i.e., white middle-class) tastes.

Like other gig workers, cam models value flexibility and working from home as individualized strategies for managing their needs. With multiple jobs and college coursework, some interviewees appreciated camming as a gig performed at night, on weekends, and during free time, allowing them to preserve normal business hours for other commitments. Working from home is also a respite from the pressures of traditional workplaces to optimize productivity at the expense of personal relationships and family matters, an expectation women negotiate alongside the persistent gendered division of labor in which they are overwhelmingly responsible for managing the household, childrearing, and elderly care in their extended families. Blair, for instance, started camming to care for her grandmother, who recently suffered a stroke and has Alzheimer's. Abbie and Stephanie homeschool their sons and cam while the boys sleep. While the flexibility of gigs is likely overstated, it is also not an abstract virtue of camming but a concrete gain that gives women control they are sorely lacking in other labor sectors. Many cam models have worked in industries without paid or unpaid leave and risk being fired if they miss a pre-assigned shift.[32] For these workers and caretakers, flexibility is all they have.

Traditional workplaces can also be inhospitable to workers with chronic physical, mental health, or behavioral conditions who might need to take more breaks. Kendrix started camming after she had two car accidents that left her with severe brain trauma. She had to quit the jobs she previously held and defer college enrollment due to physical and cognitive limitations. Jessica also suffered a car accident that halted her work as a nurse supervisor at a medical office. She began camming after a doctor told her to do less physically taxing work. Other interviewees had anxiety, depression, attention deficit disorder, bipolar disorder, or autism spectrum disorder. They all appreciate camming as a job without rigid protocols. Flexibility, then, is less about neoliberal mantras of freedom and choice and more about recognizing individual needs and limitations, an instinct that is discouraged, shamed, or even penalized in traditional workplaces. Whether camming is truly flexible is beside the point. Workers' preference for flexibility over stability calls attention to the underlying systemic failure to create humane employment policies that address their needs and reflect their values.[33]

The Pleasure of Creativity and Community

Some women frame their choices to cam in strictly economic and pragmatic terms, as survival strategies, but those who are most active in the business and community also imbue it with cultural meaning and symbolic status. Full-time models are more likely to see themselves as independent content creators, with live cam sessions representing only a fraction of their creative output and revenue, which includes more lucrative ventures such as photo and video clip production for social media and fan club subscriptions. Successful models operate like one-woman multimedia companies, perpetually creating and promoting shows, content, and merchandise. As sex work becomes more mainstream or at least more visible, some models hope to leverage their experiences in the adult industry as expertise they carry over into careers in media, sex therapy, business consulting, marketing, and sales. After a decade as a phone-sex-operator-cum-cam-model, Avery has authored two books, offers one-on-one consulting with models, and delivers an online teaching series. Callie runs an online industry publication and hosts a podcast on camming. An industry that represents the marriage of sex, performance art, business, and technology, camming is a hotbed for innovation that appeals to women invested in becoming "sexual entrepreneurs."

Sexual content creation can become a source of creativity, self-esteem, and community even if begun under financial strain. Several interviewees proudly told me how they had earned "best cam show" and "fan favorite" awards at conventions. These achievements are noteworthy since gaining recognition for female amateur content production is unusual in other creative industries. Networking with models at events or in online forums and group chats also satisfies desires for community built on shared experiences. Penny recalls feeling "empowered" while attending a convention. Struggling with the stigma of sex work, she felt a sense of belonging that helped overcome her fears. Vanessa, who also works at strip clubs, sees the camming community as less judgmental. Even amongst exotic dancers, she finds "prudes" who judge her. She speculates that women who strip are more private or ashamed than cam models, who are open and free with publicly broadcasting their sexuality, a style she admires and embodies. While her opinions and experiences regarding the limitations of stripping may not be shared, her appreciation for this community built on celebrating sexual freedom suggests it is one reason models remain loyal to this industry.

Camming is known for its permissiveness, and the anonymity of internet interactions attracts users looking to safely explore fetishes with models up to the task. Not all models I interviewed enjoyed fetish work, but many seemed proud of skillfully playing a role and providing pleasure to audiences. Nearly all models I interviewed do female domination, a roleplay fetish that eroticizes patriarchal power reversal by positioning women as "goddesses, art, and superior to men," according to Jessica. "Men are always in charge, so it's powerful," she said. In these shows, men expect women to demean them with services such as small penis humiliation, orgasm denial, sissy training, and jerk-off instruction. Fetish work can be emotionally draining, but it is also fun and different from the monotony of everyday life. Some unleash sides of themselves they otherwise repress. Recently married, Tessa finds camming to be a "safe outlet" to receive the sexual attention she craves outside of her primary romantic relationship. An accountant by day but a "flirtatious extrovert" at heart, she is free to be "an amplified version" of herself while camming: "I get to share a part of myself that I had to put away in the real world." Additionally, part of a cam model's job is to "hang out" and "have fun," highlighting self-expression and pleasure. Some showcase and practice their skills and talents for an audience; models are known to paint, sing, dance, cook, and play videogames as ways to entertain and interact with users. Acknowledging that sex workers feel pride and pleasure in providing services is sometimes elided in order to legitimize their labor as "real work." But these joys differentiated cam modeling from other gigs my interviewees considered like catering or car-share service work. The search for pleasure and passion in camming and other gig work is important to take seriously as indications of what is missing in workers' everyday lives under increasingly unstable and alienating economic conditions.[34] Still, the "freedom" to "have fun" is neither problem-free nor equally available to all models. Aspirations for money, creativity, community, and pleasure are not always achieved on cam platforms, which constrain workers' experiences in particular ways.

The Constraints of Platform-Mediated Sex Work

Camming can be lucrative, pragmatic, and meaningful, but it is also an individualized solution to systemic problems. As such, camming is subject to terms set by patriarchal capitalism; it reformulates conditions of dependence that workers seek to escape, despite appearing to offer them greater autonomy. This section examines two ways patriarchal capitalism undergirds platform-mediated sex work: (1) platform design, governance, and relations that devalue and exploit models' labor, and (2) dependence on cultivating a mostly male fan base and relationships to compensate for the lack of worker protections as independent contractors in this digital creative industry.

Platforms aim to squeeze the most value out of cam models' labor. Because they provide servers, user interface, traffic, and payment processors needed to professionally cam, they justify collecting 40 to 70 percent of models' earnings. Models whose followings drive regular traffic to cam platforms sense their worth to companies boasting billion-dollar revenues, but they fear repercussions of contesting low payouts since companies have a steady influx of workers. Some attempt to circumvent cam platforms and keep their profits by using video chat applications to perform private shows, but they do so at personal risk. Sexual transactions violate "morality clauses" in companies' terms of service, and payment processors are known to freeze and close accounts with suspected ties to individual sex workers (though some work directly with major platforms). Customers also abuse models' precarity by contesting payment after receiving services, knowing models have little recourse to regain their money.

Marginalization of sex workers gives platforms more control over their labor and the ability to institute unfair terms and conditions with little pushback. For example, Birdie revealed how a platform immediately suspended her for three months after monitoring a conversation in which she and a customer violated one of its terms by agreeing to meet on a different platform: "I was like, 'it's Christmas time! Are you kidding me? You can see he started this. I bring a lot of money to this site. No slap on the wrist?" While she scrambled to financially recover, the customer received a warning, indicating a double standard in this two-sided market. Birdie's story also epitomizes the precarity of platform labor and chronic stress caused by platform surveillance.[35] Monitoring workers' data is a form of organizational policing that is not unique to online contexts, but platform policies are opaque and inconsistently enforced. Their actions seem haphazard or even discriminatory, leading to more uncertainty for these unprotected workers.

Sociotechnical features are decisions dictated by stakeholder interests and profit motive, but they are misrecognized as inevitable, even natural, aspects of technology and of practical and aesthetic value for consumers. This paradox matters because, much like human language, platforms are not simply conduits of information and social connection, but in fact constitute and legitimize forms of sociality based on how they are designed and governed.[36] Tech companies make decisions that are not neutral or benign but *actively* construct the constraints and possibilities of digital cultural work even when they feign a passive role. For example, companies standardize platform transactions by making users pay models with tokens they purchase from the platform company. Each token costs approximately $0.10 depending on the package (of which approximately $0.05 goes to a model). This decision makes token packages affordable to buyers and likely prolongs time spent on the platform, but it also reduces the scale of models' compensation to a US dime. Token-based systems also devalue a models' labor by masking the true exchange of money for services rendered. If not in token form, paying models in such minuscule increments would perhaps too starkly reveal the low valuation of their time.

Further, some platforms require models to perform unpaid labor, entertaining users in "free chat" areas and working for tips. While tipping is expected, models complain about "freeloaders," lurkers who never tip yet frequent their rooms. Platforms give models the option to "silence" freeloaders and only interact with token-carrying "members," but this feature bypasses the larger issue and is more likely designed to persuade buyers to purchase tokens than to help models.

This solution benefits platforms in two ways: They are able to claim they "empower" models with a feature that tackles the freeloader problem and avoid addressing their unpaid labor. They also make models individually responsible for converting free users into paying members. Converting users into consumers involves promotion and marketing, the cost of which platforms conceal and offload onto workers to increase surplus value. Josie laughs at her initial naïveté, when she believed she could simply turn on her webcam, talk to people, and make money. Though she originally hoped camming would free up her schedule to make more art, she realized the job is more "time consuming" than she imagined. Now, she feels obligated to constantly create content to maintain her social media presence and grow her fan base.

According to Kitty, camming is not actually a moneymaker. Models who claim to make money actually work multiple platforms and industries—cam sites, clip subscription sites, phone/text services, panty selling and so on—to assemble a livable income. They then promote and cross-market themselves and their products, unpaid work that benefits each platform and their payment processors in user traffic and transactions. Self-promotion has worked for models. However, recently increased competition means they do even more unpaid promotion to be noticed, a dynamic that only benefits platforms.

It is also a precarious strategy: The promotion of adult content is subject to platforms' terms of service and ever-evolving public policy, making these unreliable tools. In fact, social media frequently ban or "shadowban" (hide from view, but still allow) models, both of which can greatly impact their income. Still, models accept this arrangement, believing that platforms are intermediaries and, as independent operators, they are solely responsible for their success or failure on a platform. "The pay scale really is all over the place. It really depends on how much time you put into it and how dedicated you are," Alexa admitted. This individualist logic reinforces a sense of meritocracy and autonomy, the myth that a model can create her own wage stability. Models see unpaid work as part of the entrepreneurial experience, which relieves platforms of responsibility.

Platforms conceal the investment costs workers typically incur, banking on models to front this capital in order to build their personal brands. To be successful, models invest in professional lighting, camera equipment, high-speed internet, sex toys, personal grooming and appearance and intangible resources such as IT skills, social support, and business acumen. Models working alone, with rudimentary equipment or technological literacy, have little success keeping people in their rooms, much less building a following, even if they have an attractive personality and look. Not only do users lose interest when there are technical glitches, but models are also convinced that platforms hide those with low-resolution cameras and slow internet connections from view in order to preserve a better user experience and quality brand. Platforms are close-mouthed about their algorithms, so arguments about their intentions are moot. However, platforms are not incentivized to create algorithms supporting a democratic field for models, nor do they invest in models by subsidizing resources needed to succeed. Models are simply the content that platforms offer and moderate for buyers: they are algorithmically sorted, searched, showcased, or hidden according to platforms' needs.[37] For instance, MyFreeCams uses "camscores" to rank models by a monthly calculation of time spent and money made. Jordan sometimes feels "defeated" by these algorithms because she works hard but knows there is a ceiling to her success. Not only does a low score reduce a model's visibility on the platform, but also many users confer status to high-scoring models. Preferences for high-scoring models doubly disadvantages mid- to low-tier models struggling to find an audience. Thus, the industry perpetuates a meritocratic myth that anyone can make six or even seven figures camming; in reality, camming requires more time, energy, and resources than advertised, creating hidden hierarchies of remuneration like other digital creative work.[38]

Though reaping exorbitant profits, platforms position themselves as "intermediaries" connecting sellers to buyers, making a model's income and financial stability contingent upon continued user interest. Models sometimes feel uncomfortably beholden to male users who will "hold the money over your head," according to Cora. Big tippers, she said, expect a model to bend her rules for them, pressing her for sensitive information like her real name and location and retaliating when rebuffed. Several models reflected on fans who would remind them they had discovered the models' real names and even home addresses but did not intend to use the information. Ophelia received a greeting card from a user at her home, which disturbed her, but she did not want to alienate the user who never tried to meet up, remained friendly, and continued to pay her. Models tend to downplay these threats and individually manage incidents of harassment or coercion because they fear the financial ramifications. This dynamic shows how workplace sexual harassment follows women onto online labor platforms but is not addressed, since "cyber" forms of harassment, stalking, and abuse are seen as less harmful. In this case, many see those affected as putting themselves in harm's way because they are sex workers.

Models endure such incidents due to the inconsistency of traffic and earnings on platforms. Even successful models experience days when "you're camming for six hours, and it's crickets," Birdie told me. Then, there are days when one tip from a "whale," a big spender, meets a model's weekly or even monthly goal. In these moments, Birdie will "cam for as long as it goes away." Her experience demonstrates how this unpredictability leads to not only dependencies on regular tippers, but also working erratic and sometimes grueling hours, which takes a psychic toll and causes models to burn out. Alexa trains models to "take a day off" when this happens "because you're not going to make any money." Birdie reiterated this sentiment: "If you're having a bad day, it shows. Even when you try to cover it up, if there's something else bothering you, people pick up on that." While a helpful form of self-care, this advice is moot if a model *needs* to work that day and does not have the freedom to let her emotions dictate her schedule. As Penny put it, "some girls, they depend on this to *eat* and if they don't have a good day, they're not eating or they're not paying rent." Thus, relying solely on individual consumers to pay the bills, who are almost entirely male, taps into a familiar gendered power dynamic in which models intensely manage their emotions to please a male consumer and stabilize their income.

This emotional labor is most pronounced when they confront requests for fetish work that undermine their values.[39] "We just see all of these sick guys that are into *kids*," Penny complained, "and they flock to cam sites because they can openly do it without really doing it." Penny finds pedophilic fetishes "disgusting," but she feels backed into a corner. "I *can't* react and go, 'You're fucking sick.'" Unlike the emotional labor of maintaining a cheery demeanor, pretending to accept fetishes that go against one's moral code and then *embodying* them can be mentally and spiritually draining. Recognizing these are exceptional work conditions, models are used to being containers for people's desires and seek to neutralize their feelings when they perform uncomfortable or offending acts such as incest fantasies, pedophilia, and race or religion play. Nearly all models revealed the same advice to newcomers: "Never do anything you do not want to do. You always have a choice." The popularity of this advice is apt—and telling. Models do have a choice, but the advice resonates because self-determination is notoriously slippery. Their dependence on satisfied users and good ratings to maintain their reputation on platforms softly massages their desires and decisions.

Developing a fan base is the most popular strategy cam models deploy to stabilize their incomes, illustrating the importance of relational labor to sexual content creation in the Web 2.0 era. Camming is intimate work that involves providing users digital companionship unrestricted by boundaries of time and space and professional and private selves. Many models create subscription-based fan clubs, where users get exclusive photos, videos, and live shows and access to a model via phone, text messages, and social media. Ophelia, for instance, commodifies all aspects of the process: posting behind-the-scenes photos and videos that lead up to an exclusive live show, offering those willing to pay more the option to watch her take a shower after a particularly "messy" show, and selling the lingerie she wore during it.

Nina, a former adult film actress who recently transitioned into camming, describes it as more demanding because of the intimacy models are expected to forge with fans. While she used to get paid to "pretend and leave" when her scenes were over, now she is expected to be real and never leave. Like all relationships, those between models and fans take ongoing work to maintain. The emphasis on being present, talking, and listening to users' needs and desires leads models to report feeling like an on-call therapist. Sensitive and nurturing, Kitty attracts fans who confide in her, leaving her feeling drained and underpaid for the level of care they seek. Models certainly may find the relational labor of this gig rewarding and enjoyable, but creating ongoing connections with mostly male users as sex workers heightens the ambiguity of these gendered transactions and requires models to be on guard to combat its pitfalls. As these relationships develop, models struggle to maintain their boundaries, with several reporting that some male regulars mistake them for genuine "friendships" and expect to "hang out" without paying them, while others treat it like a game, seeing how much they can get for free. Thus, being "authentic" builds a following, but the emphasis on friendship and connection can undermine a model's bottom line by subverting the value of her professional labor.

Conclusion

In this chapter, I have argued that camming is both rewarding and restricting for women who are seeking relief from the gendered expectations and disappointing results of traditional work available to them, frequently in service, care, or other feminized industries. On the one hand, this work holds economic, pragmatic, and cultural value. Not only do workers appreciate camming's low barriers to entry, potential for higher pay, flexibility, and the ability to work from home, but they also feel creatively fulfilled, supported by a community, and pleasure in doing it. For these workers, sexual labor and content creation is a gendered strategy for staking claim to their always already sexualized bodies under patriarchal capitalism. In the #MeToo era, American women are publicly exposing coercive relationships with men across many industries, making salient the ways in which sexuality is always a factor. Recognizing that sex workers are not the only women who experience sexual and gender exploitation is not groundbreaking, but it does trouble feminist aversions to talk of empowerment in sex work if we are able to see the gendered and sexualized aspects of women's work in other industries and how their positions situate them as both empowered and exploited. Cam models are arguably more inclined and better equipped to deal with these issues too, having developed tactics as sex workers that protect themselves from coercion, strategically redeploying patriarchal constructions of sexuality as a form of capital.

On the other hand, platform-mediated sex work is both a tool that women use and an artifact of patriarchal capitalism, a tension that cannot be discounted. Despite promoting themselves as "sex worker friendly" corners of the internet, cam platform companies still devalue and exploit the sexual labor of their mostly female workforce, leaving them to fend for themselves with mostly male consumers who can leverage these relationships in ways that put models at risk. Some of the constraints mentioned in this chapter—hidden hierarchies amongst workers, algorithmic bias, the vulnerabilities of visibility, offloading risks and capital costs to workers, and the labor of developing a following and fan relationships—are somewhat germane to creative work in the gig economy. But the ways they manifest in camming suggest a need to take a serious but not defensive look at how the *marginalization* of sex work, rather than sex work itself, creates barriers for women.

Ultimately, the constraints and possibilities of platform-mediated sex work reflect broader issues affecting gig workers. The inclusion of their tactics, strategies, and politics in this conversation brings a fresh perspective to the fight for bringing pleasure, dignity, and humanity to all forms of work. We might draw on these perspectives in the struggle to make all work more humane, starting with sex work.[40]

This involves challenging not only platform companies' policies, but also the marginalization of sex workers by legal, moral, and social codes that put unnecessary burden on cam models by making their gig work especially precarious despite being legal in the United States. Sex workers, activists, and allies have become adept at contesting and advocating for better legislation that impacts this marginalized community (and all citizens) even during the drafting process. For example, in spring 2020, activist groups like the Sex Workers Outreach Project

(SWOP), Hacking//Hustling, and Decriminalize Sex Work were at the forefront of tracking, protesting, and informing the public about the newly introduced EARN IT Act (S. 3398), another bill intending to chip away at platform immunity afforded by Section 230 of the Communications Decency Act in the name of ending sex trafficking. Granting the government "the power to compel online service providers to break encryption or be exposed to potentially crushing legal liability," the EARN IT Act has been called "a disaster for Internet users' free speech and security" by the internet civil liberties organization Electronic Frontier Foundation, which acknowledged how sex workers had so far been among the first and most invested groups to bring attention to the issue and fight its passage because the stakes for them are so severe.[41]

Despite these efforts, sex workers are not typically centered in discussions of gig workers' rights and the future of the gig economy. It is important that we center marginalized groups like sex workers not only to learn from their approaches, but also to ensure that the research we conduct and policies we advocate for are not in vain, offering unwelcome one-size-fits-all solutions to ideal gig worker dilemmas and resulting in unintended outcomes for those without seats at the table. Taking sex workers' perspectives and lived experiences into account, as I have attempted to do here, is imperative in order to develop an intersectional feminist framework for addressing the inequalities reproduced in the gig economy. Such an approach earnestly acknowledges how patriarchal capitalism is not uniformly felt and managed. Therefore, we must humble ourselves by asking workers better questions. Only then might we understand the peculiar appeal of compromised structures and find transformative potential in the creative ways people cope with precarity in their everyday lives.

Notes

1. Linda Pressly, "Cam-Girls: Inside the Romanian Sexcam Industry," *BBC*, August 10, 2017.
2. Uttam Bajwa, Denise Gastaldo, Erica Di Ruggiero, and Lilian Knorr, "The Health of Workers in the Global Gig Economy," *Globalization and Health* 14, no. 124 (2018), https://doi.org/10.1186/s12992-018-0444-8.
3. Aaron Smith, "Gig Work, Online Selling and Home Sharing," Pew Research Center, November 2016.
4. Nicholas Fiori, "The Precarity of Global Digital Labor," *Women's Studies Quarterly* 45, no. 3 & 4 (2017).
5. Julia Ticona and Alexandra Mateescu, "Trusted Strangers: Carework Platforms' Cultural Entrepreneurship in the On-Demand Economy," *New Media & Society* 20, no. 11 (2018).
6. Niels van Doorn, "Platform Labor: On the Gendered and Racialized Exploitation of Low-Income Service Work in the 'On-Demand' Economy," *Information, Communication & Society* 20, no. 6 (2017).
7. Helen Rand, "Challenging the Invisibility of Sex Work in Digital Labour Politics," *Feminist Review* 123 (2019).
8. Heather Berg, "Labouring Porn Studies," *Porn Studies* 1, no. 1–2 (2014): 75.
9. Elka Torpey and Andrew Hogan, "Working in a Gig Economy," *U.S. Bureau of Labor Statistics,* May 2016.

10. Ticona and Mateescu, "Trusted Strangers," 4385.
11. Steven P. Vallas, "Platform Capitalism: What's at Stake for Workers?" *New Labor Forum* 28, no. 1 (2019): 48–59.
12. Ibid.
13. Safiya Umoja Noble, *Algorithms of Oppression: How Search Engines Reinforce Racism* (New York: New York University Press, 2018).
14. Van Doorn, "Platform Labor," 907.
15. José van Dijck, David Nieborg, and Thomas Poell, "Reframing Platform Power," *Internet Policy Review* 8, no. 2 (2019): 7–8.
16. For a discussion of the limitations of this early research and the affordances and limitations of digital sex work, see Angela Jones, "Sex Work in a Digital Era," *Sociology Compass* 9, no. 7 (2015): 559.
17. Angela Jones, *Camming: Money, Power, and Pleasure in the Sex Work Industry* (New York: New York University Press, 2020), 120.
18. Niels van Doorn and Olav Velthuis, "A Good Hustle: The Moral Economy of Market Competition in Adult Webcam Modeling," *Journal of Cultural Economy* 11, no. 3 (2018).
19. Antonia Hernández, "'There's Something Compelling About Real Life': Technologies of Security and Acceleration on Chaturbate," *Social Media & Society* 5, no. 4 (2019).
20. Annette Bernhardt, "Making Sense of The New Government Data on Contingent Work," *Medium,* June 10, 2018.
21. Gina Neff, *Venture Labor: Work and the Burden of Risk in Innovative Industries* (Boston, MA: MIT Press, 2012).
22. Brooke Duffy, *(Not) Getting Paid to Do What You Love: Gender, Social Media, and Aspirational Work* (New Haven, CT: Yale University Press, 2017), 10.
23. Leslie Regan Shade, "Hop to It in the Gig Economy: The Sharing Economy and Neo-Liberal Feminism," *International Journal of Media & Cultural Politics* 14, no. 1 (2018): 45.
24. Duffy, *(Not) Getting Paid to Do What You Love*, 9.
25. Melissa Gregg and Rutvica Andrijasevic, "Virtually Absent: The Gendered Histories and Economies of Digital Labour," *Feminist Review* 123 (2019): 3.
26. Heather Berg, "A Scene Is Just a Marketing Tool: Alternative Income Streams in Porn's Gig Economy," *Porn Studies* 3, no. 2 (2016): 168.
27. Kavita Ilona Nayar, "Working It: The Professionalization of Amateurism in Digital Adult Entertainment," *Feminist Media Studies* 17, no. 3 (2017).
28. Nancy Baym, "Connect With Your Audience! The Relational Labor of Connection," *The Communication Review* 18 (2015): 20.
29. Sarah Banet-Weiser, *Authentic: The Politics of Ambivalence in a Brand Culture* (New York: New York University Press, 2012), 85–86.
30. All names provided are pseudonyms I have chosen to protect interviewees' identities.
31. See Angela Jones, *Camming*; Mireille Miller-Young, *A Taste for Brown Sugar: Black Women in Pornography* (Durham, NC: Duke University Press, 2014); Siobhan Brooks, *Unequal Desires: Race and Erotic Capital in the Stripping Industry* (Albany, NY: SUNY Press, 2010).
32. Stephanie Denton, "Workers' Access to and Use of Leave From Their Jobs in 2017–18," *U.S. Bureau of Labor Statistics,* January 2020.
33. Nicholas Fiori, "The Precarity of Global Digital Labor," 323.
34. Jones, *Camming*, 17.
35. Bajwa et al., "The Health of Workers in the Global Gig Economy."
36. Tarleton Gillespie, *Custodians of the Internet: Platforms, Content Moderation, and the Hidden Decisions That Shape Social Media* (New Haven, CT: Yale University Press, 2018): 22.
37. Ibid.
38. Duffy, *(Not) Getting Paid to Do What You Love*, 219.

39. Arlie Hochschild, *The Managed Heart: Commercialization of Human Feeling* (Berkeley: University of California Press, 1983).
40. David Burr Gerrard, "'Do What You Love'—Oh, But Not That! On Recognizing Sex Work as Work," *The AWL,* March 6, 2014.
41. Daly Barnett, "Sex Worker Rights Advocates Raise the Alarms about EARN IT," The Electronic Frontier Foundation, June 1, 2020.

11

THIS IS GIG LEISURE

Games, Gamification, and Gig Labor

Randy Nichols

In his book *The Procrastination Economy*, Ethan Tussey argues that media companies are able to leverage mobile technologies to "monetize our in-between moments."[1] Tussey's study elaborates on the ways a range of mobile-enabled devices has enabled corporate profit to extend into broader reaches of our lives. The increasing centrality of mobile technologies is, in fact, just one tendril of the ways that increasingly concentrated media industries have been able to render more and more of our time into profit. The move to convert the private, the in-between, the individual into capital is, in fact, one of the key industrial strategies available to media companies in the post-Fordist economy. The consequence of the widespread adoption of digital and mobile technologies is, first, a removal of the barriers that limited profitable time and, second, the ability to render private moments into profitable labor. Put another way, just as post-Fordist economic production created gig labor, it has also created what I call "gig leisure."

Torpey and Hogan describe gig labor as work on demand, usually via single projects and tasks found in digital marketplaces.[2] Gig leisure operates similarly and describes digitally mediated work done on demand, outside laboring hours. Digital media have been instrumental in gig labor and leisure exploitation.

This chapter examines video games and the development of gamification to better understand the dynamics of gig leisure exploitation. To do so, it examines relationships between digital technologies and labor, exploring how gamification extends that relationship. In so doing, this chapter contends that gamification is an early example of gig leisure. By examining gamification as a post-Fordist method of expanding labor productivity, I shed light on the broader contours and implications of gig leisure.

Gamification is typically defined as "the use of elements and techniques from game design in non-game contexts."[3] Gamification might include trying to create competition in situations where it isn't normally found or awarding points, badges, or other rewards for particular behaviors. This definition overlooks that these behaviors typically benefit capital. Gamification recontextualizes the value of play as a space for enjoyment, instruction, or catharsis, reimagining it as a mechanism for producing economic value. For this reason, gamification is often framed as a practice that increases productivity, and, as such, a number of critiques of it have focused on how gamification is deployed on workers.[4] Indeed, there has been considerable work done focusing on video games' use of immaterial labor, but gamification marks a significant change because it allows that immaterial labor to happen at different times and in different places, even as what it produces can be reconfigured and used to advance a range of productive goals.[5] Thus, gamification is not merely a means to expand immaterial labor; it is also a means to maximize productive capacity beyond formal labor production. Gamification incorporates leisure more fully into the cycles of production. If gig labor allows exploitation via work on demand, gamification is an example of its corollary: exploitation via productive leisure time. Gig leisure is most significant for removing the very possibility of the in-between time Tussey discussed.[6] If mobile and internet technologies are involved, all time is made available for capitalist exploitation.

From Fordism and Taylorization to Post-Fordism and Gamification

Scholars emphasize various aspects of new media technologies' impact on the economy. Among these are "creative," "digital," "information," "cognitive," "precarious," and "immaterial." Each points to a particular facet, and as such, these terms not synonymous, but rather, they privilege particular economic features over others.[7] All of these features are integral to the post-Fordist economy. Post-Fordism marks a shift from the industrialized, Fordist economy of the early to mid-20th century, especially its push from standardized, mass production to flexible, on-demand production and its reliance on digital and information technologies. Consequently, a key problematic for critical analysis is making sense of technical and cultural labor.[8] As Kline et al. have argued, video games represent the shift to post-Fordist production—they are the era's "ideal commodity."[9] Möring and Leino specify that video games' use is historically contingent.[10] Furthermore, how we construct play as a society, the purpose and value societies attribute to games and the act of play, and what different members of society take from those interactions are also products of the historical, ideological, and material circumstances in which they emerge.

Dominant Fordist practices and ideologies such as mass production, assembly lines, standardized products, and Taylorization also produced particular attitudes about play itself. In contrast, post-Fordism built on those practices, reshaping the idea of play and the tools involved to incorporate them into both the ideology of the time and the needs of production. Thus, in the post-Fordist epoch, mass production and assembly lines evolve into on-time and small-batch production. But likewise, the idea of Taylorization adapted to post-Fordist needs. One result of that adaptation is "gamification."

Similarly, the use of play might change. Under Fordist conditions, play oscillates between the need to be instructive and cathartic. Further, play takes place in a place and time distinctly different under industrial capitalism, when work has been separated from the home and leisure time has become a mechanism to help enforce consumption. It is not coincidence that Huizinga's "magic circle," a separate play space that allows us to learn without facing the consequences of the real, day-to-day world, comes to the fore during this period. But under post-Fordism, play becomes something that needs to be more than instructive: it must also be productive, and in order to be rendered productive, play must be controlled. The advance of digital and mobile technologies is ideal for this dynamic. As those technologies become increasingly central to daily life, so, too, will control of leisure time—of play itself—become a regular feature. As Hardt and Negri note, labor focusing on the manipulation of information is central to the emerging system of global production and control.[11] Information about how we play must be generated, studied, and deployed to better shape the process of play. Moreover, this process requires not just labor but also consumption by the player and of the player's actions. Much of gamification relies either on competition or on rendering leisure consumption into a new social norm. Stopping at a coffee shop, purchasing virtual goods, or even simply carrying one's mobile device is sufficient to generate the information needed to better shape one's leisure time behavior and productivity, while gamification incentivizes it. Coupled with Dyer-Witheford and De Peuter's assertion that video games "are media constitutive of twenty-first-century global hypercapitalism," it becomes clear that video games serve as a meaningful site to interrogate how these ideologies and practices have evolved.[12]

Digital Technologies and Labor

Although much scholarship treats "labor" and "work" as interchangeable, for Marx there was a distinction between the two: labor is paid; work is not.[13] Indeed, this discrepancy lies at the heart of concerns about the post-Fordist digital economy and is key to understanding "gig labor" and "gig leisure." Terranova reminds us that we should be careful in our assumptions about the innate human value of labor; labor may not be, as Marx suggested, the central humanizing force.[14] These problematics are crucial to understanding the impact of digital technology. As such, we should re-examine the question that Fast et al. ask: "Whether a productive activity should count as labor . . . depends on the answer to the question: who creates what type of value for whom?"[15] One may ask, "Is it labor when I create data for which Facebook gets paid?" or "In what way is the work of generating data passively via my leisure activities de-humanizing?"

These questions show how digital technologies complicate notions of value. First, digital technologies bridge elements of culture and information industries that typically appear disparate (such as the media, education, the arts, etc.). Therefore, digital technologies bear potential for some to profit and others to be exploited.[16] Consequently, new products such as computers and cell phones and the new networks tie them together via new types of work and workers who consume these products and networks. Second, digital technologies make a mess of work's conceptualization under Fordism, particularly how value is produced and where it occurs. While Fast et al. argue that work is that which creates use value (or value for oneself) and labor is that which creates exchange value (or value for someone else), with digital technologies it is entirely possible to create value for both at once and, potentially, to not realize you are doing so for one or either.[17] My cell phone might bring me value even as it provides information to the company that provides my cellular service and to third parties. Thus, while there are still traditional workplaces, digital technologies make any place a potential site of work, a new wrinkle on Andrejevic's idea that the workplace can be both a site of community and satisfaction even as it is exploitive.[18] When you can work any place, every place carries the potential to become a site of labor. Moreover, a workplace may be far removed from where that labor is made profitable and farther still from where the products of that labor are consumed.[19]

Digital technologies and networks increase scalability. As Fast et al. note, communication devices and the networks they create bring people into digital systems of production who may not realize they are working.[20] As such, they are particularly unlikely to realize there is a question about value and compensation. Because these technologies represent major changes to production, the value chains themselves become immensely complex. Even if you are aware that you are producing value for someone else and want to seek compensation, the possibilities of doing so are functionally difficult to trace, ideologically discouraged, and perhaps entirely masked. As Terranova explains it, the ability of these technologies to draw one into production is part of a process that is always around us, always seeking to involve us in flows of capital and always seeking to incorporate cultural practice into profitable business practice.[21] The data I generate actively and passively by owning a cell phone, for example, may be distributed via the market globally, making it difficult if not impossible for me to track and seek compensation, let alone to exercise the "right to be forgotten."

Under post-Fordism access to and awareness of information flows are important markers of class struggle. As Fast et al. argue, media consumption is increasingly about producing information flows to be exploited.[22] Thus, digital economies do not, as Tapscott claimed, rid us of the challenges of Fordism and the industrial economy.[23] Class struggle has not vanished; it has been remade and masked.[24] Whereas digital technologies may render some labor socially valued, it may proletarianize others.[25] Each digital device runs the risk of bringing us, consciously or not, further into what Bulut recognized as "the structural tendencies of capitalism," including the need for cheap labor and the financialization of virtually every commodity.[26]

Furthermore, such dynamics suggest that because products are immaterial, so is the labor that produced them. As Lazzarato explained, immaterial labor commoditizes information and produces "cultural context of the commodities."[27] Ceding privacy creates conditions for immaterial labor's production, and consequently, produces a context wherein particular articulations of privacy become unthinkable. Such labor, Terranova notes, is not tied to any particular class, but rather, signifies a kind of privilege.[28] The question of the social field—of the distribution of economic, social, and cultural capital—shapes and limits how such labor is used and valued and marks class position.[29] Video games are an illustrative example of this.[30] That much of this labor is free is significant. Examining the video game industry, from which the trend of gamification sprang, makes further sense of these trends, illuminating the idea of digital leisure.

Video Games, Work, and Labor

The rise of the video games industry serves as a primer to understanding the dynamics of gamification, free labor, and the gig economy. As game development has evolved, it has foregrounded industrial practices vital to the gig economy, including contractual labor with minimal benefits and protections, flexible hours, work-for-hire contracts, and non-compete clauses, among others. Crucially, game production, like the gig economy, increasingly relies upon single task hiring and consumers' labor. Despite—or perhaps because of—these trends, the video game industry has been treated as a desirable situation in terms of labor and policy. Game production's sheen persists despite exploiting what Kuehn and Corrigan aptly titled "hope labor," wherein people provide free labor hoping it leads to employment.[31] Players may be involved in play testing and maintenance of game worlds, often with an eye to joining the industry.[32]

From its very beginnings, video game production emphasized the commodity status of its products.[33] From the earliest days of the industry, game makers were more likely to think about how to profit than about artistic possibilities. Of course, this is not intended to suggest that even the earliest game products were without artistic merit or even intent, but rather that the goals of game production and the possibilities of games themselves were framed within the bounds of capitalist production. Both the fun of games and the goal of game production emphasized the commodities being sold. Bulut captures this relationship nicely: "video games act as a laboratory for the materialization of immaterial labor that fuses play with work."[34]

Players and producers mix work and play. Modding exemplifies this dynamic. Modding is the practice of players of developing new game content—typically levels but also modifications to how characters or in-game items appear—which are then shareable and, in some cases, available for purchase. For the game players producing mods, the goal is sometimes for fun but often focused on creating a pathway to employment within the games industry. Kücklich provides an excellent primer on the early history of modding, detailing its early history and profitability.[35] While the beginnings of the industry took shape in the late 1960s and the industry emerged in the early 1970s, modding was not far behind, becoming reasonably common by the early 1980s.[36] While modding emerged in the early 1980s, it was not until the mid-1990s that the industry found means to profit directly from the practice, when id Software published the code for its game *Doom* (1993, id Software). Thus, players' ability to create their own mods extended the game's playability for several years. One chief advantage of a mod is that it requires the original game to be played, a feature that can extend sales. As a result, id began to release level editors with subsequent games like *Quake* (1996, id Software) and *Quake II* (1997, id Software). Using the *Quake II* level editor, two players (both former programmers for Microsoft) created a complete game called *Half-Life* (1998, Valve Software) and used this to launch their own company, Valve Software, which went on to become a major player in the modern video game industry's distribution sector.[37] *Half-Life*, however, is an extremely rare exception; modders and their labor are clearly commodified by the industry, but they are almost never remunerated.[38]

The labor of modding has been thought of in a number of ways, including as "precarious labour,"[39] "social labor,"[40] "productive play,"[41] "immaterial labor,"[42] and "co-production,"[43] among other formulations. What these views share is the grounding in the post-Fordist digital economy, a reliance on audience and fan labor, and varying amounts of uncertainty for both workers in the industry and those working. Moreover, Taylor clarifies that while much of this labor is social in nature, it is still central to the game's maintenance and life cycle.[44] In other words, the game industry has come to rely on players, in addition to programmers, creating, maintaining, defending, and advancing games. As such, modding takes particular advantage of the interaction between player and game, using what Celia Pearce calls "productive play," in which the interaction between product and consumer also carries the possibility of blurring the lines between play and production.[45]

These dynamics mark one of the central challenges of productive play: the idea of "play" masks the impact of and interaction with "production."[46] As Kücklich noted, modding tends to be categorized as a hobby or leisure, hiding both the work and the precarity of the worker itself.[47] This veiling is neither new nor limited to video games, of course, as the locus of production across media industries typically centers on certain producers while excluding others. While the film industry distinguishes between "above the line" and "below the line," the example of video gaming demonstrates there is often, in fact, a third possibility, "outside the line," exemplified by the consumer who exists entirely outside the industrial, accounting lines but who is nonetheless necessary for production and profitability.[48] One such example is that modders have rarely been paid for their labor. While they might gain social and cultural capital within the field of game production, modders rarely gain employment.[49] And yet, as Tai and Hu note, fan labor continues to be a major force in the game industry that relies on the passion of gamers who are rarely treated as co-creators.[50]

Fan labor normalizes unpaid labor in the video game industry, enabling players to carry that norm into other cultural fields. That normalization makes the post-Fordist move towards exploiting leisure in other contexts for profit more accepted. This can be seen in another key development growing out of the video game industry: gamification. Gamification has become common in a wide range of industries and has extended into the leisure time of anyone using digital networked products. Gamification, however, allows unpaid labor to move beyond the work of fans actively engaged with a product to those who passively own or use digital technologies in non-game spaces. Via cell phones and other networked devices, the commodification of nearly the whole range of human activity in and outside of work is made possible.

Gamification and Ramifications

As DeWinter et al. argued, gamification has become a key organizing principle for labor in the 21st century, similar to Taylorism in the 19th and 20th centuries.[51] Taylorism is a Fordist practice geared towards maximizing productivity in the workplace, while gamification functions as a post-Fordist mechanism that extends that productivity into leisure time. In this way, gamification serves as a training method to produce productive time and resources.

Kim and Werbach rightly point out that while there is a long history of the intermingling of games and business and production, as seen in Roy's 1959 studies of factory workers playing games while at work, gamification functions differently.[52] While the factory workers in Roy's study invented games spontaneously, gamification was neither spontaneous nor instituted by the workers themselves. Rather, it was capital or management attempting to initiate something that appears as play to boost productivity. It is not play that happens during break time, it is labor that happens "on the clock."[53]

Because of its usefulness in increasing production, gamification has become its own industry. Estimates suggest that its value was US $4.9 billion in 2016 with the potential to triple by 2020.[54] Perhaps most important is the range of factors of production that gamification can target. Gamification practices might focus on relatively explicit production boosts like working faster in the checkout line, but might also be less obvious including attempts to gamify health and wellness as a way to decrease employer paid insurer costs, better communication with consumers, educational initiatives, and even working towards particular policy outcomes.[55]

If gamification were only deployed in these ways, however, it would not be significantly different from much of what was seen in the Fordist era. While much of the literature of gamification has focused on its value with workers, it is just as likely to be deployed on consumers and audiences as a way to boost productivity outside of wage labor formulations.

If it were deployed only within the confines of one's work, gamification would be little more than maximized Taylorization, an economy of scale reached. Rather, because it can be used across a range of activities—both within the confines of work and without—it becomes something else, reaching an economy of scope in its production impact. DeWinter et al. note that while many foundational works about gamification focus on its use in helping business and nonprofits, the potential for it to be employed elsewhere, particularly on consumers, was also always there.[56] Ideologically, gamification typically carries with it both an explicit focus on productivity and an implicit assumption that market forces are the ideal mechanism of correction. This is particularly true of McGonigal's book *Reality Is Broken*, which takes as a given that making work playful is a necessary starting point but that using play as work is the ideal solution to a range of social problems.[57] Game players might submit content for a game's development, for example, or consumers might boost a company's brand via reviews.

While there has been considerable focus on gamification's effects on workers, less attention has been given to its impact on audiences and consumers. Like games at work, commodifying leisure is not new. Kücklich, quoting Fulchen, notes that the idea of leisure time emerges out of the shift to capitalism, and so becomes one of the first spaces for commodification to occur.[58] Thus, gamification represents not just a method for blurring the boundaries between "real" and "virtual," as Kim and Werbach describe it, but also between work and leisure and between production and consumption.[59] Such a method takes Huizinga's "magic circle" and blurs it by the addition of other sets of practice. When play is rendered into production, failures to play equate to failures to produce. In the capitalist market, failure to produce always eventually carries consequences. What are the consequences, who issues them, and how they are felt?

This blurring makes gamification both more difficult and more vital to understand. As DeWinter et al. explain, any examination of it must understand both the context of the game allows, the practices invoked, and the real world space in which the game mechanic is deployed.[60] This may well represent a conflict, in which the frame that wins out likely enforces dominant ideology. The magic circle has the Game, in which consequences are limited because rules are agreed upon by players; gamification has "the game," which has the trappings of a game, but where rules come from an outside, more powerful force. The consequences are real even as they may never be explicitly acknowledged until the moment they are invoked.

Finally, gamification increasingly relies on digital technologies for its capability, bringing with it all the concerns over privacy, exploitation, and profit that arise with these technologies. Those concerns are especially impactful in gamification's use outside of business, where cell phones, social media, and electronic devices are vital. Marketing and surveillance are often a part. Thus, gamification in the realm of leisure seems likely to achieve an economy of scale unattainable even in the largest firms. As Fast et al. explain, value from online and digital ventures is typically less about an individual actor's behavior and more about the flow of information from large audiences.[61] The value of the former is small and limited; the value of the latter is extensive and scalable. Moreover, they note that value created in this way is poorly related to typical questions about time and productivity because the effort of one person to click or post is infinitesimal compared to the total time produced by the entire flow. Just as the Internet as described by Terranova serves as a mechanism to facilitate the gathering of human intelligence, including the knowledge and human capital at play, so, too do other digital technologies. They work to gather, focus, and amplify these forms towards capitalist productive ends.[62] While there is potential for these technologies to push back against dominant ideologies and capitalism, they begin grounded in a field defined by both.[63] Such a challenge requires a shift in how we consider labor from the classical Marxist definition to one capable of making sense of the economies of scale and scope at play.[64] The question of gig leisure suggests that labor needs to be reconsidered in order to make sense of production that occurs in play and leisure.

From Gamification to Gig Leisure

In the digital environment, the most tacit participation contributes to the flow of value production. By simply having my phone, I generate usable data, exploitable and profitable across many institutions. Gig leisure's significance is that like gig labor, access to that flow is on demand. Other forms of capital limit one's access to and ability to profit from that flow: you have to have the knowledge to design it or the wealth to buy into it. The implication, however, is clear: leisure time in the digital environment is a resource to be bought and sold similar to productive labor. The mechanisms of gamification incentivize leisure-as-production: badges, points, statuses, but rarely, if ever, is there anything that resembles actual compensation. Moreover, because digital technologies enable nearly infinite labor exploitation, leisure time might be carved up for data based on particular demand, but might also, with the simple update of an application or terms of service agreement, produce an entirely new set of on-demand data flow.[65] This is gig leisure: post-Fordist, on-demand production for capital via leisure time and the application of digital technologies. Thus, gig leisure emerges as an ideological mechanism that combines pre-existing neoliberal conceptions about the role of technology, markets, and labor with post-Fordist ideas about play and games.

Such a combination poses a few challenges for researchers. First, we need to pay increased attention to leisure time and the mechanisms the post-Fordist economy deploys to exploit it. As Möring and Leino note, the economy under Fordism advances a belief that labor and free time are one of the key oppositional dialectics in which labor productivity must be managed and maximized.[66] Management is accomplished via both technological forms and administrative practices available at the time. In the post-Fordist economy, this division is reconsidered, with leisure time becoming an area of key focus, with the goal of making it somehow productive.

Second, as Kücklich notes, scholars must differentiate between leisure that is productive and leisure that is not.[67] While this issue has been covered extensively by political economists responding to and expanding the classic blind spot debate that began with Dallas Smythe, the implications today lend new urgency to Smythe's questions about who holds power and how they make audiences work.[68] Thus, there are two poles worth considering: how is leisure time rendered productive and for whom does it produce value? Gamification provides a useful example of these dynamics and their implications.

A third aspect that has not been sufficiently examined is how all of this demands a reconsideration of employment and labor. As Terranova acknowledged, digital technologies tend to rely on a collective form of labor and production—the flow of data referenced throughout this chapter is but one form.[69] Video games rely heavily on co-production, or the interplay between players, fans, and game designers.[70] Gamification and gig leisure take this a step further, into the realm of casual, even incidental, co-production between users of digital technologies even when they are not actively engaging. Networked digital technologies bring together minute actions of individuals into aggregated data flows that result in economic value, almost exclusively to the benefit of corporate and governmental actors.[71] Such collective production necessitates rethinking the relationship of labor and productivity to employment.

Hope and potential for resistance can be seen in the contradictions of the ideological mechanisms supporting gig leisure. Gamification carries two deep contradictions, representing ideological rifts in how exploitation of leisure time has been theorized. First, proponents of gamification argue that it is about harnessing the spirit of games to solve external social and institutional problems, even as their reward system is focused on individual reward. McGonigal argues, "The more we consume, acquire, and elevate our status, the harder it is to stay happy," yet much of gamification's overt application is geared to those goals, either explicitly or implicitly.[72] Our acts of consumption generate the most useful data to capital, and our conspicuous display of gamification's shiny, valueless tokens convinces us there is some benefit in the enterprise.

The second contradiction is about participation. Again, McGonigal notes, "When you strip away the genre differences and the technological complexities, all games share four defining traits: a goal, rules, a feedback system, and *voluntary participation*" (emphasis mine).[73] But in most cases, whether in business use or otherwise, voluntary participation is far from a given. As Terranova noted, digital technologies do not automatically turn users into active producers, nor do they render every worker into an active creator.[74] The labor associated with digital technologies guarantees neither voluntary participation nor enjoyment.[75] Nor does it guarantee compensation or reward. Whether it is an employer instituting a competition to speed checkout times or a social media company creating a cell phone application to harvest data, the extent to which participation is voluntary quickly becomes unclear. The joy and benefits are, likewise, suspect. Jenson et al. note that the long history of research on the relationship between gender and game play has given us good reason to be suspect, as both digital technologies and games tend to marginalize a range of groups culturally, socially, and economically. Such a consequence seems likely to be duplicated when exploiting leisure to productive ends.[76]

As Terranova argued, digital technologies have provided a new way to rely on the public as productive subjects. The difference lies in the modes and knowledges involved.[77] As such, on-demand exploitation of leisure seems a logical consequence and corollary of gig labor.

It is incumbent on scholars to not merely acknowledge the ways in which leisure is used productively; they should also explore how gamification changes our ideas of value, exploitation, and resistance. It was once argued that the rise of the Internet and associated technologies resulted in the rise of a class of knowledge workers. It is equally apparent that the largest class to emerge is that of data generators, who exist to be exploited by old and new capital. In our leisure, digitized and commodified, we are all laborers after all.

Notes

1. Ethan Tussey, *The Procrastination Economy* (New York: New York University Press, 2018), 28.
2. Elka Torpey and Andrew Hogan, "Working in a Gig Economy," *Career Outlook*, May 1, 2016.
3. Tae Wan Kim and Kevin Werbach, "More Than Just a Game: Ethical Issues in Gamification," *Ethics and Information Technology* 18, no. 2 (2016): 157–73.
4. Work on gamification in the workplace has been undertaken across a variety of fields. To get a sense of some of the issues, see the following samples: Ethan R. Mollick and Nancy Rothbard, "Mandatory Fun: Consent, Gamification and the Impact of Games at Work," *The Wharton School Research Paper Series*, 2014; Benedikt Morschheuser and Juho Hamari, "The Gamification of Work: Lessons From Crowdsourcing," *Journal of Management Inquiry* 28, no. 2 (2019): 145–48; Mark J. Nelson, "Soviet and American Precursors to the Gamification of Work," in *Proceeding of the 16th International Academic MindTrek Conference*, 2012, 23–26; Pedro Pereira, Emília Duarte, Francisco Rebelo, and Paulo Noriega, "A Review of Gamification for Health-Related Contexts," in *International Conference of Design, User Experience, and Usability* (Cham: Springer, 2014), 742–53. Agnessa Spanellis, Viktor Dörfler, and Jillian MacBryde, "Investigating the Potential for Using Gamification to Empower Knowledge Workers," *Expert Systems with Applications* 160 (2020): 113694.
5. Again, this work has come from a variety of perspectives and fields of inquiry. Here are some useful starting points and critiques: Mathias Fuchs, "Ludic Interfaces. Driver and Product of Gamification," *G.A.M.E. (Reggio Calabria)*, April 1, 2012; Mathias Fuchs, Sonia Fizek, Paolo Ruffino, and Niklas Schrape, *Rethinking Gamification* (Lüneberg: Meson Press, 2014); Casey O'Donnell, "Getting Played: Gamification and

the Rise of Algorithmic Surveillance," *Surveillance & Society* 12, no. 3 (2014): 349–59; Rowan Tulloch, "Reconceptualizing Gamification: Play and Pedagogy," *Digital Culture & Education* 6, no. 4 (2014); Mikko Vesa and J. Tuomas Harviainen, "Gamification: Concepts, Consequences, and Critiques," *Journal of Management Inquiry* 28, no. 2 (2019): 128–30.
6. Tussey, *The Procrastination Economy*.
7. Brett Neilson and Ned Rossiter, "From Precarity to Precariousness and Back Again: Labour, Life and Unstable Networks," *Fibreculture Journal*, no. 5 (January 1, 2005).
8. Tiziana Terranova, "Free Labor," *Social Text* 18, no. 2 (2000): 33–58.
9. Stephen Kline, Nick Dyer-Witheford, and Greig De Peuter, *Digital Play* (Montréal: McGill-Queen's University Press, 2014).
10. Sebastian Möring and Olli Leino, "Beyond Games as Political Education—Neo-Liberalism in the Contemporary Computer Game Form," *Journal of Gaming & Virtual Worlds* 8, no. 2 (2016): 145–61.
11. Michael Hardt and Antonio Negri, *Empire* (Cambridge, MA: Harvard University Press, 2000).
12. Nick Dyer-Witheford and Greig De Peuter, *Games of Empire: Global Capitalism and Video Games*. Electronic Mediations; v. 29 (Minneapolis: University of Minnesota Press, 2009), xxix.
13. Karin Fast, Henrik Örnebring, and Michael Karlsson, "Metaphors of Free Labor: A Typology of Unpaid Work in the Media Sector," *Media, Culture & Society* 38, no. 7 (2016): 963–78.
14. Terranova, "Free Labor."
15. Fast et al., "Metaphors of Free Labor," 964.
16. Terranova, "Free Labor."
17. Fast et al., "Metaphors of Free Labor."
18. Mark Andrejevic, "Watching Television Without Pity," *Television & New Media* 9, no. 1 (2008): 24–46.
19. Fast et al., "Metaphors of Free Labor."
20. Ibid.
21. Terranova, "Free Labor."
22. Fast et al., "Metaphors of Free Labor."
23. Don Tapscott, *The Digital Economy: Promise and Peril in the Age of Networked Intelligence* (New York: McGraw-Hill, 1996).
24. Meg Leta Jones, *Ctrl Z: The Right to Be Forgotten* (New York: New York University Press, 2016).
25. Terranova, "Free Labor."
26. Ergin Bulut, "Glamor Above, Precarity Below: Immaterial Labor in the Video Game Industry," *Critical Studies in Media Communication* 32, no. 3 (2015): 1936.
27. Maurizio Lazzarato, "Immaterial Labor," in *Radical Thought in Italy*, NED—New ed., Vol. 7 (Minneapolis: University of Minnesota Press, 2006), 133.
28. Terranova, "Free Labor."
29. Pierre Bourdieu, *Outline of a Theory of Practice*. Cambridge Studies in Social Anthropology; 16 (Cambridge: Cambridge University Press, 1977).
30. Randy Nichols, "Bourdieu's Forms of Capital and Video Game Production," in *The Game Culture Reader* (Cambridge: Cambridge Scholars Publishing, 2013).
31. Kathleen Kuehn and Thomas F. Corrigan, "Hope Labor: The Role of Employment Prospects in Online Social Production," *The Political Economy of Communication* 1, no. 1 (2013).
32. Randy Nichols, *The Video Game Business*. International Screen Industries (New York: Palgrave Macmillan on Behalf of the British Film Institute, 2014); Judd Ruggill, Ken McAllister, Randy Nichols, and Ryan Kaufman, *Inside the Video Game Industry* (London: Taylor and Francis, 2016).
33. Nichols, *The Video Game Business*.
34. Bulut, "Glamor Above, Precarity Below," 197.

35. Julian Kücklich, "Precarious Playbour: Modders and the Digital Games Industry," *Fibreculture Journal*, no. 5 (January 1, 2005).
36. Nichols, *The Video Game Business*.
37. Ibid.
38. Ibid.
39. Ibid.
40. T. L. Taylor, *Play Between Worlds: Exploring Online Game Culture* (Cambridge: MIT Press, 2009).
41. Celia Pearce, "Productive Play," *Games and Culture* 1, no. 1 (2006): 17–24.
42. Bulut, "Glamor Above, Precarity Below."
43. Zixue Tai and Fengbin Hu, "Play Between Love and Labor: The Practice of Gold Farming in China," *New Media & Society* 20, no. 7 (2018): 2370–390.
44. Taylor, *Play Between Worlds*.
45. Pearce, "Productive Play."
46. Nick Yee, "The Labor of Fun," *Games and Culture* 1, no. 1 (2006): 68–71.
47. Kücklich, "Precarious Playbour."
48. Bulut, "Glamor Above, Precarity Below."
49. Kücklich, "Precarious Playbour."
50. Tai and Hu, "Play Between Love and Labor."
51. Jennifer DeWinter, Carly A. Kocurek, and Randall Nichols, "Taylorism 2.0: Gamification, Scientific Management and the Capitalist Appropriation of Play," *Journal of Gaming & Virtual Worlds* 6, no. 2 (2014): 109–27.
52. Kim and Werbach, "More Than Just a Game."
53. Ibid.
54. "Global Gamification Market Value of USD 11.10 Billion by 2020 - Analysis, Trends & Opportunities Report 2016–2020 - Key Vendors: Leveleleven, Arcaris Inc & Badgeville Inc," *PR Newswire (New York)*, 2016.
55. Kim and Werbach, "More Than Just a Game."
56. DeWinter et al., "Taylorism 2.0."
57. Jane McGonigal, *Reality Is Broken: Why Games Make Us Better and How They Can Change the World* (New York: Penguin Press, 2011).
58. Kücklich, "Precarious Playbour."
59. Kim and Werbach, "More Than Just a Game."
60. DeWinter et al., "Taylorism 2.0."
61. Fast et al., "Metaphors of Free Labor."
62. Terranova, "Free Labor."
63. Ibid.
64. Fast et al., "Metaphors of Free Labor."
65. Fast et al., "Metaphors of Free Labor."
66. Möring and Leino, "Beyond Games as Political Education."
67. Kücklich, "Precarious Playbour."
68. Dallas Smythe, "Communication: Blindspots of Western Marxism," *Canadian Journal of Political and Social Theory* 1, no. 3 (1977): 1–27; Terranova, "Free Labor."
69. Terranova, "Free Labor."
70. Tai and Hu, "Play Between Love and Labor."
71. Fast et al., "Metaphors of Free Labor."
72. McGonigal, *Reality Is Broken*, 16.
73. Ibid., 21.
74. Terranova, "Free Labor."
75. Fast et al., "Metaphors of Free Labor."
76. Jennifer Jenson and Suzanne De Castell, "'The Entrepreneurial Gamer': Regendering the Order of Play," *Games and Culture* 13, no. 7 (2018): 728–46.
77. Terranova, "Free Labor."

12

UPROOTING UBER

From "Data Fracking" to Data Commons

Stephen E. Rahko and Byron B Craig

Over the past decade, many scholars have noted that the emergence of "smart" devices, Big Data analytics, artificial intelligence, Cloud computing, and the Internet of Things has brought about a new digital stage of capitalism. The growing ubiquity of computers has made algorithms—the coded sequence of instructions that computers operationally perform—a new digital means of production for extracting surplus value from labor. Algorithms require what has become an increasingly valuable new raw material: data. We understand "data" as a set or collection of symbols, characters, or forms of measurable or observable quantities of information about an object or phenomenon in the world that can be converted into binary digital form and materially recorded, stored, preserved, and accumulated. Capitalism has long required data, be it for coordinating logistical supply chains or for utilizing samples of consumer preferences collected through surveys for marketing or product design. Yet, over the past three decades the technology required to convert banal processes and activities into recorded data has become increasingly inexpensive, and the expansion and permeation of the Internet into nearly all aspects of everyday life has facilitated and simplified the collection, storage, and sharing of data.

Data is to digital capitalism what oil or minerals have been to earlier industrial stages of capitalism, for it must be mined, extracted, and refined by algorithms. In fact, in 2017 *The Economist* boldly proclaimed that data *is more valuable* than oil.[1] Algorithms have enabled us to "datafy" the world, which as Kenneth Cukier and Viktor Mayer-Schoenberger define it, is to "render into data many aspects of the world that have never been quantified before."[2] "Once we datafy things," they note, "we can transform their purpose and turn the information into new forms of value" that make it possible to not only learn more about the world but also increasingly harness "an ability to predict the future."[3] Algorithms have been employed to track and catalogue a plethora of phenomena, ranging from our shopping patterns and entertainment preferences to our physical movements through space and time, for the purpose of extracting exchange value from the discovery of patterns in large volumes of data.

Capitalism's growing use of Big Data has encouraged the rise of a new business model to harness its potentialities: the platform. Platforms are data and informational intermediaries that enable multiple users or groups to connect and interact through cyberspace. As a form of digital infrastructure that can mediate customers, advertisers, service providers, suppliers, and producers, platforms often incorporate tools that enable their users to erect their own services, products, technologies, and even markets. They offer unprecedented opportunities for data extraction since they are positioned as the foundation upon which user activities transpire. Capitalist firms across all sectors of the economy have utilized the platform as a new institutional form for efficiently extracting, analyzing, and, crucially, monopolizing the colossal new expanses of data that are now available. Since platforms can also mediate physical objects designed with artificial intelligence and machine learning capabilities, capitalist firms have begun leveraging them to build device networks that link to large databases stored in the Cloud.

Through its use of app-based, on-demand cheap labor and its aspiration to leverage the power of data and algorithms, Uber stands at the intersection of the gig economy and media convergence. Uber's gig economy business model depends on flows of data it collects and leverages at the expense of its drivers. In this chapter, we critique Uber by proposing to open the proprietary data that it collects. Drawing on the Bloomington School of Political Economy, we propose the democratization of data through a reimagining of it as a "commons." Reinscribing data as a commons would move us toward a more democratic digital era with the prospect of more equitable labor relations predicated on platform experimentation.

Uber's "Data Fracking"

Uber is a transportation service that organizes a decentralized fleet of drivers into a just-in-time workforce available on demand to transport passengers and goods through the data it collects and the algorithms it manages on its platform. Founded during the widespread misery of the Great Recession, Uber has come to symbolize a form of Potemkin entrepreneurism now baked into the gig economy that promises to connect the underutilized assets, skills, and time of despondent and debt-burdened workers surviving paycheck to paycheck with strangers temporarily willing to pay for them. Uber relies on gig-based labor that is popularly called "freelancing": a vagabond form of "self-employed" work that is conducted irregularly on an *ad hoc* and as needed basis. Freelancing has historically always been a part of capitalism, but after decades of corporate downsizing and the digitalization of labor, it has become increasingly more common. As scholars have documented, Silicon Valley is creating an underclass of app-based labor that makes the gears of digital capitalism turn.[4] In an era defined by declining opportunities for social mobility, the popularity of platform-based freelancing through Uber has portended a deeper material shift in American life marked by precarity and desperation.

Uber typifies what Nick Srnicek has called a "lean platform," that is, a business model that strategically minimizes its ownership of assets and depends on services that other platforms provide. Rather than invest in capital-intensive assets such as computing equipment, Uber instead rents hardware and software from AWS's Cloud platform and relies on Google for mapping, Braintree for payments, SendGrid for emailing, and Twilio for texting. Rather than own vehicles, Uber offloads the costs of transportation to its drivers. Uber is devoid of all assets required to transport people and objects from one place to another but owns the most important asset upon which all its services depend: the platform software and data analytics.[5]

Uber engages in what we call "data fracking." Like hydraulic fracking used to extract gas from beneath the earth's surface, Uber's app penetrates deep beneath the surface of everyday life to collect, direct, and leverage valuable flows of data for competitive advantage, often creating public hazards for consumers, drivers, and municipal planners from its data hoarding in the process. As an intermediary between users, it brokers ride and delivery requests from users and dispatches drivers to serve them, managing the payment for both. With each ride or delivery transaction, Uber amasses a wealth of data such as the location where the driver picked up passengers, the time of day for the transaction, the location of rides' final destination or delivery, and the time it took to transport passengers from one destination to another. When this data is multiplied to the scale of millions of trips, it paints a complex set of patterns about rides that are extremely valuable for understanding consumer behavior as well as trends in late-capitalist urban life.[6]

Uber monetizes data about passengers into revenue streams. Geolocation data, when combined with the immense personal data Uber already collects on its users, reveals a penetrating portrait into some of the most banal and intimate details of a passenger's life that marketers crave. Anytime Uber transports a rider from point A to point B, the company collects data it can potentially sell to third-party companies that value such information. To be sure, Uber knows where its users live, dine, work, travel, and stay on vacation, and it knows to the minute what time of the day these activities transpire. Uber has commercialized this data through partnerships with hotel chains, airlines, and credit card companies, but the company also uses the data it collects to pad its profits at the expense of its users and drivers. In 2017, for example, Uber introduced "route-based pricing," which uses artificial intelligence to differentiate its users into aggregate classes of passengers that are willing to pay more for its services and charge them higher fees. These algorithmic-based price increases do not extend to drivers, however, since they are paid at set rates based on the time and distance duration of the trip.[7]

Uber also weaponizes its data in order to establish asymmetrical and exploitative power relationships with drivers. Drivers are a primary instrument for Uber's data fracking, for the data they collect shape the company's strategic position relative to riders, regulators, and competitors in the market. Uber's data fracking is best illustrated by how it monitors "dead miles," the time drivers spend driving without a fare before they receive a ride request from the Uber app. The data collected during "dead miles" is relayed back to the central platform for algorithmic analysis. Uber's routing algorithms, for example, use data on traffic patterns to derive patterns and behaviors for managing supply and demand through surge pricing (charging customers more per mile and offering slightly higher rates to drivers), for pushing out requests to determine where and when drivers work and how much they are paid, and to signal where future passengers are most likely to be.[8]

Additionally, Uber often uses data it collects against drivers when it comes to financial compensation under its route-based pricing. Since drivers are paid according to time and mileage rates rather than a set portion of the passenger fare, data collected on traffic patterns set ride prices passengers pay, decoupled from the income drivers are paid to execute the trip. Route-based pricing has provoked driver dismay and anger over the difference between their respective cut and Uber's, a discrepancy made worse by the fact that the company is not upfront about how its fluctuating algorithms calculate driver incomes, nor does it share all the data it collects on its drivers with them. The legal classification of Uber drivers in most states as "independent contractors" facilitates the company's data fracking since it enables the company to avoid financially compensating its drivers for the necessary labor time to do the work of driving, much less compensate them for overtime pay, minimum wage, payroll and social security taxes, unemployment benefits, or the data they collect during "dead miles." Uber drivers, accordingly, suffer from a "slippery wage" marked by opaque and difficult-to-track earnings and expenses.[9]

Likewise, Uber leverages data on its drivers to control them. In *Uberland: How Algorithms Are Rewriting the Rules of Work*, Alex Rosenblat documents how Uber's use of algorithmic management alters how work is both defined and organized, both supervising and coordinating its drivers in ways that standardize work. As an emerging neoliberal technique, Uber's algorithms direct not only how the driver completes the service but also the terms of the driver's behavior. Even though all drivers are dispatched through the platform's network and are in most states legally "self-employed," they have little control over their conditions of work. For example, while logged in drivers do not even determine which ride assignments they take since Uber's algorithms control the dispatch and thus incentivize drivers to work in particular places at particular times at variable wage rates. Moreover, Uber's ratings system makes management omnipresent, as it solicits customer feedback, sets performance levels, and makes driver suspensions, "deactivations," when drivers fail to meet arbitrary algorithmic performance levels set by the firm.[10] Uber's rule by algorithmic management illustrates the brutal calculating techniques of capital's micromanagement of the worker in the era of Big Data.

Rideshare Drivers United (RDU) and Service Employees International Union (SEIU)–affiliated Gig Workers Rising have resisted these measures through strategic strikes and work stoppages across the United States, most notably on the eve of Uber's initial public offering on May 8, 2019. Driver actions and lawsuits paved the way in 2019 for the passage of California Assembly Bill 5 (AB5), which temporarily recognized rideshare workers as employees before its untimely repeal with California's 2020 ballot initiative Proposition 22. Senator Bernie Sanders has introduced the Workplace Democracy Act that would in effect nationalize the AB5 standard for all employers to determine if a gig worker is an employee or an independent contractor.[11]

Data collection has figured minimally in these struggles so far. There are encouraging developments on this front, but more is required, for even if gig workers win employee status their data will continue to be extracted in the same ways at their expense. RDU and Gig Workers Rising, for example, have focused their demands on fare transparency and the establishment of minimum hourly rates and guaranteed fare rates.[12] They should collaborate with British Uber driver James Farrar's Worker Info Exchange, which pools gig worker data to resist Uber's absent data transparency in order to campaign for better terms of pay.[13] In the United States, they should join the #PayUp campaign, which has been initiated in the US by Instacart and DoorDash workers. #PayUp pools worker pay data to calculate the rate DoorDash and Instacart compensates workers against the price consumers actually pay for the service.[14] If #PayUp launches an Uber Eats pay calculator, the pooled pay data could facilitate organizing among Uber drivers. Such arrangements would empower rideshare workers to shape the uses of data as gig companies position themselves to be key players in the construction of the emerging Internet of Things.

From Uber to the Internet of Things

Uber's involvement in the so-called smart cities movement illustrates that driver organizing and resistance efforts must encompass their data fracking. In the coming decades, the Internet will be comprised of computers, smart phones, and a digital infrastructure constituted from tens of billions of quotidian objects. Everyday life in this emerging digital era will be shaped by the way these devices collect and share data about activities and phenomena within their sensor range, making the gig economy part of a deeper entanglement of human labor within a world of objects and machine learning. Most of the world's digital infrastructure is owned and controlled by Western governments and technology firms, and as more and more devices are added to the digital infrastructure, these corporations will accrue power based on the relative size of their device networks. The corporations that control the largest device networks will manage the most sensor data collected from the sociotechnical relationships between and among users and their devices. The rules and technical standards these companies are allowed to set for collecting and acting upon streams of data from users could dramatically transform the politics of everyday life in our digital era. If platforms such as Uber, Google, and Amazon are allowed to own and control the source code upon which smart cities are designed, then all organizations, workers, and citizens will in effect be paying rent to them to operate on it as they extract value from all the world's social interactions.[15]

Uber's involvement with "smart cities" can thus be understood as an effort to build out larger systems of enclosed data fracking upon which other municipal and commercial services can be privatized and monetized. The platform has joined the SharedStreets initiative and launched Uber Movement to brand itself as a socially responsible data sharing partner with cities, but the data Uber shares has limited value for urban planning.[16] Smart city initiatives also risk locking municipalities into costly technology contracts that yield little value to the public, as in the case of Toronto's canceled partnership with Google's Sidewalk Labs.[17]

The digital transformation of labor through the Internet of Things also poses a grave risk to future gig worker organizing and resistance efforts. Our analysis of Uber highlights the ways platform work is engineered to build asymmetrical relationships between consumers, employers, and gig workers. As enclosed systems of data fracking mediate digitized tasks performed by workers within device networks, organizing efforts will be hampered by asymmetries that maximize the information platforms can obtain about potential workers bidding on piecemeal work while limiting what workers can learn about each other to build associational power.

The Bloomington School and the Commons

Rather than focusing solely on changing employment law, we argue that efforts to reform Uber and other gig platforms might be best achieved through efforts to democratize data. Here, a theoretical understanding of the "commons" would prove useful. Data should be understood as a form of commons that requires protection and careful management. The commons has become an increasingly popular aspiration among Marxist, Leftist, and heterodox theorists as a response to the many crises of late capitalism, and in the past decade a growing literature has addressed the scope and organizational possibilities the commons can offer for a postcapitalist future.[18] Many theorists have framed the crisis of digital capitalism in terms of capital's appropriation of benign social cooperation and free labor into exchange value in the form of advertising.[19] Srnicek has proposed socializing specific platforms, such as Facebook, while Christian Fuchs has argued for socializing Google toward a collectively owned Internet.[20]

There are important limits to what has been proposed thus far. Allowing the state to socialize the Internet into a new Ministry of Data would not directly address the problem of data centralization, and the emerging neoliberal vision of the Internet of Things presents a crisis that will likely be far worse than that of Google and Facebook extracting value from free labor, since we can expect the future of the gig economy to be shaped by new relationships between labor, algorithms, and autonomously managed digital device networks. While these theorists have made gestures toward a "commons"-based corrective, none of them have advanced a specific model for administering a data commons.

What is a "commons"? For the past several decades, the Bloomington School of Political Economy has been a leading source of theory in commons research. Led by the late Nobel Laureate Elinor Ostrom, the Bloomington School has made important contributions to heterodox economic thought by advancing the commons as a cooperative social arrangement beyond the institutional matrices of the market and the state. The Bloomington School understands a commons as a shared resource that is inherently vulnerable to social dilemmas. Many resources are a form of "commons," including the oceans, air, and space. For our purpose here, we must additionally recognize the electromagnetic spectrum as a commons that is mediated through a vast series of networked computers and digital technologies (i.e., the Internet) that has created a historically unprecedented capacity for the collection, storage, and sharing of data. Data is a unique resource for at least three reasons. First, data is cumulative, and so long as people have access to its storage, the cumulative effect can benefit everyone. Second, data is non-rivalrous such that one person's use of it does not come at the expense of another's use. In the digital era, objects and artifacts that may have once been rivalrous can now be digitized and posted online for others to use or not use as they please. As political economist and leading commons scholar Peter Levine notes, "If the shared artifact is a digital file, then many people can view it and copy it without degrading it or otherwise detracting from others' use."[21] Indeed, as Ostrom and Charlotte Hess have argued, non-rivalrous resources are a "public good." In the specific case of data or knowledge, they argue that the "open access of information provides a universal public good: the more quality information, the greater the public good."[22]

Although it is non-rivalrous, the commons is nevertheless a fragile resource that requires forms of social cooperation to be maintained, and it is inherently threatened by improper maintenance, overuse, and especially enclosure. "Enclosure" refers to the privatization of the common resource through the ability of technologies to capture it and convert it from a resource that was previously unowned, unmanaged, and non-rivalrous into one that is both rivalrous and capable of becoming commodified. From the 1940s through the 1970s, the federal government took a principal role in facilitating the development of computer-based electronic communication, especially ARPANET, the precursor to the Internet. The rise of neoliberalism since the 1980s and 1990s, however, has led to the privatization of America's digital infrastructure, including Internet exchange points, hardware devices and software, and ultimately the data that is transmitted across networks of servers.

There are several reasons why the commodification of the Internet poses an enclosure risk that threatens a *digital* tragedy of the commons. First, commodified data is frequently un-interoperable with other forms of data when the value it represents becomes oriented to serve a narrowly specific objective, either as a return on investment or as an input for a specific platform's algorithm.[23] Accordingly, the commodification of data devalues data for wide-ranging purposes and thus contributes to its underuse. Second, the free exchange of data is threatened by the overprotection of copyright and intellectual property and thus contributes to a monopolization of data. The user agreements that are required to access the Internet and Big Data platforms usually coerce users into giving up their data with limited recourse to know how it is being used. Finally, commodification contributes to a hoarding of data. The assault on rules of net neutrality potentially enables the corporate gatekeepers of the Internet to deter free access to data by privileging some content over others with enhanced speed or storage.

If our digital social order will continue to be marked by relationships between people and networked devices, we will need a political praxis for administering democratic control over the technological means of production, value generation, and social surplus. Any sociotechnical democracy ordered around the Internet of Things must begin with a deep and enduring commitment to cultural norms, and perhaps even legal statutes, of inclusive participation. The standard for sociotechnical democratic participation should be that any individual potentially affected by decisions regarding device networks and data collection should have an equal opportunity to affect such decisions. It is perhaps unreasonable to presume that participants will be competent to make all decisions in such a technologically advanced sociopolitical order, but this should not prevent us from administering a network of devices capable of producing open source data that users can understand, and this should not warrant restrictions on what decisions individuals actually wish to participate in.

Such a participatory ideal would inform the organization and institutionalization of the data commons. Arrangements of commons management can take many forms and ultimately must be shaped according to the specific properties of the resource. We propose approaching the Internet of Things and Big Data in terms of what Levine has called an "associational commons" on a national scale.[24] An associational commons exists when a common resource is managed through organizational and institutional mechanisms that unify diverse stakeholders toward the formation of rules and responsibilities for shared use. We imagine an associational commons of civic, labor, medical, public interest, and commercial stakeholders organized into decentralized but overlapping and interlocking layers of councils.

Our vision of a council system draws inspiration from the theoretical legacy of council democracy. Council democracy has been a rich source of heterodox political and economic thought for more than a century.[25] To be clear, although the council system that we are proposing for managing a data commons is more narrowly administrative in scope than that which has been proposed by most theorists in the council democracy tradition, it does create Arendtian "spaces of freedom" for public participation in the affairs of data.[26] The council system we imagine would be organized into representative jurisdictions at the municipal, regional, state, and federal levels, and it would be chartered to establish rules and agreements that are widely reviewed and publicly approved for how device networks and data will be produced, collected, shared, managed, and made available for use. Data collected from devices operating in local cellular and Internet networks would be arranged and made publicly available by the municipal council. Members of the council would be appointed by locally elected officials who would be chosen from a list of nominees advanced by civic, labor, medical, public interest, and commercial stakeholders from the community. Data collected at the municipal level would then be pooled to be shared at the state, regional, and federal levels by councils organized to oversee, manage, and publish it for public use. Such an arrangement would create an ongoing opportunity for civic-minded stakeholders to recode our digital infrastructure according to values that transcend neoliberal norms of data commodification and enclosure.

In order to be properly maintained on a national level, however, an associational data commons must be governed by specific rules that yield more disclosure and transparency while also simultaneously decentralizing the monopolistic tendencies of platform capitalism. Rules for data sharing would need to be the cornerstone of such developments, as would rules for protecting privacy. Data sharing rules would be designed to ensure that power flows bottom up from users of the device. The user of the device should be empowered to exert control over the data collected and should have a participatory right to create the value chain stemming from his or her use. Users would simply register their device with the manufacturer's website, and from there they could identify stakeholders with whom they would like to share their data in order to enhance our collective life. Philip N. Howard has proposed that 10 percent of all data collected on all devices be made available for public use, but we believe this should be determined through democratic processes.[27]

Besides empowering individuals with the discretion to share portions of their data, the data commons would also require a data sharing mandate that encompasses all organizations participating in the digital economy. This would require every company that systematically extracts and analyzes data to share a subset of its data with the data commons on an annual basis. The mandate could be designed so that companies share their data with other companies in the same industry, as Viktor Mayer-Schonberger and Thomas Ramge have proposed; however, we propose that data be required to be shared across all sectors of society according to its relevance for addressing collective problems such as health, the environment, education, energy, or infrastructure maintenance. Such a mandate would prevent a small number of platforms from monopolizing and hoarding data. To protect privacy and encourage competition, the data "would be stripped of personal identifiers, augmented with metadata to make clear what sort of information the data provided and where it came from, and selected randomly to prevent companies from gaming the system."²⁸ Companies seeking to use the data commons would need to pay a licensing fee, but a civic exception could be implemented to allow noncommercial stakeholders access at a minimal cost. Civic-oriented stakeholders across the fields of health, labor, law, or education could register with the associational commons to access the data so long as they share their own data with the commons.

The data commons could be financed, enhanced, and expanded through data taxes specifically targeting Big Tech and other data-mining industries such as finance and industrial manufacturing. A series of graduated data taxes could be levied for every layer—municipal, regional, state, federal—of the associational data commons. At least two taxes could serve as the cornerstone of such a political economy of data: a tax on all device networks and a data transaction tax levied on every sale of data to third parties. By taxing the devices that collect and transmit data from users and taxing the sale of this data to third parties, the public revenues generated could finance a variety of public goods and services as well as public utility platforms to create more competition within the digital economy.

Taken together, the data commons could encourage a series of important developments. First, it would ensure that the large quantities of data that are collected are not underused. Second, making data a public good would likely spark innovation as more firms and people use it. As Eric Von Hippel has documented, technological innovations are often created by users and not by lead producers.[29] Third, through increased use across a multitude of different contexts of application, feedback loops would enhance the data through sharper algorithms and analytics. Finally, as more types of firms and organizations use the data, more and more will then contribute to the data commons itself.

Democratizing data through a commons would address the crises of the gig economy more effectively than other reform proposals that have either emphasized new forms of distributing social wealth, such as a universal guaranteed income (UGI), or the enforcement of antitrust law to break up Big Data platforms. A data commons would do far more to stimulate creative entrepreneurism and empower alternative models of platforms than would UGI, since access to data is far more valuable for strategic planning and product development than $500 to $1,000 per month. More importantly, UGI fails to create the proper political space for democratic interventions in the way capital circulates within platform capitalism. In his *Critique of the Gotha Programme*, Marx incisively critiqued the theoretical basis for UGI when he attacked Lassalleans for proposing it over a century ago:

> [It is] a general mistake to make a fuss about so-called distribution and put the principal stress on it . . . Any distribution whatever of the means of consumption is only a consequence of the distribution of the conditions of production themselves . . . If the material conditions of production are the cooperative property of the workers themselves, then there likewise results a distribution of the means of consumption different from the present one.[30]

The data commons offers democratic interventions in the circulation and formation of capital. Data flows are changing the way capital circulates through time and space, and in order to democratize the digitalization of capital users of devices must be empowered to direct the data that flows from their device use to whom they want. Rather than rely on a UGI that only redistributes wealth that has already been created, democratizing data through the sharing mandates of the commons would alter what Marx called "value in process," that is, the basis by which capital circulates within its circuit of value generation.[31] This would pluralize power within platform capitalism since Uber, Facebook, Amazon, and Google would be forced to share significant portions of their data for public use rather than monopolize and monetize it into finance capital at the expense of competitors, users, and gig workers.

Democratizing data through a commons would also more effectively decentralize platform capitalism than would enforcing antitrust law, as proposed by US senator Elizabeth Warren and *The Economist*. Warren's plan would apply a conventional 20th-century approach by breaking up Uber, Facebook, and Amazon through existing antitrust laws.[32] However, disbanding Silicon Valley's most dominant platforms into smaller competitors would not prevent network effects from enabling one of them to become dominant again. *The Economist*'s approach accounts for this reality, and even proposes that government enforce more data transparency with consumers, mandate limited forms of data sharing, and use data assets as a basis for considering mergers among firms.[33] Yet, antitrust enforcement, even if updated for the realities of the nature of data in the 21st century, would only at best replace platform monopolies with an oligopoly and would do little to directly address the plight of gig workers or the way firms such as Uber weaponize their data against consumers and workers.

Democratizing data for public use through a commons would more effectively change the gig economy than either UGI or antitrust enforcement would. Moreover, by enforcing new forms of data transparency, democratizing data would prevent the expansion of an enclosed Internet of Things while enhancing the organizing and negotiation position of gig workers. Democratizing data offers the best way to leverage its value for public use without enabling gross exploitation, be it through data fracking or other forms of data brokerage that would inevitably prey on the poor and most vulnerable.[34] Most importantly, it would empower gig workers to organize themselves into their own platforms and thus uproot Uber. Gig workers are already creating their own democratically managed platforms to compete against Uber and other Silicon Valley giants, but they lack the mountains of data these platforms monopolize and hoard.[35] A good example is the Montreal-based ridesharing cooperative Eva, which offers profit-sharing and voting rights to drivers and riders, enabling the platform to address the specific mobility needs of the regions it operates in while drivers negotiate their own prices and hours.[36]

A data commons would significantly close the data deficit and serve as a digital infrastructure upon which new platforms could be built. Unions, nonprofit organizations, and worker cooperatives could form platforms that are both open hardware and software and scaled to markets in ways that enable citizens to control data to better serve the needs of local communities. The data commons would incentivize platform experimentation at the local, municipal, regional, and even national levels. Srnicek, for example, has proposed the creation of public platforms that are financially and technologically supported by the state and offered as a public utility.[37] Cities could develop and support platforms that offer municipal services and that compete with commercial platforms and device networks. A data commons, coupled with Senator Sanders' Workplace Democracy Act legislation, would create a new legal and political-economic framework for the digital economy.

Conclusion

In this chapter, we have argued that challenging the maladies of the gig economy requires more than changing employment law. We have also argued that it would be a mistake to legitimize gig-based work with UGI and that it is not enough to enforce 20th-century antitrust law to break up Big Tech. Instead, it is paramount in this historical moment to take bold steps toward democratizing the very basis of capital formation and value creation in digital capitalism: data. A data commons could be a foundational step toward the emergence of a new and more humane digital way of life beyond the indigent precarity of the gig economy and the risks of an enclosed Internet of Things. It would facilitate gig worker organizing by disclosing data that platforms such as Uber refuse to publish at their expense. It would open proprietary data to anyone, including municipalities and gig workers who want to create democratically managed platforms for the public good.

Notes

1. *Economist*, "The World's Most Valuable Resource is No Longer Oil, but Data," May 6, 2017, www.economist.com/leaders/2017/05/06/the-worlds-most-valuable-resource-is-no-longer-oil-but-data.
2. Kenneth Cukier and Viktor Mayer-Schoenberger, "The Rise of Big Data: How It's Changing the Way We Think About the World" *Foreign Affairs* 92, no. 3 (2013): 29.
3. Ibid., 35.
4. Mary L. Gray and Siddarth Suri, *Ghost Work: How to Stop Silicon Valley From Building a New Global Underclass* (New York: Houghton Mifflin), 10–30; Michelle Rodino-Colocino, "Uber's $9 Billion IPO Rests on Drivers' 80-Plus Hour Workweeks and a Lot of Waiting," *Salon*, April 30, 2019, www.salon.com/2019/04/30/ubers-9-billion-ipo-rests-on-drivers-80-plus-hour-workweeks-and-a-lot-of-waiting_partner/.
5. Nick Srnicek, *Platform Capitalism* (New York: Polity Press, 2017), 49–50, 83.
6. Emily Badger, "Uber Offers Cities an Olive Branch: Your Valuable Trip Data," *Washington Post*, January 13, 2015, www.washingtonpost.com/news/wonk/wp/2015/01/13/uber-offers-cities-an-olive-branch-its-valuable-trip-data/.
7. Alex Rosenblat, *Uberland: How Algorithms Are Rewriting the Rules of Work* (Berkeley: University of California Press, 2018), 107–9.

8. Jay Cassano, "How Uber Profits Even While It's Drivers Aren't Earning Money," *Vice*, February 2, 2016, www.vice.com/en_us/article/wnxd84/how-uber-profits-even-while-its-drivers-arent-earning-money.
9. Katie Wells, et al., *The Uber Workplace in D.C.*, accessed April 29, 2020, https://lwp.georgetown.edu/wp-content/uploads/Uber-Workplace.pdf, 9.
10. Rosenblat, *Uberland*, 75, 92–95.
11. Tara Golshan, Bernie Sanders's Plan to Reshape Corporate America, Explained, *Vox*, October 14, 2019, www.vox.com/2019/10/14/20912221/bernie-sanders-corporate-accountability-ftc-merger-tax.
12. Faiz Siddiqui, "Uber and Lyft Drivers Strike for Pay Transparency—After Algorithms Made It Harder to Understand," *Washington Post*, May 8, 2019, www.washingtonpost.com/technology/2019/05/08/uber-lyft-drivers-strike-pay-transparency-after-algorithms-made-it-harder-understand/?arc404=true.
13. Sarah Holder, "For Ride-Hailing Drivers, Data Is Power," *CityLab*, August 22, 2019, www.citylab.com/transportation/2019/08/uber-drivers-lawsuit-personal-data-ride-hailing-gig-economy/594232/.
14. Bryce Covert, "Like Uber, but for Gig Worker Organizing," *American Prospect*, March 30, 2020, https://prospect.org/labor/like-uber-but-for-gig-worker-organizing/.
15. Phillip N. Howard, *Pax Technica: How the Internet of Things May Set Us Free or Lock Us Up* (New Haven: Yale University Press, 2015), 226–31.
16. Grace Dobush, "Uber Has Troves of Data on How People Navigate Cities. Urban Planners Have Begged, Pleaded, and Gone to Court for Access. Will They Ever Get it?" *Marker*, September 9, 2019, https://marker.medium.com/ubers-real-advantage-is-data-e54984ff524c.
17. Edward Ongweso, Jr., "We Really Don't Need Uber," *Vice*, December 12, 2019, www.vice.com/en/article/y3mm5x/we-really-dont-need-uber.
18. Michael Hardt and Antonio Negri, *Assembly* (Oxford: Oxford University Press, 2017), 84–90; Couze Venn, *After Capital* (London: Sage, 2018), 123–28; Evgeny Morozov, "Socialize the Data Centres!" *New Left Review* 91 (2015): 65.
19. Ibid., 143, 169.
20. Nick Srnicek, "We Need to nationalize Google, Facebook and Amazon. Here's Why," *The Guardian*, August 30, 2017, www.theguardian.com/commentisfree/2017/aug/30/nationalise-google-facebook-amazon-data-monopoly-platform-public-interest; Christian Fuchs, *Digital Labor and Karl Marx* (London: Routledge, 2014), 300.
21. Peter Levine, "Collective Action, Civic Engagement, and the Knowledge Commons," in *Understanding Knowledge as a Commons*, ed. Charlotte Hess and Elinor Ostrom (Cambridge: MIT Press, 2007), 247.
22. Elinor Ostrom and Charlotte Hess, "A Framework for Analyzing the Knowledge Commons," in *Understanding Knowledge as a Commons: From Theory to Practice*, ed. Charlotte Hess and Elinor Ostrom (Cambridge: MIT Press, 2007), 13.
23. Greg Bloom, "Towards a Community Data Commons," in *Beyond Transparency: Open Data and the Future of Civic Innovation*, ed. Brett Goldstein with Lauren Dyson (San Francisco: Code for America Press, 2013), 263.
24. Levine, "Collective Action," 250–51.
25. James Muldoon, "Council Democracy: Towards a Democratic Socialist Politics," in *Council Democracy: Towards a Democratic Socialist Politics*, ed. James Muldoon (London: Routledge, 2018), 2–15.
26. Hannah Arendt, *On Revolution* (New York: Penguin Press, 2006), 256.
27. Howard, *Pax Technica*, 240–48.
28. Viktor Mayer-Schonberger and Thomas Ramge, "The Big Choice for Big Tech: Share Data or Suffer the Consequences," *Foreign Affairs* 97, no. 5, 2018: 52.
29. Eric Von Hippel, *Democratizing Innovation* (Cambridge: MIT Press, 2005), 93–133.
30. Karl Marx, "Critique of the Gotha Programme," *Marxists Internet Archive*, accessed April 29, 2020, www.marxists.org/archive/marx/works/1875/gotha/.

31. Karl Marx, *Capital, Volume I,* accessed April 29, 2020, www.marxists.org/archive/marx/works/1867-c1/ch04.htm.
32. David, Dayden, "Monopolist's Worst Nightmare: The Elizabeth Warren Interview," *American Prospect,* June 18, 2019, https://prospect.org/economy/monopolist-s-worst-nightmare-elizabeth-warren-interview/.
33. *Economist,* "The World's Most Valuable Resource."
34. Sarah Jeong, "Selling Your Private Information Is a Terrible Idea," *The New York Times,* July 5, 2019, www.nytimes.com/2019/07/05/opinion/health-data-property-privacy.html.
35. Trebor Scholz, *Uberworked and Underpaid: How Workers Are Disrupting the Digital Economy* (Cambridge: Polity Press, 2017), 1–25.
36. Ryan Hayes, "Worker-Owned Apps Are Trying to Fix the Gig Economy's Exploitation," *Vice,* November 19, 2019, www.vice.com/en/article/pa75a8/worker-owned-apps-are-trying-to-fix-the-gig-economys-exploitation.
37. Srnicek, *Platform Capitalism,* 127–28.

V
Struggles
Organizing in the Gig Economy

13

PLATFORM ORGANIZING

Tech Worker Struggles and Digital Tools for Labour Movements

Enda Brophy and Seamus Bright Grayer

A 2017 *Management Report* editorial features words of warning from Alfred T. DeMaria, the publication's editor and a lawyer specializing in "combating union organizational campaigns."[1] Knowing "how employees can use new media tools, including social media and dedicated apps, to interact among themselves and with union organizers is absolutely necessary," DeMaria cautions, "Employers who ignore this potential stealth activity risk their union free status."[2] DeMaria's concern might seem excessive given that digital technologies' infiltration of workplaces has occurred alongside a decline in union density across developed countries since the 1980s. Moreover, "platform capitalism"[3] continues to gather strength and appears well poised to deliver yet another blow to unions. What could DeMaria be worried about in an economy where jobs are sliced into ever-smaller segments, workers are governed remotely by code, and bosses isolate workers by technological design?

Recent events occurring at the interface of digital technologies and labour organizing suggest there is some substance to DeMaria's concerns. In this chapter we call these activities, collectively, *platform organizing*. Platform organizing refers to three overlapping developments within the recent cycle of tech labour contestation: labour and solidarity organizing by the high-skill, core workforces of tech sector companies; defiance by workers at "gig economy" companies governing their labour forces through digital platforms; and the development of counter-platforms for workers dedicated to facilitating horizontal communication among workers for the purposes of labour organizing.

Drawing on six interviews conducted with platform developers, labour organizers, and tech activists between 2017 and 2018, we explore each of these developments in turn. We argue that the development of purpose-built platforms for labour organizing is necessary to the broader goal of organizing gig workers, but that it remains only one element of this project. To set the stage for this investigation, we first consider the central role played by the tech sector within capitalism more broadly and a brief history of labour struggles in this industry.

The Aristocracy of Digital Labour?

A December 2018 article in *Wired* memorialized a year marked by labour resistance in the sector as one when "tech workers realized they were workers."[4] The title alludes to the fact that from the early years of capitalism's digitization in the post–World War II era, employees fashioning the cutting-edge technologies our economy relies on have seemed like an unlikely prospect for collective organization. With their highly demanded skills, attachment to an emergent craft, and libertarian ethos, tech workers have often been cast as a privileged aristocracy of digital labour, with a broad immunity to labour politics and worker solidarity, and at times, the outright enemies of working-class communities.[5]

The tech workforce's political orientation has become a topic of scrutiny and debate as the sector played a central role in the transformed political economy of capitalism. As the digital economy developed after World War II, Silicon Valley employment ballooned from 3,000 to over 150,000 by the 1970s.[6] In the 1970s, dramatic changes in working-class composition provoked Marxist scholars to develop divergent theories of a new, technically proficient working class[7] and an increasingly de-skilled "proletariat in a new form."[8] Underscoring their political ambivalence, early programmer cultures were infused with the sensibilities of Californian counterculture, contributing to the creation of a distinctive and irreverent corporate ethos of tinkering, experimentation, and work as play.[9]

As the discourse around "creative industries" crystallized into Blairite cultural policy in 1990s Britain, scholars observed how tech sector earnings dwarfed those of the fashion, arts, culture, and media sectors it was lumped in with.[10] The take-home here was that if creativity truly constituted a new paradigm of economic development, then the sector's sharpest edge was tech. The more recent rise of companies like Amazon, Facebook, and Google to the commanding heights of the economy in the decade following the financial crisis of 2008 raises the newer question of whether platform capitalism constitutes a qualitatively new regime of accumulation premised upon strategic control of digital interfaces.[11] In the world of work, platform-based companies have the capacity to dramatically intensify the expansion of precarious employment that has been underway since the 1980s. Along with mobile communication devices, digital platforms are the emergent medium of the gig economy.

As the developers of these interfaces, the workers at the very heart of tech's rise are of critical importance to the broader labour movement. If tech workers are judged solely by the kinds of employee management interfaces they have developed at companies like Deliveroo, Upwork, and Uber, they may rightly be seen as enemies of the working class. Workers' accounts and scholarly assessments of the cutting-edge corporate platforms shaping the gig economy today reveal a series of interfaces designed to isolate, disempower, and silence employees in their organization of the labour process.[12] While platform companies are varied, both internally and among each other, management interfaces across a range of enterprises support a labour process premised upon an unprecedented degree of employee surveillance and data extraction,[13] utilization of platform channels for the distribution of management propaganda, algorithmically dictated managerial communication, and the channelling, obstruction, or even suppression of worker communication.

That workers at Deliveroo in the United Kingdom were sacked by an anthropomorphized algorithm named "Daisy" captures the dystopian possibilities of tech worker labour under the conditions of platform capitalism. The logics implanted in these technologies seek to produce the ideal situation for Alfred DeMaria: an *asymmetrical* communicative regime,[14] where management dominates labour communication both externally and internally. Indeed, the rise of digital intermediaries in the world of work, when paired with the expansion of mobile communication, appears to constitute a significant acceleration in the decades-old process of labour's decomposition, or the disintegration of the institutions, infrastructures, and social relationships from which workers had been able to defend and advance their interests. That the talents of tech workers have been put to work so decisively toward the management-dictated objective of worker disempowerment might suggest we have reached the end of the line for even the faintest trace of tech's countercultural past.

A Genealogy of Tech Sector Labour Struggles: From Tomeo to #techwontbuildit

While accurate in many respects, the widely shared image of solidarity-averse tech workers obscures a genealogy of labour contestation and collective organizing in the sector. Dig into the history and one finds more than a few examples of labour organizing, conflict, and solidarity developing out of the high-tech workforce's earliest days. These stories reveal the roots of the current upswing in tech organizing and display some striking parallels to today.

For example, union drives that flared up in the Santa Clara Valley of the early 1970s and 80s included a briefly successful one at the electronics firm Tomeo, which was quashed by a lockout and eventual closure.[15] Workers at Atari attempted to certify twice, both times stymied by their employers' anti-union tactics which ranged from lavish parties to mass layoffs and relocation to Taiwan and Hong Kong.[16]

Further, in the 1970s, workers banded together not only to propose worker control of production but also to determine the outcome of their labour in a high-tech industry. In the United Kingdom, shop stewards at Lucas Aerospace factories devised the "Lucas Plan," proposing that workers establish full control over the design of the technology they manufactured. Described as a "worker-driven response to military design, redundancy, and the primacy of profit over workers,"[17] the plan was ultimately beaten back by management and "washed over by neoliberalism,"[18] but still managed to offer an answer to the question of what a tech workplace where workers coordinated production from below might look like.

The Silicon Valley Toxics Coalition formed in 1982 after leaks at Fairchild and IBM exposed workers to toxic chemicals, and the organization has been an important player in mobilizing for occupational health and safety among the mostly immigrant, female, and people of colour labour force that has traditionally staffed silicon chip assembly in the Santa Clara Valley, one of the most polluted areas in North America.[19] Nearer to the high-skill core, temp agency–based contractors at Microsoft adopted a strategy of minority unionism at the end of the 1990s, organizing the WashTech project supported by the Communication Workers of America. Contractors were excluded from perks, benefits, and equal pay with full-time employees, but the self-defined "permatemps" organized demonstrations at the company's Redmond, Washington, campus and eventually won a significant settlement from Microsoft.[20]

These moments of tech worker unrest hardly add up to a mass labour movement, but they do reveal a series of instructive precedents for the recent flare-ups of worker organizing. Worker complaints have been building in the sector for years, including stark inequities along the lines of age, gender, sexuality, and ethnicity;[21] arbitrary divisions in labour conditions among core, permanent workers and contractors including permatemps, cooks, and cleaners;[22] and socially destructive applications of the technologies workers are developing.

Supported by record levels of wealth accumulation, the tech sector has promoted discourses of philanthropy, social entrepreneurship, and technological solutions as top-down, accumulation-friendly modes of fixing social inequalities.[23] Yet in a troubling development for platform capitalists, workers in tech's high-skill core have launched a variety of collective organizing forms, triggering the third cycle of labour unrest to hit the sector after the ones in the 1970s and 1990s. Here we survey and offer an initial typology of these struggles, moving outward from the high-skill core of full-time employees toward the considerable and growing fights generated by the app-governed gig workforce.

Each of these struggles displays shades of previous tech labour campaigns. For example, in 2017—in an effort reminiscent of those at Tomeo and Atari—software engineers at the American logistics company Lanetix began to organize through the Communication Workers of America. After filing a petition to join, 14 of the workers were laid off in January 2018 after management got wind of the campaign. According to one account, management may have been alerted to their intentions by an employee's post on an internal Slack thread (for which he was fired), an example that offers a "cautionary tale about the importance of reliable communication platforms for labour organizers."[24] While traditional single-workplace organizing campaigns have had a lower profile within the wider episodes of unrest in tech, in 2020 workers at Kickstarter certified with the Office and Professional Employees International Union after a bitter struggle that saw core organizers fired and a widespread but rejected call for voluntary recognition at the firm. Likewise, in September 2019 workers at Google contractor HCL Technologies in Pittsburgh voted to unionize with the United Steelworkers and in so doing made history as the first group of outsourced tech workers to unionize in the United States.

By the time news of the Lanetix campaign emerged, tech was in the grip of gathering controversies surrounding the application of the technologies developed by workers in the sector. Media accounts commonly attribute the emergence of tech worker unrest to the 2016 election of Donald Trump.[25] Trump's announcement of a travel ban on majority-Muslim countries galvanized the more progressive sections of workforces (and many executives) at Silicon Valley companies into taking actions that flooded airports in late January 2017 to protest the directive. In a distant echo of the Lucas Plan, between 2016 and early 2017 tech workers signed the Never Again pledge, vowing not to build technologies that might assist the Trump administration in developing a Muslim Registry, which amassed 1,300 signatures in two days. As the Trump administration's policy of mass incarceration and deportation of migrants gathered pace, Microsoft, Salesforce, Palantir, and Amazon workers petitioned their executives to cancel lucrative contracts with US Customs and Border Protection. Google employees were at the forefront of efforts to redirect the products of their labour, forcing the company to drop a contract for Project Maven, a company which developed technology to analyze drone video footage to identify human targets, and speaking out against a censored search tool the company was developing for the Chinese state.

Notable in this cycle of tech sector struggle has been the formation of groups on each coast of the United States devoted to sectoral solidarity efforts and organizing tech's workforces—especially its ancillary ones. In the Bay Area, Tech Workers Coalition (TWC) has adopted a grassroots, autonomous organizing structure and a political perspective constructed on the need for solidarity among different kinds of workers. Formed in 2014 out of a casual discussion between a cafeteria worker and an engineer, TWC has expanded rapidly to several cities in the United States and internationally.[26] Describing their approach, TWC has noted that "[i]f tech workers are to be united with their various counterparts in other segments of the supply chain," organizers need "to start from square one, and actually figure out how to start organizing ourselves as a sub-section of the working class."[27] Notable among the organization's activities was its early involvement in the successful campaign to organize over 500 cafeteria workers at a Facebook food services subcontractor through the trade union UNITE HERE.

On the East Coast, a working group of the Democratic Socialists of America's (DSA) New York chapter has formed to bring tech to the attention of socialists, and the perspective of socialism to tech workers.[28] Named Tech Action, the group has embarked on a path of counter-education for tech workers in the NYC area, organizing educational events and assisting with campaigns such as the successful coordination of resistance among community and labour groups that prevented Queens from becoming the site for Amazon's second headquarters.[29]

The collaborative network that these groups developed is a notable element of this organizing wave. When Lanetix workers were fired, Tech Action and TWC co-produced a public statement condemning the company's actions. Coworker.org (discussed in the next section) has coordinated with both organizations to host organizing workshops for tech workers. Similarly, they advised organizers of the November 2018 global demonstration where thousands of Google employees walked out in protest of gender and racial discrimination and lack of worker voice. Adding fuel to the fire, in December of the same year, temporary, vendor, and contract workers (TVCs) wrote an open letter to CEO Sundar Pichai calling for action on inequities among full-time staff and the precarious margins of Google's "shadow workforce." In April 2019, the company responded by announcing it will require its contractors to give full benefits to temporary and contract workers, including comprehensive health care, 12 weeks of paid parental leave, a minimum wage of $15 an hour, and $5,000 per year in tuition reimbursement.[30]

These wins demonstrate that although labour unrest has been the most forceful at the lower reaches of capitalism's digital workforces, the solidarity of high-skill, core workers is often crucial to these efforts. Alliances between "white collar" and "blue collar" workforces have revealed themselves to be powerful, vindicating TWC and Tech Action's orientation toward solidarity unionism. While we have only offered a thumbnail sketch of the struggles in tech, the intensifying rounds of protest and organizing by workers at the precarious, low-skill periphery of platform companies whose labour is governed by algorithmic digital interfaces, including warehouse workers at Amazon,[31] drivers at Uber,[32] and food delivery workers at Deliveroo,[33] are also notable.

Indeed, if recent surveys suggest a broader "platformization" of labour markets,[34] then we must also account for the emergence and spread of struggles among workers controlled by such platforms. The first global strike of platform workers unfolded on May 8, 2019, as drivers for Uber and Lyft organized by the independent Rideshare Drivers United union contested their labour conditions ahead of Uber's initial public offering.[35] While there is little question that work is increasingly occurring on and through platforms, as Callum Cant notes, "[t]he assumption that increased technical control of the labour process by bosses will inevitably lead to a reduction in worker resistance is unfounded."[36] Platform capital undoubtedly enjoys a "priority of agency,"[37] but its platform labour force is not quite the pushover some might have imagined.

Labour Organizing Platforms

In the context of growing tech worker unrest, the third dimension of platform organizing takes shape—the utilization of online platforms for organizing workers. We break these efforts into two main variants: The first involves labour organizing that takes place through mainstream platforms such as Facebook, Twitter, or Slack. Examples include the Fight for 15 movement's use of Twitter and Organization United for Respect at Walmart's adoption of Facebook as one of its key sites of organizing.[38] The use of corporate social networking platforms is common—so much so that the world of labour organizing would grind to a halt, at least temporarily, if these tools disappeared. Virtually every union has a digital media presence,[39] and autonomous networked labour movements use Facebook extensively, like the *Comités Unitaires sur le Travail Étudiant* (CUTEs) did to coordinate their groundbreaking 2019 internship strike.[40]

The pattern holds with labour organizing in the tech sector. At least one organizer involved in the union certification drive at Lanetix said the campaign "would not have happened without Slack,"[41] and employees at mammoth tech companies such as Google have used the firm's tools and internal worker-only forums to coordinate labour action.[42] While corporate platforms remain a necessary tool for communication with a workforce immersed in the flows of the online world, in this section we focus on a second variant of labour organizing platforms: the purpose-built, worker-to-worker communication channels developed by labour activists *for* labour movements. The development of such autonomous communication channels is important for several reasons. With respect to existing scholarship, labour's adaptation of corporate platforms has already received attention from researchers,[43] a literature that dovetails with the extensive analysis of social media utilization by networked social movements like Occupy and Black Lives Matter.[44] Strategically, our focus is inspired by the belief—expressed most powerfully by the feminist poet Audre Lorde—that "the master's tools will never dismantle the master's house." Indeed, for labour movements there are pitfalls attached to the use of these platforms, including the intertwined concerns of privacy breaches, algorithmic moderation of content, and an omnipresent commercial logic that make such platforms risky and sometimes ineffective propositions for worker organizations. As a result, the creation of autonomous communication channels designed specifically for building worker power holds more potential. After all, while corporate platforms may be useful, relying on them exclusively is, as Wobbly developer John Evans puts it, "like trying to write a novel with crayon. It's technically possible to do it, but no reasonable person would do so if they had the choice of something better."[45] The significance of the purpose-built tools for the working class we survey here is twofold: First, they represent the early stirrings of a digitally savvy labour force coming to terms with capitalism's use of platforms in labour markets. Second, they are an eloquent example of why tech workers are such strategic actors in building resistance to the broader platformization of work.

We draw on conversations we had across 2017 and 2018 with organizers involved in the development of three platforms: the union-driven social networking site Unionbase; the "platform for worker voice" Coworker.org; and the organization behind WorkIt, an AI chatbot-driven question-and-answer app for and by Walmart workers. These platforms are but a sampling of the attempts to build platforms to assist with organizing,[46] but together they provide a sense of recent efforts in the area. While these projects are ambivalent in a few key respects and their success to date has been uneven, they represent important efforts toward the establishment of a digital infrastructure for worker communication, information, and visibility organizing for those outside the established labour movement, especially in the context of rising activism in tech and gig work more broadly. Despite their different approaches, these technologies from below reveal a set of common themes that can be used to understand the logics and possibilities of these platforms. These themes cohere around three key functions: *offering entry points*, *filling gaps*, and *producing visibility*.

First, our conversations with developers and organizers underscored the challenges faced by the trade union labour movement, especially in the United States where each of the surveyed platforms are located. Organizers noted the gradual dissolution of organized labour, whether from persistent legislative attacks or the growing perception—mainly among younger workers—that unions are, in the words of Unionbase co-founder Larry Williams Jr., "out of school, out of touch." In light of these difficulties, each of these platforms strives to offer *entry points* to workplace organizing for workers who are increasingly outside the scope of organized labour.

Among the three platforms we surveyed, Coworker.org most effectively realizes the goal of providing an opening to organizing. Co-founder Jess Kutch described the platform as "the front doorstep of the labour movement." Inspired by Kutch's time at the popular campaigning site Change.org, Coworker.org's petition function was its earliest and most prominent feature, although recent iterations of the platform have featured a growing number of tools and resources for workplace campaigns.[47] Petitions have proved effective in attuning workers to struggles in their workplace (for example, employees fighting for expanded parental leave at Netflix). From there workers may seek greater involvement in organizing taking place around them. According to Kutch, such victories, however small, give people "a taste of what's possible," allowing them to decide if "they want to go further and join a union, win a contract, put some of the changes they've won in writing and have it legally protected."

WorkIt and Unionbase also use technology to bring workers into organizing. Reflecting on the challenges of a workforce as large as Walmart's, OUR Walmart co-director Dan Schlademan sees potential in getting people's attention by offering trusted communicative spaces and useful resources. Schlademan describes WorkIt's IBM Watson-powered question-and-answer chatbot as a potential starting point for a deeper engagement with organizing in the workplace:

> [W]e believe we've got to create spaces that people own, that are theirs, that allow them to build power, that allow them to be an important resource for the co-workers so that they can bring them into the organization and bring them into the bigger fights.
>
> *(Dan Schlademan, interview by authors, April 6, 2018)*

Unionbase, on the other hand, designed its platform to direct workers toward further involvement with organized labour. By adopting familiar social media features such as user profiles, posts, and "likes," the platform builds communication channels between unions and workers with the goal of leading to a more formal labour relationship such as a certification drive.

A second theme emerging from our conversations with app developers is the identification of *gaps* in what is being offered to workers, whether it is missing resources, support, or infrastructure. Organizers focused on these missing offerings and how their organizations and technologies give workers a more complete arsenal of tools at their disposal. Of the gaps identified, organizers singled out two in particular: gaps in the offerings of corporate platforms and gaps in the organizing tactics of the established labour movement.

As discussed earlier, it is easy to identify concerns with mainstream social media platforms, especially for labour movements. For an organization like OUR Walmart that was at the forefront of using Facebook for organizing, the extractive logics underlying these platforms are a concern:

> [A]s Facebook continues to try to become a money-making machine for Wall Street . . . it's just not a long-term healthy strategy to think that you're going to build the key infrastructure of your organization on a space that's owned by corporate America.[48]

In absence of reliable security on mainstream social media, dedicated labour organizing platforms can offer trusted spaces for workers to come together and organize. At the same time, none of the organizers we surveyed advocate for a complete split from corporate platforms. Kutch calls for "meeting people where they're at," adding that one needs to understand that while workers are using Coworker.org, "they're also using Facebook," and it's all "part of the toolbox."

The rise of platforms has also challenged traditional organizing strategies, exposing gaps in the offerings of the established labour movement. These difficulties are exacerbated by the changing composition of the contemporary workforce, with growing numbers of dispersed, temporary, and isolated workers presenting a critical challenge to trade union organizers. One of the primary motivations for initially developing Unionbase relates to the difficulty workers face in joining unions, not only because of disintegrating labour laws and protections, but also because of the limited visibility of the labour movement to non-unionized workers. Through his experience with the Teamsters, Williams was attuned to the union's efforts toward "turning [the organizing process] into a digital process, doing digital card signing, using cell phone apps for organizing instead of paper." Despite the fairly widespread adoption of digital tools by unions at this point, Williams was struck by the lack of an obvious digital avenue for joining a local union, an observation that eventually inspired Unionbase. Similarly, Kutch and Coworker.org identify a "space in between the folks who are actively trying to join unions, organizing into unions, and are union members" as a potential site of organizing that is not being addressed by unions themselves.

Critically, developers cannot assume such gaps. If the labour movement is "only building what we want to believe, what we think workers need and what we think unions need, we're just going to fail," says Williams.[49] Likewise, Schlademan invokes Silicon Valley tropes when he claims that WorkIt "wasn't a couple of college kids in their dorm room like, 'Oh, I've got the next million-dollar idea!'" Instead, he says that the platform comes from "low-wage workers really thinking about how to leverage technology to support their coworkers and support more workers like themselves." Part of this recognition is the aforementioned reluctance to divest from corporate social media, the convenience of which makes them such a common feature in workers' lives. Kutch spells it out plainly: "You can't just build tools and expect people to use them. People actually have to want to do the thing that you're making possible."

The third theme arising from our conversations is the need to produce *visibility*, for both workers and the labour movement. Making work visible is critical on labour platforms where management lurks behind algorithmic interfaces and can "use the spectacle of innovation to conceal the worker."[50] Moreover, as communication infrastructure, platforms have a special capacity to highlight labour campaigns or patterns of workplace exploitation. The wide reach afforded by corporate social media is a testament to this. Organizers are using their own labour-driven platforms to give working people a similar ability—though with the crucial difference of being oriented toward the accumulation of worker power.

In an environment where corporate media tend to ignore unions unless they are on strike,[51] the intent to make organized labour visible to unorganized workers was a part of Unionbase since its inception. Williams was struck by how little he knew when he got involved in the labour movement during his work with the Teamsters. This informs much of the work his platform does on behalf of unions and workers, making them visible to each other and opening communication channels. As the depletion of union resources makes it more difficult for people to identify a union local in their area, the ability to get online and contact an organization directly—something Unionbase is working on facilitating through its website—offers great potential. These channels run the other way as well, however. Williams notes how many of the unions he works with do not have a clear picture of the working people in communities around them.[52]

While Unionbase makes workers and the labour movement visible to each other, Coworker.org makes visible the problems and organizing efforts that tend to fall outside the purview of trade unions. Kutch describes this as surfacing "a more three-dimensional picture of what happens in the modern workplace" that involves "not just . . . wages, benefits, it's the total experience and how your dignity is sometimes in jeopardy." With its petition feature, Coworker has sought to raise the visibility of day-to-day problems faced by workers on the ground that a trade union might miss. This effort has included raising the profile of a workplace issue to the public, publicizing questionable employer practices, or helping workers recognize a larger issue at work. Coworker's petition and networking tools have been especially effective in the latter case. For example, Starbucks baristas were faced with brutal "clopening" shifts that saw people closing stores late at night and then opening the next morning, only a few hours later. Because their employer is so large, Kutch observes, workers were "having trouble diagnosing problems in their workplace" and asking, "Is this a problem that my store is having? Or, is this more systemic? Is this happening across the company?" Boosted by a widely circulated petition, the profile of this workplace problem became prominent to the point that the employer took action, resulting in a win for baristas as Starbucks eliminated "clopening" shifts.

Finally, knowledge about workers and their issues can become visible through these platforms. Part of the motivation behind WorkIt is simply for Walmart workers to gather information for the sake of future action. Schlademan reflects on the organizing possibilities entailed by such a rich dataset:

> I think about what collective bargaining would be like if every [worker] had this app on their phone and I had three years of data about what the biggest issues were, what the problems were, where there were all these kind of things . . . That would create a completely different set of power [relations].
>
> *(Dan Schlademan, interview by authors, April 6, 2018)*

The data labour organizing platforms provide help make visible trends, connections, and information about the workplace that can assist with organizing campaigns and strategies. At the same time, the collection of user data is one among several challenges and concerns that need to be addressed by those designing labour organizing platforms.

The Perils and Potential of Platform Organizing

While examples of insubordination and collective action occurring at the intersection of labour and digital technology are encouraging, they do not add up to a cycle of struggle capable of reversing the now decades-long process of labour movement decomposition. Vast segments of the high-tech workforce, especially those within the more privileged high-skill core, remain apolitical with a significant minority attracted to the politics of the "manosphere" and the "alt-right." As class lines become drawn more sharply within the tech workplace, employers like Google and Amazon have struck back at workers involved in collective organization through dismissals. Moreover, lurking within the instances of labour recomposition we have described are political and technological risks stemming from the corporate logics already firmly in place in Silicon Valley. To conclude then, we consider the perils and the potential we observe within the initiatives surveyed previously and identify some fixes that might advance digital labour's goal of wresting the initiative away from platform capitalism.

Perhaps the most obvious risk of organizing at the intersection between tech and labour is that platforms become seen as the ends rather than the means for developing worker power. One of the key critiques voiced against platform organizing relates to its perceived techno-centrism. As Fred, a founding member of Tech Action describes it, "[i]t's really part of this idea from *Wired Magazine* and the tech media world that everything's about tools, it's all about cryptography, it's all about substituting technology for politics."[53] That enthusiasm for digital tools can take time away from organizing on the ground is demonstrated by the early history of Tech Action itself, which at the outset was focused on building digital tools to help the DSA with its organizing efforts. As Fred notes, after a few iterations "it was clear that that was soaking up a lot of energy and attention, myself and a couple others became much more interested in vocally saying: 'Let's not do this.'" This recognition steered Tech Action away from a focus on developing technology and toward educational efforts geared to the tech workforce.

At the same time, the trade-off can, and perhaps should, be seen as a false dilemma. When it comes to organizing, as Kutch says, "[t]here's not one thing, we should do all the things." None of the platform developers we interviewed had doubts about the necessity of in-person organizing, stressing instead the importance of being omnivorous in their organizing tactics, using what is available and building what is needed. In this vein, Williams suggests, "[t]he centre and the core of the labour movement is movement building, it's organizing face-to-face" but "we have to supplement that with the use of the newest technology and the internet." Similarly, Schlademan argues it will be impossible for the labour movement to amass enough resources to organize door-knocking campaigns with the same reach offered by digital tools. So, "when we merge apps like WorkIt, when we merge online organizing with the traditional organizing model we're then creating a massive amount of efficiency that we currently don't have."

Ambivalent attitudes around labour organizing platforms also stem from their relationship with data. Compiling large amounts of information produced by and for workers holds significant potential for generating useful knowledge that can be integrated into organizing campaigns. At the same time, these technologies are not immune to the defining logics of platform capitalism, and the development of platform technology for labour organizing raises important questions around surveillance and user data. Platform organizers acknowledge the challenges but also speak to how they plan on addressing security concerns. They emphasize that their efforts do not require the exchange of vulnerable information, including WorkIt's Schlademan who says his organization knows "that the data is interesting and important and all of this, but [users are] not giving us precarious information other than details about issues they're having."[54] Similarly, Kutch says Coworker.org operates according to the principle that "there's no secrets on the Internet" and that all information is public information from the outset. Unionbase collects anonymous user data such as geographic location, type of mobile device, or demographic information so that it can provide the labour movement with information about "who [is] on the site . . . to just make sure that we are being realistic about what our challenges are and where our strengths are." When asked about the potential value of the data their platforms will collect, the organizers are unanimous that the sale of user information is off the table. While acknowledging that there are some very real concerns with the implications of data collection practices, Schlademan quips, "We're no Cambridge Analytica."

More broadly, it remains to be seen what impact the rise of technologies for labour organizing will have on the organizing process and the position of unions within it. It is tempting to suggest that digital technologies have the capacity to simplify and democratize labour organizing, enabling a possible shift away from professional, staff-driven models of trade union organizing. The remarkable expansion of the Rideshare Drivers United union in southern California, the growth of which was coordinated through an app and well-placed ads on social media platforms, is proof positive of the significant potential of labour tech to put power in the hands of unaffiliated organizers and gig workers labouring through platforms.[55] But established trade unions are sure to incorporate such technologies in their organizing strategies as well, giving them new avenues to reach out to workers and coordinate campaigns. In the end, much like the adoption of social media, it is unlikely to be an either/or scenario. Because of the potential that platforms offer to labour movement organizing, future research should continue to chart the take-up of new technologies by labour movements with a view to assessing their effectiveness in organizing new workers—especially gig workers.

The platforms we have surveyed are an uncertain yet promising avenue for building worker power in the digital space, especially when viewed alongside the recent wave of tech and gig worker struggles. While there are key tensions among the organizing approaches, communication and action are indispensable and indivisible elements of labour organizing in digital spaces. The secure forms of labour communication for which these platforms strive are crucial to organizing, allowing for the effective transmission of information and a heightened understanding of the struggles faced by workers on the ground. On the other hand, communication alone is seldom enough to bring about meaningful change at work and needs to be coupled with activism, organizing, and institutional change. As explored throughout this chapter, instances of such organizing are taking place with greater frequency, including challenges from the white-collar tech workforce that designs the platforms as well as the precarious gig workers who are governed by them. If labour organizers wish to make DeMaria's fears a reality, they will need to treat platforms as a necessary but insufficient element in building power for workers. Organizing online is not enough, but organizing digitally is clearly necessary.

Notes

1. Alfred T. DeMaria, "Organizers Increase Sophistication With Digital Communications," *Management Report for Nonunion Organizations* 40, no. 2 (2017): 3.
2. Ibid., 4.
3. Nick Srnicek, *Platform Capitalism* (Cambridge: Polity Press, 2016).
4. Nitasha Tiku, "The Year Tech Workers Realized They Were Workers," *Wired*, December 24, 2018, www.wired.com/story/why-hotel-workers-strike-reverberated-through-tech/.
5. Douglas Coupland, *Microserfs* (Toronto: HarperCollins, 1995).
    Richard Barbrook and Andy Cameron, "The Californian Ideology," *Science as Culture* 6, no. 1 (January 1996): 44–72. Douglas Rushkoff, *Throwing Rocks at the Google Bus: How Growth Became the Enemy of Prosperity* (New York: Portfolio, 2016).
6. "Rumblings of Organizing in Silicon Valley," *Science for the People*, January 1976, www.marxists.org/history/usa/pubs/science/SftPv8n1s.pdf.
7. Romano Alquati, "Struggle at Fiat," *Classe Operaia* 1 (1964); Serge Mallet, *The New Working Class* (Nottingham: Spokesman Books, 1975).
8. Harry Braverman, *Labor and Monopoly Capital: The Degradation of Work in the Twentieth Century* (New York: Monthly Review Press, 1974, 355).
9. Nick Dyer-Witheford and Greig De Peuter, *Games of Empire: Global Capitalism and Video Games*, Electronic Mediations 29 (Minneapolis: University of Minnesota Press, 2009).
10. Nicholas Garnham, "From Cultural to Creative Industries," *International Journal of Cultural Policy* 11, no. 1 (March 1, 2005): 15–29.
11. Srnicek, *Platform Capitalism*.
12. Brett Caraway, "Online Labour Markets: An Inquiry into ODesk Providers," *Work Organisation, Labour & Globalisation* 4, no. 2 (2010): 111–25; Alex Rosenblat, *Uberland: How Algorithms Are Rewriting the Rules of Work* (Berkeley: University of California Press, 2018); Facility Waters and Jamie Woodcock, "Far From Seamless: A Workers' Inquiry at Deliveroo," *Viewpoint Magazine*, September 20, 2017, www.viewpointmag.com/2017/09/20/far-seamless-workers-inquiry-deliveroo/; Callum Cant, *Riding for Deliveroo: Resistance in the New Economy* (London: Polity Press, 2020).
13. Sam Adler-Bell and Michelle Miller, "The Datafication of Employment," *The Century Foundation*, December 19, 2018, https://tcf.org/content/report/datafication-employment-surveillance-capitalism-shaping-workers-futures-without-knowledge
14. Alex Rosenblat and Luke Stark, "Algorithmic Labor and Information Asymmetries: A Case Study of Uber's Drivers," *International Journal of Communication* 10, no. 0 (July 27, 2016): 27.
15. "Rumblings of Organizing in Silicon Valley," *Science for the People*, January 1976, www.marxists.org/history/usa/pubs/science/SftPv8n1s.pdf.
16. Hossfeld quoted in Chris Benner, "Win the Lottery or Organize: Traditional and Non-Traditional Labor Organizing in Silicon Valley," *Berkeley Planning Journal* 12, no. 1 (1998), https://escholarship.org/uc/item/6z2697vb.
17. Adrian Smith, "The Lucas Plan: What Can It Tell Us About Democratising Technology Today?" *The Guardian*, January 22, 2014, www.theguardian.com/science/political-science/2014/jan/22/remembering-the-lucas-plan-what-can-it-tell-us-about-democratising-technology-today.
18. Felix Holtwell, "Bringing Back the Lucas Plan," Socialist Project, April 6, 2018, https://socialistproject.ca/2018/04/bringing-back-the-lucas-plan/.
19. David N. Pellow and Lisa S. Park, *The Silicon Valley of Dreams: Environmental Injustice, Immigrant Workers, and the High-Tech Global Economy* (New York: New York University Press, 2002).
20. Enda Brophy, "System Error: Labour Precarity and Collective Organizing at Microsoft," *Canadian Journal of Communication* 31, no. 3 (2006): 619–38; Michelle Rodino-Colocino, "Laboring Under the Digital Divide," *New Media & Society* 8, no. 3 (June 1, 2006): 487–511.

21. A. Banks, "Which Side Are They On?" *The Baffler*, August 21, 2018, https://thebaffler.com/latest/which-side-are-they-on-banks; *Silicon Valley Rising*, Tech's Invisible Workforce, March 2016, https://siliconvalleyrising.org/files/TechsInvisibleWorkforce.pdf.
22. Joshua Brustein, "What It's Like to Work Inside Apple's 'Black Site'," *Bloomberg*, February 11, 2019, www.bloomberg.com/news/features/2019-02-11/apple-black-site-gives-contractors-few-perks-little-security.
23. Anand Giridharadas, *Winners Take All: The Elite Charade of Changing the World*, First edition (New York: Alfred A. Knopf, 2018).
24. Ben Tarnoff, "Coding and Coercion," *Jacobin*, April 11, 2018, https://jacobinmag.com/2018/04/lanetix-tech-workers-unionization-campaign-firing.
25. Lizzie O'Shea, "Tech Capitalists Won't Fix the World's Problems—Their Unionised Workforce Might," *The Guardian*, November 24, 2017, www.theguardian.com/commentisfree/2017/nov/24/technology-capitalists-unionised-workforce-tech-sector.
26. Moira Weigel, "Coders of the World, Unite: Can Silicon Valley Workers Curb the Power of Big Tech?" *The Guardian*, October 31, 2017, www.theguardian.com/news/2017/oct/31/coders-of-the-world-unite-can-silicon-valley-workers-curb-the-power-of-big-tech.
27. R. K. Upadhya, "Tech Workers, Platform Workers, and Workers' Inquiry," *Medium* (blog), January 26, 2018, https://medium.com/tech-workers-coalition/tech-workers-platform-workers-and-workers-inquiry-92fbc6369647.
28. "Fred," Tech Action member, Interview by Enda Brophy, New York City, August 8, 2018.
29. J. David Goodman and Karen Weise, "Why the Amazon Deal Collapsed: A Tech Giant Stumbles in N.Y.'s Raucous Political Arena," *New York Times*, February 15, 2019, www.nytimes.com/2019/02/15/nyregion/amazon-hq2-nyc.html
30. Alexia Fernández Campbell, "Google Will Extend Some Benefits to Contract Workers After Internal Protest," *Vox*, April 4, 2019, www.vox.com/2019/4/4/18293900/google-contractors-benefits-policy.
31. Alessandro Delfanti, "Amazon Is the New FIAT," *Notes from Below*, August 16, 2018, https://notesfrombelow.org/article/amazon-is-the-new-fiat; Karen Weise, "Somali Workers in Minnesota Force Amazon to Negotiate," *The New York Times*, April 11, 2019, www.nytimes.com/2018/11/20/technology/amazon-somali-workers-minnesota.html
32. Michelle Rodino-Colocino, "Uber Drivers Report 80-Plus Hour Workweeks and a Lot of Waiting," *The Conversation*, April 29, 2019, http://theconversation.com/uber-drivers-report-80-plus-hour-workweeks-and-a-lot-of-waiting-115782
33. Cant.
34. Ursula Huws, Neil H. Spencer, and Dag S. Syrdal, "Online, On Call: The Spread of Digitally Organised Just-in-Time Working and Its Implications for Standard Employment Models," *New Technology, Work and Employment* 32, no. 2 (2018): 113–29.
35. Brian Dolber, "From Independent Contractors to an Independent Union: Building Solidarity Through Rideshare Drivers United's Digital Organizing Strategy," Media, Inequality & Change (MIC) Center (2019), www.miccenter.org/wp-content/uploads/2019/10/Dolber_final-2.pdf
36. Callum Cant, "The Wave of Worker Resistance in European Food Platforms 2016–17," *Notes from Below*, January 29, 2018, https://notesfrombelow.org/article/european-food-platform-strike-wave.
37. Srnicek, *Platform Capitalism*.
38. Brett Caraway, "OUR Walmart: A Case Study of Connective Action," *Information, Communication & Society* 19, no. 7 (2016): 907–20.
39. For discussion of the Canadian context, see Émond-Sioufi, "#Unions: Canadian Unions and Social Media" (Unpublished thesis, Simon Fraser University, BC, Canada, 2017).
40. Elizabeth Sarjeant, Enda Brophy, Jeanne Bilodeau, and Éloi Halloran, "'Autonomy Among Us': An Interview With Quebec Student Strike Organizers," *Viewpoint Magazine*, June 25, 2019, www.viewpointmag.com/2019/06/25/autonomy-among-us-an-interview-with-quebec-student-strike-organizers/.

41. Tarnoff, "Coding and Coercion," para. 23.
42. Kristen Sheets, "Inside the #MeToo Revolt at Google," *Socialist Worker.org*, November 13, 2008, http://socialistworker.org/2018/11/13/inside-the-metoo-revolt-at-google.
43. For an overview of this literature, see Émond-Sioufi. For an in-depth reflection on the overlap between labour unions and the development of autonomous communication outlets, see Lina Dencik and Peter Wilken, *Worker Resistance and Media: Challenging Global Corporate Power in the 21st Century* (New York: Peter Lang, 2015).
44. Paolo Gerbaudo, *Tweets and the Streets: Social Media and Contemporary Activism* (London: Pluto Press, 2012); Zeynep Tufekci, *Twitter and Tear Gas: The Power and Fragility of Networked Protest* (New Haven and London: Yale University Press, 2017).
45. John Evans, "An Introduction to Wobbly: An App for 21st Century Workers' Power," *Notes from Below*, 2018, 3, https://notesfrombelow.org/article/an-introduction-to-wobbly.
46. A notable omission here is Turkopticon, a program that lets workers on the Amazon Mechanical Turk platform rate, discuss, and make public their experiences with employers. For more see Lilly C. Irani and M. Six Silberman, "Turkopticon: Interrupting Worker Invisibility in Amazon Mechanical Turk," *UC San Diego*, 2015, https://escholarship.org/uc/item/10c125z3.
47. "We're not just a toolset—we offer strategic support, media outreach, we help workers win their campaigns. We provide coaching and training to help them think through: 'Okay, I have a petition. What's the best way to get this out there? How do I recruit support?' Who is the decision-maker for this campaign and what might influence them? What are the things they're thinking about?" (interview by authors, January 10, 2018).
48. Dan Schlademan, interview by authors, April 6, 2018.
49. Since the time of our interview, Unionbase has added a new "wing" of their operation: a publication titled *Workplace Leader* aimed at equipping people that are new to the labour movement to build and grow their own unions.
50. Trebor Scholz, "Think Outside the Boss," *Public Seminar*, 2015, www.publicseminar.org/2015/04/think-outside-the-boss/.
51. Deepa Kumar, *Outside the Box: Corporate Media, Globalization, and the UPS Strike* (Urbana: University of Illinois Press, 2008).
52. "Most of the unions that we've talked to have said, 'Yo, we have no idea how many members we have in X state.' Which is kind of incredible to me, right? You would think through dues and things like that folks would know" (Larry Williams Jr., interview by authors, 2018).
53. Interview by Enda Brophy, New York City, August 8, 2018.
54. When asked whether worker questions would be accessed by IBM, on whose AI technology WorkIt relies, Schlademan says that only the questions themselves are shared, "and then everything else is handled in the back-end that we've built." He clarifies that sensitive questions are an exception, such as those about sexual harassment: "We've got that set so that Watson's not going to answer that question and it's going to stay in the hands of a human . . . none of that goes to Watson. There's also a process by which people can make conversations private, and so those privacy settings allow that information to be held back from being seen by anybody else but the two people that are engaged in it" (Dan Schlademan, interview by authors, April 6, 2018).
55. Dolber, "From Independent Contractors to an Independent Union."

14

COMPETITION, COLLABORATION AND COMBINATION

Differences in Attitudes to Collective Organization Among Offline and Online Platform Workers

Kaire Holts, Ursula Huws, Neil Spencer, and Matthew Coates

In October 2018, representatives from 31 different collectives and unions in 12 European countries came together in Brussels to form the Transnational Courier Federation.[1] This represented a culmination of spreading efforts over the previous two years to unionise workers in the part of the 'gig economy' devoted to providing delivery services by bike, scooter, motorcycle or car to individual homes or businesses. Using a variety of tactics including strikes, demonstrations and court cases, these workers had achieved considerable success in drawing attention to their poor working conditions and wages and, in some cases, negotiating improvements. In doing so, they, and their organising efforts, have attracted the attention of a number of scholars and have been widely promoted as an example of successful organisation among platform workers.[2]

Similarly, there have been a number of initiatives among drivers working for platforms such as Uber and Lyft which provide taxi-type services, including the formation of new trade unions such as the UK-based App Drivers and Couriers Union (ACDU),[3] affiliated to the International Alliance of App-Based Transport Workers,[4] set up in 2019. Tactics they have used include demonstrations, mobilisation within existing trade unions and taking test cases on employment status to the courts, as well as setting up alternative platform models, such as cooperatives.[5] These drivers, too, have attracted considerable scholarly attention.[6]

These two groups are often regarded as emblematic of the new platform workforce, and, based only on this literature, it would be possible to draw relatively optimistic conclusions about the scope for development of new forms of collective organisation and representation in the 'gig economy'. Indeed, taken alongside some of the new forms of trade union organisation among other casually employed workers in the retail, warehouse, logistics and hospitality sectors,[7] it could even be regarded as heralding a new wave of trade union organisation among precarious workers, paralleling the 'new unionism' that emerged in the UK between 1889 and 1893, or the mobilisations of US workers that began in the mid-1890s and culminated in the foundation of the Industrial Workers of the World (IWW—colloquially known as 'Wobblies').[8]

Although there is an emerging body of literature on the collective agenda of platform workers in general,[9] this mostly analyses emerging organising strategies and the role of traditional trade unions among workers in public spaces. These studies often generalise to all platform workers. Apart from a few exceptions,[10] there is very little literature about collective organisation efforts or understanding about the attitudes towards unionisation of platform workers who work from their homes offering online services.

In this chapter, we draw on in-depth interviews with a range of different workers for online platforms in Europe to explore the assumption that delivery and driving platform workers' attitude represent those of working in other platforms and sectors.[11]

Home-Based Platform Work

The research we discuss here was carried out as part of a larger research project on platform work funded by the Foundation for European Progressive studies (FEPS) in partnership with the European Confederation of white-collar trade unions, UNI-Europa, which eventually included surveys in 13 European countries.[12]

We report here on results from the first seven of these.[13]

Survey questions asked whether participants had sold their labour via online platforms for a fee in three broad categories: providing driving or delivery services; providing services on other people's premises; or providing work to clients using a computer or other device from their own homes. In each case, prompts included examples of platforms that were well known in the respective countries. Respondents were asked,

> How often, if at all, do you do each of the following online?
> This may be done using any device connected to the internet, including a PC or laptop, Smartphone, Tablet Computer or Smart TV, etc.

Some examples of response options can be illustrated by these options, taken from the UK survey:

- Look for work you can carry out *from your own home* on a website such as Upwork, Freelancer, Timeetc, Clickworker or PeoplePerHour
- Look for work you can carry out for different customers somewhere *outside your home* on a website such as Handy, Taskrabbit or Mybuilder
- Offer to drive someone to a location for a fee using an app or website such as Uber or Blablacar

TABLE 13.1 Platform workers by type of platform work in Austria, Switzerland, Germany, Italy, the Netherlands, Sweden and the UK (% of working-age population)

	Offline driving/ delivery work in public spaces		Offline work on other people's premises		Online work from own home	
	At least weekly	Ever	At least weekly	Ever	At least weekly	Ever
Austria	3.3	10.6	6.7	14.0	8.2	17.7
Switzerland	3.5	10.8	7.2	15.3	8.4	16.9
Germany	2.3	7.1	4.1	9.7	4.9	11.1
Italy	5.8	14.7	9.9	19.3	10.4	19.8
Netherlands	1.4	4.4	3.0	6.6	3.9	8.2
Sweden	1.4	5.7	3.0	7.5	4.0	8.8
United Kingdom	1.5	4.8	2.9	7.1	3.9	8.4

Source: Hertfordshire Business School Crowd Work Survey, 2016–2017

Base: 1969 respondents in Austria, 2001 respondents in Switzerland, 2180 Respondents in Germany, 2199 respondents in Italy, 2126 respondents in the Netherlands, 2146 respondents in Sweden and 2238 respondents in the UK (weighted results).

Table 3.1 gives a breakdown of the answers from seven countries surveyed in 2016 and 2017 showing the proportion of the population involved in each of these broad types of platform work. It should be noted that many were involved in more than one type, so there is some double counting across categories.

As can be seen from the table, the highest numbers of platform workers are to be found doing 'virtual' online work from their homes in all countries, ranging between 3.9 and 10.4 per cent for those who said that they carried out this type of work at least weekly. The equivalent range for those doing driving/delivery-type work in public spaces was from 1.4 per cent to 5.8 per cent. In each country, therefore, this is the smallest category of platform work type, with online work constituting the largest category. Because we had only three interviews with workers in the intermediate category (working in other people's homes doing tasks such as cleaning and household repairs), in this chapter we decided to focus on those working for platforms from their own homes, in order to compare their attitudes to unionisation with platform workers in driving and delivery work.

Methodology

To explore attitudes about unionising among various platform workers, we now turn to our in-depth interviews with individual workers, drawing on the results of 36 of these interviews carried out in three countries: the UK, Germany and Estonia between February 2017 and May 2018.

Respondents were recruited by a variety of means. Some participants were identified randomly as a result of participation in a national survey carried out in the UK, in which respondents were asked if they would be willing to be re-contacted for a further in-depth interview. Others were recruited via trade unions and platforms, through snowballing methods, via online discussion group or approached in the street. Fifteen of the interviewees were women and 21 were men. Thirty-three interviewees were of European or British origin (including three who were Black and minority ethnic British people). The remainder had a variety of different national origins including South Asian and Kurdish.

Most interviews (which varied from 40 minutes to 2 hours in length) were conducted by Skype or telephone, but six were carried out face to face. Interviews were recorded (with the consent of participants), transcribed and analysed using Nvivo. All respondents were given nicknames to protect anonymity.

Fourteen interviewees were doing driving or delivery work, of whom six were drivers providing taxi-type services, one was a courier using his own van to deliver goods and packages and seven were cycle couriers, of whom one sometimes also used her car for delivery work.

The remaining 22 interviewees, making up the largest group, were working online from their own homes.

In the next section we explore the attitudes of these platform workers to collective organisation and representation. The small numbers make it difficult to generalise but there do appear to be distinctive differences between those workers who work offline in public spaces, where they have the opportunity of meeting and identifying each other, and those who work online, in more isolated and private locations.

Research Findings

In general our interviews showed contrasting attitudes towards collective organisation between online and offline platform workers. While offline workers had more positive attitudes towards trade unions and peer groups to support each other, online workers were less interested in traditional trade unions representing their interests. Eight out of 14 offline workers had organised collectively by either becoming a member of a trade union or forming a peer group such as an online Facebook group or participating in regular informal meetings with other workers. Only one out of 22 online workers was a member of a traditional trade union (and she had only become a member because of her other full-time job and was not sure whether the membership would also cover her work for online platforms). The majority of online workers had not considered joining a union because they either believed they were not entitled to it because they were self-employed or because they did not see any value in trade unions representing their interests.

The Race to the Bottom in Platform Labour Markets

Many workers in both categories presented an articulate analysis of the labour market in which they found themselves, where opportunities and threats abounded. One major theme in this analysis related to the open nature of labour markets for platform workers. On the one hand, this presents an open door to new workers seeking to enter the field. On the other, this very openness created a risk of a competitive race to the bottom. It was striking that the workers most likely to draw from this the conclusion that unionisation would be a way to help minimise these risks were offline workers, some of whom were already members of unions.

One reflection on the overall character of platform workers' labour market came from a 32-year-old male rideshare driver in the UK who was a member of a trade union. He contextualised this in a critique of the 'flexibility' that platforms purport to offer their workers:

> I mean it says that . . . it gives you full flexibility, but if you think about it, you, if everything's so low and so competitive in the terms that you've got so many drivers, you need to be out there more, and by being out there more, it doesn't guarantee you a set amount and once you, and the thing is, it's not as busy as what, as what it used to be, it's way less. So . . . you have to work more to get a decent amount, so when you're off, you're off, you're not getting any, not going to get any ex, you're not going to get any money for, you know.
>
> *(Mustafa, rideshare driver)*

John, a 25-year old delivery rider interviewed in the UK, also pointed to the way that over-recruitment of workers by platforms led to a deterioration in conditions for others.

> Like in [name of town], [name of company] have been over hiring riders, which means that there's a huge amount of people for the work that needs to be done. The only difference that makes to [name of company] is that their orders spend less time waiting until they're picked up and delivered. Of course, the effects for the riders is massive, because they get paid by delivery. So, fewer deliveries per rider means a much lower income, but I mean, [name of company] doesn't have to think twice about that, and that's, in no way can we call that efficiency, and yet it's the model.
>
> *(John, delivery rider)*

He was emphatic about the need for unionisation.

> I was instantly convinced that joining the union was the right thing to do. I mean, even though I didn't have any, you know, some people have the

like, 'ah, I might only have this job for two months so what's the point of signing up for a union?' To me, the case that the union, what it was doing was so, it was so obviously an important thing.

(John, delivery rider)

Online workers also demonstrated a strong awareness of the competitive nature of the labour market they were in.

Here, for example, is a 36-year old male graphic designer working in Estonia for online platforms.

> Competition. You live in a super expensive country in a global context—Estonia. Well, some places are more expensive . . . but . . . well, the competition is tough. For example, if you take the logo design project, which is a very specific thing. Then usually a person is hired within a few hours. For example, the opening is at 9am and if you then look at midday they have already found someone. But by then, there are 50 proposals. Well, your chances are then 1/50 whether you get it or not. Something like that. Maybe a little more, maybe a little less.
>
> *(Henry, graphic designer)*

And a 40-year-old German IT worker:

> On [name of company], there is in principle no competition but on other platforms there is. You can see that there is supply and demand and that you can make an offer. This is not the case with [name of first company]. This was probably also the reason why I stayed with [this company] as there is no competition in principle . . . The disadvantage is that you have to be really good. You have to deliver a good quality work because there are 100,000 people who apply at the same time. And whether you get selected or not is a matter of luck. You're just one of many, whether you're here or if you're not there, that's completely uninteresting. . . . They can come from all over the world, so theoretically you have a very few assignments and a million hungry mouths
>
> *(Arno, IT worker)*

While aware of the competitive pressures, however, Arno did not see trade unions as offering any solution:

> Because I see trade unions representing the interests of employees. We don't know how this is going to develop but another issue is that for me it is not a main source of income.
>
> *(Arno, IT worker)*

Competition, Collaboration and Combination 229

Interestingly, his reasoning for this draws on two arguments: first, that he is not an employee; and second, that platform work is not his main source of income. In fact both of these factors also apply in the case of John, the cycle courier quoted earlier (who was in fact combining his platform work with a full-time job in another sector), but in this case this had led to a very different form of argumentation, for reasons we speculate on later.

Arno's pessimism about trade unions was also shared by another German online worker, this time a 37-year-old woman for whom it provided the only source of income.

> I don't think there is much that can be done. I believe that for self-employed there is always the risk of not getting enough assignments, or that it doesn't work out. Thus I do not know what could be done. Last year, there was this suggestion that trade unions could do something. And last year, this trade union [name of union] had discussions with [name of company] but I am not really clear what a trade union could do or how they could support. I am not sure how something could be implemented on a practical level, and what should actually be changed. As a result, it could happen that [name of company] will have less assignments and in worst case they could stop existing. And because one is not employed with them there is no social security that one would otherwise have if one was employed.
>
> *(Manuela, IT worker)*

Similar views were expressed by another German online worker, 51-year-old Monika, who carried out a variety of tasks for several different online platforms on top of employment in another job.

> I cannot imagine it [being a member of a trade union] at all and I am not sure how it should work because if I was a member of a trade union and worked through a platform then I am not employed. The platform does not owe me anything. A trade union cannot fight for anything, as I have no right to expect work from this platform anyway.
>
> *(Monika, multitasking online worker)*

Here, her attitude might have been shaped by a limited understanding of what a trade union can achieve. In other cases, the attitudes of online workers to trade unions were more ambivalent. They recognised their value in principle but were sceptical about the possibilities for success. Here, for example, is another German online worker, a 49-year-old woman for whom IT work for online platforms constitutes the only source of income.

> It should be organised differently because this form of work is not compatible with the form of work that trade unions cover. Sometimes I wish that

there was more teaming up with other workers on the same platform . . . It would be good if there was a possibility to have a dialogue [with the platform], to have the possibility to say 'hey people, this [change or decision] was not good and I want to tell you why'. . . . However, I cannot imagine having a proper labour dispute about something because I think we are the co-creators of something that is not finished yet and where there are no ready-made solutions for everything. To be honest, I would find a trade union strange. Having contact [with other workers] is good and valuable. It would be good for letting off steam when one gets upset about something. But a traditional trade union where an outsider who is not even on the platform organises something for us . . . I would find it strange.

(Adriane, IT worker)

Thirty-eight-year-old Amelie, a German writer and translator who relies on her income from platforms as a freelancer, also expressed some scepticism about whether traditional trade unions could represent her interests, but she did see some possibilities for using online means for new forms of organisation and information exchange.

I think that traditional trade unions have all the wrong answers or no answers to these kind of problems related to digitalisation. I do not expect much but maybe that we react to digital forms of work with digital form of unionisation—so with digital trade unions. I can imagine this. Another thing that we have criticised [together with other online workers] is that platforms have closed down online forums where we could exchange our experiences. [name of platform] still has a forum but there does not seem to be any interest in bringing workers together so that they could speak with each other.
 . . . I sometimes use their forum but rather in order to get help with assignments and to understand how to interpret the instructions etc. and less in order to organise with other workers. However, I think it could be used for this but they [platforms] do not want this.

(Amelie, writer and translator)

The much higher level of pessimism about the possibility for trade unions to be able to improve their situation found among online workers seems to be linked to a perception that, without employee status, they are labour market 'outsiders'.

Tensions Between Competition and Collaboration

An important dimension of the ambivalent attitudes to collective organisation among platform workers is a tension between competition and collaboration among fellow workers. When probed about this, some respondents saw other platform workers primarily as colleagues and others saw them primarily as rivals. The majority, however, expressed considerable ambiguity, seeing them as a mixture of both, sometimes (but not always) with the allegiance varying according to their nationality. Even when other platform workers are defined primarily as colleagues this does not necessarily involve the idea that this could provide a basis for organising themselves. They often see others as colleagues for the purposes of knowledge exchange rather than fighting in solidarity for better working conditions.

A 30-year-old German product designer provides an example of an online worker who regards other platform workers primarily, and straightforwardly, as competition.

> Think about it. I think that I even enjoy a little bit this competitive nature as a whole because I can then see my own progress. I notice the change: how at the beginning it was difficult for me to get assignments and also deliver work but then how it gets better once the work becomes more familiar.
>
> *(Stefan, product designer)*

A 29-year-old platform tester, also German, who combined his work testing websites and apps for an online platform with being a student, expressed a view that is more nuanced, making a distinction between foreign competition and competition within Germany.

Interviewer: But how do you see the other people? Are they colleagues or rather competitors?

That depends a little bit on the person and on his or her character. You get the idea about the person when you read the bug reports and descriptions. Generally speaking, I consider them as colleagues and I don't like the idea of being in competition. However, when I do the tests in English (well, this certainly also happens with Germans but even more with English-speaking people) there are always people who copy things from other people and submit for themselves. This is a bit unappealing and that's when I see it more like a competition.

Interviewer: Does this mean that German-speaking people stick together and when it gets more global, then less so?

This is a very subjective view. I don't know if it's really like this. I take it a little bit like that. So also with others. For example, I do not remember what that was . . . I think he came from Poland or so or Ukraine . . . obviously there are also many nice, wonderful people . . . but there are also some . . . they are probably in minority who are exhausting because they copy content, for example. They misbehave in chats or make allegations or have a discussion about various things. And this is just annoying. But that's also the case with Germans but maybe a bit more with English speaking people [i.e. workers from other countries who speak English]. I think it is because they believe more in competition. I can see that for Germans it is usually not their main source of income, they do it as a side activity. Hence they are a bit more relaxed. And whoever makes it for a living, for example someone in Eastern Europe or somewhere like that or in India, I just think that there is a different kind of pressure. And then I can understand that their tone is a bit rougher. (Dietrich, platform tester)

Another German online worker, a 35-year-old IT worker who carried out a variety of different IT-related roles via several different platforms to supplement his income from his main job, expressed a similar ambivalence towards fellow workers. He described a relationship among colleagues which was, or at least in his view, aspired to be 'collegial', but in which there were nevertheless competitive tensions.

Interviewer: *Are they colleagues or competitors for you?*

(laughing) It's a damn good question, so . . . because I said that I do not do that full time, they are rather no competitors for me. They are more like colleagues than competitors. So I do not know, I see that rather neutral. So there is a test and who gets the job, he or she then just does it and if not, then not. Well, I see it very collegial. Maybe collegial is the wrong word because I don't know them. I sit in front of my screen and they in front of theirs and we don't know each other. Competitors—I am not sure about it. If I had to make a living out of it then they would be competitors for me but I don't. These are for me at most people who may somehow have an interest in it, maybe because of the technology, somehow want to earn extra money. That's OK too. As I can see who gets which assignments, they are not really competitors for me. . . . So in principle you have a lot of time, but the problem is that there is always competition, because every bug can only be reported only once. You are paid per error. And of course I'm not the only one testing—the later I start, the more bugs others have found. So the later I start, the less productive I am because I have to search even more and see what else I can do. And of course it is sometimes frustrating even if you find things you realise that someone else has already registered. And then you have nothing and that upsets you and you stop. So it's worth starting early, but you do not have to. But it's worth it. (Benjamin, IT multitasker)

However, it seems unlikely that this relaxed attitude to competitors is a simple by-product of the fact that Benjamin has a steady income from his main job. Manuela, a 37-year-old who lacked regular employment in Germany where she lived, expressed a similar view. She pieced together an income from advertising revenue from her blogs and a similar type of product testing, often on the same platform as Benjamin. This suggests that their attitudes may be shaped more by their similar work experiences than by their personal circumstances—experiences which are at least partly shaped by the particular business model of this company and the labour processes dictated by it.

> [Other people working for the same platform] are more like colleagues, yes. I do not see them as competitors . . . And there were people who behaved a bit as if they were competitors. One of them asked me about my approach and if I could give him hints about how he could also find better bugs. And then I thought 'no, I won't do that'. This was the first time I saw someone as a competitor because I thought that I cannot reveal all my tricks because only the one who finds it [a bug] first gets paid.

Interviewer: So there is a bit of competition?

> Yes, a little but I do not feel it that strongly. However, I found this one case blatant. I thought 'no, I'm not here to give out information about what I typically do because I've found my own way how I work and I don't want to tell anyone about it'. But I think that other workers feel even more like competitors. (Manuela, blogger and IT worker)

This ambivalence around feelings of worker solidarity is by no means restricted to online workers. Offline platform workers sometimes expressed similar views. A 42-year-old male Estonian rideshare driver clearly stated his view that other drivers were competitors:

> Well, basically they [other drivers] are my competitors. They also look for customers. And the less cars there are, the better for me. But the more cars there are, the . . . Well, I'm not . . . in a nutshell, I'm relatively neutral. I have maybe had a conversation with one or two drivers about 'well, how are you doing?' Are there a lot or a little assignments?' That's it. However, I know that two of my acquaintances also drive.
>
> *(Paul, rideshare driver)*

In general, however, offline workers exhibited a stronger sense of solidarity with fellow workers than did online workers. Another Estonian offline worker, a 35-year-old woman who carried out deliveries by bike and car, expressed it in these words:

> There is no sense of competition against other couriers. We openly talk about how many orders we have made. For instance, you have managed 120, but I have only 110. . . with 120 you get a bonus . . . there are still 10

left till a bonus. Then one delivery driver says that he/she is going home today so that I will get enough assignments. We rather help each other to get enough assignments. The one who gets enough manages his/her goal and goes home earlier. A new counting starts tomorrow. For me a team is very important in life. A collective. I have never had such a good collective, team, work. I feel I'm in the right place. I'm in Tallinn what I wanted. I can leave whenever I want—exactly the day I want (laughs) and at the time I want.

(Mia, courier)

Interestingly, none of the Estonian respondents in the survey were members of trade unions. This is not surprising in a former Soviet republic, where trade unions were often viewed with suspicion as instruments of the state. As a consequence of this legacy, trade unions are relatively weak and membership low.[14] Nevertheless, this has not prevented offline driving and delivery workers from building up a comradely, collaborative work culture.

A similar sense of camaraderie was found among couriers in other countries. One 32-year-old delivery rider, Tahim, who was interviewed in Germany but had also worked for the same platform in the UK and was interviewed in English, was combining this work with being a student. He compared the work favourably with working for a supermarket which, he said, paid more, but entailed 'lots of stress'. One of the things he enjoyed most about being a delivery rider was 'every time when I'm riding I saw lots of [name of company] drivers, when they're not busy we talk, we gossip'.

Thierry, another student/delivery rider interviewed in Germany, a 20-year-old man, also described the friendly relationships among fellow workers:

> Between [name of company] riders we always say 'hi' to each other when we meet. And if two [name of company] riders, or even [name of rival food delivery company] riders, are waiting at the restaurant we start chatting as well. . . . We have a good communication, yes.
>
> *(Thierry, food delivery rider)*

This interaction extends beyond casual greeting to include pre-arranged meetings, combining work-related and social contact.

> We talk about everything and nothing. For example, if we want to meet in a bar, or, I don't know, we ask about our experience with one of our riders, for example, I don't know, we talk about everything and nothing.
>
> *(Thierry, food delivery rider)*

It should be noted that Thierry was not a trade union member and said that he had not heard of any other food delivery rider being a member.

It is apparent that offline courier workers, even when they are not unionised, have managed to build a culture of collaboration and solidarity that could be an important precursor of collective organisation. It seems likely that the chance to interact with each other in person, in real time and real space, has played an important role in this.

The importance of face-to-face meetings for trade union recruitment was borne out by the testimony of John, the UK delivery rider quoted earlier, who was an active trade union member. Indeed, he suggests that the platform company he worked for was so concerned about this that it had taken steps to reduce the amount of direct time that riders spent together waiting for tasks.

It has changed a bit now but they [the company] used to have a lot of emphasis on what they called the zone centre, which is a spot they've calculated to be equidistant from all of the different restaurants you might pick up from. In [district in South London] it was a square, they also tried to try and, I think they used to try and make it a place you could also hang out, where there were some benches or something, and in [name of district] it happened to be a square, in [another London district] it's just off the High Street, there are no benches but there are restaurants that have outdoor seating thing, also there's a place to park your bikes and stuff, like a bike rack. I think they've tried to de-emphasise the zone centre a little bit recently.

Interviewer: Why?

> Because it was crucial in, it's like really, it facilitates communication between drivers, which is the only way really that there's a kind of tangible sense of all being in the same boat with [name of company], otherwise you're . . . you're just one rider in the city. Where you see other people in the same uniform, there's not a connection there. So it was, it has been key, that zone centre, in fermenting strike movements and resilience towards bad practices. (John, delivery rider)

Taken together, these accounts lend strong support to the hypothesis that direct social contact between workers plays a strong role in building collective identities and organisation. However, it is also clear that an employed service worker in the retail sector has more connectivity than a self-employed courier worker has. And while access to social relationships plays an important role in organising, it is not the only factor that eases unionisation. Platform workers still face barriers that range from the cultural/historical environment (as in Estonia), stereotyped ideas about the role of trade unions (as among some of the German online workers quoted earlier) to the legal classification that makes organising difficult.[15]

Conclusions

Although this study is part of a larger work in progress and draws only on some of the interviews conducted for this analysis, we believe that these results shed interesting light on the attitudes of platform workers to trade union organisation and open up important questions to be addressed in any further research. First, they caution us against generalising from the experience of one occupational group of platform workers to those in other occupations. Even when there are strong similarities in their situations as platform workers in relation, for example, to their formal status as self-employed workers, the unpredictability of work and the negative effects of competition in a flooded labour market, it cannot be assumed that the reactions to these situations will necessarily be the same. Even a similar interpretation of the problem will not necessarily lead to the same political conclusion.

There are of course many factors that shape attitudes to collective organisation. One might expect that one of the strongest of these factors might be the extent to which a platform worker is actually dependent on his or her income from platform work to make a living. Somewhat surprisingly, based on these interviews, this is a much less important factor than whether the worker is involved in delivering offline or online services. While it is beyond the scope of this chapter to investigate the many other factors that shape platform workers' attitudes to unionisation, we can surmise that the opportunity to meet with fellow workers in real time and space plays a strong role in building a sense of solidarity, mutual trust and common purpose that, in turn, can provide the basis for collective organisation. Further research will be necessary to establish this.

It would be also interesting to further explore connections between the layers of worker-perceived 'insiders' and 'outsiders' within platform labour markets and unionisation attitudes. How do perceptions of such status by other workers or by themselves impact these attitudes? How does the material status of workers as reserve armies within a reserve army or within core labour shape attitudes about labour organising and union membership?

The results of our research also raise questions about whether and how trade unions need to change in order to meet the needs of platform workers and the new and enduring landscapes of work. Would union organising campaigns benefit by conducting education campaigns about the achievements of organising digital workers and of using digital tools to organise workers? Our interview material raises these questions.

There could be other explanations for the differences we found, perhaps including a realistic assessment of the prospects for success of trade union organisation. Have platform companies raised barriers to organising so high that workers fail to even imagine how digital organising might occur? Or are there unrealised opportunities for working around or through these barriers? Here, it is possible that success breeds further success, as news spreads of successful examples of organisation and representation, inspiring others to join and follow their example is also clear that the propensity to organise is contingent on specific circumstances and cannot be read off from the simple fact of being a platform worker.

Our study suggests that, useful though it is in bringing real benefits to the workers represented and drawing public attention to the challenges facing platform workers, trade union organising is unlikely, alone, to bring about a universal improvement in conditions. Union organising should be combined with broader political action, with unions and in coalition with nonunionised workers to make policy interventions that regulate platform companies and provide basic employment rights to platform workers.

Notes

1. Labournet TV, "Riders Across Europe Unite to Form the Transnational Federation of Couriers," 2018, accessed February 9, 2019, https://en.labournet.tv/riders-across-europe-unite-form-transnational-federation-couriers.
2. Daniela Leonardi, Annalisa Murgia, Marco Briziarelli, and Emiliano Armano, "The Ambivalence of Logistical Connectivity: A Co-Research With Foodora Riders," *Work Organisation Labour & Globalisation* 13, no. 1 (2019); Facility Waters and Jamie Woodcock, "Far From Seamless: A Workers' Inquiry at Deliveroo'," *Viewpoint Magazine*, September 20, 2017, accessed February 9, 2019, www.viewpointmag.com/2017/09/20/far-seamless-workers-inquiry-deliveroo/; Caleb Goods, Alex Veen, and Tom Barratt, "'Is Your Gig Any Good?' Analysing Job Quality in the Australian Platform-Based Food-Delivery Sector," *Journal of Industrial Relations* (2019), https://doi.org/10.1177/0022185618817069; Arianna Tassinari and Vincenzo Maccarrone, "The Mobilisation of Gig Economy Couriers in Italy: Some Lessons for the Trade Union Movement," *Transfer: European Review of Labour and Research* 23, no. 3 (2017): 353–57; Anne Degner and Eva Kocher, "Arbeitskämpfe in der 'Gig-Economy'? Die Protestbewegungen der Foodora—und Deliveroo-'Riders' und Rechtsfragen ihrer kollektiven Selbstorganisation," *KJ Kritische Justiz* 51, no. 3 (2018): 247–65.
3. Formerly the United Private Hire Drivers (UPHD), the members of this union briefly joined the Independent Workers of Great Britain (IWGB) before becoming an independently registered trade union. www.adcu.org.uk.
4. https://iaatw.org/.
5. Karolien Lenaerts, Zachary Kilhoffer, and Mehtap Akgüç, "Traditional and New Forms of Organisation and Representation in the Platform Economy," *Work Organisation, Labour and Globalisation* 12, no. 2 (2018): 60–78; Jeremias Prassl, *Humans as a Service: The Promise and Perils of Work in the Gig Economy* (Oxford: Oxford University Press, 2018); Trebor Scholz, *Platform Co-Operativism* (New York: Rosa Luxemburg Stiftung, 2016).
6. Luke Munn, "I am a Driver-Partner," *Work Organisation Labour & Globalisation* 11, no. 2 (2017): 7–20; Alex Rosenblat and Luke Stark, "Algorithmic Labor and Information Asymmetries: A Case Study of Uber's Drivers," *International Journal of Communication* 10, no. 27 (2016): 3758–84; Veena B. Dubal, "The Drive to Precarity: A Political History of Work, Regulation, & Labor Advocacy in San Francisco's Taxi & Uber Economics," *Berkeley Journal of Employment and Labor Law* 38, no. 1 (2017): 73–136; Geoffrey Dudley, David Banister, and Tim Schwanen, "The Rise of Uber and Regulating the Disruptive Innovator," *The Political Quarterly* 88, no. 3 (2017): 492–99; Mareike Glöss, Moira McGregor, and Barry Brown, "Designing for Labour: Uber and the On-Demand Mobile Workforce," Paper read at *Proceedings of the 2016 CHI Conference on Human Factors in Computing Systems*, 2016, 1632–43, https://doi.org/10.1145/2858036.2858476; Jeremias Prassl and Martin Risak, "Uber, Taskrabbit, and Co.: Platforms as Employers—Rethinking the Legal Analysis of Crowdwork," *Comparative Labor Law & Policy Journal* 37 (2015–2016): 619.
7. Brett Caraway, "Collective Action Frames and the Developing Role of Discursive Practice in Worker Organisation: The Case of OUR Walmart," *Work Organisation Labour & Globalisation* 12, no. 1 (2018): 7–24; J. Slaughter, "Strikes Expose Hazards In Walmart's Supply Chain," *Labor Notes* no. 403 (October 2012): 15–16; Jake Alimahomed-Wilson and Immanuel Ness, *Choke Points: Logistics Workers Disrupting the Global Supply Chain Journal of Labor and Society* (London: Pluto Press, 2018);

Reuters Staff, "Amazon Workers Strike in Germany, Joining Action in Spain and Poland," *Reuters Business News*, July 16, 2018, 4:17 pm, accessed August 24, 2018, www.reuters.com/article/us-amazon-com-germany-strike/amazon-workers-strike-in-germany-joining-action-in-spain-and-poland-idUSKBN1K61OY; Julia Kollowe and Nicola Slawson, "McDonald's Workers to Go on Strike in Britain for First Time," September 4, 2017, 05:27 BST, accessed August 24, 2018, www.theguardian.com/business/2017/sep/04/mcdonalds-workers-strike-cambridge-crayford; Alison Moody, "Labour and the Contradictory Logic of Logistics," *Work Organisation Labour & Globalisation* 13, no. 1 (2019).

8. Derek Matthews, "1889 and All That: New Views on the New Unionism," *International Review of Social History* 36, no. 1 (1991): 24–58.
9. Hannah Johnston and Chris Land-Kazlauskas, "Organizing On-Demand: Representation, Voice, and Collective Bargaining in the Gig Economy," in *Conditions of Work and Employment Series No. 94* (Geneva: International Labour Office, 2018), www.ilo.org/travail/whatwedo/publications/WCMS_624286/lang--en/index.htm; Phoebe V. Moore, Pav Akhtar, and Martin Upchurch, "Digitalisation of Work and Resistance," in *Humans and Machines at Work: Monitoring, Surveillance and Automation in Contemporary Capitalism* (New York: Palgrave Macmillan, 2017), 1–16; Kurt Vandaele, "Will Trade Unions Survive in the Platform Economy? Emerging Patterns of Platform Workers' Collective Voice and Representation in Europe," ETUI Research Paper—Working Paper, April 2018, www.etui.org/Publications2/Working-Papers/Will-trade-unions-survive-in-the-platform-economy-Emerging-patterns-of-platform-workers-collective-voice-and-representation-in-Europe; Lenaerts et al., "Traditional and New Forms of Organisation."
10. Gemma Newlands, Christoph Lutz, and Christian Fieseler, "Collective Action and Provider Classification in the Sharing Economy," *New Technology, Work and Employment* 33, no. 3 (2018): 250–67; Lilly C. Irani and M. Silberman, "Turkopticon: Interrupting Worker Invisibility in Amazon Mechanical Turk," Paper read at *Proceedings of the SIGCHI Conference on Human Factors in Computing Systems*, ACM Digital Library, 2013, https://dl.acm.org/citation.cfm?id=2470742; Alex J. Wood, Vili Lehdonvirta, and Mark Graham, "Workers of the Internet Unite? Online Freelancer Organisation Among Remote Gig Economy Workers in Six Asian and African Countries," *New Technology, Work and Employment* 33, no. 2 (2018): 95–112; Christina Hießl, "Labour Law for TOS and HITs? Reflections on the Potential for Applying 'Labour Law Analogies' to Crowdworkers, Focusing on Employee Representation," *Work Organisation Labour & Globalisation* 12, no.(2 (2018): 38–59; P. D'Cruz and E. Noronha, "Positives Outweighing Negatives: The Experiences of Indian Crowdsourced Workers," *Work Organisation, Labour and Globalisation* 10, no. 1 (2016): 44–63.
11. The research reported here focused on the attitudes of online and offline workers to unionisation. We do not explore achievements in unionising. For that research, see Vandaele, "Will Trade Unions Survive in the Platform Economy?"; Lenaerts et al., "Traditional and New Forms of Organisation."
12. This chapter was written in 2019 when the final report with additional six countries was not published yet. In 2019, the final 13-country report was published: U. Huws, et al., *The Platformisation of Work in Europe. Highlights from Research in 13 European Countries* (Brussels: Foundation for European Progressive Studies, 2019).
13. For details of the research in the first seven countries, see Huws, Spencer, Syrdal, and Holts, 2017, www.feps-europe.eu/resources/publications/561-work-in-the-european-gig-economy-employment-in-the-era-of-online-platforms.html.
14. Raul Eamets and Epp Kalaste, "The Lack of Wage Setting Power of Estonian Trade Unions?" *Baltic Journal of Economics* 5, no. 1 (2004): 44–60.
15. Prassl, *Humans as a Service*.

15
PRECARITY BEYOND THE GIG
From University Halls to Tech Campuses

Tamara Kneese

Introduction

In 2018, Cynthia Nixon, the former *Sex and the City* actor and New York State gubernatorial candidate, tweeted, "José is an adjunct professor who has to double as a ridesharing driver because he can't make a living on a CUNY salary." With this tweet, Nixon highlighted how different kinds of precarity converge within the gig economy. Despite popular depictions of gig workers as separate from their white-collar counterparts, insecure positions are common in numerous professions, from higher education to tech, prompting workers to seek supplementary income. Such dynamics are particularly apparent in the San Francisco Bay Area—the prohibitively expensive home of major tech companies and universities, where coders also work as ride-hail drivers. One San Francisco–based Uber engineer wrote an op-ed supporting gig workers because he was once a Lyft driver himself.[1] The pandemic has made some gig work even more precarious, pushing workers to supplement their incomes with work in multiple sectors, and has hit San Francisco gig workers particularly hard.[2] However, while COVID-19 is deepening inequalities, it is also fostering creative approaches to organizing. Through my participant observation at Tech Workers Coalition (TWC) meetings and interviews with local tech workers, I argue that situating the gig economy within larger frameworks of precarity underscores possibilities for coalition building across class divides.

In this chapter, I argue that gig economy labor organizers should look to other sectors, including higher education, where contingent workers have allied, sometimes with the support of more secure employees, to fight for better wages and working conditions. Focusing on gig work's technological attributes, that is, algorithmic management, to the detriment of other forms of contingent, low-paying jobs, obfuscates the power relations that organizing efforts must also address. Beneath the privileged veneer of tech and university campuses, there exists an entire underclass of contingent workers. Tech companies employ contractor coders along with subcontracted custodial and food service staff. A similarly precarious workforce exists on university campuses, including adjuncts, grad workers, and subcontracted support staff. In both cases, precarious workers are not well paid, sometimes receive no benefits, and are employed on short-term contracts. In both academia and tech, some workers are considered valuable members of the workforce while others are disposable.[3] Gig workers are part of this larger labor ecosystem. Reflecting on the homologies between tech and higher ed workforces, I argue that labor organizers should consider precarity beyond the "gig," which is typically construed in narrow, platform-oriented, technologically determinist terms.[4] Additionally, I argue that while both tech and academia are notoriously difficult spaces in which to organize, historical and emergent examples show there is hope for cross-class movements uniting more privileged and precarious workers in both sectors.

I develop these arguments by first proposing an expansive definition of gig work, situating it in broader histories of precarity, and finding commonalities among marginalized workers in academia and tech. My research included two years of participant observation in TWC meetings and actions around the Bay Area as well as 10 semi-structured interviews with TWC volunteers and workers I encountered at TWC-sponsored events. Next, I highlight the histories of racialized, gendered, and class-based hierarchies and ideologies that inhibit organizing strategies in both contexts. Finally, I present TWC as an illustrative case study. TWC represents a model of organizing that does not necessarily depend on traditional labor unions. In the conclusion, I point to a new wave of unionizing efforts connecting gig workers to larger, more inclusive coalitions, particularly during the COVID-19 pandemic.

Converging Histories of Gig Work

In this section, I argue for the importance of understanding gig work as a form of labor casualization that affects workers across platforms and sectors, especially gig and academic workers. I contend that expanding the definition of "gig" labor is a productive step in finding common ground between platform workers and other precarious workers. Gigs predate new apps but are a defining part of enduring forms of precarious labor. Precarious labor is contract-based, contingent, freelance, part-time, or short-term work—including farm labor, home-based work, piecework, and sex work. Workers, not employers, take on risks associated with the work at hand, and such positions rarely offer benefits or protections. This section situates gig work within the history of labor casualization under post-Fordism and subsequent organizing strategies, drawing on examples from secondary historical sources and my own interviews. While the notion of "precarity" can unproductively collapse race, gender, and class-based differences between workers, viewing both tech and academic campuses through the lens of precarious labor can help identify new spaces for potential solidarity.

For many people in various professions, including those in the tech industry, work has long been insecure and unfulfilling. Tech-focused gig economy discourses obscure longer histories of systemic oppression, which cannot be reduced to one platform alone.[5] The legal argument surrounding an "independent contractor" is essential to employers' claims about their lack of responsibility; gig companies are building on precedents set by management in other sectors, including higher education, which has continuously argued that grad workers, for example, are not "real" employees.[6] Legal scholar Veena Dubal argues that the distinction between full-time employees and independent contractors is based on a series of political and legal changes throughout the 20th century, tracing how the reorganization of taxi cab companies, much like ride-hail platforms, sought to place responsibility on individual drivers rather than on companies. While post-Fordism and anti-union labor trends from the 1970s onward, along with computing technologies and automation, are often blamed for the growth of precarious labor, Dubal's historical work shows how "precarity has been the norm, not the exception" in the US.[7]

Despite growing casualization, the 1960s and 1970s simultaneously created opportunities for new organizing tactics in many fields, including academia and tech. During this period, stratification within the university, corporate managerialism, and the growing contingent workforce inspired union drives for clerical workers, service workers, adjuncts, and graduate students alike.[8] Sometimes, it brought unlikely groups together. Labor historian Zach Schwartz-Weinstein details the effects of 1960s and 1970s austerity and restructuring that fomented a series of strikes at Yale University. Black and Latinx custodians and cafeteria workers suffered pay cuts while working without benefits and pensions, while women clerical workers struggled to find adequate childcare and dealt with sexual harassment without legal protections. Students, too, became increasingly encumbered by debt. As a result of budget cuts, "Service workers, contingent academics, and students experienced the dawn of Yale's era of austerity very differently. Yet they were also linked, inasmuch as they could be, by how the cuts made apparent their value and their vulnerability."[9] Schwartz-Weinstein shows how disparate groups on campus, marked by race and gender as well as class, found common ground despite structural barriers.

As in academia, coalitions have formed between different contingent workers in the tech industry. *Processed World*, an anarchist magazine started by activist Chris Carlsson in San Francisco in 1981, offers a glimpse of how white-collar office temps joined forces with service workers, including van drivers, in Silicon Valley. *Processed World* critiqued and satirized Silicon Valley's sexist, racist culture and profiled examples of worker resistance in the Valley, including janitors unionizing at HP. The magazine covered theft, sabotage, and strikes by white-collar office workers, who sometimes attempted to form unions, although many of their efforts failed and the coalition built around *PW* dissipated.

Many of *Processed World*'s efforts resonate with the contemporary moment, particularly in the Bay Area. *Processed World* writers addressed Silicon Valley's entrenched hierarchies: "for relatively fat paychecks, skilled people design and develop new (or revolutionize old) technology that less skilled and less well-paid people manufacture and ship."[10] The architecture of separating salaried and hourly workers is also echoed in today's tech campus arrangements: "Many medium to large Valley firms maintain one set of buildings, lunchrooms, washroom and recreation facilities for exempt technical workers and another, less desirable set for production workers."[11] Despite these hierarchies, *Processed World* enlisted a diverse team of anonymous voices in tech to write for them, presenting their perspectives while finding commonalities across racial, gender, and class divides and supporting each other's organizing efforts and direct actions. One uniting factor was that white-collar and manufacturing sector workers alike had trouble paying the rent, given the high cost of living, and had lengthy commutes.

After *Processed World*, there were other waves of tech organizing. Launched in 1998, WashTech, the union for temporary workers at Microsoft, was backed by the Communication Workers of America.[12] Microsoft used various strategies to sow divisions between full-time employees and temporary workers. Temps wore orange badges to mark their status. In addition, temps didn't receive benefits and sick leave, or the other perks usually associated with Microsoft employment.[13] In light of these issues, WashTech organizers realized that traditional labor organizing strategies wouldn't suffice.[14] Because there were not enough people to form a bargaining unit at Microsoft, specifically, the union admitted anyone working in tech, finding a solution to structural limits on organizing. WashTech gave isolated workers a chance to communicate, providing the scaffolding for building worker power.

Such developments and conflicts parallel cross-campus organizing efforts at universities today, where food service workers, clerical staff, adjunct professors, and graduate students all fight for union recognition. In 2018, University of California service workers went on strike. One Cal dining hall worker said it is impossible to live in Berkeley and raise a family on service-worker wages. In addition to his job at Cal, he works two other "gigs" to survive.[15] Graduate students and faculty showed their support for workers, sometimes joining them on the picket line and using class time to discuss the strike. While the prestige and exclusivity of UC Berkeley work to create social distance between students and service workers, the shared conditions of precarity have a tendency to bring them closer together. Historical examples like *Processed World* and WashTech, along with coalitional labor organizing tactics in higher education, offer a roadmap for alternative organizing strategies within today's tech industry.

Expanding the Gig in Today's Labor Landscape

As I described previously, academia and tech have included a more precarious workforce since at least the 1960s, and systemic precarity, however counterintuitively, created new spaces for organizing. Building on these historical movements, in this section, I address the continuation of contract-based labor in both tech and academia, expanding gig labor to include other kinds of precarious work. Focusing on apps and their technological affordances or on gig workers as a distinct class reifies boundaries between people who work for gig companies and other kinds of precarious workers. Doing so may overlook shared forms of discrimination that contingent workers across sectors experience. Additionally, while there are specific modes of exploitation unique to each platform (i.e., surge pricing and indirect management), precarious workers in the "gig economy" and academia are often at the mercy of customer reviews that discriminate against members of oppressed communities. Evaluations of adjuncts who are women, queer, trans, or Black, Indigenous, People of Color (BIPOC) may be biased, just as reviews of ride-hail drivers who are immigrants can reflect riders' biases. Beyond gig platforms, many workers depend on ratings and reviews on short-term gigs in the hopes of attracting future work.

One problem with focusing on gig work in isolation from other contingent workers is that gig workers encompass a diverse group of people, some of whom perform other kinds of labor within the tech industry while driving for Lyft or delivering for DoorDash. Gig workers may have experience as software engineers or have some coding expertise. Gig economy workers can be highly educated; researchers have found that education level does not positively affect compensation earned from gig economy work, so—as in the example from the introduction—there is nothing barring people with PhDs from participating in the gig economy and they aren't better off than their fellow workers without degrees.[16] As academics and other members of the so-called creative class have known for decades,[17] prestige and training do not always translate into a decent standard of living.[18] Numerous reports show that contractors and adjuncts, along with other precarious workers, are likely to be housing and food insecure.[19] Companies' treatment of contractor coders is analogous to the plight of adjunct professors, who may have PhDs from top universities and extensive experience but remain marginalized within their departments. In academia, 75.5 percent of faculty are off the tenure track and 50 percent of those jobs are part time.[20] A disproportionate number of contingent faculty are Black and Latinx, well over half are women, and many adjuncts live in poverty.[21] Workers cannot eat prestige, and proximity to major tech firms or universities does not guarantee a high standard of living; in the cases of both academic workers and tech workers, gig work may fill in gaps in employment or supplement insufficient wages, especially for workers from oppressed groups.

Critiques distinguishing between the vaunted coder class and gig economy workers miss their crucial overlap. Bay Area gig workers I spoke with told me that high rent and student debt led them to seek platform work to supplement their incomes. Matthew picked up delivery gigs between network engineering positions after he was laid off. Still others like Roshan, an immigrant Lyft driver, do not work enough hours in their tech job, telling me, "I'm a tech worker. I work part-time in IT and drive on the side."[22] Software engineers may themselves be precarious; half of Google's workforce is comprised of temps, vendors, and contractors, or "TVCs."[23] Contractors at tech companies, like gig workers, are disproportionately Black and Latinx and/or immigrants.[24]

Precarious work can also sow divisions among groups of workers and exacerbate race and gender-based hierarchies. Much like contingent faculty members, TVCs also feel as if they are expendable and siloed from other employees. This was the case for Maya, a Black woman contractor who has attended TWC events and has worked in full-time positions at major San Francisco tech companies. She "got involved in tech almost by chance and my first after school jobs were reception jobs at software companies." Growing up in the Bay Area amid the 1990s tech boom, Maya thanks a supportive woman mentor at a software company for helping her become a quality assurance tester. As a QA tester, she "occasionally felt dismissed. My roles are generally underappreciated. QAs get the shit end of the stick. Project management is always seen as a mothering role, it's a nagging role and they give it a feminine spin." While her positions require technical expertise, she isn't considered on par with her male software engineer colleagues. She feels that her work isn't taken seriously, although she is unsure if her colleagues' dismissal of her is a result of her race, gender, status, or some combination of those.

Maya described how being a contractor affects her treatment at work, both socially and materially:

> I don't have benefits. I am paid hourly and other holidays that people take for granted I don't get paid for. There is no sense of how long I will be around or needed . . . My employer definitely treats me differently. When the company is introduced, I am the last person to be mentioned. I'm an optional attendee at company gatherings.

When she worked as a contractor at a larger company, Maya enjoyed some perks, including their free shuttle and cafeteria, but as she put it,

> there was a sense of being isolated or segregated into a different building with no windows and no one to talk to but the people who were also secreted away. I did a lot of things that employees do, but it was clear who was a real employee and who wasn't.

This treatment carried over to her experiences at her current employer: "The company I'm working for now does company retreats and I was invited one year, but not the next year." As a contractor, particularly in feminized positions, Maya experienced her position as markedly distinct from her full-time colleagues.

Maya's narrative is exemplary of the ways that entrenched hierarchies in workplaces can lead to atomization and foreclose organizing possibilities. As I will describe in the following section, systemic precarity in both tech and academia has made them hostile to organizing despite their reputations as progressive spaces.

Barriers to "Campus" Organizing

Academic and tech workers face similar barriers to formal organizing campaigns, including architectural features on campuses that encourage worker segmentation, ideologies regarding meritocracy and flexibility, and entrenched hierarchies. The very architecture of tech campuses can resemble the aesthetics of the contemporary university, with amenities intended to attract tuition-paying elites who may become future donors. Mountain View's Googleplex reflects the company's ideals of openness and flexibility, with its architects explicitly tying the Googleplex to academia: "With a system resembling the freedom found in academia to pursue one's own goals, each employee has 20 percent of the working week to dedicate entirely to projects of his or her own choosing."[25] Like academics, Googlers are expected to be passionate self-starters who are willing to work overtime without additional compensation.

Infused in many tech origins stories—from Google to Facebook—is a dorm room mythos that perpetuates a collegiate lifestyle. The Googleplex was intentionally designed to mimic the university campus.[26] Fancy cafeterias convince employees to eat on campus rather than going home, which presumes the absence of caregiving responsibilities, while tech companies offer spaces for leisure, as well as generous happy hours. Such comforts may prevent tech workers from thinking of themselves as workers, forming an ideological barrier to organizing.

The refusal to think of oneself as a worker reflects ideologies in both academia and tech. Linking academic precarity to similar circumstances in New York's Silicon Alley, Andrew Ross addressed the problem of "mental labor," which inhibits organizing.[27] As Ross described, early 1990s' tech workers were also enticed by stock options, free coffee, and the promise of a nonhierarchical office structure in exchange for insecure positions without healthcare. In a statement that could be made about gig economy workers now, Ross laments the fact that education does not guarantee a living wage or stability, as people with advanced degrees work as baristas, servers, taxi drivers, or temps. The gig economy has grown in the wake of the Great Recession and intensified with the COVID-19 pandemic. With increased austerity measures and growing casualization, PhD students compete for an ever-diminishing number of tenure-track jobs, while many more work in contingent positions. As Ross argues, the very nature of academic labor itself makes the university a perfect setting for incentivizing such a system. Again, the industry's focus on individual merit and creativity coupled with the absence of trade unions or other forms of structured organizing contribute to feelings of isolation and personal failure.

Indeed, along with these ideological barriers, the hierarchical structures of both academia and tech make them difficult places in which to organize. Both places are associated with and managed by elite white professional men, which belies the hierarchies of precarious but "essential" workers who are overshadowed by such stereotypes. A few innovators, entrepreneurs, and geniuses are put forth as representatives of the industry as a whole, whereas the majority of workers in both fields are struggling, if to various extents. Stereotypes about "tech bros" ignore the larger problem of who can be defined as a tech worker and who performs labor on tech campuses and in a globalized platform economy.

In both universities and tech companies, there are subcontracted workers on campus who have little in terms of status, but whose roles are essential to making their institutions function. Universities and tech companies rely on a globalized workforce as well as low-waged workers from the cities in which they are situated. From contractor coders and adjuncts to subcontracted cafeteria, custodial, and clerical workers, the tech or university ecosystem is a diverse, highly segregated entity. As Maya described in her account, contractors and others who are not part of the elite software engineering crowd are physically segregated from full-time employees. Similarly, on academic campuses, tenured faculty have dedicated offices while adjuncts work from cubicles or in public spaces on campus. Akin to the way Zach Schwartz-Weinstein refers to the "whitewashed, reductive metonym for intellectual labor" known as the university, the tech industry is often shorthand for privileged, cognitive labor.[28] In both universities and tech companies, undervalued, diverse workers allow for the continued reproduction of cognitive labor.

Because of physical and ideological barriers on universities and on tech campuses alike, traditional models of staff organizing don't always work. Staff union representatives may not be welcome in campus workspaces. For one, campuses are enclosed spaces. Different colored badges or limitations on access make it difficult for outsiders to organize. It may be hard to convince science, technology, engineering, and mathematics (STEM) PhD students or software engineers that they are ordinary workers who should flex their collective bargaining rights. As one TWC volunteer told me, he did not think traditional unions would be effective in tech and stressed that it would be better if organizing happened internally rather than externally.

In addition to atomizing ideologies and hierarchies, immigration status may also affect workers' willingness to participate in formal organizing campaigns. As I found through my participant observation at TWC events, many contractor coders are also immigrants who depend on visas. Experiencing xenophobia and racism at work may heighten their job insecurity and, thus, their fears about joining in organizing efforts. Gig workers can be vulnerable in the same way. In San Francisco, a majority of gig workers are BIPOC and many are immigrants.[29] As

I note in the next section, while immigration status can make some workers more vulnerable and therefore hesitant to organize, it is also an experience shared by tech workers at all levels and a potential radicalizing pressure point.

By finding commonalities across racial, gender, and class boundaries, it may be possible for workers in both industries to gain more visibility and power in their respective workplaces. Collective organizing efforts should strive to make different types of work and workers more legible to one another and to form alliances across isolated segments of the industry. As I will describe in the following section, Tech Workers Coalition may signal a new wave of more inclusive labor activism that addresses long-standing and app-based barriers to organizing.

Expanding "The Gig" With Tech Workers Coalition

TWC volunteers define gig work in an expansive way and foster connections among tech workers in all categories. In some cases, TWC volunteers have been actively involved in academic labor organizing as well, showing how there is even more kinship between the two sectors.

TWC is comprised of tech workers across the industry, including software engineers at Square and Google, product managers at Slack, and coders at fledgling startups. Members are committed to organizing their own workplaces and forming coalitions with other sectors, including cleaners and food service workers on tech campuses, gig workers, and contractors across Silicon Valley. As Ben Tarnoff describes, new rank-and-file led movements undermine the tech industry's reliance on the neoliberal—or the West Coast's blend of libertarianism and techno-optimism—which makes the sector notoriously anti-union. In the past few years, even white-collar coders "are building relationships of solidarity with their working-class colleagues in the tech industry and coordinating their efforts in order to advance their campaigns together."[30] Tarnoff notes how workers in various categories, including subcontracted service workers, subcontracted office workers, and full-time office workers, can find common ground. I would add gig workers to this larger schema, as they share many of the same concerns as other contracted workers at major companies.

TWC represents this new wave of labor mobilization. The Bay Area–based TWC was founded in 2014 by cafeteria worker Rachel Melendes and software engineer Matt Schaefer but gained more visibility in 2016, after the election of Donald Trump. The rise of xenophobic immigration policies after Trump's election, including the Muslim ban, helped spark solidarity between subcontracted janitors and white-collar coders who were also immigrants. This was followed by a wave of organizing efforts centered on refusing to build harmful tech, including technology that could be used by the US Immigration and Customs Enforcement (ICE) or other nefarious anti-immigrant entities.

TWC exemplifies a radical, more inclusive, and horizontal organizing model. In TWC's Bay Area chapter, one member often wears an IWW (Industrial

Workers of the World) hat, a signal that TWC is not aligned with mainstream labor unions but based on more anarchic principles. In fact, I first encountered TWC at the Anarchist Book Fair at Oakland's Omni Commons in the fall of 2017. At their table, TWC displayed a zine titled "Tech Workers Against White Supremacy," which immediately reminded me of *Processed World*. TWC later started a zine called *Bug Report!* with witty cartoons and anonymously written articles in the style of *Processed World*. In a January 2019 email advertising *Bug Report!*, TWC wrote,

> The industry is so big, it's harder to justify the definition of "tech worker" as solely the well-paid software engineer; it's now also the fulfillment center worker, the cafeteria staff, the rideshare driver, the independent contractor. Increasingly, we tech workers are women, leftists, immigrants, people of color, queer and trans folks. Many of us came of age during the recession, and we don't like what we're seeing.

This missive typifies the growing solidarity between different sectors within tech and the recognition that precarity affects everyone, even if it harms people to varying degrees. Like earlier movements such as *Processed World* and WashTech, TWC also actively works against the notion that tech workers are uniformly upper middle-class, white, and male, spotlighting the diverse people who comprise the industry.

TWC actions have united precarious workers from various sectors within tech. In some cases, employees at major companies used their privilege to support unionizing efforts by contract workers. As I learned through conversations with TWC volunteers, during UNITE HERE's campaign at Facebook, full-timers gave union organizers access to campus so they could more easily reach cafeteria staff. In 2018, contractors who worked for Facebook through Filter Digital collectively wrote a letter asking for better wages and sick leave. Facebook responded by intimidating them in one-on-one "meetings" in a van and threatening to fire them. In a show of solidarity, a Facebook full-timer shared the letter on an internal company board, making it more difficult for Facebook to ignore their demands.[31] TWC encourages organizing models that center gig and contract workers in addition to full-time employees, while positioning them all as rank-and-file workers as opposed to the owners and CEOs of tech platforms.[32]

Through such organizing efforts, precarious coders formed bonds with gig workers and other subcontracted campus workers, recognizing themselves as rank-and-file workers. While they may earn higher salaries than do other contractors in tech, such as people who work in tech campus cafeterias, contractor coders do not receive benefits and their rates of pay vary based on skill level and location.[33] Tech Workers Coalition hosted events focused on the problems unique to contract workers in the tech industry, including contractor coders as well as other contingent members of the workforce. At one event, one contractor said she was excluded from her company's happy hour and that none of her project team acknowledged her presence outside of working hours. Another contractor at a major company noted that he was incentivized to secretly work overtime—without pay—to finish all of his assigned tasks within his allotted hours. In an interview with me, a trans contractor said she was concerned about the possibility of gaps in her health care coverage, despite the fact that she was technically making a high hourly rate as a contractor. Immigration emerged as a major sticking point for contingent workers in all categories. For contractors on H1B visas, if they are terminated and don't find a new position within 30 days, they may be deported. In my conversations with them, immigrant contractors expressed concern that organizing in their workplaces would jeopardize their positions and, thus, their immigration status. Through Learning Club events, workers were able to find common ground regardless of their position or status and openly voice their personal concerns over immigration, making it a potential point to organize around.

In addition to the more formal aspects of Learning Clubs and other events, TWC offers a social outlet for tech workers who might feel alienated or isolated in their jobs, which may in turn plant the seeds for future organizing. Learning Clubs facilitate both scholarly and practical knowledge sharing, for example reading groups focused on leftist theory or film events along with meetings about legal rights and visa issues. Importantly, as one TWC volunteer told me, Learning Clubs offer disparate workers a chance to connect. Beyond the direct actions or petition-drafting sessions themselves, people also went out for food and beer, informally interacting and building relationships. Such settings helped create a social life around organizing work and united different kinds of tech workers, as tech workers who would ordinarily be closed off from each other on their campuses or who worked at different companies could come together and share common interests. My own involvement in TWC is based around personal relationships formed over time, including inviting TWC members to campus to speak to my classes or to attend public events at the University of San Francisco. Such informal encounters may give rise to new organizing strategies; it was through my conversations at TWC events that I began to think about the relationship between university and tech industry labor stratification.

TWC volunteers, too, see the potential relationship between university campuses and the future of tech: If STEM students enthusiastically join grad unions, then they will bring that same energy to their post-university jobs. TWC has reached out to engineering programs around the Bay, hoping to inspire future generations of tech workers to think of themselves as workers. Several TWC members are also involved in academic unionizing efforts at Bay Area universities. For example, academic and tech labor organizing converge with respect to Stanford University's (not yet formally recognized) graduate union. I interviewed Aylan, an immigrant woman of color TWC volunteer who is both an academic and a tech worker. As Aylan recounted, when the Stanford grad union formed in

2016, organizers hoped to attract STEM students, especially those in computer science. To unionize Stanford CS, as budding engineers and PhD students at an elite school, would "really say something," according to Aylan, about the changing nature of the tech industry and academia.[34]

Despite these organizing efforts at Stanford, there were still ideological barriers to graduate students thinking of themselves as workers akin to other workers on campus. For instance, Aylan noted that many graduate students refused to join in solidarity with striking cafeteria workers on campus. Students weren't afraid their faculty supervisors would retaliate; they just didn't see their concerns as related to those of other kinds of workers. Grad students weren't worried about their short-term working conditions because they believed that meritocracy would save them in the end and they would go on to earn high salaries in the tech industry because of their prestigious degrees.

Some TWC adherents think as material conditions change, these ideological barriers may fall away; given the large number of TVCs in the tech workforce, it's possible that speculative high-paying jobs won't exist in the future. Aylan said that outsourcing and a shift to contract-based engineering jobs meant that those high-paying coder positions might eventually go the way of academia, in that contractor gigs would take the place of full-time positions. Nothing guarantees the lucrative positions of software engineers if circumstances change. One TWC member told me that he pivoted to the tech industry in order to pay off his student loans. After paying for his exorbitant San Francisco rent on top of his loan payments, he had almost no savings to fall back on if he lost his job. Given this general sense of insecurity, joining forces with other workers and even users across tech may offer a way forward.

Many TWC members are from oppressed, marginalized, or underrepresented groups and therefore may not trust in the ideological and material promises of tech companies or in the strategies of traditional labor unions like SEIU or UAW. As disclosed to me by several TWC volunteers, particularly those who had experience with labor organizing in other sectors like higher education, there was a great deal of skepticism around big unions. As one TWC member put it, "We don't want this to end up like the Fight for 15, where SEIU basically took over and sold workers out." TWC members are pro union and do work in tandem with bigger labor unions, but their ultimate goal is not to follow the lead of staff union organizers. Rather, they are making their own way.

New approaches to dealing with precarity beyond the gig help unite workers at every level within the tech industry hierarchy and across companies and sectors of tech, as well as uniting tech workers with other struggles for social justice. In addition to fighting for better working conditions unique to their own jobs, tech workers are joining calls for affordable housing, pushing back against gentrification throughout the Bay Area by working together with local organizations. The end user or consumer is also a major part of ongoing efforts to make tech workplaces more equitable. If Lyft and Uber drivers go on strike, pressure from riders along with other tech workers strengthens their efforts. Organizing efforts against Proposition 22 in California, which passed in November 2020 thanks to the propaganda and financial backing of gig companies, is one example of how end users, gig workers, and other tech workers can join forces against the interests of major tech companies, who sponsored the proposition to undermine the rights of gig workers. If gig work is intended to divide the precariat while theoretically empowering a handful of free agents, these new organizing developments find ways of bringing a globalized, contingent workforce together.

TWC encourages full-time coders and people in more secure positions to support the actions of subcontracted and gig workers. The TWC Twitter account tweeted: "All workers in tech: we are stronger together! Every single worker at these billion-dollar tech companies deserves good pay and healthcare, full stop." In another tweet, the TWC account acknowledged that many programmers worked overtime, finding commonality with the cafeteria workers at Facebook: "Our coworkers in the kitchens are fighting for 8 hour shifts and better schedules. Many of us also work well beyond 40 hours a week. This erosion of workers' rights starts at the bottom and affects us all." Full-time coders at places like Google and Facebook realize that their working conditions are connected to other workers throughout the tech campus and around the world. For software engineers to consider subcontracted janitorial staff or gig workers their "coworkers" is in many respects a radical shift.

What would it mean to connect Uber drivers and riders with contractor coders at Uber, along with the cleaners and other subcontracted staff who work at Uber's headquarters? Organizing efforts must extend beyond specific companies, however, or even particular job descriptions. Relying on gigs does not mean you are managed through an app, nor are gig economy workers necessarily separate from others in the tech ecosystem. It is difficult to parse different types of gig workers and group them according to a trade or role when so many of them fulfill multiple kinds of jobs across industries.

TWC volunteers want to deepen solidarity even further. They have been in ongoing conversations with delivery and ride-hail drivers about how to strengthen support for one another. In addition to pushing back against Proposition 22 propaganda put out by gig companies, TWC members have been assisting gig workers in their applications for unemployment insurance during COVID-19, since many gig and contract workers missed out on initial unemployment benefits. TWC has also partnered with gig worker advocacy groups and coalitions to push for workplace protections and personal protective equipment (PPE) for gig workers, who are now considered "essential" workers. As one TWC volunteer told me, focusing on coders as workers is no longer a radical position. Much of the press has focused on the novelty of software engineers organizing, but TWC goes beyond that. How can they use their privilege to help more precarious workers in tech?

TWC has partnered with other local grassroots organizations in order to support less privileged tech workers and broader racial and social justice-oriented efforts. For example, TWC works with Gig Workers Collective, a group of women of color-led gig workers organizing in the Bay Area, as well as with Bay Area Amazonians, which is a Black-led organization in the East Bay. Bay Area Amazonians was started by Adrienne Williams and John Hopkins, two Black Amazon warehouse workers. Their first action was on Juneteenth, after the murder of George Floyd. For Bay Area Amazonians, racial justice is a fundamental aspect of fighting for workers' rights. The group connects marginalized workers, pushing back against meritocracy and flexibility narratives pushed by Amazon. Like gig workers, Amazon deliverers use their personal cars to deliver packages and are hired on short-term contracts, don't receive benefits, and don't have sick days. In a press interview, Hopkins stated, "I'm a technologist, and I've got a lot of ideas for how we can use technology to overcome the challenge of Amazon cracking down on organizing in our warehouses."[35] Precarious workers in tech may use their technological skills and access to thwart workplace surveillance and control.

As I discuss in the Conclusion, COVID-19 is creating new opportunities for organizing across class distinctions in both academia and in tech at the same time the dissolution of campus life is changing the nature of work and, subsequently, labor organizing.

Conclusion

Gig workers are connected to longer histories and ecosystems of precarious labor. Contractor coders and adjunct faculty, like gig workers, may work in insecure positions for insufficient pay and no benefits. Tech and university campuses are hierarchical environments built on a myth of meritocracy, making them difficult spaces to organize in. However, the recognition of shared precarity, even if it affects workers of different identities and in different positions to various degrees, may offer new opportunities for cross-class solidarity.

COVID-19 is reconfiguring labor organizing efforts around contingent workers and full-time employees. On the one hand, the loss of face-to-face encounters on campus is presenting unique barriers to organizing. Cleaners, kitchen staff, and other contractors on campuses were the first to be furloughed or laid off when the pandemic began. Meanwhile, companies and universities encouraged full-time employees to work from home. Major tech firms, including Google and Facebook, say employees can work from home indefinitely.[36] What does this mean for contractor coders, who are not allowed to bring home their work-owned laptops and who may have other security clearance issues while working remotely?[37] Adjunct faculty are putting unpaid labor into revamping their classes for remote instruction and are offered fewer classes than before, whereas full-time faculty are still receiving their full salaries, despite putting in extra hours. Organizing efforts around the campus environment may no longer be as effective, particularly with a highly stratified workforce.

On the other hand, the pandemic exposes the fact that even workers who view their positions as safe may find they have more in common with precarious colleagues than they once believed. Tenured faculty may lose their jobs when departments are eliminated and even the most lucrative tech companies, including Salesforce and Kickstarter, are laying off white-collar employees amid record-breaking profits.

I have witnessed new coalitions forming at my own university, the University of San Francisco. USF administrators forced our full-time faculty union to make concessions to save the jobs of part-time faculty and the entire tenure-track faculty. As a result of the university's hardline measures, including furloughing most staff, instating drastic pay cuts for faculty, and laying off most of the subcontracted workforce, various unions from campus are working together for the first time. We have weekly "solidarity" calls, and even some non-represented staff members have attended.

Severe cuts and attacks on labor during the pandemic means that formerly complacent tenured faculty are waking up to their position against university administrators, just as software engineers are beginning to see themselves as workers. Prestige is not a guarantee in the face of austerity. The continued actions of Tech Workers Coalition and their alliance with gig workers who are fighting against Proposition 22 and underpaid essential workers who toil in Amazon's fulfillment centers portend a way forward. If everyone is precarious, albeit to greater and lesser extents, the stakes are higher but possibilities greater for working together.

Notes

1. Kurt Nelson, "I'm a Software Engineer at Uber and I'm Voting Against Prop 22," *TechCrunch*, October 6, 2020, https://techcrunch.com/2020/10/06/im-a-software-engineer-at-uber-im-voting-against-prop-22/.
2. Jennifer McNulty, "Already Vulnerable, Gig Economy Workers in San Francisco Suffer During Coronavirus Pandemic, Survey Reveals," May 7, 2020, www.universityofcalifornia.edu/news/already-vulnerable-gig-economy-workers-san-francisco-suffer-during-coronavirus-pandemic-survey.
3. The "shadow workforce" in tech are not considered "real" employees, Mark Bergen and Josh Eidelson, "Inside Google's Shadow Workforce," *Bloomberg,* July 25, 2018, www.bloomberg.com/news/articles/2018-07-25/inside-google-s-shadow-workforce. Universities also depend on precarious workers, many of whom are women and/or BIPOC. Such workers have gone on strike to demand better pay and working conditions: Chris Brooks, "University of California Workers Strike for Racial Justice," *LaborNotes*, November 20, 2018, www.labornotes.org/2018/11/university-california-workers-strike-racial-justice.
4. Such techno-determinist discussions are part of the "future of work" discourse regarding automation, viewing a shift to contingent work as a direct result of replacing full-time jobs with machines. See: www.forbes.com/sites/jeannemeister/2019/05/07/the-future-of-work-the-rise-of-workers-who-self-automate-their-jobs/#2a0218603c23.
5. Michael Palm and I call for an expansion of platform labor to include part-time, platform-assisted retail labor connected to longer histories of gentrification in US

cities. Tamara Kneese and Michael Palm, "Brick-and-Platform: Listing Labor in the Digital Vintage Economy," *Social Media + Society* (July 7, 2020), https://doi.org/10.1177/2056305120933299. See also Julia Ticona on overlooking careworkers in the platform economy, "Essential and Untrusted," *Dissent*, Fall 2020, www.dissentmagazine.org/article/essential-and-untrusted and Tressie McMillan Cottom on the gendered and racialized aspects of "The Hustle Economy," *Dissent*, Fall 2020, www.dissentmagazine.org/article/the-hustle-economy.

6. Sarah Kessler, *Gigged: The End of the Job and the Future of Work* (New York: St. Martin's Press, 2018).
7. Veena Dubal, "Wage Slave or Entrepreneur? Contesting the Dualism of Legal Worker Identities" (April 4, 2016), *California Law Review* 105 (2017): 101; UC Hastings Research Paper No. 176, 96.
8. Randy Martin, *Chalk Lines: The Politics of Work in the Managed University* (Durham, NC: Duke University Press, 1998).
9. Zach Schwartz-Weinstein, "Beneath the University: Service Workers and the University-Hospital City" (New York University diss., New York, 2015), 276.
10. Chris Carlsson and Mark Leger, *Bad Attitude: The Processed World Anthology* (New York: Verso, 1990).
11. Ibid., 152–53.
12. Enda Brophy, "System Error: Labour Precarity and Collective Organizing at Microsoft," *Canadian Journal of Communication* 31, no. 3 (2006): 620.
13. Ibid., 624.
14. Ibid., 626.
15. Natalie Orenstein, "Workers at UC Berkeley, Other Campuses Launch 3-Day Strike," *Berkeleyside*, May 7, 2018, www.berkeleyside.com/2018/05/07/workers-at-uc-berkeley-other-campuses-launch-3-day-strike.
16. Petra Zaal, Andrea Herrmann, Maryse Chappin, and Britta Schemmann, "Does Education Still Matter in the Gig Economy?" *Reshaping Work* (2018), https://pe.reshapingwork.net/session/does-education-still-matter-in-the-gig-economy/.
17. Richard Florida, *The Rise of the Creative Class: And How It's Transforming Work, Leisure, and Everyday Life* (New York: Basic Books, 2002).
18. See Martin, *Chalk Lines*; Monika Krause, Mary Nolan, Michael Palm, and Andrew Ross, *The University Against Itself: The NYU Strike and the Future of the Academic Workplace* (Philadelphia: Temple University Press, 2005); Marc Bousquet, *How the University Works: Higher Education and the Low-Wage Nation* (New York: New York University Press, 2008); Abigail Boggs and Nick Mitchell, "Critical University Studies and the Crisis Consensus," *Feminist Studies* 44, no. 2 (2018).
19. Alastair Gee, "Facing Poverty, Academics Turn to Sex Work and Sleeping in Cars," *The Guardian*, September 28, 2017, www.theguardian.com/us-news/2017/sep/28/adjunct-professors-homeless-sex-work-academia-poverty. Alistair Barr, "An RV Camp Sprang Up Outside Google's Headquarters," *Bloomberg*, May 21, 2019, www.bloomberg.com/news/features/2019-05-21/silicon-valley-s-shame-living-in-a-van-in-google-s-backyard.
20. New Faculty Majority, "Facts About Adjuncts," n.d., www.newfacultymajority.info/facts-about-adjuncts/.
21. Colleen Flaherty, "Barely Getting By," *Inside Higher Ed*, April 20, 2020, www.insidehighered.com/news/2020/04/20/new-report-says-many-adjuncts-make-less-3500-course-and-25000-year.
22. All names are pseudonyms.
23. William Kerr and Carl Kreitzberg, "Google: To TVC or Not to TVC?" Harvard Business School, September 2019, www.hbs.edu/faculty/Pages/item.aspx?num=56878.
24. www.kqed.org/news/11740616/shadow-workforce-tech-contractors-disproportionately-people-of-color.

25. Peter Jakobsson and Fredrik Stiernstedt, "Googleplex and Informational Culture," in *Media Houses: Architecture, Media and the Production of Centrality*, ed. Staffan Ericson and Kristina Riegert (New York: Peter Lang, 2010), 113–37.
26. "The Googleplex and the Rise of the Corporate University Campus," n.d., https://officesnapshots.com/articles/the-googleplex-and-the-rise-of-the-corporate-university-campus/.
27. Andrew Ross, "The Mental Labor Problem," *Social Text* 8, no. 2 (2000): 1–31.
28. Schwartz-Weinstein, "Beneath the University," 9.
29. Megan Rose Dickey, "Gig Workers in San Francisco Are Mostly People of Color and Many Are Immigrants," *Techcrunch*, May 5, 2020, https://techcrunch.com/2020/05/05/gig-workers-survey-san-francisco/.
30. Ben Tarnoff, "The Making of the Tech Worker Movement," *Logic Magazine*, May 4, 2020, https://logicmag.io/the-making-of-the-tech-worker-movement/full-text/.
31. Julia Carrie Wong, "Facebook Contractors Faced Christmas Ultimatum: Accept Wage Offer or Lose Jobs," *The Guardian,* December 20, 2018, www.theguardian.com/technology/2018/dec/20/facebook-contractors-filter-digital-labor-dispute-christmas.
32. There are problems with the perceived novelty of software engineers as organizers, who tend to get more press attention than other tech workers who organize. Coders in privileged positions are often interviewed and profiled by journalists and academics. Some TWC members said they wanted to encourage more contractors and gig workers to attend their events, fostering more outreach to more precarious tech workers.
33. Rani Molla, "What Contract Tech Workers Get Paid in Cities Around the Country," *Recode,* September 27, 2017, www.vox.com/2017/9/27/16369664/contract-contractors-freelance-fulltime-salary-paid-tech-workers.
34. I interviewed several TWC volunteers who have experience in academic labor organizing, and we discussed the connections between the two types of institutions.
35. Bay Area Amazonians press release: www.digitaljournal.com/pr/4717172. Adrienne Williams, a former Amazon delivery driver, has since left BAA and advocates for working parents like herself and women who have suffered miscarriages on the job at Amazon fulfillment centers.
36. See Lilah Burke, "Uncertain Fate for Support Staff," *InsideHigherEd*, March 13, 2020, www.insidehighered.com/news/2020/03/13/future-unclear-support-staff-empty-college-campuses.
37. Nitasha Tiku and Elizabeth Dwoskin, "Silicon Valley's Two-Tiered System for White-Collar Workers Is Under Pressure as Coronavirus Spreads, *The Washington Post*, March 9, 2020, www.washingtonpost.com/technology/2020/03/09/tech-contractors-coronavirus/.

16
THE CYCLE OF STRUGGLE
Food Platform Strikes in the UK 2016–18

Callum Cant and Jamie Woodcock

Introduction

Mi son alzato
O bella ciao, bella ciao, bella ciao, ciao, ciao
Una mattina mi son alzato
E ho trovato l'invasor

When hundreds of strikers crowded outside Uber's East London head office, it was the Italians who started up *Bella Ciao*, the iconic song of the Italian partisans. Three of them, with their arms around each other, stared up at the glass and steel of the HQ as they sang. This was the first national Uber ride-hailing strike in the UK—but it had been built on the back of a wave of mobilisation led primarily by Uber Eats delivery workers. The two workforces were responding to each other's initiative. Amongst these striking Uber taxi workers was an Uber Eats courier from Wales, who had booked a cheap coach ticket to London at the last minute just to support their action. He had brought his own megaphone. It was an unlikely, heterogeneous movement, but it was a movement.

Food delivery has been a successful growth area in the platform economy for capital. Platforms including Deliveroo, Uber Eats, Food Panda, Swiggy, Zomato, Caviar, Meituan and so on have sprung up across the world in different contexts. The rapid spread of these platforms is changing the technical composition of work—both recomposing previous forms of food delivery, as well as drawing in new workers to the sector. While some early commentators claimed that workers could not organise (or at least not easily) on platforms, there is increasing evidence of a political recomposition of food delivery platform workers. This is something that has not come about through a service model of trade unionism that some called for.[1]

The European cycle of struggle in food delivery platforms began in London in August 2016. From that point onwards, strikes spread rapidly across the UK and then transnationally. These strikes were almost all wildcat actions led by mostly migrant workers and supported by a ramshackle infrastructure of unions, bulletins and informal networks. In the UK, the last years have seen the movement spread from London to Bristol, Brighton, Southampton, Plymouth, Leeds, Cardiff, Glasgow and Edinburgh. But so far, the exact dimensions of the struggle across the UK haven't been systematically understood. The order of events, processes of organisation and specific outcomes have all been unclear. A single account is required, so that all discussions of the phenomena can begin from the same baseline.

This chapter presents a survey of food platform strikes in the UK between August 2016 and 2018. It uses a combination of surveys, interviews and ethnographic data to develop a thorough and in-depth understanding of the workers movement from the perspective of workers themselves. In doing so, it provides the first authoritative account of this cycle of struggle. Food platform strikes demonstrate the opportunities that lie within the changing class composition of contemporary capitalism in the UK. The militancy of these platform workers is a signal development in the wider workers movement, and an analysis of that development opens the way for further discussions about overcoming long-term quiescence in working-class self-organisation. As capital develops in the direction indicated by platform capitalism, the strategies employed by food delivery platform workers will become ever more important.

Class Composition

There is an epistemic problem facing any analyst of food platform strikes: informal action organised through primarily invisible worker networks is hard to identify from the outside. Through detailed processes of inquiry we have significantly more information on the cycle of struggle than would otherwise be possible,[2] but even the extensive work done so far cannot produce a complete picture. Our account is informed by the approach of workers' inquiry and the theories of class composition. Workers' inquiry is a practice of research tied to organising, which starts from workers' 'actual struggles: their content, how they have developed, and where they are headed.'[3] While it is inspired by Marx's postal survey,[4] it was developed extensively by Italian workerists from the 1960s. Contemporary examples have explored at call centres,[5] as well as increasingly being used to make sense of the gig economy,[6] drawing on first-hand ethnographic accounts, as well as interviews and forms of co-research with workers. This involves actively engaging with workers, seeking to draw them into a process of co-research about their own struggles.

Class composition was developed as a framework to make sense of the findings of inquiries, putting forward theory of how classes are formed and relate to each other under capitalism. The framework developed by Italian workerists focused on the technical composition of the labour process and its relation to the political composition, or forms of struggle, of workers. Through our involvement as editors of *Notes from Below*,[7] we have helped to develop this to include social composition as part of

> a material relation with three parts: the first is the organisation of labour-power into a working class (technical composition); the second is the organisation of the working class into a class society (social composition); the third is the self-organisation of the working class into a force for class struggle (political composition).

We use this threefold analysis of class composition in the chapter to make sense of the inquiries that both of us have undertaken.

The account of collective action presented here is, to the best of our knowledge, as complete as possible. However, it is quite likely that over the course of two years some localised actions have taken place which were never communicated to a wider audience. The political composition of these strikes are such that workers have the capacity to use their leverage as they see fit with few, if any, procedural qualifications. So, this account should be considered a provisional survey of the most visible and best communicated examples. Food platforms are an acute example of how elements of the subterranean individual and collective trench warfare of class struggle nearly always exceed our analyses.

The First Strike

The first open moment in the struggle of food delivery platform workers started in August in London. Jamie started an inquiry with these workers, as they had become an increasingly noticeable presence on the streets of London. A Deliveroo worker that Jamie had been in contact with outlined how frustrations were building among the drivers and was convinced that action would follow soon. They visited a series of the "zone centres", algorithmically determined meeting points within each of the geographic zones assigned to workers to return to after making a delivery. At each of the zone centres, the Deliveroo driver pitched the idea of joining a union to the other workers, and they were incredibly receptive. In each conversation, grievances were aired about the payment structures, the organisation of the work, and the lack of communication from the company. In clear opposition to those early commentators who said these workers could not organise, there were already networks of workers forming across the city. From the meeting points workers got to know each other and started WhatsApp groups that kept them in contact. Like the traditional water-cooler conversations, these often turned to discussing problems with the work and what they could do about them.

From these meetings, we were added to the Deliveroo worker's WhatsApp groups. Later in the week, the sense from the meetings that something was building came to head: Deliveroo had announced they would be unilaterally changing the payment scheme from £7 an hour with £1 per drop to only £3.75 per drop. The workers found this out via text message, with no opportunity to negotiate around the changes. Workers saw this as an attempt to shift more of the risk from Deliveroo's business model onto them, meaning if there was no demand they would be standing at the zone centres without making any money. This also happened in the same month that the company raised £212m from investors, while facing increased competition from Uber Eats.[8] The idea of a strike was floated on the WhatsApp group, quickly filling with multiple messages to go on strike and meet outside the Deliveroo headquarters in central London.

As Jamie wrote about at the time,[9] the strike started on the 11th of August. When the time for the strike arrived, there were very few drivers, and it was starting to look like the excitement around it had been misplaced. However, 30 minutes later more drivers arrived on mopeds, and an hour later there were hundreds of striking workers outside of the Deliveroo headquarters. This strike had not followed any of the balloting rules required under the anti-trade union laws in the UK, as they only apply to workers with employment contracts. As Deliveroo relies upon "self-employed independent contractor" status—a form of bogus self-employment—workers did not have to organise within a registered trade union and complete the lengthy postal balloting process. Instead, they could collectively decide not to work, using the "flexibility" of the arrangement against Deliveroo.

The strike itself was chaotic and energetic. Workers drove up and down the street, with horns blaring and chants directed at the headquarters. A panicked Deliveroo manager came out to address the crowd. He walked into the middle of the group of workers, who were now crowding both sides of the street, and began to patronisingly explain that the proposed changes were actually better for workers. When workers disagreed with him, he tried again to explain how the new terms were better. What was clear from this encounter is that the manager had not previously interacted with any workers and was definitely out of his depth. The crowd got increasingly angry with his attempted PR spin, chanting over his comments. On noticing that he was now surrounded, two police officers intervened in order to shepherd him back into the headquarters.

As the strike developed, workers began discussing what the next steps would be. The impromptu speeches were translated into Portuguese, catering for the large number of Brazilian workers in attendance. The worker that Jamie had visited the zone centres with had reached out to the Independent Workers Union of Great Britain (IWGB) after seeing the successful struggles of bike couriers that they had supported.[10] An IWGB organiser addressed the crowd, explaining how they had won previous struggles at CitySprint, eCouriers, and Mach1. The organiser facilitated a discussion, and the workers settled on rejecting the changes and demanding the London living wage plus costs (£11.40 per hour) plus £1 per drop. Jamie and the worker from the zone centre agitation handed out forms for the IWGB, with many drivers signing up on the spot.

The strike lasted almost a week. Deliveroo refused to negotiate with any collective group of workers or the IWGB, only offering consultations with individual workers. The decision to change the payment system was moved into a trial in certain zones, a partial victory of the strike. However, despite the first Deliveroo strike not winning the workers' demands, it did show that sustained collective action was not only possible for platform workers, but also that they could form union structures to prepare for future action.

The Struggle Spreads

In winter 2016, it looked like the London strike might be a one-off. Despite food platform workforces in other cities around the UK facing a similar social and technical class composition, there was no evidence that they would mobilise and take collective action to fight for common demands. However, as 2016 turned into 2017, evidence would start to emerge that, under the surface, things were moving. Gradually, the same composition that gave rise to a wildcat strike in London would lead to similar outcomes elsewhere, as a common political composition of food platform workers began to emerge. The fuse was burning.

During this period, Callum was undertaking an inquiry in Brighton.[11] Whilst working part-time for Deliveroo he began to understand that there were strong underlying networks that linked workers across the city. The workerist Romano Alquati observed the role these informal networks could play in the development of apparently spontaneous wildcat strike action in Italian FIAT plants in the early 60s, and dubbed this underlying spider's web of worker-to-worker connection 'invisible organisation.'[12] The WhatsApp groups and zone centre meetings linking Deliveroo workers in Brighton appeared to play an analogous function.

The clearest evidence of the subterranean developments within food platforms was to be found in a bulletin which Callum was involved in producing. *The Rebel Roo* was a double-sided sheet of A4, written, edited and distributed by Deliveroo workers. Its goal was to 'help Deliveroo workers in the UK and internationally communicate and organise.' It made the simple argument that 'together we can build solidarity and fight for better wages and conditions.'[13] This argument found some immediate resonance, and the distribution network began to expand.

Workers with an interest in inquiry and class composition have often invested significant effort in producing bulletins and newspapers with the intention of circulating struggles. Alquati wrote about the *Wildcat* newspaper's role in catalysing the development of unofficial strikes in multiple different factories in Turin. In his analysis, the paper, first distributed in August 1963, contributed significantly to the process of militant working-class self-organisation in the workshops and foundries in which it was distributed.[14] Similar examples can be found in the history of the Johnson-Forest Tendency in Detroit (*Correspondence*) and Socialisme ou Barbarie in Paris (*Tribune Ouvrière*). The common thread between all of these examples of 'proletarian documentary literature'[15] is that they attempt to articulate the political "leap" from the everyday confrontation and antagonism of capitalist production into a broader process of class struggle.

The Rebel Roo was no different. It primarily consisted of short articles from workers in different cities, alongside a multilingual introduction and some information about which trade unions (the IWGB and Industrial Workers of the World, IWW) were supporting Deliveroo workers. The bulletin was circulated both online via the website of an autonomist political organisation, Plan C, and offline through the post to a network of local distributors.

After beginning monthly publication in November 2016, it was at its most influential in January 2017 when its circulation reached 1,500. The exact readership of the bulletin is impossible to pin down. Any estimate has to make assumptions about the percentage of paper copies which were successfully distributed, the percentage of double-views, the percentage of non-workers who got a copy and so on. However, given that the total Deliveroo workforce in February 2017 was 15,000 strong, it seems reasonable to estimate that somewhere between 6% and 10% of the workforce had some contact with the bulletin. The peak of the bulletin's distribution also coincided with the outbreak of strikes in two new cities. In Brighton and Leeds, longer-term organising process broke into the open. February saw strikes involving large numbers of workers in both cities over wages and victimisation. This further development of food platform worker mobilisation indicated that the London strike was not an isolated incident but the beginning of the cycle of struggle.

The strikes in Brighton and Leeds were followed by a series of demonstrations in both cities, but as the summer continued their strength declined. There was a lull in collective action until October, when 30 workers in Bristol went on strike to protest late wages. They won almost immediately. Then in November, Central Arbitration Court defeated an IWGB claim for a legally enforced collective bargaining agreement between the union and Deliveroo in their Camden zone.[16] A few days later, Brighton Deliveroo workers were on strike once again. Angered by a gradual decline in the number of orders available per worker and a corresponding decline in wages, 50 workers went on strike. The strike followed a familiar pattern, with a large meeting turning into a flying picket that circled around the city. One new feature was evident, however. For the first time, this strike involved a blockade of a "dark kitchen" site, owned by Deliveroo and run as a delivery-only operation.[17] As the technical composition of the labour process was transformed, new tactics of resistance developed in response.

The transnational development of the struggle also continued apace, with strikes spreading to seven countries across Europe by January 2018. Looking back from the end of the year, it was possible to discern the outline of an escalating wave of action which was bringing together workers from cities as diverse as

Milan, Bologna, Turin, Brussels, Paris, Marseilles, Berlin, Madrid, Valencia, Barcelona, Brighton, Bristol, Leeds and London.[18]

The IWW launched a new initiative directed at food platform couriers in January 2018: the IWW Courier Network. Building on the union's previous experience of attempting to organise food platform workers in Bristol and Cardiff in 2017, the union aimed to restart its approach to the sector.[19] The strategy of the network was planned through a period of inquiry. Whereas previous IWW organising efforts had focused on a struggle for legal rights, this inquiry found that workers were more interested in organising on bread and butter issues, like waiting times at restaurants. And so, in April and May of 2018, the IWW couriers network branches in Glasgow and Cardiff delivered letters of demands to their local McDonalds regarding just these issues. Then in May 2018 the Glasgow couriers network branch organised a 'critical mass' cycle ride[20] to remember Pablo Avendano—a courier from Philadelphia who died whilst working for food platform Caviar—and highlight the issue of rider safety.

In July, Deliveroo abolished the flat fee payment structure across the UK. Now, instead of a set value per drop, which varied from city to city between £3.75 and £4, workers would be paid a variable rate that included complex calculations about the distance. London Deliveroo workers responded by calling a strike, which was a mixed success. The main strike demonstration was small, but later that evening flying pickets of 50 plus workers assembled in local zones. Shortly after that, small-scale strikes broke out in Plymouth and Southampton.

The first IWW courier network-organised strike came in September, when workers in Cardiff descended on Uber's city HQ to demand collective bargaining. They carried signs with slogans like 'We Ain't Slaves' and 'Uber Eats Shit.' A few days later, the Glasgow branch of the network were on strike too against a low "Boost" (a multiplier that is applied to payments at peak or busy times in a zone).[21] Momentum was building.

A National Strike: The Fast Food Shutdown

In autumn 2018, Uber Eats changed the payment system in London. The minimum guaranteed fee per delivery dropped from £4.26 to as low as £2.62. This 40% pay cut sparked an immediate response. Workers drew on their invisible organisation to begin a strike on the 19th of September. The strike had two dynamics: first, workers picketed their local McDonalds in their own delivery zones. Second, they converged at the Uber Greenlight centre and HQ in Aldgate, East London. Day by day, the weighting of these two tactics varied.

The local picketing of McDonalds ensured that the app was non-operational in large parts of London and so had the greatest structural leverage, but by and large this action was not understood as strike action by the media and other workers. On the other hand, mass demonstrations in Aldgate gained significant media attention and so developed higher degrees of associational leverage but did little to actually prevent the operation of the app. Workers mixed and matched these two tactics to try to develop both forms of leverage simultaneously. The use of McDonalds as a focal point for self-organisation during normal working time and picketing during strikes is a feature of conflicts involving Uber Eats as a result of the centrality of McDonalds to the Uber Eats labour process. A significant percentage of all Uber Eats order volume comes from McDonalds, meaning that these restaurants are becoming informal labour concentration points where workers gather to work and wait for orders.[22]

By the second day of the strike, a set of demands had been agreed: a guaranteed minimum fee of £5 per delivery plus a £1 per mile distance payment, an end to the "Boost" system that led to wages fluctuating in response to consumer demand, and no victimisation of strikers. These demands were presented to management at a mass demonstration in Aldgate that assembled outside the Uber Greenlight centre. As always, management refused to collectively bargain with the hundreds of workers and instead proposed facilitating one-on-one meetings to discuss the new payment system.[23]

Following this refusal to negotiate, workers went on to blockade a key road junction in East London outside Uber HQ in Aldgate Tower. This caused significant traffic disruption until the police were able to gather enough resources to disperse them. The Metropolitan police then imposed conditions on the demonstration, threatening with arrest any workers who stayed outside the Uber office past 4pm. This was a significant escalation in the use of the repressive powers of the police against food platform worker collective action.[24]

Over the coming days the strike moved back to a local focus, with workers returning to picket their local McDonalds rather than converging in Aldgate. The strike also spread from city to city, with workers in Plymouth joining the fight on the third day. For the first time ever, there were food platform workers in two UK cities on strike at the same time. It was evident that there was substantial momentum building for an even larger food platform worker mobilisation. Strikes were becoming more frequent and interconnected as the downward pressure on wages continued. The IWW wanted to make use of this energy, and an opportunity arose to do just that.

The Bakers Food and Allied Workers Union (BFAWU) and Unite were coordinating strike action for October 4, about two weeks away. Workers at McDonalds, Wetherspoons and TGI Fridays would be walking out, and significant support from the Labour Party was already planned. The IWW couriers network saw the chance for food platform workforce to join this coalition of precarious service workers. Due to their independent contractor status, food platform workers and their unions had no responsibility to follow employment law. Therefore, the IWW could set a strike date at short notice without formal balloting periods without any risk of legal repercussions. They took full advantage of this flexibility and called the first ever national food platform strike. October the 4th was quickly dubbed the 'Fast Food Shutdown.'

On the day, food platform workers took significant strike action in Bristol, Cardiff, Glasgow and London with community support pickets in Birmingham, Bradford, Leeds, Manchester, Newcastle and Swansea.[25] The strike in Bristol was probably the largest ever outside of London. Workers within the food service and delivery industry built practical links of solidarity on both a rank-and-file and a union-to-union level.

Happy Birthday, Will Shu: December 2018

On December 1, Deliveroo founder Will Shu's birthday, the Transnational Courier Federation held its first day of action. Food platform workers in Paris, Turin, Milan and Bologna blockaded dark kitchens and held demonstrations in their city centres. In the UK, however, it was not until a week later that Deliveroo and Uber Eats workers in Bristol launched a spontaneous strike, following up on their action in October. Fifty workers joined a flying picket roaming around the city centre. Within an hour of the strike starting, the app was non-functional. Their demands were the same as they had been in October, with a central focus on wage increases across both platforms.

In Hanworth, West London, an unprecedentedly low "Boost" was leading to unprecedentedly low wages. Rather than the usual 1.6 payment multiplier, Uber Eats was offering them a 1.1 multiplier. Workers decided that they wouldn't continue to work for that rate. So, a small group of them pulled up in their local McDonalds—the centre for food platform work in the zone—and began localised strike action.[26] Whenever other riders arrived to take new orders, they were told a strike was on and asked to stop work. Most of the time, these other workers agreed.

The Hanworth strike was not only built on the networks of invisible organisation which underlie all food platform strikes; it was also characterised by a longer history of collective action. The workers in the zone had been on strike before—they knew what they needed to do to shut down the app through personal experience. In miniature, Hanworth provided an example of a more general phenomena: the consistency of food platform worker militancy has now led to some workers experiencing multiple strikes. The cumulative development of experience and knowledge about the processes of collective action is an emerging factor in the political composition of the workforce.

In Hanworth, however, this experience could not prevent Uber Eats using the workers' "independent contractor" legal status to enforce mass victimisation. Every worker who was reported by McDonalds to have been involved in the strike was removed from the platform. For some workers with dependents to look after, this victimisation led to them becoming suicidal. The social composition of food platform workers means that they rarely have access to the kinds of informal safety nets and buffer zones which can cushion the blow of being fired without any compensation. In response, local workers organised another strike with the IWW's support. They picketed the McDonalds to prevent orders being delivered, and fellow IWW members occupied the service area of the restaurant. This action was continued for two consecutive weekends, although it did not prove to be successful.

By developing a pattern of increasingly coordinated and significant self-organised collective action over the course of two years, food delivery platform workers lay the groundwork for potential future struggle. The social and technical factors which allow for the development of political composition based on self-organised militancy continue to define the experience of work at Deliveroo and Uber Eats.

Conclusion: Reflection on the Cycle of Struggle

Throughout this chapter we have documented the struggles of food delivery platform workers from 2016 to 2018. This started with the strike at Deliveroo in London but has since spread across Europe, as well as more recently connecting with other fast food workers. Through these different cycles of struggle there have been different intensities and forms of action. However, what is common across all of these examples is groups of workers refusing to accept the terms that platform capital has attempted to force upon them.

We have presented this account of food delivery platform workers as part of our analysis of class composition today. The militant workforce that is emerging is the organic product of class composition in platform capitalism. The technical composition that platforms have chosen to organise their workers has facilitated the emergence of this militancy. They have recruited large numbers of young and migrant workers, connected them via smartphone applications, ordered them to meet in specific places, attempted to immiserate their conditions without any space for negotiation, while claiming not to actually employ any of them. What is important to note here is that this technical composition combines at many points with what we—along with the other editors of *Notes from Below*[27]—have termed the 'social composition' of work. In this case, it means drawing attention to how the dynamics of migration, housing and community networks have played into these workers' struggles. The examination of the social composition of these workers shows that they are not isolated points on GPS maps; they are connected through common routes of migration and using technology to build new networks across the city.

This new composition initially threw up challenges for workers resisting and organising but did not resolve the conflict between labour and capital in food delivery. Instead, workers have been able to find new ways to refuse to work on capital's terms—something that these food delivery platforms have sought to organise unilaterally.

We have attempt to provide an account of the struggles of these workers, starting in 2016, as a baseline understanding of these struggles. However, given the empirical and methodological difficulties with covering workers (often spontaneous) struggles, it is likely that this an incomplete account of the open struggles that have taken place. It is also definitely an incomplete account of all the struggles and conflicts that have happened below the surface. However, as we have argued, it is a much-needed starting point for making sense of this phenomenon.

The implications of this survey are twofold. First, for understanding food delivery platforms, it provides a coherent account of how these struggles have developed. This shows that these workers are not "unorganisable," and if such an adjective were to be pushed onto these workers, the closest would be that they were "yet-to-be-organized-in-a-traditional-sense." This also highlights that in many cases, these workers are not choosing to follow routes of many of the established—and often highly bureaucratised—models of trade unionism. This political recomposition shows that there are new ways that workers can successfully organise today. There is much to be learned by traditional trade unions from this model. It also underlines a point we have made elsewhere: that 'one thing is clear for now: we need to stop talking about resistance as emerging in platform work.'[28] Instead, we need to start thinking about what forms of resistance and organisation can be successful.

The second are the implications that move beyond just food delivery platforms. Without wanting to talk in general terms about the "future of work," platform capitalism represents the sharp edge of technical recomposition. They act, as Cant has argued, as 'laboratories of class struggle.'[29] This means that the successes of management on platforms will not remain only within these dispersed workplaces. Instead, the new managerial innovations will be pushed out into more workplaces, whether in the private sector—which is already happening with the short-term staffing agency 'Uber Works'[30]—or with outsourcing and privatisation in the public sector. The ability for workers to resist this technical recomposition in food delivery (as well as taxi, care work, and other kinds of platforms) is therefore part of a wider struggle over what the future of work will look like. While a central premise of platform capitalism is that workers are no longer workers but rather independent contractors, the struggles documented here show that whether they are categorised that way or not, workers are finding new ways to collectively struggle. This points to the possibility of a wider political recomposition beyond platforms.

We have also pointed to the need for future research. By this, we do not mean abstracted academic research but rather engaged research that takes inspiration from a Marxist workers' inquiry. One part of building a more sustained struggle on these platforms may involve unpacking the different dynamics, as well as comparing with other countries, like China, that have seen strikes. As these platforms increasingly bring workers into contact beyond national boundaries—whether directly or indirectly through shared conditions—this kind of comparative analysis involves more than just academic interest.

The Cycle of Struggle **267**

Notes

1. John Park, "Trade Unions Must Adapt to the Gig Economy in Order to Survive," *The New Statesman*, July 28, 2016, www.newstatesman.com/politics/staggers/2016/07/trade-unions-must-adapt-gig-economy-order-survive.
2. Facility Waters and Jamie Woodcock, "Far From Seamless: A Workers' Inquiry at Deliveroo," *Viewpoint Magazine*, September 20, 2017, www.viewpointmag.com/2017/09/20/far-seamless-workers-inquiry-deliveroo/; Callum Cant, "The Wave of Worker Resistance in European Food Platforms 2016–17," *Notes from Below*, January 29, 2018, https://notesfrombelow.org/article/european-food-platform-strike-wave.
3. Harry Cleaver, *Reading Capital Politically* (Brighton: Harvester Press, 1979), 58.
4. Karl Marx, *A Workers' Inquiry* (1880), www.marxists.org/archive/marx/works/1880/04/20.htm.
5. Jamie Woodcock, *Working the Phones. Control and Resistance in Call Centres* (London: Pluto, 2017).
6. Callum Cant, *Riding for Deliveroo: Resistance in the New Economy* (Cambridge: Polity Press, 2020).
7. Notes from Below, "The Workers' Inquiry and Social Composition," *Notes from Below*, January 29, 2018, www.notesfrombelow.org/article/workers-inquiry-and-social-composition.
8. Jamie Woodcock, "#Slaveroo: Deliveroo Drivers Organising in the 'Gig Economy'," *Novara*, August 12, 2016, http://novaramedia.com/2016/08/12/slaveroo-deliveroo-drivers-organising-in-the-gig-economy/.
9. Ibid.
10. Independent Workers of Great Britain. 'Citysprint Announce Pay Rise!' IWGB, 2016. https://iwgb.org.uk/en/post/5aa7026fe3f28/citysprint-announce-pay-rise.
11. For more on this inquiry, see Cant, *Riding for Deliveroo*.
12. Romano Alquati, "The Struggle at FIAT (1964)," *Viewpoint Magazine*, September 26, 2013, www.viewpointmag.com/2013/09/26/struggle-at-fiat-1964/.
13. Rebel Roo, "Rebel Roo Bulletin," *Notes from Below*, 2018, https://notesfrombelow.org/article/rebel-roo-bulletin.
14. Alquati, "The Struggle at FIAT (1964)."
15. Stephen Hastings-King, *Looking for the Proletariat* (Boston, MA: Brill, 2014).
16. Sarah Butler, "Deliveroo Wins Right Not to Give Riders Minimum Wage or Holiday Pay," *The Guardian*, November 14, 2017, www.theguardian.com/business/2017/nov/14/deliveroo-couriers-minimum-wage-holiday-pay.
17. Hattie Garlick, 'Dark Kitchens: Is This the Future of Takeaway?' *The Financial Times*, June 7, 2017, www.ft.com/content/d23c44fe-4b0b-11e7-919a-1e14ce4af89b.
18. Callum Cant, "The Wave of Worker Resistance in European Food Platforms 2016–17," *Notes from Below*, January 29, 2018, https://notesfrombelow.org/article/european-food-platform-strike-wave.
19. Chris Fear, "'Without Our Brain and Muscle Not a Single Wheel Can Turn': The IWW Couriers Network," *Notes from Below*, August 16, 2018, https://notesfrombelow.org/article/without-our-brain-and-muscle.
20. Iain A. Boal and Chris Carlsson, "Critical Mass," in *The International Encyclopaedia of Revolution and Protest*, ed. Immanuel Ness (New York: Wiley-Blackwell, 2009).
21. Stan Mills, "Glasgow Couriers Strike Against Pay Cuts," *Notes from Below*, September 18, 2018, https://notesfrombelow.org/article/glasgow-couriers-strike.
22. Achille Marotta, "Struggle at UberEats: Reflections on October 4th," *Notes from Below*, October 11, 2018, https://notesfrombelow.org/article/couriers-struggle-and-iww-reflections-october-4th.
23. Callum Cant and Lydia Hughes, "'No Money, No Food!' London UberEats Workers on Strike'," *Notes from Below*, September 21, 2018, https://notesfrombelow.org/article/no-money-no-food-london-ubereats-workers-strike.

24. Ibid.
25. Jamie Woodcock and Lydia Hughes, "The View From the Picket Line: Reports From the Food Platform Strike on October 4th," *Notes from Below*, October 11, 2018, https://notesfrombelow.org/article/view-picket-line-reports-food-platform-strike-octo.
26. Callum Cant, "Sacked at Christmas: UberEats Fires Workers for Objecting to Pay Cut," *Novara Media*, December 12, 2018, https://novaramedia.com/2018/12/12/sacked-at-christmas-uber-eats-fires-workers-for-objecting-to-pay-cut/.
27. Notes from Below, "The Workers' Inquiry and Social Composition."
28. Callum Cant and Jamie Woodcock, "The End of the Beginning," *Notes from Below*, June 18, 2019, https://notesfrombelow.org/article/end-beginning.
29. Cant, *Riding for Deliveroo*.
30. Tim Bradshaw and Shannon Bond, "Uber Takes a Detour With Plan to Provide Temporary Staff," *The Financial Times*, October 18, 2018, www.ft.com/content/4f56aa7c-d2df-11e8-a9f2-7574db66bcd5.

VI
Conclusion
We Are All Gig Workers

CONCLUSION

We Are All Gig Workers

Michelle Rodino-Colocino and Chenjerai Kumanyika

"As a gig worker for the last three years, I have seen our wages decrease significantly. However, the fares have increased. . . . I want someone in office who also believes that gig workers deserve a fair pay," said Felicia, a Black woman voter in a progressive get-out-the-vote event livestreamed on YouTube and Facebook on the eve of the US elections, November 2, 2020.[1] The event was held virtually and broadcast over social media because of the health risks that a face-to-face event posed during the COVID-19 pandemic. Felicia's statement illustrated how exploitative gig working conditions have moved beyond individual and professional concerns to emerge as a political issue with wide resonance. Several weeks before Felicia made her statement, the AFL-CIO, SEIU, and other unions filed a complaint with the International Labour Organization (ILO) alleging that the Trump administration's lack of pay and safety protections for workers during the deadly pandemic violated international labor standards. The complaint emphasized labor law's inability to protect gig workers, resulting in a system of "forced labor" where workers, particularly workers of color, risked losing income as well as catching and spreading the virus.[2]

The coronavirus hit gig workers especially hard. After the first outbreaks were reported in the US, Seattle Uber driver Jewel Davis told the BBC, "We're stuck in that gig economy loop where we have no safety nets."[3] For Jewel, income loss due to COVID exposure seemed more frightening than contracting the virus because two weeks of isolation without income is not economically sustainable in a nation like the US that deprives workers of living wages, paid time off (PTO), and scant unemployment benefits. Uber's failure to equip drivers with personal protective equipment (PPE) and sanitizing equipment appeared in other industries, including healthcare. Rideshare drivers—lacking even basic employee protections—absorbed additional risk. The costs of securing protective gear added to the already high cost of driving (i.e., car payments and maintenance, insurance, gas, and incidentals), and sanitizing products were in short supply.

As the pandemic persisted, with mounting cases, hospitalizations, and deaths across the US, the prospects of rideshare driving without health insurance posed significant risk. In November 2020, Jewel told Michelle she was preparing to hit the road for Uber following a seven-month hiatus that began shortly after the BBC interview aired. She had exceeded unemployment benefits. Given the explosive surges in coronavirus cases, Jewel mused, "I'm hoping for the best." Underscoring inequities among workers, she added, "I would love to find an online at home job somehow." Here Jewel flagged how the pandemic reconfigured class divides, as "online at home" conveyed privilege, and "online in public" proffered deadly disadvantage.[4]

Gig worker activism in the US took on new urgency as the COVID-19 pandemic converged with enduring exploitation, worker demands in the 2020 US elections, and a resurgence of Black Lives Matter mobilizations following the police murders of Black Americans George Floyd and Breonna Taylor. In the early weeks of the pandemic, Amazon Flex and fulfillment center workers walked out across the country, demanding clean workplaces, PPE, and PTO. The protests built on years of prior activism, including protests led by Somalian woman and Amazon worker Hibaq Mohamed in Shakopee, Minnesota. Mohammed sought to improve safety, job security, and pay.[5] These work stoppages forced questions of labor, exploitation, and "essential work" into headlines and social media posts. The racial dimensions of this exploitation also surfaced when senior executives at Amazon's JFK8 facility in Staten Island fired Chris Smalls, a Black male manager, and attempted to discredit him, claiming he "was not smart or articulate."[6]

Gig workers further mobilized to draw attention to such converging injustices. On the eve of Juneteenth, the holiday commemorating the emancipation of the last enslaved African Americans, Lyft driver and Gig Workers Rising member Cherri Murphy electronically posted an "Open Letter to Gig Companies Regarding Black Lives Matter," calling for an end to exploitation, endangerment, and discrimination that Black and Brown workers experienced driving for Uber, Lyft, DoorDash, Instacart, Postmates, and the like.[7] The letter demanded the right to unionize, living wages, paid sick leave, unemployment insurance, and anti-discrimination protection.

The letter also demanded that gig companies drop their ballot measure (Proposition 22) in California. As discussed by Koonse et al. (Chapter 2), Uber and Lyft spent over $200 million on the legislation that would exempt them from state law (AB5) recognizing drivers as employees. Highlighting the racial implications of Prop 22, the letter stated, "Before the COVID-19 pandemic, Black gig workers already faced discrimination and abuse on the job," including racist customer complaints, lack of tipping, harassment from law enforcement, and discrimination from staff. One month later, on July 20, 2020, tens of thousands of workers in 2,000 US cities struck to demand that employers, including gig companies, dismantle systemic racism, in part by ending police brutality and instituting living wages and healthcare.[8] Such demands are not new, but they are converging in new ways.

Contributors to this volume demonstrate that the gig economy is neither novel nor exceptional in its exploitation of workers. Since the 1970s—and particularly since the 2008 crisis—capital's demands have pressed the state into new arenas for accumulation and marshaled digital technologies to hasten the extraction and circulation of value. Neoliberal discourses of "independence," "flexibility," and "creativity" have justified such mobilizations. While neoliberal policies persist, the contradictions they engender have become increasingly difficult to manage, placing gig workers at the forefront of potential political, economic, and cultural transformation of capitalism itself.

The history of capitalism is a history of worker exploitation. From capitalism's earliest days of terrorizing, torturing, and working to death African slave laborers across the globe, to the limb-wrenching safety hazards of pre-regulated industrial manufacturing, to the late twentieth/early twenty-first century demands for growth in the face of stagnation, capitalism has extracted workers' labor and life forces to generate profit. Putting it polemically, Marx described capitalism as a system of brutal labor extraction, "Capital is dead labour, that, vampire-like, only lives by sucking living labour, and lives the more, the more labour it sucks."[9] In the pandemic, driving for Uber, in the most callous terms, produces dead labor.

The set of convergences we call "the gig economy," now including the COVID-19 pandemic, increases the risk of doing business without boosting rewards in industries that have long been gig reliant. As Hannah Johnston discusses in Chapter 1 of this volume, the gig economy has heightened precarity for taxi drivers who compete with Uber and Lyft drivers. Consequently, taxi drivers are experiencing the brutality of surplus labor extraction in new extremes, producing dead labor in the double sense, as drivers' deaths by suicide tragically demonstrate. Sex workers like dominas and web cam models take on outsized risk by working in a historically deregulated and unsafe sector, rife with discrimination and abuse (see Levitt, Chapter 4, and Nayar, Chapter 10, respectively). Domestic workers in India that Tandon and Rathi interviewed (Chapter 3) underscore the double bind of working without a net. These workers identify as self-employed and, contrarily, as employees who, nevertheless, lack protections and benefits of full-time direct hires. In Chapter 9 Nuñez discusses how Latina audiobook narrators enter into precarious, opaque work arrangements that fail to compensate for long hours spent directing, editing, and engineering in addition to narrating.

Intensifying economic instability without supporting un- and underemployed workers, and doing nothing to dissolve larger structural incentives for hiring outside employment relationships, the gig economy creates material conditions for anti-left, anti-union politics and impedes class solidarity. As Dolber and Ceisel argue in their chapter on Airbnb (Chapter 7), the gig economy cultivates neofascist ideology in the US and further frustrates efforts to collectively organize workers by positioning hosts as petit bourgeois agents who advance corporate rather than working class interests. Additionally, gig workers may fail to see the benefits of organizing because they do not identify as "employees" to begin with. Such was the case with domestic workers Tandon and Rathi interviewed (Chapter 3), academics and tech workers Kneese discusses (Chapter 15), and at-home platform workers Holts et al. discuss (Chapter 14).

Academics often fail to identify as workers, a problem compounded by what Briziarelli and Guillem (Chapter 8) discuss as the "Uberizing," or gigifying, of academic positions following economic downturns. The COVID pandemic has only sharpened these dynamics. Colleges and universities across the US employ an ever-increasing menu of internet apps and startup companies to enhance socially distant teaching and enter into temporary, ad hoc, relationships with nonunionized workers who write code, manage accounts, promote apps, and work with customers (in this case, teachers and students). As Kneese shows in Chapter 15, pre-pandemic adjunct professors in New York State subsidized their incomes by rideshare driving, as co-editor of this volume Brian Dolber did while seeking secure academic employment.

Further complicating worker identification and class solidarity is the gig economy's blurring of labor and leisure, a convergence that opens new avenues for exploitation. Nichols (Chapter 11) discusses how monetization of leisure time through gamification constitutes "gig leisure." As Sullivan details (Chapter 6), podcasters advise other podcasters about how to succeed in the industry via smart consumption. As Venäläinen argues in Chapter 5, new management discourse promotes self-discipline required for workers to enjoy new flexible work arrangements, dynamics he calls a "paradox of freedom." Like gamification strategies that monetize leisure into unpaid labor, self-help guides advise gig workers to self-monitor, further eroding down time.

As the gig economy and COVID expose neoliberal capitalism's inability to meet workers' needs, gig workers challenge the authoritarian business models of giant platform-based corporations. Rideshare Drivers United (RDU), for example, grew to 19,000 members across California in 2020, after spending three years organizing Uber and Lyft drivers through app-based and face-to-face conversations. Their grassroots organizing helped push gig workers' demands from the sidelines to the headlines. National unions SEIU and the Teamsters considered making backroom deals with Uber and Lyft (to be brokered by Democratic Gov. Gavin Newsom) that would have left drivers without employee protections and resurrect a relic from the anti-labor time capsule: the company union.[10] RDU's democratic organizing model demonstrated that gig workers do not simply want workplace protections; they want a voice. RDU organizers emerged from California's passage of Prop 22 determined to win minimum wage protection, safety standards, transparency, and a say in management decisions. Like food delivery platform workers in the UK that Cant and Woodcock interviewed (Chapter 16), Prop 22's passage steels RDU's resolve to fight on.

Gig workers are poised to fundamentally transform our economy. Kneese demonstrates how gig, tech, and Black workers are mobilizing in solidarity for economic and racial justice. As Rahko and Craig argue in this volume (Chapter 12), gig companies like Uber data mined its drivers and customers to such an extreme they describe the practice as "data fracking." Recognizing this vast resource that workers and consumers are creating as common rather than private may build support for democratizing platform data. Already fluent in digital communication tools, gig workers are also creating new means to organize that combine new app and social media tools with old-fashioned one-on-one conversations (Brophy and Grayer, Chapter 13 this volume). Cant and Woodcock (Chapter 16) show how Deliveroo workers produced their own news outlets to share information and organizing strategies. Such communication was key to coordinating mass actions like the October 2018 fast food strike in the UK that Uber Eats workers initiated upon receiving a 40% pay cut. The very smartphones on which gig workers depend can help mediate strikes with little lead-time.

We are all gig workers. The COVID pandemic underscores the longstanding reality that workers around the world, including those engaged in work via platforms, doing hope labor as freelancers, and even workers with collective bargaining agreements and academics with tenure, face a tide of rising insecurity with no guarantees. It is worth noting the enduring barriers and new opportunities for organizing collectively as we attempt not just to end the gig economy's hyperexploitation but also to replace our inequitable, undemocratic political-economic system with something that works for working people.

To transform our economy, we call on academics to collectively organize around our precarity. Academic labor has been increasingly gigified, with contingent arrangements displacing secure faculty positions. Although tenured academic workers remain among the most privileged in regard to job security (and it is security worth fighting for in and beyond the academy), it is not so stable after over six decades of job destruction and continued surplus labor extraction; 75% of college and university instructors are non-tenure track (a flip from 50 years ago when 80% of instructors were tenure line). As the pandemic intensifies this trend, the American Association of University Professors (AAUP) is investigating eight universities' breach of governance for laying off full-time and tenured faculty and intends to take on the broader, pre-pandemic crisis of neoliberal, corporatized higher education.[11]

The growing precarity of work across higher education is also inspiring coalitions among academic and other college and university workers. The Coalition of Rutgers Unions in New Jersey that co-editor Todd Wolfson helped coordinate are bringing together dining staff, groundskeepers, administrative staff, and healthcare and grad workers, as well as adjuncts and tenure-stream faculty to fight for a shared vision of the university. Tamara Kneese discusses a similar coalition of campus unions at University of San Francisco emerging in the wake of COVID-era cuts (Chapter 15). Co-editors Brian Dolber, Chenjerai Kumanyika, and Michelle Rodino-Colocino are organizing faculty and gig workers around converging issues of safe, sustainable, and sustaining work, antiracism and antisexism, and issues of equity that affect students, faculty, staff, and community members on and around our campuses. Our participant activism in these struggles inspires this volume and the organizing for which we are calling.

We also call on academics and activists from across sectors to realize the potential for transformative political-economic change in new multiracial, democratic socialist coalitions. Such movements are key to making such change. First, they understand gig work as an expression of broader social conditions that demand radical transformation. Worker protections will not be sufficient in the absence of universal healthcare. Higher pay will not be sufficient without universal housing and student debt forgiveness. Yet none of these victories would sufficiently protect us from the devastating effects of climate change to which transportation companies significantly contribute. For these reasons, radical coalitions emerging in cities across the US seek reforms that are the beginning steps of a larger democratic socialist horizon. Black Lives Matter envisions democratic, collective, and community control over institutions like the police (via disarming, divesting, and reallocating funds to support public health and education initiatives). Democratic Socialists of America imagine similar collective management models in effort to build workers' power and equitably share resources such that healthcare, higher education, and voting are basic rights enjoyed by all, not only by those with privilege (i.e., economic, racial, gender, ability privilege) to secure them. As Democratic Socialist Rep. Alexandra Ocasio-Cortez says, the wealthy have the dollars to support their agenda, but "the people" have power in numbers.

The pandemic's "essential/non-essential," "stay safe/risk exposure" binaries add new class distinctions fed by dead labor. These hierarchies of risk have been in the making for decades, as transportation and education sectors (to name just two) cut labor costs and offloaded risk onto workers, using media technology and ideology to facilitate the process. Thus, organizers and activists should aim for transformation as they seek reform. The pandemic has made class distinctions and systems of precarity and risk glaringly obvious. In so doing, it opens new paths to solidarity.

"Essential workers" who have remained "on" and "out" during the COVID pandemic have demonstrated such solidarity. On May Day 2020, essential workers mobilized: delivery, grocery store, independent truckers, and health care workers struck and demonstrated to demand hazard pay, paid leave, protective gear, and cleaning supplies.[12] In so doing, "essential workers" built solidarity across sectors, skill, race, gender, and across reconfigured class lines that spotlight new hierarchical systems of precarity and risk. "Essential workers" who must work "out" during the pandemic should continue organizing around their common risks. After all, Jewel, who would risk contracting the deadly virus if she drove for Uber in Seattle, joins other transportation workers as well as teachers, janitors, and dining staff (in pre-K, K–12, and higher education) who risk their lives simply by showing up to work.

If we reimagine transportation and education as public goods rather than as commodities, we can view COVID-risky employment arrangements as "non-essential" because they needlessly risk lives. If the US defunded the police to fund education and transportation as "essential" services—essential as public goods—and funded sick leave, working "out" would become a non-essential, unproductive, and foolish risk. Transforming our political economic system into a democratic one demands that we define "essential workers" by their service to the common good instead of to capital. Redefining "essential" from a critical, anti-capitalist standpoint will be important in the struggles ahead. The workers from Walmart, who joined rallies around the US in solidarity with Uber drivers on May 8, 2019, understood that the roots of this pandemic conjuncture lay in the very foundations of capitalism. After the protest in Philadelphia's Uber lot concluded, Walmart stocker Osborne Hart told Michelle and Pooja that the struggles of Walmart were the struggles of Uber drivers. Neither company paid workers living wages. Consequently, Osborne and his colleagues typically worked for both companies. Capitalism's inability to create sustainable conditions for workers produce the very fluidity between gig and traditional workers that Osborne underscored. This longstanding, structural problem was one of the many reasons he was running for Philadelphia Mayor (for a second time) as a member of the Socialist Workers' Party. In 2015, Osborne told a public news crew that he hoped to raise the minimum wage, support universal health care, stop police brutality, and fund public education, issues that were, for him, essential to people's well-being.[13] He was also working for a socialist future.

"If we don't band together, it's only going to get crappier," Gloria told us as she waited to drive for Uber in the convergent space of Philadelphia's international airport parking lot. Her words opened this volume and resonate all the more concluding it. They sound a call to action and light a path for organizing. They point to emerging "solidarity unionism" among workers.[14] On strike day May 2019, gig workers converged with Walmart workers, labor organizers, journalists, and academics. We hailed from across PA, the Northeastern US, and nations in Africa, Europe, and the Middle East. We stood as workers on common ground. This convergent terrain provides a basis on which to build solidarity, empowering us to press on.

Notes

1. Felicia is with People's Lobby, Chicago. Bernie Sanders, "Our Agenda Is on the Ballot: Rally With Progressive Leaders," streamed on November 2, 2020, www.youtube.com/watch?v=E2y35de3c_o.
2. Catherine Powell, "Color of COVID: The Racial Justice Paradox of Our Emerging Stay-at-Home Economy," *CNN*, April 18, 2020, www.cnn.com/2020/04/10/opinions/covid-19-people-of-color-labor-market-disparities-powell/index.html.
3. Xinyan Yu and Angélica M. Casas, "Coronavirus: The Struggle of Being a Ride-Share Driver," www.bbc.com/news/av/world-us-canada-52028108.
4. In a subsequent conversation on January 25, 2021, Jewel told Michelle that she state and federal benefits helped her subsist without app-based driving during the

pandemic. Other drivers, she said, "didn't get any benefits and did have to continue to work through the pandemic."
5. Ibrahim Hirsi, "Meet Three Somali-American Women Fighting for Better Work Conditions at Amazon," *MPRNews*, July 15, 2019, www.mprnews.org/story/2019/07/15/meet-three-somaliamerican-women-fighting-for-better-work-conditions-at-amazon.
6. Julia Carrie Wong, "Amazon Execs Labeled Fired Worker 'Not Smart or Articulate' in Leaked PR Notes," *BBC*, April 2, 2020, www.theguardian.com/technology/2020/apr/02/amazon-chris-smalls-smart-articulate-leaked-memo.
7. "Sign On: Open Letter to Gig Companies Regarding Black Lives Matter," accessed November 26, 2020, https://docs.google.com/forms/d/e/1FAIpQLSfsRgu68wjPClH7jQjVbcl0y2GaQuy8aVySHK_e0BGCzwiGkQ/viewform. See also: Sasha Lekach, "Gig Workers to Companies after BLM Statements: 'Prove It'," *Mashable*, June 18, 2020, https://mashable.com/article/blm-gig-workers-open-letter.
8. Jacob Bogage, "Thousands of U.S. Workers Walk Out in 'Strike for Black Lives'," July 20, 2020, www.washingtonpost.com/business/2020/07/20/strike-for-black-lives/.
9. Karl Marx, *Capital, Volume 1* (1867), *Marxists.org*, www.marxists.org/archive/marx/works/1867-c1/ch10.htm.
10. Brian Dolber, "Most Expensive Ballot Initiative in California History Pits Uber and Lyft against Drivers Who Built a Union From Scratch," *Labor Notes,* November 3, 2020, https://labornotes.org/blogs/2020/11/most-expensive-ballot-initiative-california-history-pits-uber-and-lyft-against-drivers.
11. Colleen Flaherty, "A Non-Tenure-Track Profession?" *Inside Higher Ed*, October 12, 2018, www.insidehighered.com/news/2018/10/12/about-three-quarters-all-faculty-positions-are-tenure-track-according-new-aaup; "AAUP Launches a COVID-19 Governance Investigation," *AAUP.org,* September 21, 2020, www.aaup.org/media-release/aaup-launches-covid-19-governance-investigation#.X8LRxy9h3fZ; Colleen Flaherty, "Faculty Group Will Investigate U of Akron," *Inside Higher Ed*, October 28, 2020, www.insidehighered.com/quicktakes/2020/10/28/faculty-group-will-investigate-u-akron.
12. Scott Neuman, "Essential Workers Plan May Day Strikes; Others Demand End to COVID-19 Lockdowns," *NPR.org,* May 1, 2020, www.npr.org/sections/coronavirus-live-updates/2020/05/01/848931228/essential-workers-plan-may-day-strikes-others-demand-end-to-covid-19-lockdowns.
13. Brian Hickey, "A Socialist Walmart Employee Explains Why He's Running for Philly Mayor," *WHYY*, August 31, 2015, https://whyy.org/articles/a-socialist-walmart-employee-explains-why-hes-running-for-philly-mayor/.
14. Staughton Lynd, *Solidarity Unionism: Rebuilding the Labor Movement From Below* (Oakland, CA: PM Press), 2015.

BIBLIOGRAPHY

"AAUP Launches a COVID-19 Governance Investigation." *AAUP.org*. September 21, 2020. www.aaup.org/media-release/aaup-launches-covid-19-governance-investigation#.X8LRxy9h3fZ;

Adams, Abi, Judith Freedman, and Jeremias Prassl. 2018. "Rethinking Legal Taxonomies for the Gig Economy." *Oxford Review of Economic Policy* 34 (3): 475–94.

Adler-Bell, Sam, and Michelle Miller. 2018. "The Datafication of Employment." *The Century Foundation*, December 19, 2018. https://tcf.org/content/report/datafication-employment-surveillance-capitalism-shaping-workers-futures-without-knowledge

Alakovska, Ana, and Rosalind Gill. 2019. "De-Westernizing Creative Labour Studies: The Informality of Creative Work From an Ex-Centric Perspective." *International Journal of Cultural Studies* 22 (2): 195–212.

Alimahomed-Wilson, Jake, and Immanuel Ness. 2018. *Choke Points: Logistics Workers Disrupting the Global Supply Chain Journal of Labor and Society*. London: Pluto Press.

Allen, David. 2001. *Getting Things Done: The Art of Stress-Free Productivity*. New York: Viking.

Allen, Samantha. "The Mysterious Way Uber Bans its Drivers." *The Daily Beast*, January 15, 2015. www.thedailybeast.com/the-mysterious-way-uber-bans-drivers.

Allmer, Thomas. 2018. "Precarious, Always-On and Flexible: A Case Study of Academics as Information Workers." *European Journal of Communication* 33 (4): 381–95.

Aloisi, Antonio. 2015. "Commoditized Workers: Case Study Research on Labor Law Issues Arising from a Set of on-Demand/Gig Economy Platforms." *Comparative Labor Law & Policy Journal* 37: 653.

Alquati, Romano. 1961. "Organic Composition of Capital and Labor-Power at Olivetti." *Viewpoint Magazine*. www.viewpointmag.com/2013/09/27/organic-composition-of-capital-and-labor-power-at-olivetti-1961/

———. 1964. "The Struggle at FIAT." *Viewpoint Magazine*. www.viewpointmag.com/2013/09/26/struggle-at-fiat-1964/

American Associations of University Professors (AAUP). 2017. "Visualizing Change: The Annual Report on the Economic Status of the Profession, 2016–17." *aaup.com*. www.aaup.org/file/FCS_2016-17.pdf

Andrejevic, Mark. 2008. "Watching Television Without Pity." *Television & New Media* 9 (1): 24–46.
———. 2009. "Exploiting YouTube: Contradictions of User-Generated Labor." In *The YouTube Reader*, edited by Patrick Vonderau, Pelle Snickars, and Jean Burgess, 406–23. Stockholm: National Library of Sweden.
———. 2011. "The Work That Affective Economics Does." *Cultural Studies* 25 (4–5): 604–20. https://doi.org/10.1080/09502386.2011.600551.
Aravopoulou, Eleni, Fotios V Mitsakis, and Charles Malone. 2017. "A Critical Review of the Exit-Voice-Loyalty-Neglect Literature: Limitations, Key Challenges and Directions for Future Research." *International Journal of Management* 6 (3): 1–10.
Archer, Louise. 2008. "The New Neoliberal Subjects? Young/er Academics' Constructions of Professional Identity." *Journal of Education Policy* 23 (3): 265–85.
Arendt, Hannah. 2006. *On Revolution*. New York: Penguin Press.
Audio Publishers Association. 2019a. "New Survey Shows 50% of Americans Have Listened to an Audiobook." April 24, 2019.
———. 2019b. "U.S. Publishers Report Nearly $1 Billion in Sales as Strong Industry Growth Continues." July 17, 2019.
———. n.d. "A History of Audiobooks." Accessed March 9, 2018. www.audiopub.org/uploads/pdf/A-HISTORY-OF-AUDIOBOOKS.pdf.
Austin, S. 1990. "' . . . The Law Is All Over': Power, Resistance and the Legal Consciousness of the Welfare Poor." *Yale Journal of Law & the Humanities* 2 (2). https://digitalcommons.law.yale.edu/cgi/viewcontent.cgi?article=1039&context=yjlh
Badger, Emily. 2015. "Uber Offers Cities an Olive Branch: Your Valuable Trip Data." *Washington Post*, January 13, 2015. www.washingtonpost.com/news/wonk/wp/2015/01/13/uber-offers-cities-an-olive-branch-its-valuable-trip-data/
Báez, Jillian M. 2018. *In Search of Belonging: Latinas, Media, and Citizenship*. Urbana: University of Illinois Press. https://doi.org/10.5406/j.ctt21h4z2j.
Báez, Jillian M., and Mari Castañeda. 2014. "Two Sides of the Same Story: Media Narratives of Latinos and the Subprime Mortgage Crisis." *Critical Studies in Media Communication*, 31 (1): 27–41.
Bailey, Michael, and Des Freedman. 2011. *The Assault on Universities: A Manifesto for Resistance*. London: Pluto Press.
Bainbridge, Alan, Anastosios Gaitanidis, and Elizabeth Chapman Hoult. 2018. "When Learning Becomes a Fetish: The Pledge, Turn and Prestige of Magic Tricks." *Pedagogy, Culture & Society* 26 (3): 345–61. https://doi.org/10.1080/14681366.2017.1403950
Bajwa, Uttam, Denise Gastaldo, Erica Di Ruggiero, and Lilian Knorr. 2018. "The Health of Workers in the Global Gig Economy." *Globalization and Health* 14 (124). https://doi.org/10.1186/s12992-018-0444-8.
Banet-Weiser, Sarah. 2011. "Convergence on the Street: Rethinking the Authentic/Commercial Binary." *Cultural Studies* 25 (4–5): 641–58.
———. 2012. *Authentic™: The Politics of Ambivalence in a Brand Culture*. New York: New York University Press.
Banks, David A. 2018. "Which Side Are They On?" *The Baffler*. August 21, 2018. https://thebaffler.com/latest/which-side-are-they-on-banks.
Barbrook, Richard, and Andy Cameron. 1995. "The Californian Ideology." *Mute*, September 1, 1995.
———. 1996. "The Californian Ideology." *Science as Culture* 6 (1): 44–72.

Barnett, Daly. 2020. "Sex Worker Rights Advocates Raise the Alarms about EARN IT." *The Electronic Frontier Foundation*, June 1, 2020. www.eff.org/deeplinks/2020/06/sex-worker-rights-advocates-raise-alarms-about-earn-it

Barr, Alistair. 2019. "An RV Camp Sprang Up Outside Google's Headquarters." *Bloomberg*, May 21, 2019. www.bloomberg.com/news/features/2019-05-21/silicon-valley-s-shame-living-in-a-van-in-google-s-backyard.

Basolne, A. 2018. "The Skilled and the Schooled." *The Caravan*. www.magzter.com/article/News/The-Caravan/The-Skilled-And-The-Schooled

Bay Area Amazonians. 2020. "Bay Area Amazonians Hold Juneteenth Vigil Featuring Installation by AE Marling." *Digital Journal*, June 18, 2020. www.digitaljournal.com/pr/4717172.

Baym, Nancy K. 2015. "Connect With Your Audience! The Relational Labor of Connection." *The Communication Review* 18 (1): 14–22.

Bednar, Lucy. 2010. "Audiobooks and the Reassertion of Orality: Walter J. Ong and Others Revisited." *CEA Critic* 73 (1): 74–85.

Benkler, Yochai. 2006. *The Wealth of Networks: How Social Production Transforms Markets and Freedom*. New Haven, CT: Yale University Press.

Benner, Chris. 1998. "Win the Lottery or Organize: Traditional and Non-Traditional Labor Organizing in Silicon Valley." *Berkeley Planning Journal* 12 (1): 50–71. https://escholarship.org/uc/item/6z2697vb.

Berg, Heather. 2014. "Labouring Porn Studies." *Porn Studies* 1 (1–2): 75–79.

———. 2016a. "Porn Work: Adult Film at the Point of Production." PhD. diss., University of California, Santa Barbara.

———. 2016b. "A Scene Is Just a Marketing Tool: Alternative Income Streams in Porn's Gig Economy." *Porn Studies* 3 (2): 160–74.

Bergen, Mark, and Josh Eidelson. 2018. "Inside Google's Shadow Workforce." *Bloomberg*, July 25, 2018. www.bloomberg.com/news/articles/2018-07-25/inside-google-s-shadow-workforce.

Berlant, Lauren. 2011. *Cruel Optimism*. Durham, NC: Duke University Press.

Berliner, Rosaria M., and Gil Tal. 2018. "What Drives Your Drivers: An In-Depth Look at Lyft and Uber Drivers." UC Davis Institute of Transportation Studies. https://steps.ucdavis.edu/wp-content/uploads/2018/02/BERLINER-TAL-What-Drives-Your-Drivers.pdf

Bernal, Dolores Delgado. 1998. "Using a Chicana Feminist Epistemology in Educational Research." *Harvard Educational Review* 68 (4): 555–83. https://doi.org/10.17763/haer.68.4.5wv1034973g22q48.

Bernhardt, Annette. 2018. "Making Sense of The New Government Data on Contingent Work." *Medium*, June 10, 2018. https://medium.com/@a.d.bernhardt/making-sense-of-the-new-government-data-on-contingent-work-97209bb0c615

Bernhardt, Annette, and Sarah Thomason. 2017. "What Do We Know About Gig Work in California? An Analysis of Independent Contracting." UC Berkeley Labor Center. http://laborcenter.berkeley.edu/what-do-we-know-about-gig-work-in-california/.

Bernstein, Elizabeth. 2007. *Temporarily Yours: Intimacy, Authenticity, and the Commerce of Sex*. Chicago: University of Chicago Press.

Beverungen, Armin, Birke Otto, Sverre Spoelstra, and Kate Kenny, eds. 2013. "Special Issue on 'Free Work'." *Ephemera: Theory & Politics in Organization* 13 (1).

Bhattacharya, S., and S. Sinha. 2009. *Domestic Workers in India: Background and Issues*. New Delhi: ILO.

Bhattarai, Abha. 2018. "Now Hiring, for a One-Day Job: The Gig Economy Hits Retail." *The Washington Post*, May 4, 2018. www.washingtonpost.com/business/economy/now-hiring-for-a-one-day-jobthe-gig-economy-hits-retail/2018/05/04/2bebdd3c-4257-11e8-ad8f-27a8c409298b_story.html?utm_ term=.ba2225d9df44.

Bliss, Laura. 2018. "Cities Have to Get Creative When Uber and Lyft Won't Release Trip Data." *The Atlantic*, January 13, 2018. www.theatlantic.com/business/archive/2018/01/uber-lyft-cities-data/550433/.

Bloom, Greg. 2013. "Towards a Community Data Commons." In *Beyond Transparency: Open Data and the Future of Civic Innovation*, edited by Brett Goldstein with Lauren Dyson, 255–70. San Francisco: Code for America Press.

Boal, I., and C. Carlsson, C. 2009. "Critical Mass". In *The International Encyclopaedia of Revolution and Protest*, edited by Immanuel Ness. New York: Wiley-Blackwell.

Bogage, Jacob. "Thousands of U.S. Workers Walk Out in 'Strike for Black Lives'." July 20, 2020. www.washingtonpost.com/business/2020/07/20/strike-for-black-lives/.

Boggs, Abigail, and Nick Mitchell. 2018. "Critical University Studies and the Crisis Consensus." *Feminist Studies* 44 (2): 432–63.

Bologna, Sergio, and Andrea Fumagalli. 1997. *Il lavoro autonomo di seconda generazione. Scenari del postfordismo in Italia*. Milano: Feltrinelli.

Bonini, Tiziano. 2015. "The 'Second Age' of Podcasting: Reframing Podcasting as a New Digital Mass Medium." *Quaderns Del CAC* 41 (18): 21–30.

Boris, Eileen. 1994. *Home to Work: Motherhood and the Politics of Industrial Homework in the United States*. Oxford: Cambridge University Press.

Borkholder, Joy, Mariah Montgomery, Miya Saika Chen, and Rebecca Smith. 2018. *Uber State Interference: How Transportation Network Companies Buy, Bully, and Bamboozle Their Way To Deregulation*. New York: National Employment Law Project.

Bourdieu, Pierre. 1977. *Outline of a Theory of Practice*. Cambridge Studies in Social Anthropology No. 16. Cambridge: Cambridge University Press.

Bousquet, Marc. 2008. *How the University Works: Higher Education and the Low-Wage Nation*. New York: New York University Press.

Bradshaw, Tim, and Shannon Bond. 2018. "Uber Takes a Detour With Plan to Provide Temporary Staff." *The Financial Times*, October 18, 2018.

Braverman, Harry. 1974. *Labor and Monopoly Capital: the Degradation of Work in the Twentieth Century*. New York: Monthly Review Press.

Briziarelli, Marco. 2018. "Spatial Politics in the Digital Realm: Or the Productive Tension Between Logistics and Precarity." *Cultural Studies* 4: 1–19.

Bröckling, Ulrich. 2016. *The Entrepreneurial Self: Fabricating a New Type of Subject*. Los Angeles, CA: Sage.

Brooks, Chris. 2018a. "Meet the Militant Taxi Drivers Union That Just Defeated Uber and Lyft." *Working in These Times*, August 15, 2018. http://inthesetimes.com/working/entry/21386/militant_taxi_drivers_union_uber_lyft_alliance_new_york_city.

———. 2018b. "University of California Workers Strike for Racial Justice." *Labor-Notes*. November 20, 2018. www.labornotes.org/2018/11/university-california-workers-strike-racial-justice.

Brooks, Siobhan. 2010. *Unequal Desires: Race and Erotic Capital in the Stripping Industry*. Albany, NY: SUNY Press.

Brophy, Enda. 2006. "System Error: Labour Precarity and Collective Organizing at Microsoft." *Canadian Journal of Communication* 31 (3): 619–38.

Bruns, Axel. 2006. "Towards Produsage: Futures for User-Led Content Production." In *Creative Industries Faculty*, edited by Fay Sudweeks, Herbert Hrachovec, and Charles Ess, 275–84. Tartu, Estonia: Murdoch University. http://eprints.qut.edu.au/4863/.

———. 2008. *Blogs, Wikipedia, Second Life, and Beyond*. New York: Peter Lang.

Brustein, Joshua. 2019. "What It's Like to Work Inside Apple's 'Black Site'." *Bloomberg*, February 11, 2019. www.bloomberg.com/news/features/2019-02-11/apple-black-site-gives-contractors-few-perks-little-security.

Bulut, Ergin. 2015. "Glamor Above, Precarity Below: Immaterial Labor in the Video Game Industry." *Critical Studies in Media Communication* 32 (3): 193–207.

Bureau of Labor Statistics. 2018. "Contingent and Alternative Employment Arrangements Summary." *Bureau of Labor Statistics*, June 7, 2018. www.bls.gov/news.release/conemp.nr0.htm.

Burgess, Jean, and Joshua Green. 2009. *YouTube: Online Video and Participatory Culture*. Cambridge, MA: Polity Press.

Burke, Lilah. 2020. "Uncertain Fate for Support Staff." *Inside Higher Ed*, March 13, 2020. www.insidehighered.com/news/2020/03/13/future-unclear-support-staff-empty-college-campuses.

Butler, Nick, and Sverre Spoelstra. 2014. "The Regime of Excellence and the Erosion of Ethos in Critical Management Studies." *British Journal of Management* 25 (3): 538–50. https://doi.org/10.1111/1467-8551.12053.

Butlers, Sarah. 2017. "Deliveroo Wins Right Not To Give Riders Minimum Wage or Holiday Pay." *The Guardian*, November 14, 2017. www.theguardian.com/business/2017/nov/14/deliveroo-couriers-minimum-wage-holiday-pay

Caldwell, John Thornton. 2008. *Production Culture: Industrial Reflexivity and Critical Practice in Film and Television*. Durham, NC: Duke University Press.

California Public Utilities Commission. 2018. "Current TNC Permits." Accessed November 26, 2018. www.cpuc.ca.gov/tncpermitsissued/.

Cam, V. V. 2018. *Because Money Matters: How to Earn More Money as a Freelancer in a Gig Economy*. Self-published, Kindle.

Caminiti, Susan. 2018. "4 Gig Economy Trends That Are Radically Transforming the US Job Market." *CNBC*, October 29, 2018. www.cnbc.com/2018/10/29/4-gig-economy-trends-that-are-radically-transforming-the-us-job-market.html.

Campbell, Alexia Fernández. 2019. "Google Will Extend Some Benefits to Contract Workers After Internal Protest." *Vox*, April 4, 2019. www.vox.com/2019/4/4/18293900/google-contractors-benefits-policy.

Cant, Callum. 2018a. "The Wave of Worker Resistance in European Food Platforms 2016–17." *Notes from Below*, January 29, 2018. https://notesfrombelow.org/article/european-food-platform-strike-wave

———. 2018b. "Sacked at Christmas: Uber Eats Fires Workers for Objecting to Pay Cut." *Novara Media*. https://novaramedia.com/2018/12/12/sacked-at-christmas-uber-eats-fires-workers-for-objecting-to-pay-cut/

———. 2020. *Riding for Deliveroo: Resistance in the New Economy*. London: Polity Press.

Cant, Callum, and Lydia Hughes. 2018. "'No Money, No Food!' London UberEats Workers on Strike." *Notes from Below*. https://notesfrombelow.org/article/no-money-no-food-london-ubereats-workers-strike

Cant, Callum, and Jamie Woodcock. 2019. "The End of the Beginning." *Notes from Below*. https://notesfrombelow.org/article/end-beginning

Caraway, Brett. 2010. "Online Labour Markets: An Inquiry into ODesk Providers." *Work Organisation, Labour & Globalisation* 4 (2): 111–25.

———. 2016. "OUR Walmart: A Case Study of Connective Action." *Information, Communication & Society* 19 (7): 907–20.

———. 2018. "Collective Action Frames and the Developing Role of Discursive Practice in Worker Organisation: The Case of OUR Walmart." *Work Organisation Labour & Globalisation* 12 (1): 7–24.

Carey, James. 1989. *Communication as Culture. Essays on Media and Society*. Boston: Unwin Hyman.
Carlsson, Chris, and Mark Leger. 1990. *Bad Attitude: The Processed World Anthology*. New York: Verso.
Carney, Brian M., and Isaac Getz. 2016. *Freedom, Inc.: How Corporate Liberation Unleashes Employee Potential and Business Performance*. 2nd ed. New York: Somme Valley House.
Carr, Austin. 2014. "Inside Airbnb's Grand Hotel Plans." *Fast Company*, March 17, 2014. Accessed March 10, 2019.www.fastcompany.com/3027107/punk-meet-rock-airbnb-brian-chesky-chip-conley
Carragee, Kevin M and Lawrence R. Frey. 2011. "Introduction: Communication Activism for Social Justice Scholarship." In *Communication Activism: Vol. 3: Struggling for Social Justice Amidst Difference*, edited by Lawrence R. Frey and Kevin Carragee, 1–67. New York: Hampton Press.
Carson, Biz. "Uber Is Making Changes to Eliminate the Fear Factor for Drivers." *Business Insider*, November 27, 2016. www.businessinsider.com/uber-is-recommitting-itself-to-putting-its-drivers-first-2016-11.
Casey, Catherine. 1995. *Work, Self and Society: After Industrialism*. New York: Routledge.
Casilli, Antonio. 2017. "How Venture Labor Sheds Light on the Digital Platform Economy." *International Journal of Communication* 11: 2067–70.
Cassano, Jay. 2016. "How Uber Profits Even While It's Drivers Aren't Earning Money." *Vice*, February 2, 2016. www.vice.com/en_us/article/wnxd84/how-uber-profits-even-while-its-drivers-arent-earning-money
Cederström, Carl, and Peter Fleming. 2012. *Dead Man Working*. Winchester: Zero Books.
Cederström, Carl, and André Spicer. 2015. *The Wellness Syndrome*. Cambridge: Polity Press.
Chandler, David, and Christian Fuchs, eds. 2019. *Digital Objects, Digital Subjects: Interdisciplinary Perspectives on Capitalism, Labour and Politics in the Age of Big Data*. London: University of Westminster Press.
Chapkis, Wendy. 1997. *Live Sex Acts: Women Performing Erotic Labor*. New York: Routledge.
Cheng, Denise. 2014. "Is Sharing Really Caring? A Nuanced Introduction to the Peer Economy." *Open Society Foundation Future of Work Inquiry*, 12–13. https://static.opensocietyfoundations.org/misc/future-of-work/the-sharing-economy.pdf.
Circella, Giovanni, et al. 2018. "The Adoption of Shared Mobility in California and Its Relationship With Other Components of Travel Behavior." National Center for Sustainable Transportation. https://ncst.ucdavis.edu/wp-content/uploads/2016/10/NCST-TO-033.1-Circella_Shared-Mobility_Final-Report_MAR-2018.pdf.
City News Service. 2018. "After Three Years of Debate, LA Approves Airbnb Rules." December 11, 2018. Accessed March 10, 2019. www.nbclosangeles.com/news/local/Airbnb-Home-Sharing-Los-Angeles-Rules-Travel-Homes-Housing-502458851.html
Clark, Christopher. 1990. *The Roots of Rural Capitalism: Western Massachusetts, 1780–1860*. Ithaca: Cornell University Press.
Clark, Dorie. 2013. *Reinventing You: Define Your Brand, Imagine Your Future*. Boston, MA: Harvard Business Review Press.
Cleaver, H. 1979. *Reading Capital Politically*. Brighton: Harvester Press.
Clegg, Sue. 2008. "Academic Identities Under Threat?" *British Educational Research Journal* 34 (3): 329–45.
Clewlow, Regina R., and Gouri S. Mishra. 2017. "Disruptive Transportation: The Adoption, Utilization, and Impacts of Ride-Hailing in the United States." UC Davis Institute of Transportation Studies. https://itspubs.ucdavis.edu/wp-content/themes/ucdavis/pubs/download_pdf.php?id=2752.

Cloud, Dana. 2010. "The Only Conceivable Thing to do: Reflections of Academics and Activism." In *Activism and Rhetoric: Theories and Contexts for Political Engagement*, edited by JongHwa Lee and Seth Kahn, 11–24. New York: Routledge.

Codeluppi, Vanni. 2007. *La vetrinizzazione sociale, Il processo di spettacolarizzazione degli individui e della società*. Torino: Bollati Boringhieri.

Cohen, Cathy J., and Sarah J. Jackson. 2016. "Ask a Feminist: A Conversation With Cathy J. Cohen on Black Lives Matter, Feminism, and Contemporary Activism." *Signs: Journal of Women in Culture and Society* 41 (4): 775–92.

Collins, Patricia Hill. 2012. *On Intellectual Activism*. Philadelphia: Temple University Press.

Conger, Kate, and Michael de la Merced. 2019. "Uber Aims for Valuation of Up to $91 Billion in I.P.O." *The New York Times*, April 26, 2019. www.nytimes.com/2019/04/26/technology/uber-ipo-valuation-price-range.html.

Conger, Kate, and Noam Scheiber. "California Bill Makes App-Based Companies Treat Workers as Employees." *The New York Times*, September 11, 2019, sec. Technology. www.nytimes.com/2019/09/11/technology/california-gig-economy-bill.html.

Conger, Kate, Vicky Xiuzhong, and Zach Wichter. "Uber Drivers' Day of Strikes Circles the Globe before the Company's I.P.O." *The New York Times*, May 8, 2019. www.nytimes.com/2019/05/08/technology/uber-strike.html.

Cooper, Brittney C., Susanna M. Morris, and Robin M. Boylorn. 2017. *The Crunk Feminist Collection*. New York: The Feminist Press.

Corrigan, Thomas F. 2018. "Making Implicit Methods Explicit: Trade Press Analysis in the Political Economy of Communication." *International Journal of Communication* 12 (0): 22.

Cottom, Tressie McMillan. 2020. "The Hustle Economy." *Dissent Magazine*. www.dissentmagazine.org/article/the-hustle-economy

Coupland, Douglas. 1995. *Microserfs*. Toronto: HarperCollins.

Covert, Bryce. 2020. "Like Uber, but for Gig Worker Organizing." *American Prospect*, March 30, 2020. https://prospect.org/labor/like-uber-but-for-gig-worker-organizing/

Crea, Thomas M., and Neil Sparnon. 2017. "Democratizing Education at the Margins: Faculty and Practitioner Perspectives on Delivering Online Tertiary Education for Refugees." *International Journal of Educational Technology in Higher Education* 14: 43. https://doi.org/10.1186/s41239-017-0081-y

Cukier, Kenneth, and Viktor Mayer-Schuenberger. 2013. "The Rise of Big Data: How It's Changing the Way We Think About the World." *Foreign Affairs* 9 (3): 28–40.

Davidson, Nestor M., and John J. Infranca. 2015. "The Sharing Economy as an Urban Phenomenon." *Yale Law & Policy Review* 34 (2): 215–79.

Dåvila, Arlene and Yeidy M. Rivero. 2014. *Contemporary Latina/o Media: Introduction*. New York: New York University Press. www.jstor.org/stable/pdf/j.ctt9qfn6s.3.pdf?refreqid=excelsior%3Ade3932c151426448ffd7b27501b6c5ff.

Dayden, David. 2019. "Monopolist's Worst Nightmare: The Elizabeth Warren Interview." *American Prospect*, June 18, 2019. https://prospect.org/economy/monopolist-s-worst-nightmare-elizabeth-warren-interview/

D'Cruz, P., and E. Noronha. 2016. "Positives Outweighing Negatives: The Experiences of Indian Crowdsourced Workers." *Work Organisation, Labour and Globalisation* 10 (1): 44–63.

DeBlasio, Bill, and Meera Joshi. 2016. "2016 NYC Taxicab Factbook." In *NYC Taxicab Factbook*. New York: Taxi and Limousine Commission.

DeCicco, James. 2018. *Master the Gig Economy: How a Next Generation Entrepreneur Builds Wealth*. Scotts Valley, CA: CreateSpace. Kindle.

Deem, Rosemary, Sam Hillyard, and Michael Reed. 2007. *Knowledge, Higher Education, and the New Managerialism: The Changing Management of UK Universities*. Oxford: Oxford University Press.

Degner, Anne, and Eva Kocher. 2018. "Arbeitskämpfe in der 'Gig-Economy'? Die Protestbewegungen der Foodora- und Deliveroo-'Riders' und Rechtsfragen ihrer kollektiven Selbstorganisation." *KJ Kritische Justiz* 51 (3): 247–65.

Deleuze, Gilles. 1992. "Postscript on the Societies of Control." *October* 59: 3–7.

Delfanti, Alessandro. 2018. "Amazon Is the New FIAT." *Notes from Below*, August 16, 2018. https://notesfrombelow.org/article/amazon-is-the-new-fiat

"Demand Coronavirus Relief for Platform Workers." *Drivers-United.org*. Accessed November 26, 2020. https://drivers-united.org/a/demand-coronavirus-relief-for-platform-workers?r=2uHzpZoN&fbclid=IwAR3bm6gxqqhU27sQYf1dLEpCGZhOf3JQBHeAonJou2BpjHfDTe7ZFm9BWiI

DeMAnuelle-Hall, Joe. "Strike by Drivers Disrupts Uber Launch." *Labor Notes*, May 31, 2019. www.labornotes.org/2019/05/strike-drivers-disrupts-uber-launch

DeMaria, Alfred T. 2017. "Organizers Increase Sophistication With Digital Communications." *Management Report for Nonunion Organizations* 40 (2): 3–5.

Dempsey, Paul Stephen. 1996. "Taxi Industry Regulation, Deregulation, and Reregulation: The Paradox of Market Failure." *University of Denver College of Law, Transportation Law Journal* 24 (1): 73–120.

Dencik, Lina, and Peter Wilken. 2015. *Worker Resistance and Media: Challenging Global Corporate Power in the 21st Century*. New York: Peter Lang.

Denton, Stephanie. 2020. "Workers' Access to and Use of Leave From Their Jobs in 2017–18." U.S. Bureau of Labor Statistics, January 2020.

De Souza Santos, Boaventura. 2018. *The End of the Cognitive Empire: The Coming of Age of Epistemologies of the South*. Durham, NC: Duke University Press.

De Stefano, Valerio. 2015. "The Rise of the 'Just in Time Workforce': On-Demand Work, Crowdwork, and Labor Protection in the 'Gig-Economy'." Paper presented at *Crowd-Sourcing, the Gig Economy, and the Law, Philadelphia, November 7, 2015*. http://ssrn.com/abstract=2682602. *Comparative Labor Law & Policy Journal* 37: 471–504.

DeWinter, Jennifer, Carly A. Kocurek, and Randall Nichols. 2014. "Taylorism 2.0: Gamification, Scientific Management and the Capitalist Appropriation of Play." *Journal of Gaming & Virtual Worlds* 6 (2): 109–27.

De Wolff, Alice. 2000. "Breaking the Myth of Flexible Work: Contingent Work in Toronto." Contingent Workers Project. http://workersactioncentre.org/wp-content/uploads/2016/07/BreakingTheMyth_eng.pdf.

Dickey, Megan Rose. 2020. "Gig Workers in San Francisco Are Mostly People of Color and Many Are Immigrants." *Techcrunch*, May 5, 2020. https://techcrunch.com/2020/05/05/gig-workers-survey-san-francisco/.

Dickson, Gordon, "Experts Warn of Rising Demand for Amazon, Lyft, Uber Drivers." *Fort Worth Star-Telegram*, April 13, 2018. www.star-telegram.com/news/business/growth/article208321194.html.

Dobush, Grace. 2019. "Uber Has Troves of Data on How People Navigate Cities. Urban Planners Have Begged, Pleaded, And Gone to Court for Access. Will They Ever Get It?" *Marker*, September 9, 2019. https://marker.medium.com/ubers-real-advantage-is-data-e54984ff524c

Dolber, Brian. 2016. "Blindspots and Blurred lines: Dallas Smythe, the Audience Commodity, and the Transformation of Labor in the Digital Age." *Sociology Compass* 10 (9): 747–55.

———. 2017. *Media and Culture in the US Jewish Labor Movement: Sweating for Democracy in the Interwar Era*. New York: Springer.

———. 2019a. "From Independent Contractors to an Independent Union: Building Solidarity Through Rideshare Drivers United's Digital Organizing

Strategy." Media, Inequality & Change (MIC) Center. www.miccenter.org/wp-content/uploads/2019/10/Dolber_final-2.pdf
———. 2019b. "Precarity and Solidarity at Neoliberalism's Twilight: The Potentials of Transnational Production Autoethnography." *Cultural Studies Critical Methodologies*, February 22. https://doi.org/10.1177/1532708619829781.
———. 2020. "Most Expensive Ballot Initiative in California History Pits Uber and Lyft Against Drivers Who Built a Union From Scratch." *Labor Notes*, November 3, 2020, https://labornotes.org/blogs/2020/11/most-expensive-ballot-initiative-california-history-pits-uber-and-lyft-against-drivers.
Dowling, Emma, Rodrigo Nunes, and Ben Trott. 2007. "Immaterial and Affective Labour: Explored." *Ephemera: Theory & Politics in Organization* 7 (1): 1–7.
Dubal, Veena B. 2017a. "The Drive to Precarity: A Political History of Work, Regulation, & Labor Advocacy in San Francisco's Taxi & Uber Economies." *Berkeley Journal of Employment and Labor Law* 38 (1): 73–136. https://repository.uchastings.edu/faculty_scholarship/1589
———. 2017b. "Wage Slave or Entrepreneur? Contesting the Dualism of Legal Worker Identities." UC Hastings Research Paper No. 176. University of California Hastings College of the Law, September 23, 2017. https://ssrn.com/abstract=2796728.
———. 2019. "Gig Worker Organizing for Solidarity Unions." *Law and Political Economy*, June 19, 2019. https://lpeblog.org/2019/06/19/gig-worker-organizing-for-solidarity-unions/
Duchêne, Alexandre, and Monica Heller. 2012. *Language in Late Capitalism: Pride and Profit*. London: Routledge.
Dudley, Geoffrey, David Banister, and Tim Schwanen. 2017. "The Rise of Uber and Regulating the Disruptive Innovator." *The Political Quarterly* 88 (3): 492–99.
Duffy, Brooke Erin. 2015. "Amateur, Autonomous, and Collaborative: Myths of Aspiring Female Cultural Producers in Web 2.0." *Critical Studies in Media Communication* 32 (1): 48–64. https://doi.org/10.1080/15295036.2014.997832.
———. 2017. *(Not) Getting Paid to Do What You Love: Gender, Social Media, and Aspirational Work*. New Haven: Yale University Press.
Duffy, Brooke Erin, and Jefferson D. Pooley. 2017. "'Facebook for Academics': The Convergence of Self-Branding and Social Media Logic on Academia. Edu." *Social Media+Society* 3 (1): 2056305117696523.
Duffy, Brooke Erin, and Urszula Pruchniewska. 2017. "Gender and Self-Enterprise in the Social Media Age: A Digital Double Bind." *Information, Communication & Society* 20 (6): 843–59. https://doi.org/10.1080/1369118X.2017.1291703.
Duncan, P. 2014. "Hot Commodities, Cheap Labor: Women of Color in the Academy." *Frontiers: A Journal of Women's Studies* 35 (3): 39–63.
Dyer-Witheford, Nick. 2005. "Cognitive Capitalism and the Contested Campus". In *Engineering Culture: On the Author as (Digital) Producer*, edited by Geoff Cox and Joasia Krysa, 71–93. New York: Autonomedia.
Dyer-Witheford, Nick, and Greig De Peuter. 2009. *Games of Empire: Global Capitalism and Video Games*. Electronic Mediations, No. 29. Minneapolis: University of Minnesota Press.
Eamets, Raul, and Epp Kalaste. 2004. "The Lack of Wage Setting Power of Estonian Trade Unions?" *Baltic Journal of Economics* 5 (1): 44–60.
Economist. 2017. "The World's Most Valuable Resource is No Longer Oil, but Data." May 6, 2017. www.economist.com/leaders/2017/05/06/the-worlds-most-valuable-resource-is-no-longer-oil-but-data

Edelman, Benjamin, Machael Luca, and Dan Svirsky. 2017. "Racial Discrimination in the Sharing Economy: Evidence from a Field Experiment." *American Economic Journal: Applied Economics* 9 (2): 1–22. https://doi.org/10.1257/app.20160213

Edu-factory Collective. 2009. *Towards a Global Autonomous University*. New York: Autonomedia.

Egelko, Bob. "Gig Workers Could Gain Employee Status With California Supreme Court Ruling." *San Francisco Chronicle*, April 30, 2018. www.sfchronicle.com/business/article/Gig-workers-could-gain-employee-status-with-12875715.php

Émond-Sioufi, Veronique. 2017. "#Unions: Canadian Unions and Social Media." PhD diss., Simon Fraser University, BC, Canada.

Eurofound. 2017. "Atypical Work." *Eurofound,* November 24, 2017. www.eurofound.europa.eu/observatories/eurwork/industrial-relations-dictionary/atypical-work

Evans, John. 2018. "An Introduction To Wobbly: An App For 21st Century Workers' Power." *Notes from Below* 3. https://notesfrombelow.org/article/an-introduction-to-wobbly

Evetts, Julia. 2003. "The Sociological Analysis of Professionalism: Occupational Change in the Modern World." *International Sociology* 18 (2): 395–415. https://doi.org/10.1177/0268580903018002005.

Ewick, P., and Susan S. Silbey. 1991. "Conformity, Contestation, and Resistance: An Account of Legal Consciousness." *New England Law Review* 26: 731.

Fairclough, Norman, and Ruth Wodak. 1997. "Critical Discourse Analysis." In *Discourse and Social Interaction*, edited by Teun A. van Dijk, 103–36. London: Sage.

Farrell, Diana, and Fiona Greig. 2016. *Paychecks, Paydays, and the Online Platform Economy: Big Data on Income Volatility*. Washington, DC: JP Morgan Chase Institute.

Fast, Karin, Henrik Örnebring, and Michael Karlsson. 2016. "Metaphors of Free Labor: A Typology of Unpaid Work in the Media Sector." *Media, Culture & Society* 38 (7): 963–78.

Fear, Chris. 2018. '"Without Our Brain and Muscle Not A Single Wheel Can Turn: The IWW Couriers Network." *Notes from Below*. https://notesfrombelow.org/article/without-our-brain-and-muscle

Federici, Silvia. 2011. "On Affective Labor." In *Cognitive Capitalism, Education, and Digital Labor*, edited by Michael Peters and Ergin Bulut, 57–74. New York: Peter Lang.

Fernández Vitores, David. 2019. "El Español Una Lengua Viva: Informe 2019." Instituto Cervantes, Spain. Accessed August 26, 2020. www.cervantes.es/imagenes/File/espanol_lengua_viva_2019.pdf.

Fierro, Cindy O., and Dolores Delgado Bernal. 2016. "Vamos a Platicar: The Contours of Pláticas as Chicana/Latina Feminist Methodology." *Chicana/Latina Studies*. 15 (2): 98–117.

Fine, Janice. 2006. *Worker Centers: Organizing Communities at the Edge of the Dream*. Ithaca: ILR Press/Cornell University Press.

Fine, Janice, and Jennifer Gordon. 2010. "Strengthening Labor Standards Enforcement through Partnerships With Workers' Organizations." *Politics & Society* 38 (4): 552–85.

Fiori, Nicholas. 2017. "The Precarity of Global Digital Labor." *Women's Studies Quarterly* 45 (3/4): 321–26.

Fisher, Eran. 2012. "How Less Alienation Creates More Exploitation? Audience Labour on Social Network Sites." *TripleC: Open Access Journal for a Global Sustainable Information Society* 10 (2): 171–83.

Fitzpatrick, Alex. 2016. "Airbnb CEO: 'Bias and Discrimination Have No Place Here." *Time*, September 8, 2016. http://time.com/4484113/airbnb-ceo-brian-chesky-anti-discrimination-racism/

Fitzsimmons, Emma. 2018. "Suicides Get Taxi Drivers Talking: 'I'm Going to Be One of Them.'" *The New York Times*, October 2, 2018. www.nytimes.com/2018/10/02/nyregion/suicides-taxi-drivers-nyc.html.

Flaherty, Colleen. 2018. "A Non-Tenure-Track Profession?" *Inside Higher Ed*, October 12, 2018. www.insidehighered.com/news/2018/10/12/about-three-quarters-all-faculty-positions-are-tenure-track-according-new-aaup.

———. 2020a. "Barely Getting By." *Inside Higher Ed*, April 20, 2020. www.insidehighered.com/news/2020/04/20/new-report-says-many-adjuncts-make-less-3500-course-and-25000-year.

———. 2020b. "Faculty Group Will Investigate U of Akron." *Inside Higher Ed*, October 28, 2020. www.insidehighered.com/quicktakes/2020/10/28/faculty-group-will-investigate-u-akron.

Fleming, Peter. 2009. *Authenticity and the Cultural Politics of Work: New Forms of Informal Control*. Oxford: Oxford University Press.

Florida, Richard. 2002. *The Rise of the Creative Class: And How it's Transforming Work, Leisure, and Everyday Life*. New York: Basic Books.

Florini, Sarah. 2015. "The Podcast 'Chitlin' Circuit': Black Podcasters, Alternative Media, and Audio Enclaves." *Journal of Radio & Audio Media* 22 (2): 209–19. https://doi.org/10.1080/19376529.2015.1083373.

Foucault, M. 1988. *Technologies of the Self: A Seminar With Michel Foucault*. Edited by Luther H. Martin, Huck Gutman, and Patrick H. Hutton. Amherst: University of Massachusetts Press.

———. 2005. *The Hermeneutics of the Subject: Lectures at the Collège de France; 1981–1982*. Edited by Frédéric Gros. Translated by Graham Burchell. New York: Picador.

Franklin, Paul. 2008. "Amazon to Buy Audible for $300 Million." *Reuters*, January 31, 2008.

Fraser, Nancy. "From Progressive Neoliberalism to Trump—and beyond." *American Affairs Journal* 1 (4). Accessed October 27, 2018. https://americanaffairsjournal.org/2017/11/progressive-neoliberalism-trump-beyond/

Frazer, John. 2019. "How the Gig Economy Is Reshaping Careers for the Next Generation." *Forbes*, February 15, 2019. www.forbes.com/sites/johnfrazer1/2019/02/15/how-the-gig-economy-is-reshaping-careers-for-the-next-generation/.

Freedman, Des. 2012. "Web 2.0 and the Death of the Blockbuster Economy." In *Misunderstanding the Internet*, edited by James Curran, Natalie Fenton, and Des Freedman, 74–94. Communication and Society. New York: Routledge.

Freidson, Eliot. 2001. *Professionalism, the Third Logic: On the Practice of Knowledge*. Chicago: University of Chicago Press.

Freire, Paulo. 1970. *Pedagogy of the Oppressed*. Translated by M. B. Ramos. New York: Herder and Herder.

Frey, Lawrence R., and Kevin M. Carragee, eds. 2007. *Communication Activism*. 2 vols. Cresskill: Hampton Press.

Friedman, Daniel. 2014a. "Resisting the Lure of the Paycheck: Freedom and Dependence in Financial Self-Help." *Foucault Studies* 18: 90–112.

———. 2014b. "Workers Without Employers: Shadow Corporations and the Rise of the Gig Economy." *Review of Keynesian Economics* 2 (2): 171–88. https://doi.org/10.4337/roke.2014.02.03.

Fuchs, Christian. 2014. *Digital Labor and Karl Marx*. London and New York: Routledge.

Fuchs, Christian, and Vincent Mosco. 2016. *Marx in the Age of Digital Capitalism*. Leiden: Brill.

Fuchs, Mathias. 2012. "Ludic Interfaces. Driver and Product of Gamification." *G.A.M.E: The Italian Journal of Game Studies* 1: 19–26.

Fuchs, Mathias, Sonia Fizek, Paolo Ruffino, and Niklas Schrape. 2014. *Rethinking Gamification*. Lüneberg: meson press.

Gajjala, R. 2017. "The Problem of Value for 'Women's Work'." *GenderIT*. www.genderit.org/node/4907/

Garlick, Hattie. 2017. "Dark Kitchens: Is This the Future of Takeaway?" *The Financial Times*, June 8, 2017. www.ft.com/content/d23c44fe-4b0b-11e7-919a-1e14ce4af89b

Garnham, Nicholas. 2005. "From Cultural to Creative Industries." *International Journal of Cultural Policy* 11 (1): 15–29.

Gee, Alastair. 2017. "Facing Poverty, Academics Turn to Sex Work and Sleeping in Cars." *The Guardian*, September 28, 2017. www.theguardian.com/us-news/2017/sep/28/adjunct-professors-homeless-sex-work-academia-poverty.

Geiger, Roger L. 2004. *Knowledge and Money: Research. Universities and the Paradox of the Marketplace*. Palo Alto: Stanford University Press.

Gerbaudo, Paolo. 2012. *Tweets and the Streets: Social Media and Contemporary Activism*. London: Pluto Press.

Gerrard, David Burr. 2014. "'Do What You Love'—Oh, But Not That! On Recognizing Sex Work as Work." *The Awl*, March 6, 2014. www.theawl.com/2014/03/do-what-you-love-oh-but-not-that-on-recognizing-sex-work-as-work/

Geymonat, G., S. Marchetti, and Penelope Kyritsis. 2017. "Out From the Shadows: Domestic Workers Speak in the United States." *Open Democracy*. www.opendemocracy.net/en/beyond-trafficking-and-slavery/out-from-shadows-domestic-workers-speak-in-united-states/

Gibson, Rich. 2010. "Education Versus Schooling as a Commodity Fetish." *richgibson.com*. Accessed July 5, 2019. http://richgibson.com/EducationFetish.pdf

Gill, Rosalind, and Ngaire Donaghue. 2016. "Resilience, Apps and Reluctant Individualism: Technologies of Self in the Neoliberal Academy." *Women's Studies International Forum* 54 (1): 91–99. https://doi.org/10.1016/j.wsif.2015.06.016

Gillespie, Tarleton. 2010. "The Politics of 'Platforms'." *New Media & Society* 12 (3): 347–64.

———. 2018. *Custodians of the Internet: Platforms, Content Moderation, and the Hidden Decisions That Shape Social Media*. New Haven: Yale University Press.

Gilroy, Paul. 2004. *After Empire: Melancholia or Convivial Culture?* London: Routledge.

Gingrich-Philbrook, Craig. 2005. "Autoethnography's Family Values: Easy Access to Compulsory Experiences." *Text and Performance Quarterly* 25 (4): 297–314.

Giridharadas, Anand. 2018. *Winners Take All: The Elite Charade of Changing the World*. 1st ed. New York: Alfred A. Knopf.

Giroux, Harry A. 2002. "Neoliberalism, Corporate Culture, and the Promise of Higher Education: The University as a Democratic Public Sphere." *Harvard Educational Review* 72 (4): 425–64.

Glenn, Evelyn Nakano. 1992. "From Servitude to Service Work: Historical Continuities in the Racial Division of Paid Reproductive Labor." *Signs: Journal of Women in Culture and Society* 18 (1): 1–43.

Glöss, Mareike, Moira McGregor, and Barry Brown. 2016. "Designing for Labour: Uber and the On-Demand Mobile Workforce." In *CHI'16: Proceedings of the 2016 CHI Conference On Human Factors in Computing Systems, San Jose, CA, May 2016*, 1632–43. New York: Association for Computing Machinery. https://doi.org/10.1145/2858036.2858476.

Glusac, Elaine. 2016. "As Airbnb Grows, So Do Claims of Discrimination." *The New York Times*, September 26, 2016. www.nytimes.com/2016/06/26/travel/airbnb-discrimination-lawsuit.html

Godin, Seth. 2011. "Reject the Tyranny of Being Picked: Pick Yourself." *Seth's Blog* (blog), March 21, 2011. https://seths.blog/2011/03/reject-the-tyranny-of-being-picked-pick-yourself/.

Golshan, Tara. 2019. "Bernie Sanders's Plan to Reshape Corporate America, Explained." *Vox*, October 14, 2019. www.vox.com/2019/10/14/20912221/bernie-sanders-corporate-accountability-ftc-merger-tax

Goodman, J. David, and Karen Weise. 2019. "Why the Amazon Deal Collapsed: A Tech Giant Stumbles in N.Y.'s Raucous Political Arena." *New York Times*, February 15, 2019. www.nytimes.com/2019/02/15/nyregion/amazon-hq2-nyc.html

Goods, Caleb, Alex Veen, and Tom Barratt. 2019. "'Is Your Gig Any Good?' Analysing Job Quality in the Australian Platform-Based Food-Delivery Sector." *Journal of Industrial Relations* 61 (4): 502–27. https://doi.org/10.1177/0022185618817069.

Graeber, David. 2002. "The New Anarchists." *New Left Review* 13 (1): 61–73.

Graham, Mark. 2013. "Geography/Internet: Ethereal Alternate Dimensions of Cyberspace or Grounded Augmented Realities?" *The Geographical Journal* 179 (2): 177–82. https://doi.org/10.1080/10462930500362445

Graham, Mark, Isis Hjorth, and Vili Lehdonvirta. 2017. "Digital Labour and Development: Impacts of Global Digital Labour Platforms and the Gig Economy on Worker Livelihoods." *Transfer: European Review of Labour and Research* 23 (2): 135–62. https://doi.org/10.1177/1024258916687250.

Gray, Mary L., and Siddharth Suri. 2019. *Ghost Work: How to Stop Silicon Valley From Building a New Global Underclass*. New York: Houghton Mifflin.

Green, Venus. 2001. *Race on the Line: Gender, Labor, and Technology in the Bell System, 1880–1980*. Durham, NC: Duke University Press.

Gregg, Melissa. 2009. "Learning to (Love) Labour: Production Cultures and the Affective Turn." *Communication and Critical/Cultural Studies* 6 (2): 209–14. https://doi.org/10.1080/14791420902868045.

———. 2011. *Work's Intimacy*. Cambridge: Polity Press.

———. 2018. *Counterproductive: Time Management in the Knowledge Economy*. Durham, NC: Duke University Press.

Gregg, Melissa, and Rutvica Andrijasevic. 2019. "Virtually Absent: The Gendered Histories and Economies of Digital Labour." *Feminist Review* 123 (1): 1–7.

Griswold, Alison. "Uber Drivers Make About as Much Money as Minimum Wage Workers." *Quartz*, May 16, 2018. https://qz.com/1278707/the-uber-economy-is-actually-just-the-low-wage-economy/.

Gupta, Monisha Das. 2006. *Unruly Immigrants: Rights, Activism, and Transnational South Asian Politics in the United States*. Durham, NC: Duke University Press.

Gutelius, Beth, and Theodore, Nik. 2017. "The Future of Work: Urban Economies in Transition." In *Jobs and the Labor Force of Tomorrow: Migration, Training, Education*, edited by Michael A. Pagano, 3–22. Urbana: University of Illinois Press.

Gutiérrez y Muhs, Gabriella, Yolanda Flores Niehmann, Carmen G. González, and Angela Harris, eds. 2012. *Presumed Incompetent: The Intersections of Race and Class for Women in Academia*. Boulder: University of Colorado Press.

Haber, Julian. 2018. *Gigonomics: A Field Guide for Freelancers in the Gig Economy*. Self-published, Kindle.

Hall, G. Brent, and Michael Leahy. 2008. *Open Source Approaches in Spatial Data Handling*. Berlin: Springer.

Hall, Jonathan V., and Alan B Krueger. 2016. *An Analysis of the Labor Market for Uber's Driver-Partners in the United States*. Cambridge, MA: National Bureau of Economic Research.

Hall, Stuart. 1986. "The Problem of Ideology: Marxism Without Guarantees" *Journal of Communication Inquiry* 10 (2): 28–44.

Hardt, Michael, and Antonio Negri. 2000. *Empire*. Cambridge, MA: Harvard University Press.
———. 2017. *Assembly*. Oxford: Oxford University Press.
Hartsman, Avery. "10 Ways Uber Drivers Can Get Kicked Off the App." *Business Insider*, July 23, 2017.
Harvey, David. 2006. "Value Production and Struggle in the Classroom: Teachers Within, Against and Beyond Capital." *Capital & Class* 30 (1): 1–32.
———. 2008. "The Right to the City." *New Left Review* 53: 23–40.
———. 2010. *The Enigma of Capital and the Crises of Capitalism*. London: Profile Books.
Hastings-King, Stephen. 2014. *Looking for the Proletariat*. Boston, MA: Brill.
Hatton, Erin. 2011. *The Temp Economy: From Kelly Girls to Permatemps in Postwar America*. Philadelphia: Temple University Press.
Hayes, Ryan. 2019. "Worker-Owned Apps Are Trying to Fix the Gig Economy's Exploitation." *Vice*, November 19, 2019. www.vice.com/en/article/pa75a8/worker-owned-apps-are-trying-to-fix-the-gig-economys-exploitation
Healy, Joshua, Daniel Nicholson, and Andreas Pekarek. 2017. "Should We Take the Gig Economy Seriously?" *Labor and Industry* 27 (3): 232–48.
Hearn, Alison. 2010. "Structuring Feeling: Web 2.0, Online Ranking and Rating, and the Digital 'Reputation' Economy." *Ephemera: Theory & Politics in Organization* 10 (3–4): 421–38.
Heeremans, Lieven. 2018. "Podcast Networks: Syndicating Production Culture." In *Podcasting: New Aural Cultures and Digital Media*, edited by Dario Llinares, Neil Fox, and Richard Berry, 57–79. London: Palgrave Macmillan.
Hernández, Antonia. 2019. "'There's Something Compelling About Real Life': Technologies of Security and Acceleration on Chaturbate." *Social Media & Society* 5 (4). https//doi.org/10.1177/2056305119894000.
Herrera, Lucero, et al. 2020. *Worker Ownership, COVID-19, and the Future of the Gig Economy*. Los Angles: UCLA Labor Center. www.labor.ucla.edu/wp-content/uploads/2020/10/UCLA_coop_report_Final-1.pdf
Hesmondhalgh, David. 2010. "User-Generated Content, Free Labour and the Cultural Industries." *Ephemera: Theory & Politics in Organization* 10 (3/4): 267–84.
Hess, Charlotte, and Elinor Ostrom. 2007. *Understanding Knowledge as a Commons: From Theory to Practice*. Cambridge, MA: MIT Press.
Hickey, Brian. 2015. "A Socialist Walmart Employee Explains Why He's Running for Philly Mayor." *WHYY*, August 31, 2015. https://whyy.org/articles/a-socialist-walmart-employee-explains-why-hes-running-for-philly-mayor/
Hicks, Marie. 2017. *Programmed Inequality: How Britain Discarded Women Technologists and Lost Its Edge in Computing*. 1st ed. Edited by William Aspray. Cambridge, MA: MIT Press.
Hießl, Christina. 2018. "Labour Law for TOS and HITs? Reflections on the Potential for Applying 'Labour Law Analogies' to Crowdworkers, Focusing on Employee Representation." *Work Organisation Labour & Globalisation* 12 (2): 38–59.
Hill, Steven. 2018. "Ridesharing vs. Public Transportation." *American Prospect*, March 27, 2018. http://prospect.org/article/ridesharing-versus-public-transit.
Hinsliff, Gaby. 2018. "The Gig Economy Can Be Changed after All—Thanks to Unions and Activists." *The Guardian*, March 27, 2018. www.theguardian.com/commentisfree/2018/mar/27/gig-economy-unions-activists-courier-dpd-precarious-employment
Hirschman, Albert. 2016. *Exit, Voice, and Loyalty: Responses to Decline in Firms, Organizations, and States*. Cambridge: Harvard University Press.
Hirsi, Ibrahim. 2019. "Meet Three Somali-American Women Fighting for Better Work Conditions at Amazon." *MPRNews*, July 15, 2019. www.mprnews.org/story/2019/07/15/meet-three-somaliamerican-women-fighting-for-better-work-conditions-at-amazon.

Hochschild, Arlie Russell. 1983. *The Managed Heart: Commercialization of Human Feeling*. Berkeley: University of California Press.

Hodges, Graham Russell. 2007. *Taxi!: A Social History of the New York City Cabdriver*. Baltimore: The Johns Hopkins University Press.

Holborn Gray, Hanna. 2011. *Searching for Utopia: Universities and Their Histories*. Berkeley: University of California Press.

Holder, Sarah. 2019. "For Ride-Hailing Drivers, Data Is Power." *CityLab*, August 22, 2019. www.citylab.com/transportation/2019/08/uber-drivers-lawsuit-personal-data-ride-hailing-gig-economy/594232/

Holley, Peter. 2018. "New Rules Guarantee Minimum Wage for NYC Uber, Lyft Drivers." *The Washington Post*, December 4, 2018. www.washingtonpost.com/technology/2018/12/04/new-rules-guarantee-minimum-wage-nyc-uber-lyft-drivers/?noredirect=on&utm_term=.e243e179e3cb.

Holling, Michelle A. 2018. "'You Intimidate Me' as a Microaggressive Controlling Image to Discipline Womyn of Color Faculty." *Southern Communication Journal* 84 (2): 99–112. https://doi.org/ 10.1080/1041794X.2018.1511748

Holman Jones, Selma. 2005. "Autoethnography: Making the Personal Political." In *Handbook of qualitative research*, edited by Norman K. Denzin and Yvonna S. Lincoln, 763–91. Thousand Oaks, CA: Sage.

Holtwell, Felix. 2018. "Bringing Back the Lucas Plan." *Socialist Project*, April 6, 2018. https://socialistproject.ca/2018/04/bringing-back-the-lucas-plan/.

Howard, Phillip N. 2015. *Pax Technica: How the Internet of Things May Set Us Free or Lock Us Up*. New Haven: Yale University Press.

Hua, Julietta, and Kasturi Ray. 2018. "Beyond the Precariat: Race, Gender, and Labor in the Taxi and Uber Economy." *Social Identities* 24 (2): 271–89. https://doi.org/10.1080/13504630.2017.1321721.

Hurst, Mark. 2007. *Bit Literacy: Productivity in the Age of Information and e-Mail Overload*. New York: Good Experience Press.

Huws, Ursula. 2014. *Labor in the Global Digital Economy: The Cybertariat Comes of Age*. New York: New York University Press.

———. 2019. *Labour in Contemporary Capitalism: Where Next?* London: Palgrave Macmillan.

Huws, Ursula, Neil H. Spencer, and Dag S. Syrdal. 2018. "Online, On Call: The Spread of Digitally Organised Just-in-Time Working and Its Implications for Standard Employment Models." *New Technology, Work and Employment* 32 (2): 113–29.

Huws, Ursula, Neil H. Spencer, Dag S. Syrdal, and Kaire Holts. 2017. *Work in the European Gig Economy: Research Results from the UK, Sweden, Germany, Austria, the Netherlands, Switzerland and Italy*. Brussels: Foundation for European Progressive Studies. www.feps-europe.eu/resources/publications/561:work-in-the-european-gig-economy-employment-in-the-era-of-online-platforms.html.

Hyman, Louis. 2018. *Temp: How American Work, American Business, and the American Dream Became Temporary*. New York: Viking.

Illouz, Eva. 2008. *Saving the Modern Soul: Therapy, Emotions, and the Culture of Self-Help*. Berkeley: University of California Press.

Independent Workers of Great Britain. 2016. "Citysprint Announce Pay Rise!" *IWGB*, February 12, 2016. https://iwgb.org.uk/post/5aa7026fe3f28/citysprint-announce-pay-rise

International Labour Organisation. 2015. *Indispensable yet Unprotected: Working Conditions of Indian Domestic Workers at Home and Abroad*. Geneva: ILO. www.ilo.org/global/topics/forced-labour/publications/WCMS_378058/lang-en/index.htm

Intuit and Emergent Research. "Dispatches from the New Economy: The On-Demand Workforce." January 28, 2016. www.slideshare.net/IntuitInc/dispatches-from-the-new-economy-the-ondemand-workforce-57613212.

Irani, Lilly C., and M. Silberman. 2013. "Turkopticon: Interrupting Worker Invisibility in Amazon Mechanical Turk." In *CHI'13: Proceedings Of The SIGCHI Conference On Human Factors In Computing Systems, Paris, France, April 2013*, 611–20. New York: ACM Digital Library. https://dl.acm.org/citation.cfm?id=2470742.

———. 2015. "Turkopticon: Interrupting Worker Invisibility in Amazon Mechanical Turk." UC San Diego. https://escholarship.org/uc/item/10c125z3.

Jacobs, Ken, and Michael Reich. 2020. "The Uber/Lyft Ballot Initiative Guarantees Only $5.64 an Hour." UC Berkeley Labor Center. https://laborcenter.berkeley.edu/the-uber-lyft-ballot-initiative-guarantees-only-5–64-an-hour-2/.

Jakobsson, Peter, and Fredrik Stiernstedt. 2010. "Googleplex and Informational Culture." In *Media Houses: Architecture, Media and the Production of Centrality*, edited by Staffan Ericson and Kristina Riegert, 113–37. New York: Peter Lang.

James, Owain. 2017. "Public and Private Transit: Better Together." The Eno Center for Transportation. www.enotrans.org/2017/07/public-private-transit-better-together/.

Jarzombek, Mark. 2016. *Digital Stockholm Syndrome in the Post-Ontological Age*. Minneapolis: University of Minnesota Press.

Jenkins, Henry. 2006. *Convergence Culture: Where Old and New Media Collide*. New York: New York University Press.

Jenkins, Henry, Sam Ford, and Joshua Green. 2013. *Spreadable Media: Creating Value and Meaning in a Networked Culture*. New York: New York University Press.

Jenson, Jennifer, and Suzanne De Castell. 2018. "'The Entrepreneurial Gamer': Regendering the Order of Play." *Games and Culture* 13 (7): 728–46.

Jeong, Sarah. 2019. "Selling Your Private Information Is a Terrible Idea." *The New York Times*, July 5, 2019. www.nytimes.com/2019/07/05/opinion/health-data-property-privacy.html

Johnston, Hannah. 2018. "Workplace Gains Beyond The Wagner Act: The New York Taxi Workers Alliance and Participation in Administrative Rulemaking." *Labor Studies Journal* 43 (2): 141–65.

Johnston, Hannah, and Chris Land-Kazlauskas. 2018. *Organizing On-Demand: Representation, Voice, and Collective Bargaining in the Gig Economy*. Conditions of Work and Employment Series, No. 94. Geneva: International Labour Office. www.ilo.org/travail/whatwedo/publications/WCMS_624286/lang-en/index.htm.

Jones, Angela. 2015. "Sex Work in a Digital Era." *Sociology Compass* 9 (7): 558–70.

———. 2020. *Camming: Money, Power, and Pleasure in the Sex Work Industry*. New York: New York University Press.

Jones, Meg Leta. 2016. *Ctrl Z: The Right to Be Forgotten*. New York: New York University Press.

Jørgensen, Marianne, and Louise Phillips. 2002. "Critical Discourse Analysis." In *Discourse Analysis as Theory and Method*, by Marianne Jørgensen and Louise Phillips, 60–95. London: Sage.

Kacher, Nicholas, and Stephan Weiler. 2017. "Inside the Rise of the Gig Economy." Regional Economic Development Institute, Colorado State University. https://redi.colostate.edu/wp-content/uploads/sites/50/2017/06/REDI-report-April-gig-economy.pdf

Kadakia, P. 2016. "Bai On Call: How Home Service Apps Are Changing Domestic Help Market." *Hindustan Times*, February 21, 2016. www.hindustantimes.com/

more-lifestyle/bai-on-call-how-home-service-apps-changing-the-maids-market/story-s6zz6kmWw1aEamZ1yLxjaL.html

Kafka, Peter. 2019. "Spotify Has Bought Two Podcast Startups and It Wants to Buy More." *Recode* (blog), February 6, 2019. www.recode.net/2019/2/6/18213456/spotify-podcast-gimlet-anchor-q4-results.

Kalanick, Travis. "Uber LA Officially Launched." *Uber Blog*, March 8, 2012. www.uber.com/blog/los-angeles/uber-la-officially-launched/

Kalleberg, Arne L. 2003. "Flexible Firms and Labor Market Segmentation: Effects of Workplace Restructuring on Jobs and Workers." *Work and Occupations* 30 (2): 154–75.

Kane, Kat. 2015. "The Big Hidden Problem With Uber? Insincere 5-Star Ratings." *Wired*, March 19, 2015. www.wired.com/2015/03/bogus-uber-reviews/.

Kapoor, Dip, and Aziz Choudry. 2010. *Learning From the Ground Up: Global Perspectives on Social Movements and Knowledge Production*. Berlin: Springer.

Katz, Lawrence F., and Alan B. Krueger. 2019. "Understanding Trends in Alternative Work Arrangements in the United States." *NBER Working Paper* 25425, National Bureau of Economic Research, January. www.nber.org/papers/w25425.pdf.

Kelley, Robin D. G. 1996. *Race Rebels: Culture, Politics, and the Black Working Class*. New York: Free Press.

Kelly, John. 2012. *Rethinking Industrial Relations: Mobilisation, Collectivism and Long Waves*. London: Routledge.

Kerr, William, and Carl Kreitzberg. 2019. "Google: To TVC or Not to TVC?" Harvard Business School Case 820–048. Harvard Business School, September 2019. www.hbs.edu/faculty/Pages/item.aspx?num=56878.

Kessler, Sarah. 2018. *Gigged: The End of the Job and the Future of Work*. New York: St. Martin's Press.

Kiang, Peter Nien-chu. 2008. "Crouching Activists, Hidden Scholars: Reflections on Research and Development With Students and Communities in Asian American Studies." In *Engaging Contradictions: Theory, Politics, and Methods of Activist scholarship*, edited by Charles R. Hale, 299–318. Berkeley: University of California Press.

Kim, Tae Wan, and Kevin Werbach. 2016. "More than Just a Game: Ethical Issues in Gamification." *Ethics and Information Technology* 18 (2): 157–73.

Kline, Stephen, Nick Dyer-Witheford, and Greig De Peuter. 2014. *Digital Play*. Montréal: McGill-Queen's University Press.

Kneese, Tamara and Michael Palm. 2020. "Brick-and-Platform: Listing Labor in the Digital Vintage Economy." *Social Media + Society*. https://doi.org/10.1177/2056305120933299.

Kollowe, Julia, and Nicola Slawson. 2017. "McDonald's Workers to Go on Strike in Britain for First Time." *The Guardian*, September 4, 2017. www.theguardian.com/business/2017/sep/04/mcdonalds-workers-strike-cambridge-crayford

KPMG for Ministry of Skill Development and Entrepreneurship. n.d. *Human Resources and Skill Requirements in the Domestic Help Sector (2013–17, 2017–22)*. New Delhi: National Skill Development Corporation. www.ugc.ac.in/skill/SectorReport/Domestic%20Help.pdf

Krause, Monika, Mary Nolan, Michael Palm, and Andrew Ross. 2008. *The University Against Itself: The NYU Strike and the Future of the Academic Workplace*. Philadelphia: Temple University Press.

Kücklich, Julian. 2005. "Precarious Playbour: Modders and the Digital Games Industry." *Fibreculture Journal* 5.

Kuehn, Kathleen, and Thomas F. Corrigan. 2013. "Hope Labor: the Role of Employment Prospects in Online Social Production." *The Political Economy of Communication* 1 (1): 9–25. www.polecom.org/index.php/polecom/article/view/9/64

Kuiper, Dick. 2018. *Gig Economy: The Good, The Bad and the Ugly*. Self-published, Kindle.
Kumanyika, Chenjerai. 2020. "The Instacart Strike and Gig work during the COVID-19 Pandemic." *Soundcloud.com*. Accessed November 27, 2020. https://soundcloud.com/chenjeraikumanyika/instacart-strike
Kumar, Deepa. 2008. *Outside the Box: Corporate Media, Globalization, and the UPS Strike*. Urbana: University of Illinois Press.
Labour Bureau, Ministry of Labour & Employment. 2016. *Report on Fifth Annual Employment-Unemployment Survey (2015–16), Volume I*. Chandigarh: Labour Bureau. http://labourbureaunew.gov.in/UserContent/EUS_5th_1.pdf
Labournet TV. 2018. "Riders Across Europe Unite to Form the Transnational Federation of Couriers." https://en.labournet.tv/riders-across-europe-unite-form-transnational-federation-couriers.
Laclau, Ernesto and Chantal Mouffe. 1985. *Hegemony and Socialist Strategy*. London: Verso.
Laloux, Frederic. 2014. *Reinventing Organizations: A Guide to Creating Organizations Inspired by the Next Stage in Human Consciousness*. Brussels: Nelson Parker.
Larson, Magali S. 1977. *The Rise of Professionalism: A Sociological Analysis*. Berkeley: University of California Press.
Lazzarato, Maurizio. 2006. "Immaterial Labor." In *Radical Thought in Italy*, edited by Paolo Virno and Michael Hardy, 133–47. New ed. Theory Out of Bounds, Vol. 7. University of Minnesota Press.
———. 2012. *The Making of the Indebted Man: An Essay on the Neoliberal Condition*. Translated by Joshua David Jordan. Los Angeles, CA: Semiotext(e).
Leadbeater, Charles, and Paul Miller. 2004. *The Pro-Am Revolution: How Enthusiasts Are Changing Our Economy and Society*. London: Demos. www.demos.co.uk/publications/proameconomy.
Lederman, Doug. 2018. "Who is Studying Online." *insidehighered.com*. Accessed July 5, 2019. www.insidehighered.com/digital-learning/article/2018/01/05/new-us-data-show-continued-growth-college-students-studying
Lee, Jaesub, and Amy L. Varon. 2020. "Employee Exit, Voice, Loyalty, and Neglect in Response to Dissatisfying Organizational Situations: It Depends on Supervisory Relationship Quality." *International Journal of Business Communication* 57 (1): 30–51.
Lee, JongHwa, and Seth Kahn. 2019. *Activism and Rhetoric: Theories and Contexts for Political Engagement*. 2nd ed. New York: Routledge.
Lekach, Sasha. 2020. "Gig Workers to Companies after BLM Statements: 'Prove It'." *Mashable*, June 18, 2020. https://mashable.com/article/blm-gig-workers-open-letter.
Lenaerts, Karolien, Zachary Kilhoffer, and Mehtap Akgüç. 2018. "Traditional and New Forms of Organisation and Representation in the Platform Economy." *Work Organisation, Labour and Globalisation* 12 (2): 60–78.
Leonardi, D., Annalisa Murgia, M. Briziarelli, and Emiliano Armano. 2019. "The Ambivalence of Logistical Connectivity: A Co-research With Foodora Riders." *Work Organisation Labour & Globalisation* 13 (1): 155–71.
Levine, Peter. 2007. "Collective Action, Civic Engagement, and the Knowledge Commons." In *Understanding Knowledge as a Commons: From Theory to Practice*, edited by Charlotte Hess and Elinor Ostrom, 247–76. Cambridge: MIT Press.
Lina, Dencik and Peter Wilken. 2015. *Worker Resistance and Media: Challenging Global Corporate Power in the 21st Century*. New York: Peter Lang.
Lobato, Ramon, and Julian Thomas. 2015. *The Informal Media Economy*. 1st ed. Cambridge and Malden, MA: Polity Press.

Lobato, Ramon, Julian Thomas, and Dan Hunter. 2012. "Histories of User-Generated Content: Between Formal and Informal Media Economies." In *Amateur Media: Social, Cultural and Legal Perspectives*, edited by Dan Hunter, Ramon Lobato, Megan Richardson, and Julian Thomas, 3–17. New York: Routledge.

Lobel, Orly. 2017. "The Gig Economy & the Future of Employment and Labor Law." *University of San Francisco Law Review* 51 (1): 51–74.

Loh, Dylan. 2020. "Gig Economy Workers Fall on Hard Times in Singapore and Australia." *Nikkei Asian Review*, April 8, 2020. https://asia.nikkei.com/Economy/Gig-economy-workers-fall-on-hard-times-in-Singapore-and-Australia2

Lopdrup-Hjorth, Thomas, Marius Gudmand-Høyer, Pia Bramming, and Michael Pedersen. 2011. "Governing Work Through Self-Management." *Ephemera: Theory & Politics in Organization* 11 (2): 97–104.

Lorde, Audre. 2007. "The Master's Tools Will Never Dismantle the Master's House." In *Sister Outsider: Essays and Speeches*, 112. Berkeley: Crossing Press.

Lorenz, Chris. 2013. "If You're So Smart, Why Are You Under Surveillance? Universities, Neoliberalism, and New Public Management." *Critical Inquiry* 38 (3): 599–629.

Lorey, Isabelle. 2015. *State of Insecurity. Government of the Precarious*. Translated by A. Derieg. New York: Verso.

Los Angeles Alliance for a New Economy. 2015. "Airbnb, Rising Rent and the Housing Crisis in Los Angeles." March 2015. Accessed November, 27, 2020. www.laane.org/wp-content/uploads/2015/03/AirBnB-Final.pdf

Los Angeles Metropolitan Transit Authority. 2017. "On Board Survey Results Trend Report." http://media.metro.net/projects_studies/research/images/infographics/2017_fall_onboard_survey_results.pdf.

Lucas, Lisa. 2006. *The Research Game in Academic Life*. Maidenhead: McGraw-Hill International.

Lyft. 2018a. "Lyft Help Center." Accessed May 15, 2018. https://help.lyft.com/hc/en-us/articles/115013080008-How-and-when-driver-pay-is-calculated#calculations.

———. 2018b. "Lyft Terms of Service." Accessed May 18, 2018. www.lyft.com/terms.

Lynd, Staughton. 2015. *Solidarity Unionism: Rebuilding the Labor Movement From Below*. Oakland: PM Press.

Mac, Juno, and Molly Smith. 2018. *Revolting Prostitutes: The Fight for Sex Workers' Rights*. London: Verso.

MacDonald, Robert, and Giazitzoglu, Andreas. 2019. "Youth, Enterprise and Precarity: Or, What Is, and What Is Wrong With, the 'Gig Economy'?" *Journal of Sociology* 1–17. https://doi.org/10.1177/1440783319837604

Macek, Steve. 2006. "From the Weapon of Criticism to Criticism by Weapons: Critical Communication Scholarship, Marxism, and Political Activism." In *Marxism and Communication Studies: The Point is to Change it*, edited by Lee Artz, Steve Macek, and Dana Cloud, 217–42 New York: Peter Lang.

Magnacca, Mark, and gigCMO Team. 2018. *The Gig Economy: Things You Should Know to Make Your Business Grow*. gigCMO. Kindle.

Maher, John. 2018. "Audiobook Revenue Jumped 22.7% in 2018." *Publishers Weekly*, June 21, 2018. www.publishersweekly.com/pw/by-topic/industry-news/audiobooks/article/77303-audiobook-revenue-jumped-22-7-in-2018.html.

Mallet, Serge. 1975. *The New Working Class*. Nottingham: Spokesman Books.

Maloney, Jennifer. 2016. "The Fastest-Growing Format in Publishing: Audiobooks." *Wall Street Journal*, July 21, 2016. www.wsj.com/articles/the-fastest-growing-format-in-publishing-audiobooks-1469139910.

Marazzi, Christian. 2001. *Capital and Language*. Cambridge, MA: MIT Press.
———. 2015. *Diario della crisi infinita*. Verona: Ombrecorte.
Markman, Kris M. 2012. "Doing Radio, Making Friends, and Having Fun: Exploring the Motivations of Independent Audio Podcasters." *New Media & Society* 14 (4): 547–65. https://doi.org/10.1177/1461444811420848.
Marotta, A. 2018. "Struggle at UberEats: Reflections on October 4th." *Notes from Below*. https://notesfrombelow.org/article/couriers-struggle-and-iww-reflections-october-4th
Martin, Chris J., Paul Upham, and Leslie Budd. 2015. "Commercial Orientation in Grassroots Social Innovation: Insights from the Sharing Economy." *Ecological Economics* 118: 240–51. https://doi.org/10.1016/j.ecolecon.2015.08.001.
Martin, Randy, ed. 1998. *Chalk Lines: The Politics of Work in the Managed University*. Durham, NC: Duke University Press.
Marx, Karl. 1867. *Capital, Volume I*. Moscow: Progress Publishers. www.marxists.org/archive/marx/works/1867-c1/ch10.htm
———. 1875. "Critique of the Gotha Programme." Marxists Internet Archive. Accessed April 29, 2020. www.marxists.org/archive/marx/works/1875/gotha/
———. 1880. "A Workers' Inquiry." Marxists Internet Archive. www.marxists.org/archive/marx/works/1880/04/20.htm
Massey, Doreen. 2007. *World City*. Cambridge: Polity Press.
Mathew, Biju. 2008. *Taxi! Cabs and Capitalism in New York City*. Ithaca: ILR Press.
Matthew, Zoie. "If You Make Money Through an App, You Might Want to Pay Attention to This Bill." *Los Angeles Magazine*, June 6, 2019. www.lamag.com/citythinkblog/ab-5-freelancers-bill/
Matthews, Derek. 1991. "1889 and All That: New Views on the New Unionism." *International Review of Social History* 36 (1): 24–58.
Matthews, Dylan. 2017. "Europe Could Have The Secret to Saving American Unions." *Vox.com*. Accessed July 5, 2019. www.vox.com/policy-and-politics/2017/4/17/15290674/union-labor-movement-europe-bargaining-fight-15-ghent
Mayer-Schonberger, Viktor and Thomas Ramge. 2018. "The Big Choice for Big Tech: Share Data or Suffer the Consequences." *Foreign Affairs* 97 (5): 48–54.
McConnell, Kathleen. 2018. "Labored Speech: Reconsidering How Communication Studies Works." *Review of Communication* 18 (2): 67–84. https://doi.org/10.1080/15358593.2018.
McGonigal, Jane. 2011. *Reality Is Broken: Why Games Make Us Better and How They Can Change the World*. New York: Penguin Press.
McGovern, Marion. 2017. *Thriving in the Gig Economy: How to Capitalize and Compete in the New World of Work*. Wayne, NJ: Career Press. Kindle.
McKercher, Catherine, and Mosco Vincent. 2007. *Knowledge Workers in the Information Society*. Lanham: Lexington Books.
McNulty, Jennifer. 2020. "Already Vulnerable, Gig Economy Workers in San Francisco Suffer During Coronavirus Pandemic, Survey Reveals." *University of California News*, May 7, 2020. www.universityofcalifornia.edu/news/already-vulnerable-gig-economy-workers-san-francisco-suffer-during-coronavirus-pandemic-survey.
McRobbie, Angela. 2016. *Be Creative: Making a Living in the New Creative Industries*. Cambridge: Polity Press.
Meister, Jeanne. 2019. "The Future of Work: The Rise of Workers Who Self Automate Their Jobs." *Forbes*, May 7, 2019. www.forbes.com/sites/jeannemeister/2019/05/07/the-future-of-work-the-rise-of-workers-who-self-automate-their-jobs/#443c0923c23a.
Milkman, Ruth, and Ed Ott. 2014. *New Labor in New York: Precarious Workers and the Future of the Labor Movement*. Ithaca: Cornell University Press.

Miller-Young, Mireille. 2014. *A Taste for Brown Sugar: Black Women in Pornography*. Durham, NC: Duke University Press.

Millot, Jim. 2018. "For Publishers, 2018 Is Off to a Decent Start." *Publishers Weekly*, May 18, 2018. www.publishersweekly.com/pw/by-topic/industry-news/publisher-news/article/76924-for-publishers-2018-is-off-to-a-decent-start.html.

Mills, Stan. 2018. "Glasgow Couriers Strike Against Pay Cuts." *Notes from Below*. https://notesfrombelow.org/article/glasgow-couriers-strike

Mishel, Lawrence. 2018. "Uber and the Labor Market: Uber Drivers' Compensation, Wages, and the Scale of Uber and the Gig Economy." Economic Policy Institute, May 15, 2018. www.epi.org/files/pdf/145552.pdf.

Mizrahi, Olga. 2018. *The Gig Is Up: Thrive in the Gig Economy, Where Old Jobs Are Obsolete and Freelancing Is the Future*. Austin, TX: Greenleaf Book Group Press. Kindle.

Molla, Rani. 2017. "What Contract Tech Workers Get Paid in Cities Around the Country." *Recode*. www.vox.com/2017/9/27/16369664/contract-contractors-freelance-fulltime-salary-paid-tech-workers.

Mollick, Ethan R., and Nancy Rothbard. 2014. *Mandatory Fun: Consent, Gamification and the Impact of Games at Work*. Wharton School Research Paper Series. Philadelphia, PA: University of Pennsylvania.

Moody, Alison. 2019. "Labour and the Contradictory Logic of Logistics." *Work Organisation, Labour & Globalisation* 13 (1): 79–95.

Moore, Phoebe V., Pav Akhtar, and Martin Upchurch. 2017. "Digitalisation of Work and Resistance." In *Humans and Machines at Work: Monitoring, Surveillance and Automation in Contemporary Capitalism*, edited by Phoebe Moore, Martin Upchurch and Xanthe Whittaker, 17–44. London: Palgrave Macmillan.

Moorman, Evan. 2016. "A More Fair Sharing Economy: Ensure Equal Access to Uber and Lyft." UCLA Institute of Transportation Studies. www.its.ucla.edu/wp-content/uploads/sites/6/2016/12/PB_TNC_EQUITY_FINAL.pdf.

Möring, Sebastian, and Olli Leino. 2016. "Beyond Games as Political Education—Neo-Liberalism in the Contemporary Computer Game Form." *Journal of Gaming & Virtual Worlds* 8 (2): 145–61.

Morozov, Evgeny. 2015. "Socialize the Data Centres!" *New Left Review* 91: 45–66.

Morris, Eric A. 2009. "Cash and Cabbies." *Freakonomics*. http://freakonomics.com/2009/10/29/cash-and-cabbies/

Morschheuser, Benedikt, and Juho Hamari. 2019. "The Gamification of Work: Lessons From Crowdsourcing." *Journal of Management Inquiry* 28 (2): 145–48.

Mosco, Vincent. 2004. *The Digital Sublime: Myth, Power and Cyberspace*. Cambridge, MA: MIT Press.

Mounk, Yascha. 2018. *The People vs. Democracy: Why Our Freedom is in Danger and How to Save it*. Cambridge, MA: Harvard University Press.

Mountz, Alison, Anne Bonds, Becky Mansfield, Jenna Loyd, Jennifer Hyndman, Margaret Walton-Roberts, Ranu Basu, Risa Whitson, Roberta Hawkins, Trina Hamilton, and Winifred Curran. 2015. "For Slow Scholarship: A Feminist Politics of Resistance Through Collective Action in the Neoliberal University." *ACME: An International Journal for Critical Geographies* 14 (4): 1235–59. Accessed July 5, 2019. www.acme-journal.org/index.php/acme/article/view/1058.

Mulcahy, Diane. 2016. *The Gig Economy: The Complete Guide to Getting Better Work, Taking More Time Off, and Financing the Life You Want!* New York: AMACOM. Kindle.

Muldoon, James. 2018. "Council Democracy: Towards a Democratic Socialist Politics." In *Council Democracy: Towards a Democratic Socialist Politics*, edited by James Muldoon, 1–30. London: Routledge.

Munn, Luke. 2017. "I am a Driver-Partner." *Work Organisation, Labour & Globalisation* 11 (2): 7–20.

Muntaner, Carles. 2018. "Digital Platforms, Gig Economy, Precarious Employment, and the Invisible Hand of Social Class." *International Journal of Health Services* 48 (4): 597–600. https://doi.org/10.1177/0020731418801413.

Nayar, Kavita Ilona. 2017. "Working It: The Professionalization of Amateurism in Digital Adult Entertainment." *Feminist Media Studies* 17 (3): 473–88.

Neetha, N. 2008. *Regulating Domestic Work*. Mumbai: Economic and Political Weekly.

Neff, Gina. 2012. *Venture Labor: Work and the Burden of Risk in Innovative Industries*. Cambridge, MA: MIT Press.

Negrón-Muntaner, Frances. 2014. *The Latino Media Gap: A Report on the State of Latinos in U.S. Media*. The Center for the Study of Ethnicity and Race, Columbia University. https://asit-prod-web1.cc.columbia.edu/cser/wp-content/uploads/sites/70/2020/03/Latino-Gap.pdf.

Nehring, Daniel, Emmanuel Alvarado, Eric C. Hendriks, and Dylan Kerrigan. 2016. *Transnational Popular Psychology and the Global Self-Help Industry: The Politics of Contemporary Social Change*. London: Palgrave Macmillan.

Neilson, Brett, and Rossiter, Ned. 2005. "From Precarity to Precariousness and Back Again: Labour, Life and Unstable Networks." *Fibreculture Journal* 5.

Nelson, Kurt. 2020. "I'm a Software Engineer at Uber and I'm Voting against Prop 22." *TechCrunch*, October 6, 2020. https://techcrunch.com/2020/10/06/im-a-software-engineer-at-uber-im-voting-against-prop-22/

Nelson, Laura J. 2016. "Uber and Lyft Have Devastated L.A.'s Taxi Industry, City Records Show." *Los Angeles Times*, April 14, 2016. www.latimes.com/local/lanow/la-me-ln-uber-lyft-taxis-la-20160413-story.html

———. 2018. "Southern Californians are on a Car-buying Spree, and That's Cutting Deeply into Transit Ridership, Study Says." *Los Angeles Times*, February 1, 2018. www.latimes.com/local/lanow/la-me-ln-transit-car-ownership-20180201-story.html

———. 2019. "L.A. is Hemorrhaging Bus Riders—Worsening Traffic and Hurting Climate Goals." *Los Angeles Times*, June 27, 2019. www.latimes.com/local/lanow/la-me-ln-bus-ridership-falling-los-angeles-la-metro-20190627-story.html

Nelson, Mark J. 2012. "Soviet and American Precursors to the Gamification of Work." In *Mind Trek'12: Proceeding of the 16th International Academic MindTrek Conference, Tampere, Finland*, 23–26. New York: Association for Computing Machinery.

Neuman, Scott. 2020. "Essential Workers Plan May Day Strikes; Others Demand End To COVID-19 Lockdowns." *NPR.org*, May 1, 2020. www.npr.org/sections/coronavirus-live-updates/2020/05/01/848931228/essential-workers-plan-may-day-strikes-others-demand-end-to-covid-19-lockdowns.

New Faculty Majority. n.d. "Facts About Adjuncts." www.newfacultymajority.info/facts-about-adjuncts/.

Newlands, Gemma, Christoph Lutz, and Christian Fieseler. 2018. "Collective Action and Provider Classification in the Sharing Economy." *New Technology, Work and Employment* 33 (3): 250–67.

NFIB. 2019. "Limiting the Damage of California's Dynamex Decision." *NFIB*, January 18, 2019. www.nfib.com/content/legal-blog/labor/limiting-the-damage-of-californias-dynamex-decision/

Nichols, Randy. 2013. "Bourdieu's Forms of Capital and Video Game Production." In *The Game Culture Reader*, edited by Jason C. Thompson and Marc A. Ouellette, 30–46. Newcastle-upon-Tyne: Cambridge Scholars Publishing.

———. 2014. *The Video Game Business (International Screen Industries)*. New York: Palgrave Macmillan on behalf of the British Film Institute.

Noble, Safiya Umoja. 2018. *Algorithms of Oppression: How Search Engines Reinforce Racism*. New York: New York University Press.

Notes from Below. 2018. "The Workers' Inquiry and Social Composition." *Notes from Below* 1, January 29, 2018. www.notesfrombelow.org/article/workers-inquiry-and-social-composition

Nylund, Mats. 2017. "Jakamistalous ja työelämä [The Sharing Economy and the Working Life]." In *Jakamistalous [The Sharing Economy]*, edited by Minna-Maari Harmaala, Tuija Toivola, Maija Faehnle, Petri Manninen, Pasi Mäenpää, and Mats Nylund. Helsinki: Alma Talent.

O'Donnell, Casey. 2014. "Getting Played: Gamification and the Rise of Algorithmic Surveillance." *Surveillance & Society* 12 (3): 349–59.

Office Snapshots. n.d. "The Googleplex and the Rise of the Corporate University Campus." https://officesnapshots.com/articles/the-googleplex-and-the-rise-of-the-corporate-university-campus/

Ongweso, Jr., Edward. 2019. "We Really Don't Need Uber." *Vice*, December 12, 2019. www.vice.com/en/article/y3mm5x/we-really-dont-need-uber

Oppong, Thomas. 2018. *Working in the Gig Economy: How to Thrive and Succeed When You Choose to Work for Yourself*. London: Kogan Page Limited. Kindle.

Orenstein, Natalie. 2018. "Workers at UC Berkeley, Other Campuses Launch 3-Day Strike." *Berkeleyside*, May 7, 2018. www.berkeleyside.com/2018/05/07/workers-at-uc-berkeley-other-campuses-launch-3-day-strike.

O'Shea, Lizzie. 2017. "Tech Capitalists Won't Fix the World's Problems—Their Unionised Workforce Might." *The Guardian*, November 24, 2017. www.theguardian.com/commentisfree/2017/nov/24/technology-capitalists-unionised-workforce-tech-sector

Paasonen, Susanna. 2010. "Labors of Love: Netporn, Web 2.0 and the Meanings of Amateurism." *New Media & Society* 12 (8): 1297–312. https://doi.org/10.1177/1461444810362853.

Pager, Tyler, and Emily Palmer. 2018. "Uber Driver's Death Marks Seventh For-Hire Driver Suicide Within a Year." *The New York Times*, October 7, 2018. www.nytimes.com/2018/10/07/nyregion/uber-driver-suicide-for-hire-taxis-new-york.html

Park, John. 2016. "Trade Unions Must Adapt To The Gig Economy In Order To Survive." *New Statesman*, July 28, 2016. www.newstatesman.com/politics/staggers/2016/07/trade-unions-must-adapt-gig-economy-order-survive

Parsons, Talcott. 1951. *The Social System*. New York: Free Press.

Pearce, Celia. 2006. "Productive Play." *Games and Culture* 1 (1): 17–24.

Pellow, David N., and Lisa S. Park. 2002. *The Silicon Valley of Dreams: Environmental Injustice, Immigrant Workers, and the High-Tech Global Economy*. New York: New York University Press.

Pereira, Pedro, Emília Duarte, Francisco Rebelo, and Paulo Noriega. 2014. "A Review of Gamification for Health-Related Contexts." In *Design, User Experience, and Usability. User Experience Design for Diverse Interaction Platforms and Environment. Third International Conference, DUXU 2014, Held as Part of HCI International, Heraklion, Crete, Greece, June 22–27, 2014, Proceedings, Part II*, edited by Aaron Marcus, 742–53. Lecture Notes in Computer Science, vol. 8518. Cham, Switzerland: Springer.

Perlberg, Steven. 2016. "E.W. Scripps Buys Podcast Company Stitcher." *Wall Street Journal*, June 6, 2016, sec. Business. www.wsj.com/articles/e-w-scripps-buys-podcast-company-stitcher-1465239600.

Peters, Tom. 1992. *Liberation Management: Necessary Disorganization for the Nanosecond Nineties*. New York: Alfred A. Knopf.
Pine, B. Joseph., and James H. Gilmore. 2011. *The Experience Economy*. Updated ed. Brighton, MA: Harvard Business Review Press.
Pink, Daniel H. 2001. *Free Agent Nation: How America's New Independent Workers are Transforming the Way we Live*. New York: Warner Books.
Piore, Michael J., and Charles F. Sabel. 1984. *The Second Industrial Divide: Possibilities for Prosperity*. New York: Basic Books.
Poulantzas, Nicos. 2018. *Fascism and Dictatorship: The Third International and the Problem of Fascism*. New York: Verso Books.
Powell, Catherine. 2020. "Color of COVID: The Racial Justice Paradox of Our Emerging Stay-at-Home Economy." *CNN*, April 18, 2020. www.cnn.com/2020/04/10/opinions/covid-19-people-of-color-labor-market-disparities-powell/index.html.
Prassl, Jeremias. 2018. *Humans as a Service: The Promise and Perils of Work in the Gig Economy*. Oxford: Oxford University Press.
Prassl, Jeremias, and Martin Risak. 2015. "Uber, Taskrabbit, and Co.: Platforms as Employers—Rethinking the Legal Analysis of Crowdwork." *Comparative Labor Law & Policy Journal* 37: 619.
Pressly, Linda. 2017. "Cam-Girls: Inside the Romanian Sexcam Industry." *BBC*, August 10, 2017. www.bbc.com/news/magazine-40829230
Prokop, Andrew. 2018. "Michael Cohen's Taxi Business Partner Just Agreed to Cooperate With Investigators." *Vox*, May 22, 2018. www.vox.com/2018/5/22/17382138/michael-cohen-evgeny-freidman-taxi-king
PT Editors. 2011. "Keeping Up With the New Demand for Audiobooks—Publishing Trends." *Publishing Trends*, August 1, 2011. www.publishingtrends.com/2011/08/keeping-up-with-the-new-demand-for-audiobooks-2/.
Quintana, Alvina E. 2003. "Book Review *The Decolonial Imaginary: Writing Chicanas Into History*. By Emma Pérez. Bloomington and Indianapolis: Indiana University Press, 1999. *Speaking Chicana: Voice, Power, and Identity*. Edited by D. Letticia Galindo and María Dolores Gonzales. Tucson: University of Arizona Press, 1999. *Feminism on the Border: Chicana Gender Politics and Literature*. By Sonia Saldívar-Hull. Berkeley: University of California Press, 2000." *Signs: Journal of Women in Culture and Society* 28 (2): 724–28. https://doi.org/10.1086/342586.
Rand, Helen. 2019. "Challenging the Invisibility of Sex Work in Digital Labour Politics." *Feminist Review* 123 (1): 40–55.
Rapanta, Chrisy, Luca Botturi, Peter Goodyear, et al. 2020. "Online University Teaching During and After the Covid-19 Crisis: Refocusing Teacher Presence and Learning Activity." *Postdigital Science Education* 2: 923–45. https://doi.org/10.1007/s42438-020-00155-y.
Rebel Roo. 2018. "Rebel Roo Bulletin." *Notes from Below*. https://notesfrombelow.org/article/rebel-roo-bulletin
Reich, Robert. 2015. "The Share-the-Scraps Economy." February 2, 2015. http://robertreich.org/post/109894095095.
Research and Markets. 2016. "Global Gamification Market Value of USD 11.10 Billion by 2020 — Analysis, Trends & Opportunities Report 2016–2020—Key Vendors: Leveleleven, Arcaris Inc & Badgeville Inc." *PR Newswire*, February 19, 2016. www.prnewswire.com/news-releases/global-gamification-market-value-of-usd-1110-billion-by-2020-analysis-trends-opportunities-report-2016-2020-key-vendors-leveleleven-arcaris-inc-badgeville-inc-300222904.html

Reuters Staff. 2018. "Amazon Workers Strike in Germany, Joining Action in Spain And Poland." *Reuters Business News*, July 16, 2018. www.reuters.com/article/us-amazon-com-germany-strike/amazon-workers-strike-in-germany-joining-action-in-spain-and-poland-idUSKBN1K61OY.

Reyes, Emily Alpert. "At L.A. City Hall, It's the Visionary vs. the Lawmakers." *Los Angeles Times*, August 18, 2015. www.latimes.com/local/california/la-me-adv-sharing-economy-20150818-story.html.

Rhoades, Gary, and Sheyla Slaughter. 2004. *Academic Capitalism And The New Economy: Markets, State, And Higher Education*. Baltimore: JHU Press.

Rimke, Heidi Marie. 2000. "Governing Citizens Through Self-Help Literature." *Cultural Studies* 14 (1): 61–78. https://doi.org/10.1080/095023800334986.

Ritzer, George. 2004. *The McDonaldization of Society*. Thousand Oaks, CA: Pine Forge Press.

Rivero, Yeidy M. 2009. "Havana as a 1940s-1950s Latin American Media Capital." *Critical Studies in Media Communication* 26 (3): 275–93. https://doi.org/10.1080/15295030903015070.

Roberts, Sarah T. 2019. *Behind the Screen: Content Moderation in the Shadows of Social Media*. New Haven: Yale University Press.

Robertson, Brian J. 2015. *Holacracy: The New Management System for a Rapidly Changing World*. New York: Henry Holt and Co.

Rodino-Colocino, Michelle. 2006. "Laboring Under the Digital Divide." *New Media & Society* 8 (3): 487–511.

———. 2008. "Technomadic Work: From Promotional Vision to WashTech's Opposition." *Work Organization, Labour and Globalization* 2 (1): 104–16.

———. 2012. "Participant Activism: Exploring a Methodology for Scholar-activists through Lessons Learned as a Precarious Labor Organizer." *Communication, Culture & Critique* 5 (4): 541–62.

———. 2016. "Communication Activism| Critical-Cultural Communication Activism Research Calls for Academic Solidarity." *International Journal of Communication* 10: 10.

———. 2019a. "Uber Drivers Report 80-Plus Hour Workweeks and a Lot of Waiting." *The Conversation*, April 29, 2019. http://theconversation.com/uber-drivers-report-80-plus-hour-workweeks-and-a-lot-of-waiting-115782

———. 2019b. "Uber's $9 Billion IPO Rests on Drivers' 80-Plus Hour Workweeks and a Lot of Waiting." *Salon*, April 30, 2019. www.salon.com/2019/04/30/ubers-9-billion-ipo-rests-on-drivers-80-plus-hour-workweeks-and-a-lot-of-waiting_partner/

Roediger, David R., and Elizabeth D. Esch. 2012. *The Production of Difference: Race and the Management of Labor in US History*. Oxford: Oxford University Press.

Roediger, David R., and Philip Sheldon Foner. 1989. *Our own time: A History of American Labor and the Working Day*. New York: Verso.

Rogers, Brishen. 2015. "The Social Costs of Uber." *University of Chicago Law Review Dialogue* 82 (1) Art. 6: 98. https://lawreview.uchicago.edu/page/social-costs-uber.

Roggero, Gigi. 2009. *La produzione del sapere vivo. Crisi dell'università e trasformazione del lavoro tra le due sponde dell'Atlantico*. Verona: Ombrecorte.

Rosaldo, Renato. 1994. "Cultural Citizenship in San Jose, California." *PoLAR: Political and Legal Anthropology Review* 17 (2): 57–64.

Rose, Nikolas. 1992. "Governing the Enterprising Self." In *The Values of the Enterprise Culture: The Moral Debate*, edited by Paul Heelas and Paul Morris, 141–64. London: Routledge.

Rosenblat, Alex. 2018. *Uberland: How Algorithms Are Rewriting the Rules of Work*. Berkeley: University of California Press.

Rosenblat, Alex, and Luke Stark. 2016. "Algorithmic Labor and Information Asymmetries: A Case Study of Uber's Drivers." *International Journal of Communication* 10 (27): 3758–84.

Rosenfeld, Jake, and Kleykamp, Meredith. 2012. "Organized Labor and Racial Wage Inequality in the United States." *AJS: American Journal Of Sociology* 117 (5): 1460–502.

Ross, Andrew. 2000. "The Mental Labor Problem." *Social Text* 18 (2): 1–31.

———. 2004. *No-Collar: The Humane Workplace and Its Hidden Costs*. Paperback ed. Philadelphia, PA: Temple University Press.

———. 2009. *Nice Work If You Can Get It: Life and Labor in Precarious Times*. 1st ed. New York: New York University Press. https://muse.jhu.edu/book/10930.

Rubin, Gayle. 1984. "Thinking Sex: Notes for a Radical Theory of the Politics of Sexuality." In *Pleasure and Danger: Exploring Female Sexuality*, edited by Carole S. Vance, 276–319. Boston, MA: Routledge.

Ruggill, Judd, Ken McAllister, Randy Nichols, and Ryan Kaufman. 2016. *Inside the Video Game Industry*. London: Taylor and Francis.

Rushkoff, Douglas. 2016. *Throwing Rocks at the Google Bus: How Growth Became the Enemy of Prosperity*. New York: Portfolio.

Ryzik, Melena. "How Uber Is Changing Night Life in Los Angeles." *The New York Times*, December 21, 2017. www.nytimes.com/2014/11/02/fashion/how-uber-is-changing-night-life-in-los-angeles.html.

Sabeel Rahman, K., and Kathleen Thelen. 2019. "The Rise of the Platform Business Model and the Transformation of Twenty-First-Century Capitalism." *Politics & Society* 47 (2): 1–28. https://doi.org/10.1177/0032329219838932

SAG-AFTRA. n.d. "SAG-AFTRA: Audiobooks." Accessed November 21, 2020. www.sagaftra.org/audiobooks.

Sanders, Bernie. 2020. "Our Agenda Is on the Ballot: Rally With Progressive Leaders." Streamed on November 2, 2020. www.youtube.com/watch?v=E2y35de3c_o.

Sarjeant, Elizabeth, Enda Brophy, Jeanne Bilodeau, and Éloi Halloran. 2019. "'Autonomy Among Us': An Interview With Quebec Student Strike Organizers." *Viewpoint Magazine*, June 25, 2019. www.viewpointmag.com/2019/06/25/autonomy-among-us-an-interview-with-quebec-student-strike-organizers/.

Schaller, Bruce. 2007. "Entry Controls in Taxi Regulation: Implications of US and Canadian Experience for Taxi Regulation and Deregulation." *Transport Policy* 14 (6): 490–506.

Schechner, Sam. "Uber's 'Not a Taxi Company' Defense on Trial in EU." *Wall Street Journal*, November 29, 2016. www.wsj.com/articles/ubers-not-a-taxi-company-defense-on-trial-in-eu-1480427094.

Scheiber, Noam. "Debate Over Uber and Lyft Drivers' Rights in California Has Split Labor." *The New York Times*, June 29, 2019. www.nytimes.com/2019/06/29/business/economy/uber-lyft-drivers-unions.html

Scheurich, James Joseph, and Michelle D. Young. 1997. "Coloring Epistemologies: Are Our Research Epistemologies Racially Biased?" *Educational Researcher* 26 (4): 4. https://doi.org/10.2307/1176879.

Schneider, Todd. 2016. "Taxi, Uber, and Lyft Usage in New York City: Open TLC Data Reveals the Taxi Industry's Contraction, Uber's Growth, and the Scramble for Market Share." Todd W. Schneider. Last updated April 5, 2016. http://toddwschneider.com/posts/taxi-uber-lyft-usage-new-york-city/.

Scholz, Trebor. 2015. "Think Outside the Boss." *Public Seminar*, April 25, 2015. www.publicseminar.org/2015/04/think-outside-the-boss/

———. 2016. *Platform Co-operativism*. New York: Rosa Luxemburg Stiftung.

———. 2017. *Uberworked and Underpaid: How Workers Are Disrupting the Digital Economy*. Cambridge and Malden, MA: Polity Press.

Schor, Juliet B., and William Attwood-Charles. 2017. "The 'Sharing' Economy: Labor, Inequality, and Social Connection on for-Profit Platforms." *Sociology Compass* 11 (8): e12493. https://doi.org/10.1111/soc4.12493.

Schwartz, Morissa. 2016. *The Gig Economy: Our Road to Financial Freedom*. Self-published, Kindle.

Schwartz-Weinstein, Zach. 2015. "Beneath the University: Service Workers and the University-Hospital City, 1964–1980." PhD diss., New York University, New York.

Science for the People. 1976. "Rumblings of Organizing in Silicon Valley." 8 (1): 10–31. www.marxists.org/history/usa/pubs/science/SftPv8n1s.pdf.

Scolere, Leah, Urszula Pruchniewska, and Brooke Erin Duffy. 2018. "Constructing the Platform-Specific Self-Brand: The Labor of Social Media Promotion." *Social Media + Society* 4 (3): 1–11. https://doi.org/10.1177/2056305118784768.

Sennett, Richard. 1998. *The Corrosion of Character: The Personal Consequences of Work in the New Capitalism*. New York: W. W. Norton & Company.

Shade, Leslie Regan. 2018. "Hop to It in the Gig Economy: The Sharing Economy and Neo-Liberal Feminism." *International Journal of Media & Cultural Politics* 14 (1): 35–54. https://doi.org/10.1386/macp.14.1.35_1.

Shade, Leslie Regan, and Jenna Jacobson. 2015. "Hungry for the Job: Gender, Unpaid Internships, and the Creative Industries." *The Sociological Review* 63: 188–205. https://doi.org/10.1111/1467-954X.12249.

Shannon, Claude E. 1948. "A Mathematical Theory of Communication." *Bell System Technical Journal* 27 (3): 379–423.

Shared-Use Mobility Center. 2016. *Shared Mobility Plan for Los Angeles County*. Chicago, IL: Shared Use Mobility Center.

Sheets, Kristen. 2008. "Inside the #MeToo Revolt at Google." *SocialistWorker.org*, November 13, 2008. http://socialistworker.org/2018/11/13/inside-the-metoo-revolt-at-google.

Shirky, Clay. 2008. *Here Comes Everybody: The Power of Organizing Without Organizations*. New York: Penguin Press.

Siddiqui, Faiz. 2018. "Falling Transit Ridership Poses an 'Emergency' for Cities, Experts Fear." *The Washington Post*, March 24, 2018. www.washingtonpost.com/local/trafficandcommuting/falling-transit-ridership-poses-an-emergency-for-cities-experts-fear/2018/03/20/ffb67c28-2865-11e8-874b-d517e912f125_story.html?utm_term=.ea682db928b7.

———. 2019. "Uber and Lyft Drivers Strike for Pay Transparency—After Algorithms Made It Harder to Understand." *Washington Post*, May 8, 2019. www.washingtonpost.com/technology/2019/05/08/uber-lyft-drivers-strike-pay-transparency-after-algorithms-made-it-harder-understand/?arc404=true

"Sign On: Open Letter to Gig Companies Regarding Black Lives Matter." Accessed November 26, 2020. https://docs.google.com/forms/d/e/1FAIpQLSfsRgu68wjPClH7jQjVbcl0y2GaQuy8aVySHK_e0BGCzwiGkQ/viewform

Silicon Valley Rising. 2016. *Tech's Invisible Workforce*. https://siliconvalleyrising.org/files/TechsInvisibleWorkforce.pdf

Singer, Natasha. 2014. "In the Sharing Economy, Workers Find Both Freedom and Uncertainty." *The New York Times*, August 16, 2014. www.nytimes.

com/2014/08/17/technology/in-the-sharing-economy-workers-find-both-freedom-and-uncertainty.html.
Sinicki, Adam. 2019. *Thriving in the Gig Economy: Freelancing Online for Tech Professionals and Entrepreneurs*. New York: Apress. Kindle.
Sisario, Ben. 2015. "WNYC to Open New Podcast Division." *The New York Times*, October 12, 2015. www.nytimes.com/2015/10/13/business/media/wnyc-to-open-new-podcast-division.html.
Slaughter, J. 2012. "Strikes Expose Hazards In Walmart's Supply Chain." *Labor Notes* 403: 15–16.
Smith, Aaron. 2016a. "Gig Work, Online Selling and Home Sharing." Pew Research Center, November 2016. www.pewresearch.org/internet/2016/11/17/gig-work-online-selling-and-home-sharing/
———. 2016b. "Shared, Collaborative and On Demand: The New Digital Economy." Pew Research Center. http://assets.pewresearch.org/wp-content/uploads/sites/14/2016/05/PI_2016.05.19_Sharing-Economy_FINAL.pdf.
Smith, Adrian. 2014. "The Lucas Plan: What Can It Tell Us About Democratising Technology Today?" *The Guardian*, January 22, 2014. www.theguardian.com/science/political-science/2014/jan/22/remembering-the-lucas-plan-what-can-it-tell-us-about-democratising-technology-today.
Smith, Kristin. 2018. "Slowing Things Down: Taming Time in the Neoliberal University Using Social Work Distance Education." *Social Work Education* 37 (2): 691–704.
Smith, Kristin, and Donna Jeffrey. 2013. "Critical Pedagogies in the Neoliberal University: What Happens When They Go Digital?" In *Critical Geographies of Education*, edited by Tyler McCreary, Ranu Basu, and Anne Godlewska. Special issue, *Canadian Geographer/Le Géographe canadien* 57 (3): 372–80.
Smythe, Dallas. 1977. "Communication: Blindspots of Western Marxism." *Canadian Journal of Political and Social Theory* 1 (3): 1–27.
Somerville, Heather. "True Price of an Uber Ride in Question as Investors Assess Firm's Value." *Reuters*, August 23, 2017. www.reuters.com/article/us-uber-profitability/true-price-of-an-uber-ride-in-question-as-investors-assess-firms-value-idUSKCN1B3210.
Spanellis, Agnessa, Viktor Dörfler, and Jillian MacBryde. 2020. "Investigating the Potential for Using Gamification to Empower Knowledge Workers." *Expert Systems With Applications* 160: 113694.
Spross, Jeff. "Uber and Municipal Government: Super Friends?" *The Week*, February 21, 2018. https://theweek.com/articles/756344/uber-municipal-government-super-friends
Srniceck, Nick. 2017a. *Platform Capitalism*. Malden, MA: Polity Press.
———. 2017b. "We Need to Nationalize Google, Facebook and Amazon. Here's Why." *The Guardian*, August 30, 2017. www.theguardian.com/commentisfree/2017/aug/30/nationalise-google-facebook-amazon-data-monopoly-platform-public-interest
Stanford, Jim. 2017. "The Resurgence of Gig Work: Historical and Theoretical Perspectives." *The Economic and Labor Relations Review* 28 (3): 382–401.
Steinberger, Ben Z. 2018. "Redefining 'Employee' in the Gig Economy: Shielding Workers from the Uber Model." *Fordham Journal of Corporate & Financial Law* 23 (2): 577–96.
Steinmetz, Katy. 2016. "Exclusive: See How Big the Gig Economy Really Is." *Time*, January 6, 2016. http://time.com/4169532/sharing-economy-poll/.
Stolzoff, Stephen. 2018. "One Thing Millennials haven't Killed: Labor Unions." *qz.com*. Accessed July 2019. https://qz.com/work/1399288/labor-unions-are-on-the-rise-for-people-under-age-35/

Stone, Brad. 2008. "Amazon to Buy Audiobook Seller for $300 Million." *New York Times*, February 1, 2008.
Storey, David, Tony Steadman, and Charles Davis. 2018. "How the Gig Economy Is Changing the Workforce." *EY Global*, November 20, 2018. www.ey.com/en_gl/tax/how-the-gig-economy-is-changing-the-workforce.
Storper, Michael. 2016. "The Neo-liberal City as Idea and Reality." *Territory, Politics, Governance* 4 (2): 241–63. https://doi.org/10.1080/21622671.2016.1158662
Strangleman, Tim. 2007. "The Nostalgia for Permanence at Work? The End of Work and its Commentators." *The Sociological Review* 55 (1): 81–103.
Sullivan, John L. 2018. "Podcast Movement: Aspirational Labour and the Formalisation of Podcasting as a Cultural Industry." In *Podcasting: New Aural Cultures and Digital Media*, edited by Dario Llinares, Neil Fox, and Richard Berry, 35–56. London: Palgrave Macmillan.
———. 2019. "The Platforms of Podcasting: Past and Present." *MediArxiv*, May. https://doi.org/10.33767/osf.io/4fcgu.
"Supporting You During the Coronavirus." *Uber.com*. Last modified March 17, 2020. www.uber.com/blog/supporting-you-during-coronavirus/
Szymusiak Tomasz. 2015. *Prosumer—Prosumption—Prosumerism*. Düsseldorf: OmniScriptum GmbH & Co. KG.
Tai, Zixue, and Hu Fengbin. 2018. "Play Between Love and Labor: The Practice of Gold Farming in China." *New Media & Society* 20 (7): 2370–390.
Tapscott, Don. 1996. *The Digital Economy: Promise and Peril in the Age of Networked Intelligence*. New York: McGraw-Hill.
Tarnoff, Ben. 2018. "Coding and Coercion." *Jacobin*, April 11, 2018. https://jacobinmag.com/2018/04/lanetix-tech-workers-unionization-campaign-firing.
———. 2020. "The Making of the Tech Worker Movement." *Logic Magazine*, May 4, 2020. https://logicmag.io/the-making-of-the-tech-worker-movement/full-text/
Tassinari, Arianna, and Vincenzo Maccarrone. 2017. "The Mobilisation of Gig Economy Couriers in Italy: Some Lessons for the Trade Union Movement." *Transfer: European Review of Labour and Research* 23 (3): 353–57.
Taylor, T. L. 2009. *Play Between Worlds: Exploring Online Game Culture*. Cambridge, MA: MIT Press.
Team, Trefis. 2018. "As a Rare Profitable Unicorn, Airbnb Appears to be Worth $38 Billion." *Forbes*, May 11, 2018. Accessed February 23, 2019. www.forbes.com/sites/greatspeculations/2018/05/11/as-a-rare-profitable-unicorn-airbnb-appears-to-be-worth-at-least-38-billion/#2d991a642741
Terranova, Tiziana. 2000. "Free Labor: Producing Culture for the Digital Economy." *Social Text* 18 (2): 33–58. https://doi.org/10.1215/01642472-18-2_63-33.
———. 2013. "Free Labour." In *Digital Labour: The Internet as Playground and Factory*, edited by Trebor Schotz, 33–57. New York: Routledge.
———. 2014. "Algorithms, Capital, and the Automation of the Common." *EuroNomade*, March 8, 2014. www.euronomade.info/?p=2268
Theodore, Nik. 2015. "Rebuilding the House of Labor: Unions and Worker Centers in the Residential Construction Industry." *WorkingUSA* 18 (1): 59–76.
The People's Choice Podcast Awards. 2018. "Podcast Awards—The People's Choice." Podcast Awards, 2018. www.podcastawards.com/.
Tiaynen-Qadir, Tatiana, and Suvi Salmenniemi. 2017. "Self-Help as a Glocalised Therapeutic Assemblage." *European Journal of Cultural Studies* 20 (4): 381–96.

Ticona, Julia. 2020. "Essential and Untrusted." *Dissent Magazine*, Fall 2020. www.dissentmagazine.org/article/essential-and-untrusted.

Ticona, Julia, and Alexandra Mateescu. 2018. "Trusted Strangers: Carework Platforms' Cultural Entrepreneurship in the On-Demand Economy." *New Media & Society* 20 (11): 4384–404.

Ticona, Julia, Alexandra Mateescu and A. Rosenblat. 2018. "Beyond Disruption: How Tech Shapes Labor Across Domestic Work & Ridehailing." *Data & Society*. https://datasociety.net/wp-content/uploads/2018/06/Data_Society_Beyond_Disruption_FINAL.pdf

Tiku, Nitasha. 2018. "The Year Tech Workers Realized They Were Workers." *Wired*, December 24, 2018. www.wired.com/story/why-hotel-workers-strike-reverberated-through-tech/.

Tiku, Nitasha, and Elizabeth Dwoskin. 2020. "Silicon Valley's Two-Tiered System for White-Collar Workers Is Under Pressure as Coronavirus Spreads." *The Washington Post*, March 9, 2020. www.washingtonpost.com/technology/2020/03/09/tech-contractors-coronavirus/.

Todolí-Signes, Adrián. 2017. "The 'Gig Economy': Employee, Self-Employed or the Need for a Special Employment Regulation?" *Transfer: European Review of Labour and Research* 23 (2): 193–205. https://doi.org/10.1177/1024258917701381.

Tokumitsu, Miya. 2015. *Do What You Love: And Other Lies About Success and Happiness*. New York: Regan Arts.

Torpey, Elka, and Andrew Hogan. 2016. "Working in a Gig Economy." Career Outlook, US Department of Labor Statistics. Last modified May 2016. www.bls.gov/careeroutlook/2016/article/pdf/what-is-the-gig-economy.pdf.

Trachtenberg, Jeffrey A. 2018. "Amazon Already Disrupted the Sale of Print Titles. Up Next: Audiobooks." *Wall Street Journal*, February 5, 2018. www.wsj.com/articles/readers-listen-up-amazon-wants-to-extend-its-dominance-in-audiobooks-1517832000.

Trumka, Richard L. 2018. "Can Organized Labor Come Back?" *Yale Insights*. Accessed July 5, 2019. https://insights.som.yale.edu/insights/can-organized-labor-come-back

Tufekci, Zeynep. 2017. *Twitter and Tear Gas: The Power and Fragility of Networked Protest*. New Haven: Yale University Press.

Tulloch, Rowan. 2014. "Reconceptualising Gamification: Play and Pedagogy." *Digital Culture & Education* 6 (4): 317–33.

Tussey, Ethan. 2018. *The Procrastination Economy*. New York: New York University Press.

Uber. 2018. "Uber Help." Accessed May 15, 2018. https://help.uber.com/h/33ed4293-383c-4d73-a610- d171d3aa5a78

Upadhya, R. K. 2018. "Tech Workers, Platform Workers, and Workers' Inquiry." *Medium*, January 26, 2018. https://medium.com/tech-workers-coalition/tech-workers-platform-workers-and-workers-inquiry-92fbc6369647.

U.S. Census Bureau. 2017. "American Community Survey 1-year Estimates." Accessed January 23, 2019 from Census Reporter Profile page for Los Angeles, CA. https://censusreporter.org/profiles/16000US0644000-los-angeles-ca/.

———. 2018a. "ACS Demographic and Housing Estimates." https://data.census.gov/cedsci/table?q=hispanics%20in%20US&tid=ACSDP1Y2018.DP05&hidePreview=false.

———. 2018b. "Languages Spoken at Home." Table ID: S1601, 2018. https://data.census.gov/cedsci/table?q=languages%20spoken%20at%20home&tid=ACSST1Y2018.S1601&hidePreview=false.

Vallas, Steven P. 2019. "Platform Capitalism: What's at Stake for Workers?" *New Labor Forum* 28 (1): 48–59.

Vandaele, Kurt. 2018. *Will Trade Unions Survive In The Platform Economy? Emerging Patterns Of Platform Workers' Collective Voice And Representation In Europe*. ETUI Working Papers, No. 2018.05. Brussels: ETUI, the European Trade Union Institute. www.etui.org/Publications2/Working-Papers/Will-trade-unions-survive-in-the-platform-economy-Emerging-patterns-of-platform-workers-collective-voice-and-representation-in-Europe

Van Dam, Piran. 2017. *Freelancing in the Gig Economy: The Practical, Fact-Based Guide to Launching Your Career by Understanding the New Rules of the Game*. Self-published, Kindle.

Van Dijck, José, David Nieborg, and Thomas Poell. 2019. "Reframing Platform Power." *Internet Policy Review* 8 (2): 1–18.

Van Dijk, Teun A. 2015. "Critical Discourse Analysis." In *The Handbook of Discourse Analysis*, edited by Deborah Tannen, Heidi E. Hamilton, and Deborah Schriffin, 466–85. John Wiley & Sons, Ltd. https://doi.org/10.1002/9781118584194.ch22.

Van Doorn, Niels. 2017. "Platform Labor: On the Gendered and Racialized Exploitation of Low-Income Service Work in the 'On-Demand' Economy." *Information, Communication & Society* 20 (6): 898–914.

———. 2019. "On the Conditions of Possibility for Worker Organizing in Platform-Based Gig Economies." *LogOut!* https://notesfrombelow.org/article/conditions-possibility-worker-organizing-platform

Van Doorn, Niels, and Olav Velthuis. 2018. "A Good Hustle: The Moral Economy of Market Competition in Adult Webcam Modeling." *Journal of Cultural Economy* 11 (3): 177–92.

Van Mourik Broekman, Pauline, Gary Hall, Ted Beyfield, Shaun Hides, and Simon Worthington. 2015. *Open Education: A Study in Disruption (Disruptions)*. New York: Rowman and Littlefield.

Varon, Elana. 2018. *The Ultimate Side Hustle Book: 450 Moneymaking Ideas for the Gig Economy*. New York: Adams Media. Kindle.

Venn, Couze. 2018. *After Capital*. London: Sage.

Vesa, Mikko, and J. Tuomas Harviainen. 2019. "Gamification: Concepts, Consequences, and Critiques." *Journal of Management Inquiry* 28 (2): 128–30.

Villa-Nicholas, Melissa. 2017. "Ruptures in Telecommunications: Latina and Latino Information Workers in Southern California." *Aztlan: A Journal of Chicano Studies* 42 (1): 73–97.

Von Hippel, Eric. 2005. *Democratizing Innovation*. Cambridge, MA: MIT Press.

Vranjes, Toni. "California Bill Would Exempt Certain Occupations from Dynamex Ruling." *Society for Human Resource Management*, April 9, 2019. www.shrm.org/resourcesandtools/legal-and-compliance/state-and-local-updates/pages/california-bill-would-exempt-certain-occupations-from-dynamex-ruling.aspx

Wachsmuth, David, David Chaney, Danielle Kerrigan, Andrea Shillolo, and Robin Basalaev-Binder. 2018. *The High Cost of Short-Term Rentals in New York City*. Urban Politics and Governance Research Group, McGill University. https://mcgill.ca/newsroom/files/newsroom/channels/attach/airbnb-report.pdf

Waheed, Saba, et al. 2015. "Ridesharing or Ridestealing? Changes in Taxi Ridership and Revenue in Los Angeles 2009–2014." UCLA Labor Center. www.labor.ucla.edu/taxi-brief/.

Wajcman, Judy. 2015. *Pressed for Time: The Acceleration of Life in Digital Capitalism*. Chicago: University of Chicago Press.

Watanabe, Chihiro, et al. 2016. "Co-Evolution of Three Mega-Trends Nurtures Un-Captured GDP—Uber's Ride-Sharing Revolution." *Technology in Society* 46: 164–85.

Waters, Facility, and Jamie Woodcock. 2017. "Far From Seamless: A Workers' Inquiry at Deliveroo." *Viewpoint Magazine*, September 20, 2017, www.viewpointmag.com/2017/09/20/far-seamless-workers-inquiry-deliveroo/.

Weber, Max. 2004. *Science as Vocation*. Wood Dale, IL: Hackett Books.

Webster, Juliet. 2016. "Microworkers of the Gig Economy: Separate and Precarious." *New Labor Forum* 25 (3): 56–64. https://doi.org/10.1177/1095796016661511.

Weeks, Kathi. 2011. *The Problem With Work: Feminism, Marxism, Antiwork Politics, and Postwork Imaginaries*. Durham, NC: Duke University Press.

Weigel, Moira. 2017. "Coders of the World, Unite: Can Silicon Valley Workers Curb the Power of Big Tech?" *The Guardian*, October 31, 2017. www.theguardian.com/news/2017/oct/31/coders-of-the-world-unite-can-silicon-valley-workers-curb-the-power-of-big-tech.

Weise, Karen. 2019. "Somali Workers in Minnesota Force Amazon to Negotiate." *The New York Times*, April 11, 2019. www.nytimes.com/2018/11/20/technology/amazon-somali-workers-minnesota.html

Welch, Matt. "Op-Ed: Democrats These Days Hate Reregulation, But Once Upon a Time They Loved It." *Los Angeles Times*, February 8, 2018. www.latimes.com/opinion/op-ed/la-oe-welch-deregulation-carter-20180208-story.html

Wells, Katie, Kafui Attoh, and Declan Cullen. 2019. *2019 Public Report: The Uber Workplace in D.C.*, 1–21. Washington, DC: Georgetown University. https://lwp.georgetown.edu/wp-content/uploads/Uber-Workplace.pdf

Wikipedia. n.d. "Audiobook Creation Exchange." Accessed May 29, 2019. https://en.wikipedia.org/w/index.php?title=Audiobook_Creation_Exchange&oldid=899386904.

Williams, Raymond. 1977. *Marxism and Literature*. Oxford: Oxford University Press.

Winn, Josh. 2015. "Writing About Academic Labor." *Workplace: A Journal for Academic Labor* 25: 1–15.

Wolfson, Todd. 2019. "The Gig Economy and Class (De) Composition." In *The Routledge Companion to Media and Class*, edited by Erika Polson, Lynn Schofield Clark and Radhika Gajjala, 192–202. New York: Routledge.

———. 2020. "Introduction: Class Struggle Before Class." *South Atlantic Quarterly* 119 (2): 394–400.

Wong, Julia Carrie. 2018. "Facebook Contractors Faced Christmas Ultimatum: Accept Wage Offer or Lose Jobs." *The Guardian*, December 21, 2018. www.theguardian.com/technology/2018/dec/20/facebook-contractors-filter-digital-labor-dispute-christmas

———. 2020. "Amazon Execs Labeled Fired Worker 'Not Smart or Articulate' in Leaked PR Notes." *BBC*, April 2, 2020. www.theguardian.com/technology/2020/apr/02/amazon-chris-smalls-smart-articulate-leaked-memo.

Wood, Alex J., Vili Lehdonvirta, and Mark Graham. 2018. "Workers of the Internet Unite? Online Freelancer Organisation Among Remote Gig Economy Workers in Six Asian and African Countries." *New Technology, Work and Employment* 33 (2): 95–112.

Woodcock, Jamie. 2016. "#Slaveroo: Deliveroo Drivers Organising in the 'Gig Economy'." *Novara Media*. http://novaramedia.com/2016/08/12/slaveroo-deliveroo-drivers-organising-in-the-gig-economy/

———. 2017. *Working the Phones: Control and Resistance in Call Centres*. London: Pluto.

Woodcock, Jamie, and Lydia Hughes. 2018. "The View From the Picket Line: Reports From the Food Platform Strike on October 4th." *Notes from Below*. https://notesfrombelow.org/article/view-picket-line-reports-food-platform-strike-octo

Yee, Nick. 2006. "The Labor of Fun." *Games and Culture* 1 (1): 68–71.
Yeung, Ken. 2013. "With 8.5m Guests, Airbnb Seeks to Build a More Uniform Customer Experience Via Its Hospitality Lab." *The Next Web*, September 17, 2013. Accessed March 10, 2019. https://thenextweb.com/insider/2013/09/17/with-8-5m-guests-airbnb-seeks-to-build-a-more-uniform-customer-experience-with-its-hospitality-lab/
Yu, Xinyan, and Angélica M. Casas. 2020. "Coronavirus: The Struggle of Being a Ride-Share Driver." www.bbc.com/news/av/world-us-canada-52028108
Zaal, Petra, Andrea Herrmann, Maryse Chappin, and Britta Schemmann. 2018. "Does Education Still Matter in the Gig Economy?" *Reshaping Work*. https://pe.reshapingwork.net/session/does-education-still-matter-in-the-gig-economy/
Zuboff, Shoshana. 2019. *The Age of Surveillance Capitalism: The Fight for a Human Future at the New Frontier of Power*. London: Profile Books.
Zwick, Austin. 2018. "Welcome to the Gig Economy: Neoliberal Industrial Relations and the Case of Uber." *GeoJournal* 83 (4): 679–91. https://doi.org/10.1007/s10708-017-9793-8.

INDEX

ableism 133
academia 12, 124, 125, 127, 128, 131, 132, 133, 134, 135, 240–243, 245–246, 250, 252, 254, 287, 290, 291
ACLU 112
activism 160, 214, 219; editors' 8, 9–10, 276; gig worker 3–5, 9–13, 256–268, 271–273, 274–277; trade union and labor 54–55, 247, 252, 253; *see also* organizing, platform
Adams, A. 66
adjunct 239–243, 246, 252, 274–275
affect *see* affective impacts; labor; precarious
African American 3, 9, 111, 112, 113, 272; *see also* race; Black workers
Airbnb 107–121; Airbnb Citizen 112–115; brand community 109, 113–115, 117, 119–120; branding strategy 109–112; Chesky, Brian (CEO) 107, 111, 112, 121; founding 107–108; Gebbia, Joe 107; homesharing policy 115–119; Lehane, Chris 110, 115, 118, 121n8, 122n28; political strategy 112–115; racial discrimination 108, 111–112, 115, 121, 122n17, 122n18; revenue 110
algorithmic management *see* management, algorithmic management
American Association of University Professors (AAUP) 127, 136n28, 275
antiracism 6, 10, 71n32, 127, 252, 253n3, 276

Asian workers 63, 113, 161, 238n10; South Asian workers 20, 226; *see also* people of color; race
Assembly Bill 5 (AB5) 4, 5, 34, 41–42, 194, 272
assembly lines 86, 178
Audacity to Podcast, The (podcast) 93, 97, 99, 105–106
audience 7, 83, 93–94, 97, 99–104, 105–106, 107, 141, 143–146, 159, 167–168, 170, 182, 184–186, 258
audience commodity *see* audience; labor, fan; Smythe, Dallas
Audiobook Creation Exchange (ACX) 143
Audio Publishers Association (APA) 143
austerity 241, 245, 253
authentic 86, 93, 97, 103–104, 105, 111, 159, 163, 172, 175n29
autonomy 81, 104–105, 159, 168, 170

Bakers Food and Allied Workers Union (BFAWU) 263
Banet-Weiser, Sarah 7, 14n25, 163, 175n29
Bay Area Amazonians 252
Baym, Nancy 106, 163, 175n28
benefits 22, 27, 34, 35, 40, 42, 51, 52, 54, 58, 60–61, 69, 70, 78, 111, 119, 132, 134, 143, 156, 159, 160–163, 169, 170, 181, 187, 210, 212, 216, 221, 236, 240–242, 244, 248, 252, 273,

274, 277–278n4; of gig work 164–168; health insurance 58, 61–62; paid leave 58, 61–62; unemployment 193, 251, 271–272
Benkler, Yochai 94
Berg, Heather R. 59, 61, 68, 70n7, 174n8, 175n26
Berlant, Lauren 86, 91n103
Bernhardt, Annette 45n30, 162
Bernstein, Elizabeth 59, 70n5
Big Data 190–191, 194, 197, 199, 201n2
Big Tech 199, 201
biocracy 85
Black, Indigenous, People of Color (BIPOC) *see* People of Color
Black Lives Matter 14n39, 213, 272, 276
Black workers 9, 14n39, 59–60, 63, 64, 68, 111, 145, 161, 165, 226, 241, 243, 244, 252, 271, 272, 275; *see also* African American; antiracism; Black Lives Matter; People of Color; race; white supremacy
Bloomington School of Political Economy 191, 195–196
Bristol (UK) 257, 261, 262, 264

Caldwell, John T. 96
Californian ideology 107, 208, 247
cam modeling 159–174
capital 8, 54–55, 106, 108, 113, 125, 126, 130, 131, 132, 134, 164, 170, 173, 177, 178, 180, 183, 185–186, 187, 192, 199–200, 201, 212, 256, 257, 265, 273, 277; cultural 181, 183; economic 181; finance 200; human 185; monopoly 119–120; platform 265; social 120, 181, 183; venture 5
capitalism 5, 6, 7, 8, 61, 69, 76, 125, 128, 134, 148, 149, 181, 184, 185, 190–191, 208, 212, 213, 257, 258, 273; academic 125, 135n14; corporate 107, 120; digital 192, 201; frictionless 78; hypercapitalism 179; industrial 179; late 59–60, 195; neoliberal 8, 11, 12, 15n47, 19–20, 22, 36, 47, 55, 58–59, 61, 70n8, 87n18, 90n90, 107–110, 112–115, 119–121, 124, 125–127, 129, 135n11, 135n14, 135n18, 136n29, 136n47, 136n51, 142, 162, 185, 188n10, 193, 196, 198, 210, 247, 273, 274, 275; patriarchal 161, 168, 173, 174; platform 7, 190–200, 207, 208, 209, 218, 257, 265, 266; surveillance 7; venture 125
Casey, Catherine 81, 89n55

Cederström, Carl 78, 85, 87n8, 87n10, 90n82, 90n97
cell phones 39, 180, 183, 184, 187, 215; *see also* smartphone
Chapkis, Wendy 60–61, 70n13
Clark, Dorie 81, 89n48
class 5, 6, 8, 9, 12, 52, 59, 68–69, 111, 113, 114, 119, 130, 131, 144, 148, 159, 160, 163, 181, 187, 217, 239, 240, 241, 242, 243, 247, 252, 272, 273, 274, 276; class composition 208, 257, 260, 265; creative class 120, 243; higher education stratification 239–243; petty bourgeois 109, 112, 117, 120, 121; professional 92, 96; social, middle- 55, 59, 69, 113–115, 117, 120, 121, 166, 248; working-class 55, 68, 69, 112, 113, 115, 116, 118, 120, 121, 129, 208, 211, 213, 247, 257, 258, 274; *see also* class composition; class struggle; essential work; intersectionality; workers
class struggle 180, 258, 261, 266
Coalition of Rutgers Unions 275
cognitive economy 178; *see also* capitalism
commodification 52, 70, 125, 126, 183, 184, 197, 198; intensive 52
commodity 125, 181; *see also* audience commodity
Communications Decency Act *see* Section 230
Communication Workers of America (CWA) 210, 242, 254
communicativeness 76, 82–83
community 10, 11, 67, 83, 93, 94, 95, 97, 101–103, 107, 109, 110–120, 129, 133, 159, 162–168, 173, 180, 198, 202n23, 212, 264, 265, 276; community engagement 127; *see also* Airbnb, brand community
competition 19, 21, 27, 39, 31, 64–65, 160, 162, 170, 175n18, 178, 187, 198, 199, 223, 228–235, 236, 259
connectivity/connectedness 124, 128, 129, 130, 134, 136n30, 136n33, 235
consumers 5, 7, 10, 24, 27, 35, 42, 131, 169, 171, 183, 184, 192, 194, 195, 200, 275; *see also* labor, by consumers
consumption 7, 92, 128, 129, 143, 144, 179, 180, 184, 186, 199, 274
contracts 40, 51, 56, 146, 148, 157, 181, 181, 195, 211, 240, 252, 259; *see also* contractual; informational asymmetry
contractual 127, 150, 181

control 4, 6, 21, 22, 34, 35, 40, 43, 49, 50, 53, 56, 58, 66, 86–87n5, 91n100, 120, 126, 130, 137, 147, 153, 162, 163, 166, 168, 179, 193, 194, 195, 197, 198, 208, 209, 212, 252, 267n5, 276; self- 83–84
convergence 1, 3, 4, 6–8, 69, 119, 191, 273, 274; convergent space 277
cooperatives 200–201, 223
co-production/co-creation 182–183, 186
Corrigan, Thomas F. *see* labor, hope
council democracy 197–198
COVID-19 pandemic 5, 10, 12, 42, 46n42, 120, 136n40, 239–240, 245, 251–253, 271–277, 277–278n4; *see also* essential work; pandemic
Coworker.org 212–218
creative economy 114, 178; *see also* class, creative class
creativity 11, 59, 61, 67–68, 93, 112, 133, 141, 155, 166–168, 173, 208, 245, 273
Crenshaw, Kimberlé 71n32
criminalization 68–69; *see also* EARN IT Act
critical discourse analysis *see* discourse analysis
cruel optimism 86, 91n103
cycles of production 178

dark kitchen 261
data 7, 12, 31n3, 32n23, 36, 43n7, 48, 55, 57n5, 60, 76–77, 97, 169, 175n20, 179, 180, 184, 185–186, 187, 196–201, 201n1, 202n13, 202n16, 202n18, 202n20, 203n34; Big Data 5, 32n21, 190–191, 194, 197, 199; data commons 195–201; "data fracking" 190–195; democratization of data 191
Davis, Jewel 271–272, 276
deactivation 34, 36, 39–40, 43, 51, 193
dead labor *see* labor, dead labor
debt 20, 22, 26–27, 31, 84, 90, 164; student 191, 241, 244, 276
Decriminalize Sex Work 174; *see also* criminalization
Deliveroo x 208, 209, 212, 220n12, 237n2, 256, 258–262, 264–265, 267n2, 267n6, 267n8, 267n10, 267n16, 268n29
De Peuter, Greig 178, 179, 188n9, 220n9
De Stefano, Valerio 60, 62, 65, 70n9, 71n21, 71n24, 71n34, 71n35, 87n19
digital economy 32n16, 178–179, 182, 188n23, 198–199, 201, 203n35, 208; *see also* capitalism; digital

digital media 136n50, 142, 177; digital media presence 213
digital placement agency 50–51, 53, 55
digital technology 11, 119, 125, 126, 128, 134, 177, 179–181, 183, 184–185, 186–187, 207, 217, 219, 273
digital tragedy of the commons 197
discourse analysis 11, 56, 76, 97, 109, 142
discrimination 34, 62–64, 78, 145, 212, 272, 273; *see also* Airbnb, racial discrimination; gender; patriarchy; race; racism; sexism; white supremacy
disruption 5, 22, 57, 79, 84, 111, 134, 136n43, 263
diversity 122n12, 133, 161, 165; *see also* race
Dolber, Brian 3, 4, 9–10, 13n5, 13n7, 13n9, 14n23, 15n40, 15n41, 15n47, 221n35, 222n55, 273, 274, 275–276, 278n10
Doom (video game) 182
DoorDash 194, 243, 272
Dubal, Veena 13n9, 32n14, 44n10, 55, 57n12, 237n6, 241, 254n7
Duffy, Brooke 9, 14n37, 92, 96, 99, 101, 102, 106, 175n22, 175n25, 175n38
Dungeon X 59–70, 70n1
Dyer-Witheford, Nick 135n17, 135n21, 137n56, 179, 188n9, 188n12, 220n9

EARN IT Act 174, 176n41; *see also* criminalization
Economist, The 190, 200
economy of scale 184, 185
economy of scope 184, 185
Electronic Frontier Foundation 174
e-mail 82–83
employee 4, 5, 9, 22, 24, 25, 32n19, 34, 35, 40, 42, 43n1, 45n38, 55, 56, 58, 61, 66, 75, 78–79, 119, 127, 194, 207, 208, 209, 210–214, 228, 229, 230, 239, 241, 242, 244–246, 248, 252, 253, 271, 272, 273, 274; *see also* Assembly Bill 5 (AB5); employment; independent contractor; Proposition 22; workers
employment 6, 7, 9, 21, 22, 24, 36, 37, 40, 41, 42, 54, 55, 56, 59, 60, 68, 76, 86, 128, 161, 164, 166, 182, 186, 208, 223, 229, 232, 237n13, 243, 259, 277; academic 274; contingent 75; employment law 195, 201, 263; employment relationship 48–49, 60, 273; self-, 54, 58, 66, 83, 84, 259;

see also Assembly Bill 5; employee; employment law; employment relationship; Proposition 22; unions
empowerment 163, 167, 173
entrepreneurial 8, 9, 12, 76, 79–80, 85, 94, 101, 103, 105–107, 110, 115–118, 120, 135n14, 152–154, 159, 162–163, 167, 170; *see also* entrepreneurship
entrepreneurship 57n6, 79–80, 107, 108, 119, 120, 159, 174n5; sexual 173; social 210
essential work 246, 251, 253, 254n4, 272, 276–277
Estonia 225, 228, 233–235
ethnicity *see* race
ethnography 11, 60, 257
exploitation 3, 5, 7, 8, 9, 11, 12, 19, 24, 25, 26–29, 42, 47, 48, 52, 53, 56, 61–63, 65, 69–70, 78, 142, 146, 149, 162–163, 168, 177–178, 184, 185, 186, 187, 200, 216, 243, 272–275; sexual and gender 173; *see also* income; working hours

Facebook 7, 19, 96, 179, 195–196, 200, 208, 211, 213, 215, 226, 245, 248, 251–252, 271
fan base 165, 168, 169, 172
fares 3, 19, 21–22, 28, 30, 38, 193, 194, 271
Farrar, James 194
fascism 11, 120; *see also* neofascism
feminism 14n39, 49, 56, 58–60, 69, 88n22, 90n93, 107, 159, 160, 161, 163, 175n23; Black feminism 145; Chicana/Latina feminism 142, 145, 155, 157n28, 157n31, 157n32, 157n33, 157n34; popular feminism 160; *see also* feminist; gender
feminist 6, 11, 14n39, 49, 56, 58–60, 69, 71n32, 126, 136n51, 142, 145, 155, 163, 173, 174n7, 175n25, 175n27, 254n18; intersectional 142, 145, 155, 160–161, 163, 174; liberal 145; neoliberal 163; and race financialization 22, 181; *see also* feminism; gender
Fleming, Peter 78, 85, 86n5, 87n8, 90n97
flexibility 6, 11, 25, 28, 42, 51, 59, 65, 66–67, 70, 81, 84, 104, 119, 127, 130, 131, 159, 161, 162, 163, 166, 173, 227, 245, 252, 259, 263, 273
flow 213; of capital 180; of content 7; of data 186, 191, 192, 200; of information 185; of money 164; of power 198

Floyd, George 272
Ford, Henry 8
Fordist 126, 130, 177–179, 181, 183, 185, 78–80, 183, 185; post-Fordist 126, 130, 177–179, 182, 183, 185–186
for-hire vehicle (FHV) 4, 19–21, 24; *see also* transportation network companies (TNCs)
formalization 48, 52–53, 93–96, 104–106
FOSTA-SESTA 160 *see* Section 230
Fraser, Nancy 107–108, 109, 121, 121n4, 123n36; *see also* neoliberalism, populism
Freedman, Judith 66, 71n25, 94
freelance 65–66, 68, 82, 83, 93, 103, 104, 150, 159, 113, 191–192, 275; freelancer 83, 87n17, 88n28, 88n33, 89n47, 89n50, 89n59, 89n60, 90n72, 90n73, 90n79, 104, 224, 230, 238n10, 255n33
friendship *see* relationships

game development 181
gamification 12, 177, 179, 181, 183–184, 185–187, 187n4, 187–188n5, 189n54, 274
gender 6, 8, 9, 11, 12, 14n34, 14n37, 20, 44n11, 44n23, 57n9, 69, 78, 130, 154, 159, 160, 89n65, 157n29, 157n33, 160, 163–164, 172–173, 174n6, 175n22, 175n25, 187, 189n76, 210, 247, 254, 276; bias 160; cisgender 159, 161; inequality 161; division of labor 47, 166; power dynamics 171–172; and race 131, 142, 145, 153, 155, 212, 240–242, 244, 247, 254n5; and sexuality 160; *see also* feminism; feminist; feminization of; intersectionality; labor
gig economy 93–95, 105, 181, 223; definition of gig 3, 7, 78–79; gig mindset 79; getting things done guidebook genre 78, 87n14; history of gig work 7–8, 19–71; ideal gigger 77, 79–81; vs. mainstream economy 59–60, 68–70; methods 8; *see also* participant activism, pláticas
gig labor *see* labor, gig
gig leisure 177–179, 185, 274; *see also* gig labor; leisure
Gig Workers Collective 252
Gig Workers Rising 194, 272
Google 7, 93, 98, 145, 192, 195, 196, 200, 202n20, 208, 211–213, 217, 220n5, 221n30, 222n42, 244, 245, 247, 251–255, 278n7; *see also* Googleplex

Googleplex 245, 255n25, 255n26
Great Recession 21–23, 36–37, 39, 113, 191, 245, 248

Hacking/ /Hustling 174
Half-Life (video game) 182
Hall, Stuart 108, 121n6
Hart, Osborne 277
Harvey, David 113, 122n22, 135n12; *see also* right to the city
Healy, Joshua 60, 70n10, 70n17, 71n26
Hirschman, Albert 20, 24, 27, 28, 31n2
Holder, Eric 112, 122n9
Huizinga, Johan 179, 184; *see also* magic circle
hustle 66; side hustle 8, 9, 68, 82, 89n62, 90n96, 98, 159, 163

ideology 9, 11–12, 73, 95, 108, 119, 120, 124, 125, 178, 184, 185, 276; *see also* Californian ideology; connectivity/connectedness; neofascism; petty bourgeois; progressive neoliberal
id Software 182
immaterial economy 178 *see also* labor, immaterial
immigrant 6, 8, 11, 14n10, 30, 35, 37, 38, 42, 51, 55, 118, 210, 220n19, 244, 249; anti-immigrant 247; South Asian 20; *see also* race, gender; immigration status
immigration status 246, 247, 249
income 21, 22, 23, 25, 29, 32n21, 58–60, 62, 68–69, 82, 84, 96, 110, 113, 114, 141, 154, 160, 162, 164, 165, 170, 171; basic 5; low- 47, 48, 58, 69, 160, 174n6; income tax 58; insecurity 36; multiple income streams 59, 60, 67–69; *see also* wages; tips
independent contractor 5, 13n5, 13n7, 15n41, 22, 24, 34, 40, 41, 42, 55, 56, 58–59, 61–62, 64, 66–67, 159, 160, 168, 170, 193, 221n35, 222n55, 241, 248, 259, 263, 264, 266; "1099" workers 160; *see also* Assembly Bill 5; employee; Proposition 22
Independent Workers of Great Britain (IWGB) 237n3, 259–261, 267n10
inductive coding 76
industry 132, 160, 163, 198; audiobook and publishing 141–144, 149, 151, 152, 156n4; camming 159, 161, 165, 167, 168, 170, 174n1; domestic 8–9, 14n30, 47–57; food service and delivery 264; hotel/hospitality 115, 117, 118; information 180; media/entertainment 7, 94, 142, 148, 158n43, 177; movie/film 96, 182; podcast 10–11, 105, 274; rideshare 3–6, 9, 10, 34–46, 192–194, 200–201, 202n13, 227, 233, 271–273, 274, 277; self-help 87n13; service 66; sex 59–63, 65, 68–70, 167, 175n17, 175n31; taxi v 19–31, 32n23; technology 86, 208, 209, 241–243, 245–250; telecommunications 9; videogame 12, 96, 181–183, 188n26, 188n32, 189n35
industrial economy 180 *see also* capitalism; industrial
Industrial Workers of the World (IWW) 224, 247, 261, 262; IWW Courier Network 262–263; *see also* Wobblies
inequality 4, 20, 130, 132, 174; gender 161–163; racial 165–166
informality 52, 56, 127
information 124, 179, 151, 169, 171, 179, 180, 181, 190, 192, 195, 196, 198, 217, 218, 219, 222n54, 257, 275; asymmetry 128–129, 146–149, 195; control of 49; information and communications technologies (ICTs) 126, 178; information economy 178 (*see also* capitalism); information flows 180, 185 (*see also* flows); information industry 180; sharing of (research methods) 36, 60; transmission of 128–129, 219
insecurity 22, 35, 36, 42, 60, 69, 127, 160, 246, 250, 275; *see also* precarious labor
Instacart 10, 15n42, 194, 272
International Alliance of App-Based Transport Workers (IAATW) 223, 237n4
International Labour Organization (ILO) 57n8, 271
Internet 56, 111, 147, 164, 167, 170, 173, 174, 178, 185, 187, 194–198, 218, 224, 274
Internet of Things 190, 194–197, 200–201, 202n5
intersectionality 6, 69, 71n32, 142, 145, 153, 155, 160, 161, 163, 174; *see also* feminist, intersectional

Jackson, Dave 93, 97–106
Johnson-Forrest Tendency, the 261

Keep Neighborhoods First coalition 115, 121, 122n29
Kelley, Robin D. G. 68, 71n30
Kelly Girls 8, 14n30
Kline, Stephen 178, 188n9
Kuehn, Kathleen *see* labor, hope
Kumanyika, Chenjerai 3, 10, 15n42, 271, 275–276
Kutch, Jess 214–218

labor 7, 8, 177, 179–181, 183, 185–187; above the line labor 182; academic labor 11, 124–128, 131, 134, 136, 245, 247, 255, 275; affective 83, 100, 101, 104–106, 171–172; affective impacts of 154–155; blue-collar 212; by consumers 181; contractual 181; costs 5; cultural 93, 103, 105; dead labor 273, 276; on demand 185; discipline 8; division of 47; fan 183, 106, 181; feminized 47, 59; free 126; gig 3, 177–179, 185; hope 92; immaterial 178, 181, 182; labor force 6; labor market 21, 26, 27, 32, 44n13, 44n14, 45n29, 45n32, 45n35, 45n36, 50, 59, 97, 227–230; labor market 'outsiders' 230, 236; labor organizing 8; labor relations 7, 54; labor relationships 56; labor power 55; labor process 124, 126, 142, 209, 212, 233, 258, 261, 263; labor struggle 7; outside the line 182–183; platform 53; relational labor 163, 172; slave 7; social 182; surplus 8, 148, 273, 275; unpaid labor 149–152, 164, 164, 169–170, 183; wage labor 184; white-collar 212, 219, 224; *see also* contracts-imprecise; essential work; gig leisure; industry; Marx, Karl; precarious labor; sex work; workers; unions
Lanetix 210–213, 221n24
Latina 63–66, 141–142, 144–145, 149, 153, 154, 155, 161, 273; *see also* feminism, Chicana/Latina feminism; Latino; Latinx; race
Latino 144, 145
Latinx 108, 111, 144, 154, 241, 243, 244
Lease Drivers Coalition 20; *see also* New York Taxi Workers Alliance
leasing: cars and drivers 20, 22–23, 25, 26, 27, 28, 30, 39; real estate 110
leisure 7, 178–179, 183–186, 245, 274; *see also* gig leisure
Lewis, Daniel J. 93, 97–99, 101–104
liberation management 78, 87n11

lifelong learning 80
Lopdrup-Hjorth, Thomas 83, 90n75
London 3, 10, 235, 256, 257, 258, 259, 260–261, 262, 263, 264, 265, 267n23, 265
Lorde, Audre 13n13, 213
Los Angeles 3, 4, 6, 10, 34–36, 42, 43n2, 43n4, 43n5, 45n8, 45n34, 45n41, 46n41, 108–109, 110, 113–119, 121n8, 121n9, 121n10, 123n30, 123n31
low barriers to entry 93, 100, 164, 173 *see also* competition
Lucas Plan 209, 211, 220n17, 220n18
Luna, Fausto 31
Lyft 3, 4, 5, 7, 9, 10, 12n1, 14n37, 25, 26, 29, 30, 32n23, 33n32, 33n33, 33n34, 35, 36, 39, 40, 43n7, 45n30, 45n39, 45n41, 46n43, 61, 202n12, 212, 223, 239, 243–244, 250, 272, 273, 274, 278n10

Mac, Juno 69, 71n33
malleability 76, 81–82, 85
management 183, 186; algorithmic management 193–194
marginalization 12, 112, 142, 153, 160, 163, 168, 173–174; marginalized workers 240, 243, 250, 252
marketing 35, 64, 65, 80, 81, 94, 96, 97, 98–100, 160, 167, 169, 175n26, 185, 190
marketplace 3, 49, 50, 55, 135, 143, 162, 177
Maron, Marc 95
Marx, Karl 8, 14n28, 90n93, 115, 119, 156n9, 158n41, 179, 199–200, 202n20, 202n30, 203n31, 257, 267n4, 273, 278n9; and capitalism 148–149; labor theory of value 143; surplus value 148, 273, 275; *see also* labor, dead labor, labor, surplus labor; Marxism
Marxism 14–15n39, 86n14, 119, 121n6, 127, 185, 189n68, 195, 208, 220n6, 220n15, 266
mass production 128, 178; *see also* capitalism; Fordist
McDonalds 237–238n7, 262–264; McDonaldization 125–126, 135n14
McGonigal, Jane 184, 186, 189n57
McRobbie, Angela 61, 70n15
medallion 21–22, 24–28; *see also* industry; taxi
meritocracy 93, 105, 106, 119, 170, 245, 250, 252

meta-work 83; *see also* work
Microsoft 182, 210, 211, 242, 282
Miller-Young, Mireille 59, 60, 70n6, 70n12, 71n25, 175n31
misclassification 34, 42, 61–62; *see also* employee; independent contractor
mobile: application 51; capital 54; communication devices 208, 209, 219; platforms 92; technologies 126, 127, 177–179; *see also* capital; cell phones
modding (video games) 181–182
Mohammed, Hibaq 272
multihoming 27
Murphy, Cherri 272
MyFreeCams 166, 170

Neff, Gina 9, 14n36, 70n3, 175n21
neofascism 107, 108, 109, 112, 115–116, 120–121; *see also* fascism
neoliberalism *see* capitalism, neoliberal
New York 3, 19–22, 25–27, 29, 31, 94, 122n16, 132, 211, 239, 245, 274
New York Taxi Workers Alliance (NYTWA) 12n4, 19–21, 23, 26, 30–31; *see also* industry, taxi; Lease Drivers Coalition; New York
Nicholson, Daniel 60, 70n10, 71n34
Noble, Safiya 8, 14n26, 145, 157n30, 175n13
non-compete clauses 181; *see also* competition; contracts
Notes from Below 258, 265

occupational segregation 47; *see also* gender, division of labor; labor, division of
Office and Professional Employees International Union 211
online education 124, 126, 128, 131
online reviews 82
Operation Choke Point 160; *see also* criminalization; marginalization
Organization United for Respect Walmart (OUR Walmart) 213–215
organizing 20, 22, 29, 30, 35, 36, 42, 83, 240, 242, 243, 277; academic 132–134, 276; Airbnb 112, 115, 121; barriers to 43, 132, 244–245; "campus" organizing 245–247; committee 10, 21; COVID-19 239; driver 194; by editors 10; gig work 9, 12, 41–43, 194–195, 200–201, 274; informal groups 41; labor 8, 95; models 8, 240, 274; participant activism 276; platform organizing 207–219; sex workers 173–174; strategy 4, 6, 240, 275; tactics 241; tech 242, 247–252; tools 4; union 3, 10, 12n1, 142, 155, 219, 240–241, 246–250, 253, 273–277, 277
Ostrom, Elinor 196, 202n21, 202n22

pandemic *see* COVID-19 pandemic
paradox of freedom 84, 274
passive income *see* financial independence
patriarchy 8, 9, 66–67, 121n3, 145, 161, 165, 167, 168, 173, 174; *see also* capitalism, patriarchal; intersectionality
#PayUp campaign 194
Pearce, Celia 182, 189n41, 189n45
Pekarek, Andreas 60, 70n10, 71n34
people of color 64, 69, 111, 112–113, 115, 118, 120, 121, 133, 248; Black, Indigenous, People of Color (BIPOC) 243–244 *see also* African American; Asian workers, South Asian workers; Black workers; Latina; Latino; Latinx; race; women of color
personal finances *see* financial independence
petty bourgeoisie 109, 110, 115–116; *see also* class
Philadelphia 3, 4, 10, 262, 277
Philadelphia Drivers Union (PDU) 10, 12n1
platform capitalism 7, 198–201, 207, 208, 209, 218, 257, 265–266; *see also* capitalism; platforms
platform organizing *see* organizing, platform
platforms 134; algorithms 164, 170, 173, 190–194, 197, 199, 201; constraints 168–171; control 169; on-demand platforms 49, 50–51, 53, 55; democratically managed 200–201; hierarchies 162, 170–171, 173; platform capitalism 198–201; surveillance 169; typology of 55; *see also* Audiobook Creation Exchange (ACX); labor, on demand; management, algorithmic management
pláticas: method 142, 145; narration from narrators POV 146–155
play 178–179, 181
players (video games) 181
play testing 181
pleasure 82, 161, 163, 166–168, 173

podcasting 10, 11, 92, 93, 94–106
pomodoro *see* time management
pop-management literature *see* popular management literature
popular management literature 75–76, 78, 85
populism 108–109, 120–121
Poulantzas, Nicos 119–120, 122n27, 123n32
precarious labor 8–9, 10, 35–36, 39, 44, 51, 58–61, 69, 78, 86, 141, 144, 146, 149, 150, 154–155, 159–161, 168–174, 174n4, 175n33, 178, 182, 224, 239–243, 245, 247–253; precariat 9, 119, 251; *see also* labor
privacy 118, 162, 181, 184, 198, 213, 222n54
pro-ams 95–96
Processed World 241–242, 248, 254
Procrastination Economy, The (book) 177
production cultures 92–93, 95–96
productive play 182
product testing 233
professionalism 92, 93, 95–96, 97, 99, 101, 104–106
Proposition 22, 34, 42, 194, 251, 253
prosumption 129–130
prudence 76, 83–85
public assistance 37

Quake (video game) 182; Quake II (video game) 182

race 9, 11, 12, 14n30, 20, 69, 78, 131, 144, 145, 153, 155, 160, 161, 163, 165, 172, 240–241, 242, 243–244, 247, 251–252, 254n5, 276; multiracial 113; *see also* African American; Asian workers; Black Lives Matter; Black workers; gender; intersectionality; Latina; Latino; Latinx; People of Color; White workers
race to the bottom 28, 30, 31, 227
racism 8, 9, 14n26, 63–64, 69, 133, 112, 121n3, 241, 246, 272–273; *see also* antiracism
Reality is Broken (book) 184
Rebel Roo, The 260–261
recession *see* Great Recession
Rideshare Drivers United (RDU) 4, 10, 194, 212, 219, 274
right to the city 109, 112–113, 115, 118, 120; *see also* Harvey, David

risk 86, 117, 126, 130, 132, 160, 162, 166, 168, 173, 180, 195, 197, 207, 227, 229, 263, 273; COVID-19 42, 272, 276; demutualization of 59–60, 161, 162, 168, 173; employment-related 22; exploitation 25; organizing 218; shifted onto workers 259, 271; workers' lives 12, 277
Roberts, Sarah 14n27, 145, 155, 157n29
Rodino-Colocino, Michelle 3, 10, 12n1, 12n3, 13n7, 13n14, 14n24, 14n38, 15n43, 15n44, 15n46, 271–272, 275–276, 277
Rosenblat, Alex 13n7, 32n18, 45n40, 57n5, 193, 201n7, 202n10, 220n12, 220n14, 237n6
Ross, Andrew 245, 254–255

SAG-AFTRA 141–142; and Latina insights 155; talent representation 149; taller de audiolibros 144, 152
Sanders, Bernie 194, 201, 277n1
San Francisco 107, 239, 241, 244, 246, 248, 250; Bay Area 211, 239–240, 242, 243, 244, 247, 249, 250, 252; University of 249, 253, 275
scalability 180
Schifter, Douglas 19, 28–29, 30
Schlademan, Dan 214, 216–219
School of Podcasting (podcast) 93, 97, 99, 105, 106
Schwartz-Weinstein, Zach 241, 246, 254n9, 255n28
Section 230 of the Communications Decency Act 160, 174
Seeing White (podcast) 10
self-actualization 93, 97, 103
self-development 76, 80–81, 85, 87n13
self-help 78, 84–85, 86, 274
self-management 83, 85, 133
self-promotion 79, 102, 169–170; *see also* visibility
seniority 36, 64
Sennett, Richard 81, 88n29, 89n54
Service Employees International Union (SEIU) 194, 250, 271, 274; *see also* Gig Workers Rising
service industry 66
sexism 66–67, 69, 133, 241, 273, 276; *see also* patriarchy
sex work 11, 58–70, 71n29, 160–163, 165–173, 159–174; *see also* industry, sex; labor; underground economy

Sex Workers Outreach Project (SWOP) 173–174
Shirky, Clay 92, 94
Silicon Alley 59, 245
Silicon Valley 4, 6, 8, 12, 92, 107, 108, 125, 192, 200, 208, 211, 216–217, 241–242, 247, 254, 255
Silicon Valley Toxics Commission 210
slavery 7, 272
small batch production 179
smartphone 4, 36, 224, 265, 275; *see also* cell phones; mobile
Smith, Molly 69, 71n33
Smythe, Dallas 7, 13n22, 14n23, 186, 189n68
Socialisme ou Barbarie 261
social media 29, 99, 102, 105–106, 184, 187, 272; cam workers 163–164, 166, 169, 170, 172; social movements 213; worker organizing 4, 207, 215, 216, 219, 271, 275; *see also* unions
solidarity 4, 5, 10, 12, 119–121, 134, 231, 233, 235, 236, 241, 247–248, 250–253, 260–264, 275–276, 277; audiobooks 147, 151; competition 65; impediments to 273–274; taxi industry 20; tech sector 207, 208, 209, 211, 212; *see also* unionism, solidarity unionism; unions
South Asian workers *see* Asian workers, South Asian workers
Srnicek, Nick 13n20, 192, 195, 201, 202n20, 203n37, 220n2, 221n37
standardized products 178; *see also* Fordist
Stanford, Jim 60, 70n11, 71n23
Stanford University 249–250
stigma 58, 69, 160, 163, 165, 167; *see also* sex work
Strategic Alliance for a Just Economy (SAJE) 115
strikes 235, 242, 257, 275; food platform strikes 256–266; internship 213; May 1, 2020 276; media coverage 216; Strike for Black Lives, July 20, 2020 272–273; teacher 132–133; Transnational Courier Federation 223; Uber strike 3–4, 5, 10, 12n1, 194, 212, 250; Yale University 241
structures of feeling 75
subjectivities 55, 126, 163
suicide 19, 29–30, 273

surveillance 7, 40, 51, 52, 124, 132, 133, 162, 169, 185, 209, 218, 252; *see also* capitalism, surveillance capitalism

Tapscott, Don 180, 188n23
Tarnoff, Ben 7, 13n17, 221n24, 222n41, 247, 255n30
Taxi and Limousine Commission (TLC) 23, 26, 28, 29; *see also* industry, taxi
Taylor, Breonna 272
Taylor, T.L. 182, 189n40
Taylorism 125, 178–179, 183–184
Teamsters 10, 215, 216, 274
Tech Action 211–212, 218
technologies of the self 86
Tech Workers Coalition (also *see* TWC) 211–212, 239–240, 244, 246–253, 255n32
Terranova, Tiziana 92, 96, 106, 135n24, 179, 180, 181, 185, 186, 187, 188n8, 188n14, 188n16, 188n21, 188n25, 188n28, 189n62, 189n68, 189n69, 189n74, 189n77
time blocking *see* time management
time management 83–84, 165
tip 5, 50, 62–63, 160, 164, 169, 171; *see also* income
Tomeo 209–210
training 21, 51, 65, 83, 95, 97, 148, 167, 183, 222n47, 243
Transnational Courier Federation 223
transportation network companies (TNCs) 34–43; *see also* industry, taxi; Lyft; Rideshare Drivers United; strikes, Uber strike; Uber
Trump, Donald 108, 110, 160, 211, 247, 271
turnover 8, 38, 62, 64–65
Tussey, Ethan 177–178, 187n1, 188n6; *see also Procrastination Economy, The* (book)
TVCs 212, 240–241, 243–252, 254–255; *see also* contractors

Uber 2–6, 7, 9–10, 12n1, 117, 208, 212; connect with tech workers and riders 250–251; data 191–195, 200–201; driver experience 34, 35, 36, 39–40; engineer 239; model of gig economy 49, 61, 92, 110; neoliberalism 59; New York 19, 21–22, 23–26, 26–29, 30; platform organizing 223–224; United Kingdom 256, 271–277; *see also* industry, taxi; strikes, Uber strike;

Transportation Network Companies (TNCs); Uber Eats; "Uber University"; Uber Works
Uber Eats 194, 256, 262–265, 275
"Uber University" 124–134
Uber Works 266
UC Berkeley 242, 254
Uncivil (podcast) 10
underground economy 59, 69
union organizing *see* organizing, union
Unionbase 213–216, 219
unionism: minority 210; new 224, 238n8; solidarity 5, 212, 277; trade 256, 266
unions *see* American Association of University Professors (AAUP); Bakers Food and Allied Workers Union; Bay Area Amazonians; Communication Workers of America (CWA); Gig Workers Collective; Gig Workers Rising; Independent Workers of Great Britain(IWG B); Industrial Workers of the World (IWW); International Alliance of App-Based Transport Workers; International Labour Organization (ILO); Lease Drivers Coalition; New York Taxi Workers Alliance (NYTWA); Office and Professional Employees International Union; Rideshare Drivers United (RDU); Organization United for Respect Walmart (OUR Walmart); Philadelphia Drivers Union (PDU); Rutgers Coalition of Unions; SAG-AFTRA; Service Employees International Union (SEIU); Teamsters; Tech Action; Tech Workers Coalition; Transnational Courier Federation; Unite Here; United Autoworkers; Washington Alliance of Technology Workers (WashTech); Wobblies (IWW)
United Autoworkers (UAW) 250
United Kingdom (UK) 108, 209, 223, 224, 225, 226, 227, 234, 235, 256–266, 274, 275; *see also* Bristol (UK); London
United States Bureau of Labor Statistics 86n3, 161
Unite Here 211, 248; Unite Here Local 11 109, 115–119
universal guaranteed income (UGI) 199–201
University of San Francisco 249, 253
user-generated content 93–94

value 82, 152, 162, 178–181, 197, 201, 219; extraction and circulation of 7, 100, 119, 126, 162, 191, 195, 273; gamification industry 183–187; hosting 110–111; labor theory 142–143; in process 200; surplus 8, 119, 148, 190; use 134; value chains 180, 198
value chains *see* value, value chains
Valve Software 182
video games 177, 179, 181, 186; as commodity 181; development 181; as "ideal commodity" 178; industry 182–183; production 181
visibility 164, 167, 170, 173

wages 26, 28, 35, 39, 58–59, 61–63, 65–66, 68–69
wage theft: low-wage work 37; *see also* labor, uncompensated
Wales 256
Warren, Elizabeth 200
Washington Alliance of Technology Workers (WashTech) 10, 210, 242, 248; *see also* Microsoft; organizing, tech
Web 2.0 93, 101, 162, 172
WhatsApp 258–260
white supremacy 8, 108, 248; *see also* antiracism; racism
White workers 5, 8, 9, 10, 59–60, 63–64, 96, 108, 111, 112, 118, 145, 154, 161, 165, 166, 246, 248; "white femininity" 163, 165; *see also* race; racism
Williams Jr, Larry 214–216, 218, 222n52
Wobblies 224; *see also* Industrial Workers of the World (IWW)
Wolfson, Todd 4, 10, 13n8, 13n15, 14n35, 275
women 47, 51, 58–70, 131, 135n23, 136n41, 145, 146, 153, 155; *see also* gender; feminism; feminist; intersectionality; women's work
women of color 8, 9, 63, 69, 118, 131, 133, 136n41, 137n53, 145, 161, 163, 165–166, 175n31, 244, 252; *see also* Latina; women's work
women's work 6, 8–9, 14n30, 47–48, 57n9, 58–61, 66–67, 69, 131, 133
work: work from home 8, 14n30, 146–147, 151, 154, 156n2, 166, 173, 224–226, 234, 252; work hours 62–63, 65, 68, 249; work-related expenses 35–39, 42, 84, 193; *see also* labor; workers

worker center 21
Worker Info Exchange 194
workers: workers' agency 20, 24–26, 30; *see also* activism; Asian workers; Black workers; class; class struggle; employees; entrepreneurial; entrepreneurship; essential work; exploitation, freelance, flexibility; gig economy; gig economy, ideal gigger; immigrant; independent contractor; industry; labor; Latina; Latinx; people of color; organizing; petty bourgeoisie; precarious labor; unions; White workers; women; women's work
Workers' inquiry 257–258, 260, 262, 266
WorkIt 213–214, 216–218, 222n54
Workplace Democracy Act 194, 201

Zwick, Austin 59, 69, 70n8, 70n17, 71n22, 71n31, 87n18

331.25729 GIG
The gig economy :
workers and media in

07/28/21

CPSIA information can be obtained
at www.ICGtesting.com
Printed in the USA
LVHW050611060721
691876LV00019B/3571